EUTOPIA

WRITING WALES IN

CREW series of Critical and Scholarly Studies
General Editors: Kirsti Bohata and Daniel G. Williams (CREW, Swansea University)

This CREW series is dedicated to Emyr Humphreys, a major figure in the literary culture of modern Wales, a founding patron of the Centre for Research into the English Literature and Language of Wales. Grateful thanks are due to the late Richard Dynevor for making this series possible.

Other titles in the series

Stephen Knight, *A Hundred Years of Fiction* (978-0-7083-1846-1)
Barbara Prys-Williams, *Twentieth-Century Autobiography* (978-0-7083-1891-1)
Kirsti Bohata, *Postcolonialism Revisited* (978-0-7083-1892-8)
Chris Wigginton, *Modernism from the Margins* (978-0-7083-1927-7)
Linden Peach, *Contemporary Irish and Welsh Women's Fiction* (978-0-7083-1998-7)
Sarah Prescott, *Eighteenth-Century Writing from Wales: Bards and Britons* (978-0-7083-2053-2)
Hywel Dix, *After Raymond Williams: Cultural Materialism and the Break-Up of Britain* (978-0-7083-2153-9)
Matthew Jarvis, *Welsh Environments in Contemporary Welsh Poetry* (978-0-7083-2152-2)
Harri Garrod Roberts, *Embodying Identity: Representations of the Body in Welsh Literature* (978-0-7083-2169-0)
Diane Green, *Emyr Humphreys: A Postcolonial Novelist* (978-0-7083-2217-8)
M. Wynn Thomas, *In the Shadow of the Pulpit: Literature and Nonconformist Wales* (978-0-7083-2225-3)
Linden Peach, *The Fiction of Emyr Humphreys: Contemporary Critical Perspectives* (978-0-7083-2216-1)
Daniel Westover, *R. S. Thomas: A Stylistic Biography* (978-0-7083-2413-4)
Jasmine Donahaye, *Whose People? Wales, Israel, Palestine* (978-0-7083-2483-7)
Judy Kendall, *Edward Thomas: The Origins of His Poetry* (978-0-7083-2403-5)
Damian Walford Davies, *Cartographies of Culture: New Geographies of Welsh Writing in English* (978-0-7083-2476-9)
Daniel G. Williams, *Black Skin, Blue Books: African Americans and Wales 1845–1945* (978-0-7083-1987-1)
Andrew Webb, *Edward Thomas and World Literary Studies: Wales, Anglocentrism and English Literature* (978-0-7083-2622-0)
Alyce von Rothkirch, *J. O. Francis, realist drama and ethics: Culture, place and nation* (978-1-7831-6070-9)
Rhian Barfoot, *Liberating Dylan Thomas: Rescuing a Poet from Psycho-Sexual Servitude* (978-1-7831-6184-3)
Daniel G. Williams, *Wales Unchained: Literature, Politics and Identity in the American Century* (978-1-7831-6212-3)
M. Wynn Thomas, *The Nations of Wales 1890–1914* (978-1-78316-837-8)
Richard McLauchlan, *Saturday's Silence: R. S. Thomas and Paschal Reading* (978-1-7831-6920-7)
Bethan M. Jenkins, *Between Wales and England: Anglophone Welsh Writing of the Eighteenth Century* (978-1-7868-3029-6)
M. Wynn Thomas, *All that is Wales: The Collected Essays of M. Wynn Thomas* (978-1-7868-3088-3)
Laura Wainwright, *New Territories in Modernism: Anglophone Welsh Writing, 1930–1949* (978-1-7868-3217-7)
Siriol McAvoy, *Locating Lynette Roberts: 'Always Observant and Slightly Obscure'* (978-1-7868-3382-2)
Linden Peach, *Pacifism, Peace and Modern Welsh Writing* (978-1-7868-3402-7)
Kieron Smith, *John Ormond's Organic Mosaic* (978-1-7868-3488-1)
Georgia Burdett and Sarah Morse (eds), *Fight and Flight: Essays on Ron Berry* (978-1-7868-3528-4)

EUTOPIA

STUDIES IN CULTURAL EURO-WELSHNESS, 1850–1980

WRITING WALES IN ENGLISH

M. WYNN THOMAS

UNIVERSITY OF WALES PRESS
2021

www.uwp.co.uk

British Library CIP Data
A catalogue record for this book is available from the British Library.

ISBN: 978-1-78683-614-4
e-ISBN: 978-1-78683-615-1

THE *A*SSOCIATION FOR
*W*ELSH *W*RITING IN *E*NGLISH
*C*YMDEITHAS *L*LÊN *S*AESNEG *C*YMRU

Typeset by Marie Doherty
Printed by CPI Antony Rowe, Melksham

CONTENTS

SERIES EDITORS' PREFACE

The aim of this series, since its founding in 2004 by Professor M. Wynn Thomas, is to publish scholarly and critical work by established specialists and younger scholars that reflects the richness and variety of the English-language literature of modern Wales. The studies published so far have amply demonstrated that concepts, models and discourses current in the best contemporary studies can illuminate aspects of Welsh culture, and have also foregrounded the potential of the Welsh example to draw attention to themes that are often neglected or marginalised in anglophone cultural studies. The series defines and explores that which distinguishes Wales's anglophone literature, challenges critics to develop methods and approaches adequate to the task of interpreting Welsh culture, and invites its readers to locate the process of writing Wales in English within comparative and transnational contexts.

Professor Kirsti Bohata and Professor Daniel G. Williams

Founding Editor: Professor M. Wynn Thomas (2004–15)

CREW (*Centre for Research into the English*
Literature and Language of Wales)
Swansea University

CREW

Richard Huws, Beetham Plaza Fountain, Liverpool.

Richard Huws (1902–80) was an artist and designer of European outlook. Born on Anglesey, he was influenced by the unifying design vision of the Dessau Bauhaus during his period of study at the Vienna Kunstgewerbeschule (school of applied arts) between 1927 and 1931, before returning to live and work in London. Among his several designs for kinetic water sculpture, the Beetham Plaza Fountain (or 'Bucket Fountain') is the last surviving, completed in 1967. (DJ)

'Hanes gwareiddiad Ewrop, hanes delfryd ysbrydol ydyw.'
(Saunders Lewis)

QUESTIONER: The Italian artist Michelangelo was born in
which European country?
CONTESTANT: France.

The Time it Takes, BBC1
(with thanks to 'Dumb Britain', *Private Eye*)

'To be European, we need first to be more Welsh.'
(Emyr Humphreys, *Conversations and Reflections*)

Preface

This volume is intended as a corrective to the habit, long established
but exacerbated by the prolonged Brexit debates, of considering
Wales's relationship to Europe by concentrating exclusively, narrowly
and suffocatingly, on its social, political and economic aspects.

The intention here is to explore the rich and exhilarating spectrum
of pro-European sentiment evident for more than a century in the
writings of Welsh intellectuals and creative writers. And the hope in
so doing is that this disclosure will put paid, once and for all, to the
tired, clichéd view of Welsh culture as insular and parochial. To the
contrary, not only has Wales long welcomed very substantial inward
migration, it has also been hospitably internationalist, driven in such
direction by a mixture of curiosity, necessity and deep conviction.

As the very title *Eutopia* concedes, there have of course often
been utopian aspects of Wales's dreams of Europe. But while some
may therefore choose to dismiss them as examples of mere wishful thinking, others may fruitfully appreciate their aspirational and
inspirational features.

Introduction

While I was writing this book, a memory from over thirty years ago returned to me with some force, and with some point. I was at that time a member of the Arts Council of Wales, and chair of its influential Literature Committee, and it was in this latter capacity that I had occasion to preside over an international conference at Aberystwyth attended by representatives of many of the less used languages of Europe – and indeed beyond. There were, I recall, delegates there from such states as Greece and Sri Lanka, from aspiring or re-emergent countries such as Ukraine and Georgia, and from such small and distinctly marginal cultures as that of Friesland.

Several of them seemed to me to speak to my own condition, as a Welsh-speaker struggling to survive in an anglophone and anglocentric environment. The Georgians and Ukrainians represented countries that were at that time politically and culturally subordinate to the dictates of the Soviet Union, and most particularly to the will of Russia. The Greeks – whom I never would have expected to attend – spoke of their anxiety at the growing power of English as promoted globally by Anglo-American culture. As for the Friesans, theirs, they freely admitted, was a language already largely dead as a contemporary social medium. But as they were creative writers, they found a paradoxical freedom in this circumstance. It meant, they explained, that they could experiment with the language at will, without worrying about the social consequences.

Most illuminating of all, however, was the realisation that came to me when I accompanied several of the delegates to an Aberystwyth pub. As we sat there happily socialising, it suddenly struck me that while I felt I was in congenial company amongst these bilingual and bicultural Europeans, my English-speaking compatriots, by whom I found myself surrounded, could well be feeling distinctly uneasy at this invasion of their social space by a group of foreigners. And never before had I so fully registered the implications of being a bicultural native of what had long become a very largely monocultural country. I suddenly felt both isolated in my own country and heartened by a new experience of transnational cultural solidarity. It had never previously occurred to me either, in my innocence, that my own Europhilia, whatever its very obvious deficiencies, might be starkly at odds with the attitude towards Europe that had become the default stance of anglophone Welsh society. And then there was another obvious aspect to the case. Champions of our own, native, less used languages though we all were, we were able to communicate with each other only through the *lingua franca* of English, the 'common tongue' of us all, and yet the very language, of course, that so very seriously threatened our own.

This book is as much a belated product of such realisations as these as it is a response to the recent Brexit fiasco – which, at least from my own particular point of view, seemed, and seems, an obvious by-product of resurgent insular English nationalism. Fintan O'Toole confirmed this in his witty philippic, *Heroic Failure: Brexit and the Politics of Pain*:

> survey data showed a very strong link between identification as 'English only' and hostility to the EU. Fully 64 per cent of people with an exclusively English identity in 2012 said the EU was 'a bad thing', compared to just 28 per cent of those who chose a British-only identity.[1]

That Wales should have voted to align itself with such attitudes came, sadly, as no great surprise: for me, it was not only a woefully misdirected expression of the understandable anger and resentment felt by the abandoned post-industrial communities of south Wales, but also the most recent evidence of how far down the road to total assimilation by England contemporary Wales (long England's 'little butty', in Harri Webb's bitter gibe) has now travelled. While that assimilative process is most directly evident, of course, in Wales's relations to England, it is undoubtedly greatly reinforced and accelerated by Wales's relationship, via England, to Anglo-American culture.

Not that such a state of affairs is by any means the legacy of Wales's post-industrial slump alone. The truth is that Euro-Welshness has never made a serious, sustained attempt to anchor itself in the consciousness of the Welsh public at large. It has remained a fringe movement, the preserve of middle-class academics, writers and intellectuals, many of whom have been working in the Welsh language. Indeed at times – notably during the 1930s – some of its leading adherents seem to have displayed an almost offensive disregard for the general condition of their compatriots. While readily admitting this, the present volume tries nevertheless to demonstrate that what has remained a minority variant of Welsh identity has produced contributions to Welsh culture that continue to be potentially very productive.

The hard-core English nationalism of the extreme Brexiteers, to which Fintan O'Toole shrewdly pointed, was amusingly exposed in a *Private Eye* column listing some of the egregious historical allusions that were featured in the speeches and comments by several prominent figures, including the serenely self-satisfied Jacob Rees-Mogg: The 'brave but mistaken dash against all the odds' was actually the Chequers plan, he wrote in the *Daily Telegraph* on 29 September, 2018. 'Eurosceptics to the Right, the Labour Party to the Left and the European Union in front have all stormed at it with shot and shell.'[2]

If you don't fancy that historical analogy, Rees-Mogg has had plenty more to offer – ever since his maiden speech in 2010 when he paid tribute to 'Alfred the Great, the first Eurosceptic, who got rid of the Danes and made England independent'. In September 2017 he wrote that Brexit was 'as worthy for celebration as victory at Waterloo or the Glorious Revolution'. A month later he told Tory conference delegates that 'Brexit is Magna Carta, it's the burgesses coming at Parliament, it's the Great Reform Bill, it's the Bill of Rights, it's Waterloo, it's Agincourt, it's Crécy. We win all these things.' *Audience member*: 'Trafalgar!' *Rees-Mogg*: 'And Trafalgar, absolutely.' In March 2018 he said a diluted Brexit would be a worse national humiliation than the Suez crisis.[3]

As for the European Union, a shrewd and amusing summary of the many different 'mental universes' out of which it was born and which it continues to instantiate was posted online on 12 December 2018 by Andreas Kluth as a *Handelsblatt Today* blog:

1950s, the six founding members: The West Germans, happy to be part of any club again, were eager to atone for invading everybody by proving what great post-nationalist Europeans they now were. The French, having recently been trounced by the Germans and (possibly worse) rescued by

Yankees, and having then lost an empire, were thrilled to keep projecting global French power via a new 'Europe'. (The deal was that the Germans, even with a mightier economy, would always play second fiddle to the French in diplomacy.)

The Italians, reeling from one collapsing government to another and mired in corruption, were trying to outsource governance to the cleaner north. The BeNeLux three were overjoyed to be, finally, at the table with the French and Germans at all.

1973: After long dithering, the Brits, still chuffed about their 'splendid isolation' but also chafing at their waning empire, pragmatically re-defined 'Europe' as no more than a customs union, and dipped in a reluctant toe, to buy and sell more stuff. (Besides, the French were running that club, so better keep an eye on them!) If the English were in, the Irish felt they should be more in. The Danes, in their continental appendage, opted to tag along at a safe distance (although Greenland, 12 years later, would stage the first Grexit).

1980s: The Greeks, Portuguese and Spanish, having got rid of their dictators only in the 1970s, couldn't wait to re-join the rest of Europe, and thus modernity. 1990: The East Germans hadn't even thought about it; they just wanted to join the other Germans. 1995: The Swedes and Finns, seeing that the Danes were in and the Norwegians not, decided to check it out. The Austrians wanted to show that they could do Anschluss right. (During golf and ski season the border delays between Munich and Kitzbühel had been such a nuisance!)

2004, 2007, 2013: The Iron Curtain was gone, hurrah, so it was about time for the Poles, Hungarians and other easterners to get the heck away from the Russians and into the West. (But they had for so long been part of empires – Ottoman, Austrian, Russian, German, Soviet – that they now wanted to build their own nations, not slide into a new Eurocrat empire.)

As for my own involvement with 'the matter of Europe' viewed from a Welsh perspective, there is a certain symmetry to the fact that this book was in preparation at the very juncture when a continuing future for Britain within the European Union was coming to seem but a dim and distant possibility, because I was first introduced to such issues at the very outset of my own intellectual journey. One of the very few books I read outside the A-level syllabus when a sixth-former at grammar school, preparing for interview for admission to the then University College of Swansea, was John Gunther's *Inside Europe Today*. Sadly, my proud reference to this reading failed to impress my interviewer, who pointed out fairly enough that I was applying for a place to read English Literature rather than International Politics. But Gunther's book provided me with an invaluable introduction to the crucial post-war process, still at an embryonic stage in the late sixties, of forging a union between the major nations of Europe that would help prevent the possibility of yet further murderous international conflict.

He opened the chapter he entitled 'At Sixes and Sevens' with a reminder of how the 'European Community' had begun.[4] Two of the key figures were Jean Monnet, a visionary French economist, and Robert Schuman, a native of Luxemburg with family roots in the long-contested region of Lorraine, who had been Prime Minister of France before becoming its Foreign Minister. In May 1950 they proposed the creation of 'a common authority for French and German coal and steel'. Italy, Belgium, the Netherlands and Luxembourg rallied to the idea, and so on 18 April 1951 a formal treaty was agreed at intergovernmental level on the establishment of the European Coal and Steel Community (ECSC). To consolidate this development, a European Parliament was formed, which first met, with Paul-Henri Spaak as its president, in September 1952 (*IET*, 247). Gunther then proceeded to trace the stages by which, under the Treaty of Rome on 25 March 1957, the 'European Community' still existent at the date his book appeared (1961) had come into being. This consisted of 'three different but closely interlocked instruments – the ECSC for coal and steel, the Common Market, and Euratom' (*IET*, 248). Even though this present study at no point addresses the development of the European Union, or of the related phenomena of 'Europeanisation'[5] and anti-Europeanisation, it may nevertheless be useful, and indeed salutary, to remind ourselves of that admirable, idealistic vision of a viable, practical 'Europeanness' from which that Union originated all of those sixty and more years ago.

Those who wish a people to lose their identity cause them first to lose their memory. In both the lead-up to and the aftermath of the fateful Brexit vote in Wales, I was forcibly struck by two things: first, the complete ignorance displayed of the long history of Wales's own distinctive and complex relationship with Europe; and second, the virtually exclusive concentration on the political and economic implications of Wales's European associations. Little awareness, if any, was shown of the cultural aspects of Wales–Europe relations. And it is to these, and these alone, in particular as addressed by selected writers and intellectuals, that this book proposes to pay some preliminary attention.

I have for some time found it convenient to distinguish very crudely but highly suggestively between two kinds of Welshness – one that orientates itself towards the USA, the other that orientates itself towards Europe. The former is evidently very much the stronger, grounded as it largely is in the socially influential anglophone monoculture of an industrial, and latterly post-industrial south Wales that, from the 1920s onwards, has boasted the label of 'American Wales'. When Dai Smith presented a series of programmes on the making of industrial south Wales a few decades back, it opened with a shot of him speaking while standing on the Brooklyn Bridge. And a few years ago, when he published his important personal memoir of his south Wales industrial experience, *In the Frame*, the connections of that region with the US again loomed large.[6]

But that same year, the multilingual Ned Thomas published his own personal memoir, *Bydoedd*, which outlined his impressive career as a lifelong Europhile and Euro-traveller, convinced that his Wales needed to link itself not to the States, and not to the Europe of the large powers, but to a Europe constituted of a rich multitude of small nations and subnational regions.[7] It was that vision in part that prompted him to launch *Planet*, his influential periodical of the seventies, and that subsequently drove him to work within the administrative structures of the newly established European Commission to bring to Aberystwyth the unit charged by the Commission with monitoring the media output of so-called less used languages across Europe. His protégée Sioned Puw Rowlands became founding Director of the Literature Exchange project in Aberystwyth for translating key Welsh texts into several of Europe's languages. She later became domiciled in Paris, as did Owen Martell, the leading Welsh-language novelist who initially edited with her the cutting-edge cultural periodical *O'r Pedwar Gwynt* – which could therefore be regarded as a Parisian production. And there are many other important recent cultural initiatives stemming from this vision of Wales's place in Europe that are worth mentioning. One relates to the ERASMUS student placement scheme so long important to British universities. And who was one of its visionary founders? It was Hywel Ceri Jones, a Welsh-speaker from Pontardawe, and at one time head of the European Commission's Department of Education and Youth Policy.

It was as official representatives of Britain, and not Wales, that other Welshmen made notable contributions to the development of the European Community. During his time as an MEP, Wayne David spent a period as leader of the Labour Group in the European Parliament. Roy Jenkins (Lord Jenkins of Hillhead) served from 1977 until 1981 as president of the European Commission, the only Briton to hold that post. (Lord) Neil Kinnock served for a period first as a European commissioner and later (1999–2004) as vice-president of the European Commission under Romano Prodi. Welsh-speakers of distinguished European pedigree include the eminent British diplomat Sir Emyr Jones Parry, whose senior position in Brussels was as director European Union during the 1998 United Kingdom presidency of the European Union, with overall responsibility for policy, coordination and organisation of the presidency. Aneurin Rhys Hughes is another, who filled a number of key posts in the European civil service. Hughes served as EU ambassador to various countries, including Norway, Australia and New Zealand, and was chief of staff to Ivor Richard (another Welshman) when he was European commissioner for employment, social affairs and inclusion. Finally, there is the case of Rob (now Sir Rob) Wainwright, the Welsh-speaker from Pontyberem, who was head of Europol from 2009 to 2018.

The fundamental division in Welsh self-perception and positioning implicated in the division between American Wales and European Wales has long fascinated me. Consequently I have published several works that have highlighted Wales's American dreams, including a chapter in my book *Corresponding Cultures* and the volume *Gweld Sêr: Cymru a Chanrif America*, important because it included the testimony of many of the leading writers of contemporary Wales to the enduring fascination and inspiration of the United States.[8] My own pioneering work on such cultural interactions has of course been significantly augmented and enriched by Daniel Williams's brilliant subsequent study of the links between Wales and African America.[9]

My intention after publishing *Gweld Sêr* in 2002 had been to edit a similar volume on Wales's European dreams, but I was sidetracked by other interests, and so my venture at outlining what I had in mind was limited to a lecture, entitled 'Ewtopia: Cyfandir Dychymyg y Cymry', delivered to mark the new millennium at the Centre for Advanced Welsh and Celtic Studies in Aberystwyth. Eighteen years later, that lecture found printed form in the collection of Welsh-language essays I published under the title *Cyfan-dir Cymru*.[10]

This present book is an attempt to carry the subject a little further, by studying some of the most striking models of relationship between Wales and Europe that have been developed by writers and intellectuals over the last century and a half. What it clearly is not, is a comprehensive, authoritative treatment of the subject. And so, as if to set the tone of the following discussion, let me begin with a typically bold and sweeping assertion that Saunders Lewis made in 1937: 'Wales can understand Europe, because she is one of the family.' He glossed this by adding: 'The Welsh are the only nation in Britain who have been part of the Roman Empire.'[11] And then, by way of counterpoint, it is interesting to note a comment made by Jan Morris sixty years later: 'I found myself in Welshness and came to realize that I had also been an European all the time.'[12]

Two more different authors and characters than Lewis and Morris you'd be hard pushed to find, yet they concur on the primacy for them of the Welsh European identity. Morris's handy term for it is 'Euro-Welshness' (*FYE*, 359). And they further concur in their (no doubt fanciful) conviction that such a European identity is foreign to the English. In Lewis's case that is because the Welsh, having been fashioned within the Roman Empire, are the legitimate heirs of that culture's pan-Europeanism. Whereas, as the descendants of one of those 'barbarian' tribes that dismantled the empire, the Saxon English are not. In short, Lewis is elaborating a powerful myth of origin for the Welsh. Morris, on the other hand, believes that the outlook of the English is still influenced by a recent imperial history of world domination that, along with their supposed special relationship with the USA, convinces them of their continuing difference from (and superiority to) their European neighbours. For both Lewis and Morris, therefore, the image of a Wales in Europe is in part a kind of back-construction; an important and powerful alternative to the current state of affairs, which is a Wales in England. To be a Welsh European is, among other things, an effective means of not being English. This is a seminal dimension of Welsh Europeanism that, we will find, keeps recurring. And we can go one step further. With the rise of the United States to imperial, hegemonic power after World War II, Welsh Europeanism offered to some writers and intellectuals an alternative to an erosive Welsh relationship to global Anglo-Americanism. Just as, for them, pre-war Welsh Europeanism was an alternative to British jingoism and Imperialism.

I think it may be useful at the outset to distinguish between several different versions of Welsh Europeanism that we find operative in the culture between the mid- nineteenth century and the late twentieth century, some of which will be examined in greater detail in the body of this book. Needless to say this is a very rough-and-ready, home-made kind of taxonomy. Some of these models obviously interlock, while others are nakedly conflicting.

THE HOME RULE MODEL

The great uprising of peoples across Europe in 1848 fascinated and appalled Nonconformist Wales in equal measure. The immediate response was not, as it was in Ireland, to emphasise the struggles of subordinated peoples for recognition, but rather to view these revolutions as popular agitations for greater representative government along British lines. Later in the century, however, some of the intelligentsia of the day – most of whom were Nonconformist ministers – found much to admire in figures they considered to be constructive moderates and progressives, such as Mazzini and Kossuth (and Ireland's Thomas Davis). But the abject desire of the middle class of Victorian Wales, whose rural population and industrial proletariat alike were regarded as dangerously unruly by the English establishment, was to prove its undying loyalty to the British state and empire. And this was reinforced at this very time by the publication of the notorious Blue Books Report, which found one of the many shortcomings of the primitive Welsh to be their stubborn adherence to a native tongue that was not only barbarous but also an obstacle to their smooth assimilation into English society.

By the end of the nineteenth century, a desire for a degree of home rule was being voiced, and actively pursued, by some sections of the Young Wales/Cymru Fydd movement. But any incipient Europeanism could not compete with the stubborn determination of the Welsh, still ancient Britons to the core, to trust to the evolution of another multi-state collective, that of the British empire. The hope was that over the course of time the empire would evolve into a worldwide Commonwealth of erstwhile colonised subject peoples that had been granted a polite degree of tractable self-government.

THE POSTCOLONIAL MODEL

There were, however, one or two powerful dissenting opinions, trenchantly expressed by the fiery proto-nationalist Michael D. Jones and the important late Victorian journalist and polemicist Emrys ap Iwan. His was a prescient reading. The most electrifying controversialist ever produced by Wales, he inveighed against the way in which the Welsh mind had been thoroughly colonised by the English. The Welsh were, he argued, a conquered, assimilated and thoroughly cowed people. Saisaddoliaeth – English-worship – was the national disease. His Nonconformist colleagues, afraid of their own shadows, were obsessed with toeing the English line and with slavishly imitating English manners. And they were in thrall to the big sugar daddy beyond their border.

The only remedy for this, Emrys ap Iwan claimed, was for them to raise their modestly downcast eyes and look beyond their insolent neighbours to a continental Europe that had been fashioned in the image of his hero, Napoleon. Proud of his own French ancestry, the exasperated and cholerically impatient ap Iwan assured his cowed compatriots that the England by which they were overawed looked altogether different and very much smaller when viewed from a European point of view.

THE NONCONFORMIST MODEL

The great fashioner of this form of late Victorian Welsh Europeanism was O. M. Edwards, a giant of the time on the cultural scene in Wales. An Oxford don of brilliant intellectual gifts and lowly Welsh origins, he well-nigh killed himself to produce an extraordinary range of popular periodicals and histories of Wales, in both Welsh and English, in order to educate his people in their past and orientate them in their present. He also produced three popular travelogues, in which he outlined his view of Europe as seen through the lens of the Nonconformist convictions that reinforced his Whiggish view of history as the divinely ordained progress of all peoples towards the representative government already enjoyed by Britain. Catholic Europe, for him instanced by the Brittany and the Italy that he visited, clearly fell well short of this blessed state. For Edwards, true progress remained confined to northern, Protestant Europe, having radiated out from the free mercantile towns of the Low Countries. But the true powerhouse of progress had been Calvin's Geneva, in which Edwards spent some considerable time.

In one way, Edwards's outlook was typical of the rural Wales of the chapels that had recently seen the rising of small tenant farmers, like his father, against their oppressive foreign landlords. In another way, though, Edwards's model of Welsh Europeanism actually contrasted with that which was dominant in the Nonconformist Wales of his time, which placed Germany, contemporary powerhouse of the most progressive theology and most advanced biblical scholarship, firmly at the centre of its vision of Europe. By the end of the nineteenth century the most brilliant of Welsh chapel ministers were completing their training at the great universities of Germany, and there imbibing the new scholarship that was actually steadily undermining the Calvinism that Edwards espoused. And German philosophy appealed as much to Welsh intellectuals as German theology. Hegel, in particular, with his progressivist vision of the advance of national communities in accordance with the evolutionary laws of a spiritualised universe, spoke appealingly to the 'religiose' Welsh, and so it is no surprise to learn that one of the most prominent of late Victorian British Hegelians was Henry Jones, who had risen from poverty in rural Wales to the giddy heights of the Regius Chair in Philosophy at Edinburgh University.

THE SMALL NATION MODEL

As was evidenced in the case of O. M. Edwards, the late nineteenth century had seen the opening of Europe up to middle-class travellers. But this terminated abruptly with the First World War, as did Nonconformist Wales's infatuation with things German. The focus now switched to imaginary Welsh affinities with poor persecuted little Belgium, and even with poor persecuted little Serbia, as Lloyd George played unscrupulously on 'local' national sentiment by representing Wales, too, as one of the little countries of Europe perpetually threatened with bullying by the big boys. As minister of munitions and then secretary of state for war, he campaigned to create a 50,000-strong Welsh corps, but the plan was modified to produce the 38th Infantry Division that went on to carnage and fame at Mametz Wood, Pilckem Ridge and Ypres.

In his tub-thumping, he was staunchly aided and abetted by the *Welsh Outlook*, the leading cultural periodical of the day, which was an organ of the Liberal Party in Wales. Following the outbreak of war, it began to feature articles about prominent Belgian refugees, such as the leading visual artists who had sought refuge in Wales. These were however but the beginning, and over the next few years the *Outlook* published a stream of fascinating articles about the languages, cultures and, above all, the politics, of contemporary Europe. Then, as the Great War drew to an end, the *Welsh Outlook* worked itself into a paroxysm of ecstatic Welsh Europeanism. Its confident supposition was that Lloyd George, sometime famed nationalist and champion of small peoples, would take advantage of Woodrow Wilson's wish to empower the latter to ensure that little Wales, too, would be guaranteed a significant degree of home rule, just like Poland, Serbia and the other new nations. We all know how that dream ended.

PEACE MOVEMENT WELSH EUROPEANISM

An important by-product of the home rule model of Welsh Europeanism favoured during the Great War was the Peace Pledge Movement of the 1930s in which prominent Welsh intellectual and cultural leaders took part. This movement, which actually began during the last phase of the war, was particularly strong in Wales, naturally dovetailing as it did with the activities of the pre-existing indigenous pacifist society Cymdeithas y Cyfamod. There had, after all, been a strong tradition of internationalist and pan-European solidarity for peace in Wales building up in Welsh Nonconformity ever since the tireless campaigning of Henry Richard of Tregaron, the legendary late Victorian 'Apostle of Peace', whose contribution was eventually recognised by the League of Nations. And one of the founding figures of that League was Lord Davies of Llandinam (and Gregynog), grandson of the pioneering industrialist 'Top-Sawyer' David Davies. He it was in due course who both funded and thus founded the Temple of Peace in Cardiff (which opened in 1938), and established the world's first Chair of International Politics in the University College of Wales, Aberystwyth. An associate of Lord Davies, the Rev. Gwilym Davies, was one of the organisers of the Youth Message of Peace and Goodwill first broadcast to the world in 1922, which continues to be broadcast on 18 May every year (the date of the first peace conference at the Hague in 1899). Along with Lord Davies, Gwilym Davies was a founder (1920–2) of the Welsh League of Nations Union and a strong proponent of the view that Wales had a mission to spread the message of international peace throughout the world. During the 1920s, the Union grew to include 1,014 local organisations and to boast a membership of some 60,000. In 1923 it supported the Welsh Women's Peace Petition to

America, which featured 390,000 signatories, urging the US to join the League of Nations. Then in 1926 Wales hosted the League of Nations International Peace Congress in Aberystwyth.[13]

Lord Davies also played a prominent part during the 1930s in attempts to construct a pan-European political order that would curb the aggressive power of the great nation states. So, when the pacifist politician Gwynfor Evans became leader of Plaid Cymru after the war, he was very conscious of following in the footsteps of such distinguished Welsh Europeans as this. And he – with rather touching naivety – supposed that the breakdown of Europe's great endlessly warring feuding states into an alliance of small peoples would provide the foundation of a new peaceful European order. The Welsh, as a stateless people with no strong, established tradition of militarism of their own, were, or so he (like Davies) fondly chose to believe, particularly well placed to become one of the leaders of post-war Europe in this peacefully internationalist direction.

CULTURAL RENAISSANCE MODEL

Even before the war, a brilliant young generation of writers and scholars was emerging for the first time from the newly established University of Wales. These then often went on to Oxford, and further afield to Freiburg and the Sorbonne, where they became excited by their discovery of the wealth of strikingly innovative creative talent available on the continent. Figures such as John Morris-Jones, an accomplished lyricist as well as a major scholar, were belatedly discovering German Romanticism, and T. H. Parry Williams was encountering modernist experimentation, the philosophy of Bergson in Paris and the psychoanalysis of the Freudians in Freiburg. T. Gwynn Jones, whose 1902 *awdl* 'Ymadawiad Arthur' was the harbinger of a remarkable Welsh-language literary renaissance, went on to translate poetry from French, German, Italian, Spanish, Breton and Gaelic into Welsh.

This momentum was subsequently maintained during the interwar period, not least through the publication of translations. Over the decades these embraced not only literatures in the usual major western European languages but also materials from Romania, Russia and Czechoslovakia. And when Emyr Humphreys became producer of drama for the BBC in Wales in the late 1950s he set about commissioning a number of groundbreaking contemporary plays from

Europe, inspiring his mentor and friend Saunders Lewis to produce his own major European play, *Brad/Treachery*, about the German officers' plot to kill Hitler in 1944, a piece that was very well received when performed in Germany.

THE RADICAL CONSERVATIVE MODEL

The most powerful, influential, controversial and magisterial version of Welsh Europeanism to have been constructed to date is without doubt that developed by Saunders Lewis between the two World Wars. His view was that Wales had become the first victim of the nation state of England constructed by Henry VIII, and his vision was of a recovery by Wales of decisive powers of self-determination under the auspices of a restored pan-European order sponsored by a resurgent Catholicism.

Beginning by seconding Emrys ap Iwan's view that Wales was hopelessly in thrall to England and things English, Lewis developed a highly idealistic model of a Wales that experienced the golden age of its culture when it was embedded in the pan-European Catholic culture of the Middle Ages. It was an attempt to instil in his compatriots a degree at least of cultural pride sufficient to kick-start the slow process of rebuilding a national confidence that could result in political action to secure a much greater degree of self-government. And it was a model developed against the background of what might be called the culture wars of the inter-war period, a period when English literature was, under the powerful auspices of Eliot and Leavis, busily claiming to lie at the very core of Anglo-British identity. Lewis's model was, therefore, a very powerful enabling myth with considerable political as well as cultural potential, and, for all its very obvious drawbacks and dubious implications and associations, it needs to be treated seriously as such.

THE RADICAL LEFT MODEL

In 1941 Cyril P. Cule published his book of continental travel, *Cymro ar Grwydr*.[14] In it he contrasts the reactions of Welsh nationalists to the Penyberth incident of 1936 with their disregard of the bombing of Guernica that occurred that same year. Guernica, he pointedly notes, was not just a Spanish city; it was the ancient capital of Euskadi and the Basques, another of Europe's small peoples. Yet 1930s nationalists had shown little interest in its reduction to rubble, perhaps because theirs was an ideology largely rooted in rural, Welsh-speaking Wales, whereas Euskadi was, like anglophone south Wales, a heavily industrialised region. He praised the courage of the Welsh section of the International Brigade who had fought against Franco during the Spanish Civil War, and wholeheartedly endorsed the fighters' vision of a Europe composed of the transnational solidarity of industrial workers. Cule thus added a European dimension both to the myth of the 'gwerin' that had been inherited from nineteenth-century Wales and to the cause of an international socialism with a distinctively Welsh face preached by the likes of that legendary character Niclas y Glais.

   In Cule's work, then, we have one of the earliest, and most attractive, of distinctively Welsh textual expressions of a Europe of the workers. His is a model of Welsh Europeanism to be later embraced, for example, by that most charismatic of modern Welsh historians, Gwyn A. Williams, whose version of Welsh Europeanism was in part a response, late in his career, to the retreat, and then effective rout, of the traditional British left in the face of triumphal Thatcherism. It is a model that overlaps with that developed by those left-wingers in Plaid Cymru who, from the 1930s onwards, had found themselves at odds with the values of their party's sometime leader Saunders Lewis, in that they were increasingly attracted to the progressive socialist models of society beginning to be favoured by Scandinavian countries. With Plaid's decisive swing to the left from the 1970s onwards came an interest in the New Left policies of cognate national movements across Europe, and in the eminent Welsh cultural critic Raymond Williams the party found a new, persuasive advocate of this socialist model of a 'Welsh Europeanism'.

MULTICULTURAL MODEL

I began by quoting Jan Morris to the effect that once she'd shed her British imperialism and had found her Welshness, she had also discovered herself to be a European. She made this remark in connection with her deep attachment to Trieste, a city she has come to regard as the real cultural capital of Europe, because of its strong insistence on its liminal identity. Unwilling to be attached to any single large centralist state, it has become for her the epitome of fluid cultural pluralism and multiculturalism. Viewing Wales from that vantage point

has allowed Morris to see it as one of the many 'minority nations'
of Europe –

> not just enclavists, or ethnic segmentarians, or members of compulsory
> federations, or islanders, but people who, though clamped within the
> frontiers of greater states, still consider themselves complete nations in
> themselves, inhabiting their native territories. They have all been mucked
> about by history in one way or another. (*FYE*, 98)

Her eclectic version of Euro-Welshness continues to be attractive to
sections of contemporary Welsh intellectual society because it is so
clearly in keeping with the spirit of our time.[15]

While this rough taxonomy of Welsh Europeanism is unlikely to prove
exhaustive, it does at least offer us a map for orientating the provi-
sional discussion that follows, a discussion that is confined to those
instances of this complex and pressingly important subject that I
personally have found most interesting, and most rewarding to study.
To the eyes of a professional economist, sociologist or historian, these
versions of Welsh Europeanism cannot but seem hopelessly naive and
impractical. And indeed the title of this present volume – *Eutopia*
– implicitly draws attention to the idealistic and fantastical aspect
of these models, products as they very largely are of the creative
thinking of artists and related intellectuals. Many of them clearly do
not provide a credible blueprint for practical action, nor are any of
them reflective of 'mainstream' opinion in Wales of any period. But
to dismiss them in consequence as mere castles in the air would be to
mistake their real function and significance – to fail to realise the valuable 'cultural work' they are performing. Because they are all attempts
– as Saunders Lewis amongst others quite consciously realised – to
shift the axis of the Welsh mind; to persuade the thinking Welsh man
and woman to look, for once at least, not in the usual, imprisoning
direction of England for a reflection, but rather at the very different
social forms and traditions on offer across continental Europe, and to
begin to uncover there new parallels to, and insights into, the peculiar
circumstances of Wales; circumstances that have long been occluded
by traditional Welsh preoccupations with England.
    To deal with 'the matter of Europe' at all involves inescapably
sailing into waters that are both immensely deep and worryingly

treacherous. While this book lays no claim to plumbing these depths, it would nevertheless seem sensible to take one or two preliminary soundings of the subject so as to be better able to navigate. While the chapters that follow do not map exactly onto the taxonomy of Welsh Europeanism offered above, when considered as a whole they cover very much the same territory.

Where exactly does Europe begin and where does it end? The question acquired new point in the immediate aftermath of the collapse of the Soviet empire in Europe. For decades until then, 'Europeanism' had been primarily confined to the western region of the continent, 'Eastern Europe' being out of bounds and accordingly regarded – at least unconsciously – as being as remote, marginal and 'alien' as it was inaccessible. And yet countries such as Poland had, until the Second World War, seemed to cosmopolitan intellectuals to be a primary site of 'Mitteleuropa', the very heartland of Europe and the great, rich melting-pot of many national languages and cultures. Once the Cold War was over and the nations of 'Eastern Europe' had begun to be readmitted, via the European Union, to the European fold, questions began to be asked as to where, then, the boundaries of Europe could be safely said to terminate? Was Russia part of Europe or not? And what about Turkey? As for 'Eastern Europe', it migrated eastward as nations such as Ukraine and Georgia began to assert their liberated presence. But so far, the Welsh have demonstrated precious little interest in such developments. As Professor Robin Okey, himself an acknowledged international authority on Slavic and other peoples, has ruefully pointed out, Welsh Europeans have long stubbornly ignored the clutch of small central and eastern European nations many of which re-emerged into view and into modern nationhood following the collapse of the Habsburg empire.[16]

As for the European union, what kind of 'Europe' exactly did it represent? What function did it perform? Having been born as an urgent post-war initiative intended to minimise the possibility of future bloody conflicts between the great nations of Europe, it had therefore initially been a hybrid of social, cultural, economic and political developments. But as it grew, so it seemed increasingly to be driven primarily by economic interests, even as it developed ever more ambitious programmes of cultural support. And as far as its political structure was concerned, it became a bulwark of the established order of nation states, led, as ever, by the more powerful. While 'regionalism' was certainly recognised and catered for, this Europe had no sympathy with any genuinely advanced empowerment of minority peoples, let alone with a deliberate shift towards a politico-cultural pluralism much greater than ever before. Its alarm when both the small countries of Scotland and Catalonia began to agitate in earnest, and with very real success, for self-government, was immediately manifest and very palpable.

What concept of 'Europe' do, and did, the 'Europeans' themselves have in reality? Is any such concept currently recognised by the peoples at large, or indeed has it ever been? Or has the idea of a Europe always been confined in reality to a small, and privileged, intellectual elite? The events of the last few years – including, most obviously, Brexit – strongly suggest the latter. The Europeanism of the peoples of Europe seems to have been exposed as primarily pragmatic in character and merely economic in orientation. Nor is this surprising, if one believes that the modern concept of a 'Europe' is actually a derivative of the 'prior' concept of a 'nation', even though a cadre of intellectuals argued the exact opposite during the inter-war years, insisting that modern 'nations' were a secondary formation, the products of a collapse of a 'prior', pan-European, Catholic civilisation. One of the drivers of this radically reactionary ideology, of course, was a healthy antipathy to the kind of malign and immensely powerful cult of the nation being aggressively cultivated at that time in fascist Germany. In other words, the very idea of a 'Europe' has undoubtedly at times operated as a defensive intellectual formation, constructed and vigorously promoted in order to protect an important, but vulnerable, body of values.

And then there is the 'Europe' which, it could be argued, is a product of the imagination of the United States. Indeed, throughout the period covered in this volume, the States have functioned as the 'other' of Europe, silently shaping both a Europe made in its own image and, by reaction, a Europe that has been enabled, for the first time, to become self-conscious through its awareness of being *unlike* the States. Three of the great, sophisticated, exponents of the former kind of American Europeanism were Henry James, T. S. Eliot and Ezra Pound. While supposing that in 'Europe' they had discovered the civilised antithesis of everything they detested about the vulgar, dollar-mad, populist United States of their own age, which they had so precipitately fled, these three were in fact treating Europe as if its respective national cultures and collectives related to the European whole much as the constituent states of the Union related to the United States as a whole. In other words, they treated these cultures as if their deep linguistic differences and profoundly different pasts were of no more than superficial concern; all were mere local variants of some primary European social, cultural and political collective. 'Who do I call if I want to call Europe?' Henry Kissinger once exasperatedly enquired.

For Americans, the cultural unity of Europe was accordingly unproblematic – as, of course, it could never be for Europeans themselves. And so powerful was the influence of their thinking on the literary and intellectual culture of the post-war anglophone world – and on Britain in particular – that it left its indelible mark on the Europeanism of some impressive thinkers of the inter-war generation, including, as we shall see, the Welsh writer Saunders Lewis. For these thinkers, the Europe they vigorously imagined into being provided an escape from all the ills of a 'modernity' the dark incarnation of which was the United States.

Finally, it is worth registering the vexed issue of Eurocentrism, while noting that an awareness of it began to loom large in Western consciences only during the closing decades of the twentieth century. To examine the history of Welsh Europeanism in the light of a newly sharpened awareness of the ignorance and arrogance long ingrained in the settled supposition of European intellectuals that all major human initiatives and achievements had originated in a Europe that could therefore safely be regarded as the cradle of advanced civilisation is certainly to realise its prejudices and limitations. It was a weakness compounded in many cases – such as that of Saunders Lewis – by the additional confident assumption that even within Europe the only true custodians of civilised living were such majestic nations of western Europe as France and Germany. Nowhere do we find recorded either an acknowledgement of the astonishing achievements of so many profoundly 'other' cultures across the world or a realisation that many of the major developments in the arts and sciences traditionally attributed to Europe were in fact imports from the neighbouring Muslim world and even further afield.

When situated in such contexts as those superficially outlined above, the variants of Welsh Europeanism with which this volume is concerned cannot but seem piddling, provincial and hopelessly naive exercises in a variety of utopianisms. So indeed in one important sense they undeniably are. But viewed as politico-cultural strategies, creatively stimulating by-products of the long struggle by Wales to retain some small remnants, at least, of a cultural specificity long remorselessly threatened by English hegemony within Britain, they do nevertheless possess, or so at least I would argue, some compelling power and continuing relevance.

Norman Davies is one of the most distinguished of contemporary British historians. Sometime professor of History at the School of Slavonic Studies, University of London, and Supernumerary Fellow of Wolfson College, Oxford, he is now professor at the Jagiellonian University at Cracow, an Honorary Fellow of St Antony's College, Oxford, and a Fellow of the British Academy. Particularly well known and admired in Poland, having written a definitive history of that country, he became a best-seller when he published in short order a history of Europe and a highly distinctive history of Britain under the title *The Isles*. Long an admirer of his, I was therefore eager to read the new book he published in 2011, not only because it appeared under his name but also because it was entitled *Vanished Kingdoms: The History of Half-Forgotten Europe*.

The subject fascinated me not least because it spoke to my under-standing of my own cultural situation. In some ways I feel I belong to a 'survivor culture', one that has had to live with the very real danger of extinction virtually from the date of its inception in the immediate aftermath of the Roman withdrawal from Britain not far off 2,000 years ago. Mine has always therefore been a world perman-ently existing on the very brink of vanishing, perhaps more so than ever today, because of the ever-increasing, encroaching and eroding power of a global English, the spread of which threatens the exist-ence of many, if not most, of the world's languages. As I repeatedly try to explain in this volume, the Welsh Europeanism with which it is concerned can only be understood, and properly appreciated, as a product of this perilous situation; as a cultural 'survival strategy' if you will; an attempt to save Welsh culture, along with the Welsh identity of which it could still arguably be said to be a vital sustaining element, from the void.

Norman Davies's work of cultural salvage therefore naturally appeals to me, concentrating as it does on recovering a few long-vanished cultures from the void of historical unknowing to which they have long been consigned. As he explains in his Preface, the vanished kingdoms of Europe are legion, and his own study can concern itself only with a handful of examples. 'I have', he writes, been at pains to present vanished kingdoms drawn from as many of the main periods and regions of European history as space would allow. Tolosa, for example, comes from Western Europe, Litva and Galicia from the East, Alt Clud and Eire are based in the British Isles, Borussia in the Baltic, Tsernagora in the Balkans, and Aragon in Iberia and the Mediterranean. The chapter covering the 'Five, Six or Seven Kingdoms' of Burgundia tells a medieval story that straddles modern France and Germany; Sabaudia deals mainly with the early modern period while linking France, Switzerland and Italy; and Rosenau and CCCP [USSR] are confined to the nineteenth and twentieth centuries.[17]

It is, then, a dizzying glimpse into the vortex of oblivion that he offers us, and it is accompanied by a warning that our own cultures are historically predestined to be swallowed up by the same void.

But if I was naturally disposed by my own cultural situation to be interested in such a theme, imagine my pleasure, on obtaining a copy of Davies's book, in discovering that it was prefaced by an epigraph in Welsh, accompanied by its English translation: 'I'r anghofiedig'/'For those whom historians tend to forget'. In penning that Welsh epigraph it is very unlikely that he was unaware he was vaguely echoing a famous line from a poem by the great Welsh-language writer of the twentieth century, the remarkable Waldo Williams. Entitled 'Cofio' (Remembrance) it brings to mind the myriad forgotten inhabitants of distant past centuries, on whose lips so many long-dead languages were once vivid with life. And in its powerful ending it recollects, in both senses of that word, the innumerable multitude of the mute dead, 'a'u breuddwyd dwyfol a'u dwyfoldeb brau' ('with their divine dreams and their fragile divinity'):

> Mynych ym mrig yr hwyr, a mi yn unig,
> Daw hiraeth am eich 'nabod chwi bob un;
> A oes a'ch deil o hyd mewn Cof a Chalon,
> Hen bethau anghofiedig teulu dyn?

> (Often, on brink of night and lonely
> A longing grips to know you every one;
> Is there a soul who holds you still in heart and memory
> You old forgotten things of human kind?)[18]

But the epigraph was far from being the sole acknowledgement of Wales in this study. On the very first page of his Introduction, Davies explained that his interest in the subject covered by his book could be traced back to the repeated experience he'd enjoyed as a boy of visiting his Welsh-speaking relatives in Bethesda, in north Wales. Not only did it leave him with a lifelong interest in the Welsh language and its literature, past and present; it also predisposed him to identify with the conquered, not with the conquerors – that is with the losers of history, not the victors. 'As someone brought up in English surroundings', he writes, 'I never ceased to be amazed that everywhere which we now call "England" was once not English at all. The amazement underlines much of what is written in *Vanished Kingdoms*. Dover, after all, or the Avon, are pure Welsh names' (p. 2).

So, then, Davies's observations, along with his book as a whole, throws an interesting new light on the complex phenomenon of Welsh Europeanism. Whereas I, like the thinkers whose ideas are examined in this volume, was predisposed to view Europe through Welsh eyes, Davies is, in a way, inviting Europe to view itself through Welsh eyes; to see important aspects of its past, and also indeed of its future, mirrored in Welsh history, which is the history of a people who have long lost that which once was theirs, and who have ever since perforce had to learn – and to learn anew from generation to generation – what it is to survive as a 'diminished thing'; the perilous art of hovering on the edge of extinction. It is an art, Norman Davies implies, that contemporary Europe, increasingly threatened both from the east by the rise of long-suppressed civilisations and nations and from the west (and other points of the compass) by global Anglo-Americanism, may itself be well advised to begin learning. It is also an art that contemporary Britain – dramatically diminished, having lost all its imperial possessions, and also in real and ever-increasing danger of being swallowed up by Americanism – might itself do worse than begin cultivating. Instead of which, at least at the time of writing my own study, it seems hell-bent on a pig-headed isolationism and anti-Europeanism that currently finds expression as a defiant Brexit.

But there is also another, equally compelling, context into which the pro-Brexit vote in Wales might be put. Far more genuinely and widely reflective of mainstream opinion in Wales down the centuries than any of the models offered in this study is the belief that Wales belongs not to Europe but to a Britain that is usually positioned ideologically as well as geographically off-shore of the continent and decidedly wary of its relationship with it. One might go so far as to suggest (as Gwyn A. Williams has done) that just as the Welsh were, or so for more than 1,000 years they boasted of themselves, the first and therefore 'original' Britons, so they show every inclination to be the last. They are, and have always been, far more British than their neigh-bours the English, whose Britishness has more often than not been a code-word for a Greater Englishness. The pro-British identity of the Welsh that had its origins for a millennium in recollections of, and mournful longing for, the Britain-wide domination they once had sup-posedly enjoyed, was reinvigorated and, so to speak, retooled, during the eighteenth century and most particularly during the Napoleonic Wars. And in its new, revised, updated form, it continued to be a very influential factor in the whole history of Liberal, Nonconformist Wales before undergoing yet another major metamorphosis during the industrial period, when the centralist character of all the levels of growth, 'progress', and power clearly lay outside Wales and mostly well beyond its direct, 'personal' influence. Viewed in the light of this long, stubborn, history of Britishness, the pro-Brexit vote should have come as no surprise. Whereas in England it may clearly have been an expression of a resurgent, specifically English, nationalism, and the product of English nostalgia for Empire and the glorious super-nation heroics of the Second World War – and, as conceded earlier, this vision did indeed appeal to many of the Welsh as well – in crucial regions of Wales the anti-European vote was rather an unconscious resurgence of the nation's ancient loyalty to the idea of Britain.

To note this is, inevitably, to underline the fantastical nature of the models of European integration considered in this volume. Viewed in the harsh light of historical realities they appear to be no more than fond mirages. But as has already been emphasised their inter-est, and indeed their usefulness, does not really depend on sound alignment with social, economic and political realities. Rather they are cultural constructs, whose function it was, and still is, to open the Welsh mind to the possibility of future realities alternative to those that have become so familiar to us from our past that they have made circumstances that in reality are merely contingent seem permanent, inevitable and immutable. They are stimulating examples of what it might mean for us to 'dwell in possibility', which is what Emily Dickinson once memorably described as being any artist's true func-tion. In that sense, all these models belong in reality more to the realm of the creative arts than to history, politics or economics.

*

A brief word about the dates chosen to bracket the period covered
by this study. While their exactness is undeniably spurious, they
serve as useful markers of two significant stages in the development
of a Welsh Europeanism in the cultural sector. During the middle
decades of the nineteenth century, Welsh Nonconformist denominations very belatedly developed a political consciousness. While this
had momentous political consequences, it also slowly resulted in a
new kind of interest in European affairs. Heavily mediated though
this interest originally was by the strong loyalty felt in high Victorian
Wales to the cause of a Great Britain and its glorious global Empire,
by the end of the nineteenth century, and with the appearance of
the Cymru Fydd movement, it had evolved into a significantly more
independent Welsh outlook on Europe. Hence the choice of 1850 to
indicate the beginning of this phase of the development of a Welsh
Europeanism.

As for 1980, it represents the end of the phase, following Britain's
entry into membership of the European Union in 1973, of initial
adjustment by Wales to this new state of affairs. Thereafter, the country began very slowly to learn how to take advantage of this new
situation, although it remained hampered, as well as being advantaged, by the fact that Wales remained embedded in a powerfully
anglocentric British state. In the same period, availability of cheap
travel resulted in a radical change in popular Welsh perception, as
well as experience, of a continent to which access was now thoroughly
'democratised' as never before. With that democratisation of continental experience, it could be argued, came the 'disenchantment' of
Europe. That was soon followed by casual familiarity, if only with
the obvious hot holiday destinations and tourist spots, and with that
familiarity there came in due course, if not contempt, then at least
a blasé attitude towards all things European. Fundamental to this
whole reductive process was the stubborn refusal of most Welsh visitors to the continent to make even the most rudimentary attempt
to learn any of its languages or to probe the depth and richness of
any of its distinctive cultures. To have attempted to map and evalu-
ate the impact of all these startling transformations on the cultural
life of Wales would probably have meant doubling the size of a volume that is already unwieldy enough. Hence the decision to conclude
this discussion around 1980, the date at which *Planet*, the important
anglophone Welsh periodical of the seventies which was dedicated
to the promotion of a new kind of Welsh Europeanism, ceased

publication. (At the instigation of the Welsh Arts Council, and with
its handsome support, the periodical subsequently resumed publication in 1985.)

Welsh involvement with, and indeed in, Europe did not, of course,
begin in the nineteenth century. It is a feature of life as old as Wales
itself, and any account of it, however superficial, would be bound to
include mention at least of a series of glamorous examples. While
the Irish may in modern times have successfully given the world
the impression that all the legendary peregrine Celtic saints set sail
from their own Emerald Isle, there were Celtic saints from Wales
too, involved in the epic project of bringing Christianity, along with
the cultural legacy of the Classical period, to the attention of the
'barbarians' of the post-Roman continent. The Cistercian monks
who gradually went native and whose great Abbeys made important
contributions to late medieval culture had originally been brought to
Wales by the Normans from their religious headquarters at Cîteaux in
Burgundy. The highly imaginative and colourful fabrications woven by
Geoffrey of Monmouth, partly out of the ragged remnants of some
old Welsh traditions about a warrior-hero named Arthur became the
toast of Europe once they had been spruced up and richly embroi-
dered, and had assumed glossy new form in stylishly sophisticated
French romances and German tales of chivalry. The letter addressed
from Pennal, near Machynlleth, by Owain Glyndŵr in March 1406, in
the brief heyday of his power, to Charles VI of France and preserved
in the French National Archives, remains one of the greatest visionary documents to have been produced in Wales. While some may
proudly recall the key role played by Gwent archers in the English victories at Agincourt and Crécy, others may prefer to remember Owain
Lawgoch. Known on the continent as Yvain de Galles, this last heir
of the House of Gwynedd was a mercenary of legendary reputation
who served with great distinction in the forces of the French king.
Dafydd ap Gwilym and his contemporaries in a multicultural Wales
that was largely dominated by the Normans were very alive to contemporary literary fashions in Europe. The late eighteenth-century
group of Welsh Jacobins that included Iolo Morganwg looked to
revolutionary France for inspiration. Richard Price, the scandalously
overlooked eighteenth-century Welsh Dissenter from the Garw valley who remains arguably the greatest of Welsh philosophers, was a
radical political thinker as admired in revolutionary France as he had
previously been in revolutionary America.

Nowhere in these examples, however, can one readily discern the rudiments of what is nowadays known as Welsh Europeanism. For evidence of that one would need to consider the case of Gruffydd Robert, canon of Milan Cathedral, confessor and adviser of Cardinal Borromeo, and a leading figure of the Counter-Reformation. A distinguished Welsh Recusant, he was also a major Renaissance humanist and a fervent Welsh patriot. It was in Milan that he laboured on the first great grammar of the Welsh language, and it was in that city that he published it from 1567 onwards. Like all the leading European scholars of his day, he saw himself as a member of the pan-European community of learning that was one of the most glorious products of the Renaissance and a powerful engine of human advancement. And as a Welsh patriot, he passionately wished his own people to benefit from the revolution being effected by this new, enlightened scholarly project. His particular concern was for the well-being of the Welsh language, to which he actually gave voice in his famous Preface. 'Seeing myself disregarded and neglected for many long years by all in the land of the Welsh', the language there plaintively asserts, 'And without any fruitful writings [in me] that would serve to educate my people in learning and skill, I saw well to travel the countries of Europe and to discover if other languages were as unheeded and as unbeneficial to their speakers as I was.'[19] Robert was far from being alone in his time in viewing Wales in a European context. It was an outlook shared by all the great Welsh humanist scholars of his generation, both Protestant and Catholic. William Morgan, Richard Davies, William Salesbury, Siôn Dafydd Rhys (who himself spent several years in Italy), Maurice Kyffin, Morys Clynnog (the first rector of the English College in Rome) and John Davies (Mallwyd), in their way, and in their day, they were great Welsh Europeans all.

Sadly, however, over three centuries were to pass before Wales became capable of embracing such a vision again, and it is with that very belated re-emergence of Welsh Europeanism that this volume is concerned. In the overview that is on offer here there are undoubtedly several lacunae, of some of which I am already perfectly aware. For instance, in an important, and sadly neglected, article, the late R. Tudur Jones conclusively demonstrated that from the beginning of the nineteenth century onwards religious leaders from Wales's various Nonconformist denominations not only showed a lively interest in contemporary theological developments on the continent but actually travelled to Europe in order to learn more about such matters.[20] A seminal figure in Welsh historiography is Thomas Stephens, the mid-nineteenth-century Merthyr Unitarian chemist, who was a brilliant amateur scholar. He transformed understanding of the Welsh past when he coolly deconstructed and thoroughly discredited several of the myths relating to it that had previously been revered as gospel by the cultural establishment in Wales. These included belief in the Druidic origins of the Gorsedd and the legend of Prince Madoc's discovery of America. Ongoing research by Dr Marion Löffler at Cardiff University into Stephens's achievements is uncovering a body of the instructive correspondence he maintained with some of the eminent scholars who were engaged in developing a new 'scientific' historicism in the great German universities of the day.

This study therefore lays no claim to being either exhaustive in scope or authoritative in its treatment of its subject. It is merely indicative in intention: it does no more than rough out an interesting area of Welsh intellectual history. The hope is that some scholar of the future may be tempted to embark on a much fuller and better-informed examination of Welsh Europeanism in its many fascinating manifestations.

Notes

1 Fintan O'Toole, *Heroic Failure: Brexit and the Politics of Pain* (London: Head of Zeus, Apollo Book, 2018), pp. 190–1. It is to be noted, however, that O'Toole's text is potentially misleading in relation to Wales; as a corrective, I refer to the July/August 2019 article for Barn magazine written by Richard Wyn Jones, Director of the Wales Governance Centre at Cardiff University, https://nation.cymru/opinion/richard-wyn-jones-brexit-wales-identity/ (accessed 17 June 2020).

2 The Chequers Plan, officially 'The Future Relationship between the United Kingdom and the European Union', was agreed by the UK Government Cabinet in July 2018 to detail the UK/EU trading relationship after the UK's formal departure from the economic bloc.

3 *Private Eye* (11–24 January 2019), 9.

4 John Gunther, *Inside Europe Today* (London: Hamish Hamilton, 1961), Chapter 19. Hereafter *IET*.

5 See Martin Conway and Kiran Klaus Patel (eds), *Europeanization in the Twentieth Century: Historical Approaches*, Transitional History Series (London: Palgrave Macmillan, 2010).

6 Dai Smith, *In the Frame: Memory in Society, Wales 1910 to 2010* (Cardigan: Parthian, 2010)

7 Ned Thomas, *Bydoedd: Cofiant Cyfnod* (Talybont: Y Lolfa, 2010).

8   M. Wynn Thomas, *Corresponding Cultures: The Two Literatures of Wales* (Cardiff: University of Wales Press, 1999); and ed., *Gweld Sêr: Cymru a Chanrif America* (Cardiff: University of Wales Press, 2001).

9   Daniel G. Williams, *Black Skin, Blue Books: African Americans and Wales, 1845–1945* (Cardiff: University of Wales Press, 2012); (ed.), *Canu Caeth: Affro-Americaniaid a'r Cymry* (Llandysul: Gwasg Gomer, 2010).

10 'Ewtopia: Cyfandir Dychymyg y Cymry', in M. Wynn Thomas, *Cyfan-dir Cymru: Ysgrifau ar Gyfannu Dwy Lenyddiaeth Cymru* (Cardiff: University of Wales Press, 2017), pp. 149–70.

11 Saunders Lewis, 'Lloegr ac Ewrop a Chymru', in *Canlyn Arthur* (Llandysul: Gomer, 1938; reprinted 1985), p. 31.

12 Jan Morris, *Fifty Years of Europe: An Album* (London: Viking, 1998), p. 7. Hereafter *FYE*.

13 J. E. Meredith, *Gwilym Davies, 1879–1955* (Llandysul: Gomer, 1972).

14 Cyril P. Cule, *Cymro ar Grwydr* (Llandysul: Gomer, 1941). Hereafter *CG*.

15 Further, see Richard Robinson, *Narratives of the European Border: A History of Nowhere* (London: Palgrave Macmillan, 2007).

16 Robin Okey, 'Wales and Eastern Europe: Small Nations in Comparison', in T. M. Charles-Edwards and R. J. W. Evans (eds), *Wales and the Wider World: Welsh History in an International Context* (Bodmin and King's Lynn: Shaun Tyas, 2010), pp. 184–217.

17 Norman Davies, *Vanished Kingdoms: The History of Half-Forgotten Europe* (London: Allen Lane, 2011), p. 9.

18 Waldo Williams, 'Cofio', in *Dail Pren* (Llandysul: Gomer, 2010), p. 65.

19 Quoted in Angharad Price, 'Welsh Humanism after 1536', in Helen Fulton and Geraint Evans (eds), *The Cambridge History of Welsh Literature* (Cambridge: Cambridge University Press, 2019), pp. 176–93; p. 186.

20 R. Tudur Jones, 'O Genefa i'r Bala: Marchnad Rhydd y Diwinyddion', in Densil Morgan (ed.), *Grym y Gair a Ffydd y Fflam* (Bangor: Centre for Advanced Studies of Religion in Wales, Bangor University, 1998).

1

THE EUROPE OF WELSH NONCONFORMITY

The landscape of contemporary Wales is littered with empty chapels. So alien and remote do they seem to members of the younger generation that very few of them nowadays even understand that these abandoned buildings are the sad relics of a once powerful religious culture that held Wales firmly in its grip for most of the nineteenth century. Yet the immensely powerful 'Nonconformist Wales' of which these hollow shells are the sole remnants prepared the ground, in many different respects, for the eventual emergence of the modern nation of today.

Not the least significant of this culture's productions was the first truly indigenous, and largely Welsh-speaking, middle class in the long history of Wales. And the kingpins of this new social formation were the influential cadre of ministers who were the giants of the Welsh pulpit. These were the charismatic opinion-shapers and social and political leaders of their day. During the early decades of the nineteenth century they were very largely self-educated, but by the middle of the century they were increasingly the products of a system of religious education organised along denominational lines and centred on the colleges, particularly concentrated in Bala, that had been established to produce an educated ministry. Several powerful weekly and monthly journals were also established to provide this new intelligentsia with a forum for debate and to help educate the 'laity'. And while many of the strongest denominations had committed themselves throughout the first half of the nineteenth century to an otherworldliness that involved a renunciation of any involvement in social and political affairs, a sea change occurred during the second half of the century, and this saw them largely united in their loyal and impassioned support for the progressive policies of British Liberalism. It was therefore from the ranks of Welsh Nonconformity that there eventually emerged stellar political talents such as T. E. Ellis (who was Liberal chief whip at Westminster at the time of his early death) and, of course, the incomparable and incorrigible Lloyd George.

Then, in 1848, at the very tipping-moment of Welsh Nonconformity, a series of political upheavals rippled across the continent of Europe and beyond, reaching far-flung places from Hungary to Colombia (1849) and Chile (1851). While historians have come to doubt the accuracy of the utopian epithet 'the springtime of peoples' traditionally applied to these events, and have also sceptically examined the supposition that they together constituted a 'revolution' truly pan-European in scope, they nevertheless agree on the historic significance of this chain of happenings, even though they eventually proved to be far less momentous in their consequences than the early enthusiastic participants had hoped. Historians also remain persuaded that there was a nodal cluster of five themes underlying all these convulsive upheavals, although the different regions and centres involved varied in the intensity of their individual adherence to them. These themes were: (1) the overthrow of *anciens régimes* by enlightened and progressive forces; (2) political reforms centred on the widening of popular participation in political affairs; (3) initiatives of social amelioration; (4) assertions of national self-determination and emergence of new national collectives; and (5) concern at the growing possibility of counter-revolutionary measures.[1]

Of these, it was the first three, particularly as evidenced in the turbulent events in Paris, that came most to interest Welsh Nonconformists, thus confirming their proud, loyal identification at this juncture of their history with mainstream British Liberalism. By instructive contrast, insurrectionary separatists in Ireland were primarily attracted to the fourth issue, and were thus particularly excited by the incipient nationalism evident in the dramatic developments on the Italian peninsula. The almost craven British loyalism of Welsh Nonconformists owed a great deal, no doubt, to the circumstances in the Wales of the time. A year or so before the outbreak of revolution in Europe, an infamous three-volume report commissioned by Parliament into the state of Welsh education, ended up roundly condemning the chapel Welsh for their pig-ignorance, extreme moral laxity, general filthiness and stubborn adherence to a supposedly primitive *patois* of a foreign language. The result was an outburst of indignant protest by the Nonconformists at the findings of this alien group of commissioners, all of whom were Anglicans and monoglot English-speakers. But, shaken to the very core, and in effect collect-ively traumatised, the Nonconformists also began immediately to favour activities (such as pious, four-part congregational hymn sing-ing and the great public performances of mass choirs) that would gain the respect of the 'cultivated' middle classes of England.

Moreover, the 'Treachery of the Blue Books', as it became known in popular Welsh memory, occurred at the end of a period that had seen a series of violent social protests alike in rural Wales (the Rebecca Riots of 1839–43), in proletarian industrial Wales (the Merthyr Rising of 1831), and among a frustrated middle class (the Chartist march on Newport in 1839 had ended in bloodshed). These were vivid examples of the kinds of unrest that so deeply alarmed the members of the English middle class, who accordingly supported the modest pro-gramme of ameliorative measures favoured by the Liberal Party. In the minds of such, cautious reforms along the lines advocated by some of the more moderate leaders of the European revolutionary movements were needed if a conflagration of unrest was not to erupt that might in due course engulf the rest of Britain as well. No wonder, then, that the leaders of Welsh Nonconformity should hurriedly and loudly encourage their followers, in line with middle-class English Liberals, to view the events on the continent as a manifestation of Divine Providence, a long-overdue replay of the events of the sup-posedly Glorious Revolution of 1688 in English history.

There was no more powerful figure in mid-century Wales than the magisterial Rev. Lewis Edwards, the undisputed doyen of Welsh Calvinistic Methodists.[2] An incisive thinker and theologian who had completed his education at Edinburgh University, he was an influen-tial educator and founding principal of a seminal training college for Calvinistic Methodist ministers at Bala. He was also a heavyweight essayist, who established in 1845 a monthly journal, *Y Traethodydd*, which quickly became the mouthpiece of Welsh Nonconformity at its most sophisticated. Edwards's lengthy and magisterial commentary in the columns of *Y Traethodydd* on the events of 1848 therefore constitute an authoritative record of Welsh Nonconformity's response to the European revolutions of that year.

His essay reads much more like a sermon than political commen-tary. It abounds in sonorous declarations paraphrasing well-known biblical passages.[3] Justice, we are told, has not yet fled the earth; as the evil sow, so shall they reap; a house built on deceit and hypocrisy cannot stand for long. Edwards sees evidence everywhere in the European unrest of the mysterious operations of Divine Providence, not least in the unlooked-for overthrow in France of Louis Philippe's regime that had seemed so unassailably secure. The French monarch is accused of having betrayed, on his assumption of power, all the liberal values and constitutional principles he had previously sworn to protect. As well as persecuting the French press the king also, Edwards adds, began to amass a personal fortune, sinking his poor nation deep into debt in the process. But even while Edwards the stern moralist was excited by the events on the far side of the Channel, he was also worried that once any population at large began to realise its power, then violent anarchy could ensue unless government proved enlightened enough to bring in reforms by sensible degrees. It is with some trepidation that Edwards notes how the great army of the disempowered in Italy and Germany is beginning to agitate for political change. Left implicit was Edwards's concern with contemporary signs that similar unrest among the disempowered and disenfranchised might grow among both the middle class and the working class in Britain too. After all, Wales itself had recently furnished several alarming examples of such.

In every important respect, therefore, Edwards views the happenings on the continent through the lens of the classic English Whig version of history that had been enthusiastically adopted by the English liberals of his own age. According to this model, the supposedly bloodless 'Glorious Revolution' – contrasting, of course, with the later and eventually bloodthirsty French Revolution – had in 1688 replaced the Catholic reactionary James II with the progressive settlement of William of Orange and Mary, thus ushering in a new, rational and enlightened era of progress in Britain towards a truly liberal democracy and constitutional monarchy. This historiography was given important new impetus in 1848 with the publication of Thomas Babington Macaulay's volume *The History of England from the Accession of James II*. 'The history of our country during the last hundred years', the historian proudly asserted in the opening chapter, 'is eminently the history of physical, of moral, and of intellectual improvement.' In associating himself with such a reading of British and European history, Edwards was also in effect endorsing the kind of English nationalism that gloried in the British Empire as the providential instrument of a process of general human improvement involving the forcible civilising of primitive peoples worldwide.

By January 1849, reverend contributors to the *Traethodydd* were beginning to shift their attention from France to Italy, their Protestant antennae twitching as the chaotic early steps towards national unity taken in Piedmont began to lead to confrontation with Austria and to affect the papal states of Pope Pius IX. Although no liberal, this humble, beloved 'pope of the people' ('Pio Non'), had begun to respond to popular clamour for reforming measures in his territories. But in a military showdown with Austria he quickly backtracked, thereafter leaving the leadership of the Risorgimento to secularists and anticlericals like Mazzini. His political territories reduced to a rump, he eventually promoted both the cult of the Immaculate Conception and adopted the new dogma of papal infallibility.

It was the supposed reversal of policy by Pius IX in 1848 that attracted the excited attention of Gwilym Hiraethog, a Congregational minister, based in Liverpool and with a passion for social justice, who later acquired a deservedly high reputation as a militant supporter of radical social protests in Wales and a furious enemy of slavery. He was also to meet with Mazzini, to correspond with Garibaldi and to support Kossuth's work in Hungary – in turn a deputation from that country visited him to thank him for his support. Never one to offer merely passive support for a cause in which he passionately believed, Hiraethog became a member of the Society of the Friends of Italy, founded by Mazzini in 1851 during one of his periodic stays in London in an attempt to ensure solid, influential backing for his aims and activities amongst British radical thinkers and intellectuals. At its peak (it disbanded in 1855) the society could boast some 800 members.

A shrewd manipulator of influential British opinion, Mazzini was careful to couch his message in terms that were religiose (to attract the Christians) without ever being truly religious (so as not to alienate his 'freethinking' followers). A fierce opponent of socialism (a stance calculated to appeal to the staunchly Liberal Hiraethog, whose politics were grounded in twin commitments to the individual and the nation), Mazzini advanced

> a notion of democracy . . . based on the view that all men were equally God's children and only became ordered in civil society by the knowledge of His intentions. Religion ought, therefore, to be the guiding light of reform, not an 'exclusively political idea' (p. 232)

such as that which animated the Chartist movement (whose aggressive militancy, evidenced at Newport, had startled and alarmed Welsh Nonconformists like Hiraethog).[4]

Mazzini's opposition to governmental despotism also appealed to those mid-century radicals who were strongly advocating a localism that would entrust more power to municipal authority in the many great towns and cities across Britain that the Industrial Revolution had produced. Consequently, Hiraethog's experience as a Liverpudlian Welshman also naturally inclined him to sympathise with Mazzini's sociopolitical vision. But it is clear that the core of his support for Mazzini was Hiraethog's passionate sympathy with nations struggling to extricate themselves from foreign domination. In an unpublished study of Garibaldi, he praised Mazzini for warming 'y galon genedlaethol a fuasai yn oer a marw am oesau, a dechreuodd guro yn wanaidd dan fron y wlad' ('the national heart that had for ages seemed cold and dead, and that began to beat weakly beneath the country's breast').[5] He was equally attracted to the cognate national vision of Kossuth, another of the 'democratic exiles' who had fled to London for sanctuary and support following the failed revolutions of 1848.

But in 1849 it was Pius IX that Hiraethog had firmly in his sights. Indeed, among the attributes of Garibaldi's vision that attracted the arch-Protestant Hiraethog was his anticlericalism and fierce hostility to the papacy. One of the series of rustic, racily colloquial letters addressed by Hiraethog's noted and highly popular creation 'Rhen Ffarmwr' ('Old Farmer') to a number of prominent political figures in the pages of *Yr Amserau* was directed at 'Y Pab o Ryfen' ('The Pope of Rome'), who is referred to, in pointedly demeaning familiar terms, as 'Mistar Non.'[6]

Much of the *Traethodydd* article is taken up with an embarrassing paean of praise for Hiraethog's own enlightened age, which he believed had reached the very highest pinnacle of human history. 'Erioed', he asserted, 'ni roddodd y natur ddynol y fath brofion ymarferion o'i mawredd a'i hurddas ag a roddodd yn yr ystod hwn o amser'[7] ('Never before has human nature afforded such practical proofs of greatness and of dignity as it has during this period of time'). And it is Britain, of course, that Gwilym Hiraethog regards as the lucky site of this glorious, unprecedented achievement. Ever since the Elizabethan Francis Bacon had first begun to practise experimental science, thus ridding the world of its previous superstitious beliefs, England had been in the very vanguard of human progress. By contrast, Hiraethog implicitly suggests, many continental countries, notably including the several different territories of the Italian peninsula, had remained sunk in reactionary torpor.

Pope Pius IX had been briefly moved to some mild ameliorative measures, but he had now quickly reverted to arch-reactionary practices, alarmed to discover that both his spiritual authority and his temporal power were being undermined because the scriptures had begun for the first time to become accessible to ordinary people. In truth, however, Hiraethog's attacks on the papacy were occasioned by his alarm at developments much nearer home. He was greatly exercised by contemporary evidence that Catholicism was beginning to re-establish itself threateningly just across the Welsh border in neighbouring England, thanks to Puseyism, the Oxford Movement and the High Church Anglicans of the day.

Then, in July 1849, Hiraethog returned to the fray with a retrospective review of the events of the previous year. It is a discussion worthy of careful summary, not because it would nowadays be accounted reliable history – modern academics would almost certainly want to take issue with its every detail – but precisely because it is instructively unreliable. Its very tendentiousness makes it a valuable document for unmasking several of the basic underlying assumptions of the historiography of early nineteenth-century British Liberalism and Welsh Nonconformity. Here we find Britain depicted as the beacon of hope for all European peoples in their journey towards the freedoms flowing from a genuinely representative democracy, while a benevolent divine providence is invoked as the hidden guide and guarantor of such inevitable progress towards enlightenment. Also evident is the dark side of this vision in the form of a deep concern that the model stability of Britain itself might be undermined by the disruptive energies of the lower, disenfranchised orders – Hiraethog clearly has in mind memories of the recent revolutionary actions of the Merthyr proletariat – and such disaffected and discontented sections of the middle class as had led to the fateful Chartist march on Newport.

In analysing the events of 1848 Hiraethog's tone is consistently apocalyptic. Not content with mere revolution, he opted for Revelation. The Lamb, it seemed, had opened one of the seven seals in preparation for the End of Days. Then he switches to a naturalistic mode of explanation, comparing these great political explosions to the processes that occasion earthquakes. In both cases long-pent-up energies and forces are seeking a dramatic release.[7] What has been imprisoned is demanding its freedom. Oppressive government, the denial of the national rights of men, the curtailing of the liberties of civic and religious freedom that are every man's inheritance, these are the main causes of the current reaction.

Then, having thus switched to explanations assuming that the concept of justice is providentially ingrained in the natural laws of the universe as well as in human realms of law and government, Hiraethog reverts again to a battery of biblical quotations to buttress his arguments. Only when a nation – such, Hiraethog implies, as contemporary England – is governed by enlightened means is it able to grow in honour, trade, wealth, internal peace, knowledge and morality. But even the most advanced nations, he sternly warns, can fall prey to the demonic wiles of Belial, who sows discord, disorder, anarchy and rampant immorality wherever he goes. Wherever this happens, the poor end up turning on the rich, the industrious are attacked by the idle, all the bonds of society are broken, and humans become no better than animals and use the catchword of liberty to justify every manner of iniquity. But the just and stable structure of progressive nations are in the end guarantors that chaos will not prevail. Integral to such a structure is a political system granting a say to every deserving individual of appropriate age in the choice of representatives for the national assembly, thus assuring a degree of influence in key areas such as law and the levying of taxes.

Britain's adoption of these principles and practices had resulted in its being the most advanced nation in Europe before 1848, and this had saved it from like social and political turmoil. That, however, Hiraethog adds, is not to say that Britain is free from internal oppression. The press may be allowed an enviable degree of freedom, and the population at large may be allowed to form civic societies and to elect parliamentary representatives, but the aristocracy, along with the mighty in government and the established Church, still retain an oppressive grip on a power denied to ordinary people. Nevertheless, compared to the benighted countries of Europe, Britain is exemplary in its inclusiveness and tolerance. And lacking a similar safety valve – here Hiraethog parades his familiarity with that new-fangled experiment, the steam engine – the populations of the continent had been left no choice but to turn to sword and gun for redress, turning their own flesh and blood in the process into bloodily eloquent pleas for freedom (273). But it would be sheer madness for the British to take

a similar route, since they already had means sufficient at their dis-
posal, in the form of a free press and a popular vote, to make their
grievances known.

Having clearly advertised his position as a cautious gradualist in
reform matters and thus on balance as a defender of the established
order, and having also equally clearly indicated his own fearful awareness of the possibility of unrest among deeply dissatisfied sections
(such as the industrial workers of the Merthyr area, or the Chartists
of Newport) of the British population, Gwilym Hiraethog proceeds
further to inoculate his readers against the malign bacillus of revolution by instructing them in the history of Europe from the French
Revolution onwards. Having noted how Napoleon had for ever undermined the authority of monarchies across Europe, and how following
his final overthrow Russia, Prussia and Austria had hastened to form
their sinister reactionary Holy Alliance to prevent any further manifestations of such radicalism, Hiraethog describes how the age of
Metternich had come into being. Its most disturbing initiative, he
argues, was to establish a Europe-wide system of education cunningly
designed to instruct the people in the divine right of monarchs to
govern and the divine obligation of populations to obey. Worst of all,
this initiative was underpinned by a wholly spurious appeal to biblical authority, possible only because the populace was denied direct
access to the scriptures. In consequence, Christianity appeared to be
an instrument of oppression, so that many liberal rebels were driven
to seek succour in secularism and anticlericalism. Metternich had
turned the press into the obedient voice of authority, and the armed
forces were his powerful instruments of enforcement.

In spite of this, the Austrian arch-schemer had failed to quell the
desire for freedom native to the human spirit, and it was in France
that his policies of repression had begun to unravel first. The year
1830 saw the toppling of one of the tyrannical Bourbons, Charles X,
from power, only for him to be replaced by another family member,
Louis Philippe, who was acclaimed as the people's monarch and who
swore, following his bitter educative experiences of exile in England
and America, to govern as a champion of popular liberty. But no
sooner was he enthroned than he began to change course, trampling
on justice in his headlong pursuit of wealth and power – the latter
taking the form of his opportunistic military adventures in Africa.
Meanwhile his wife was arranging a bloody attack on the Protestant
evangelists of Tahiti in a determined effort to recover the island for

her benighted form of Catholicism. So much, Hiraethog scathingly adds, for the pacific pretensions of 'the Napoleon of peace'. In the meantime, Louis Philippe reorganised Paris into a military stronghold and began to infiltrate Spain, seeking to undermine the reforming work of the administration of the famous military hero Espartero and also scheming to gain control of the Spanish monarchy by engineering forced marriages of the sickly young queen and her sister to French men of his choosing.

So corrupt and dissolute did his court become that in the end the French people could stand his rule no longer. Agitation for change grew in intensity and volubility as reform societies proliferated, and matters came to a head in February, 1848 when Louis Philippe had tried to ban a special banquet that had been arranged by the reformers. In the clash that ensued, an increasingly enraged Parisian crowd had turned on the soldiers and routed them, prompting the king himself to flee in disguise, ignominy and disgrace. Thus was the spark of rebellion kindled that spread in due course to Austria, Berlin, the states of Germany, Sicily, Naples, Lombardy, Tuscany and, last but not least, to Rome. And in consequence, Europe had advanced centuries in the space of one short year, thanks to the secret ministrations of divine providence. By year's end, a degree of popular representative government had been established in many of the participating countries; the Press was largely freed from its shackles; liberty of conscience came to be respected; and the scriptures were made available for people to read, with the result that the Bible Society in London was requested to send 14,000 bibles to Austria and 10,000 to Rome and the papal states. Much remained to be achieved, but nothing could prevent the eventual triumph of divine providence, for the hand of the Lord could be clearly discerned in all these events. He had awakened as one from slumber and like a strong man who roars after imbibing wine, he had lifted his hand from his waist and struck his enemies as from the rear, condemning them to everlasting scorn. He had swept up thrones, and that of Louis Philippe was now no more than fragments borne aloft on the wings of the wind.

Visceral hatred of Catholicism fuses with apocalyptic fervour in the inflamed rhetoric of Hiraethog's response to 1848. In his view, the Church of Rome has always been the greatest enemy not only of true religion but also of human rights and representative government. In his lengthy 1850 essay 'Cyflawniad Prophwydoliaethau yn nygwyddiadau [sic] yr Amser presennol' ('The fulfilment of prophecies in the events of the present time') he draws upon both the Book of Daniel and the Book of Revelation.[9] From information encoded in the Book of Revelation he calculates that 1848 is the date there prophesied as marking the end of the rule of the Great Dragon over the world. To arrive at this date he assumes the Dragon's reign of terror had begun when in AD 606 Pope Boniface III had been declared the supreme head of the Church. Convinced that he can correctly so interpret the prophecies as to be able to read the signs of the times, Gwilym Hiraethog concludes that his age is the age of the opening of the Sixth Seal and the time of the pouring of the seventh vial, the period so memorably described in symbolic terms in Revelation:

> And I beheld when he had opened the sixth seal, and, lo, there was a great earthquake; and the sun became black as sackcloth of hair, and the moon became as blood; And the stars of the heavens fell unto the earth, even as a fig tree casteth her untimely figs, when she is shaken of a mighty wind.

The eclipse of the sun and the blood-red moon, he asserts, stand respectively for the overthrow of the French monarch Louis Philippe and his satellite ministers. Reverting to the old practice in Protestant propaganda of identifying Babylon, that notorious city of vice, with the Church of Rome, Hiraethog argues that Mazzini had indeed briefly succeeded in engineering its downfall, only for the old Catholic autocracies of Europe, led by France, to intervene to reinstate it. However such restoration will not, he confidently predicts, be of very long duration.

Given Hiraethog's passionate commitment to the spread of those political liberties he believed to be the inalienable right of every human being, it is not perhaps surprising to discover that one of his great heroes was the colourful British foreign minister of the day, the canny, cavalier and charismatic Lord Palmerston, who was ever eager to intervene in European affairs whenever he believed he could not only best realise the interests of Britain but also advance the cause of the freedoms to which he, an ardent Liberal like Hiraethog, was devoutly committed. And roguish womaniser though Palmerston, the dashing aristocrat, was well known to be, his egregious moral shortcomings were obviously trumped, in the impeccably moral Hiraethog's admiring opinion, by his altogether admirable political principles. What is also telling is that Hiraethog seems wholly unin-terested in the many examples of Palmerston's willing support of the struggles for self-determination by national minorities right across Europe – always excepting the Irish, of course.

At mid-century, then, there was very little to distinguish reaction in Nonconformist Wales to the European convulsions from that of mainstream English Liberalism, apart from the intense – not to say extreme in Hiraethog's case – religious overtones of the Welsh understanding of events. Move on some forty years, however, and there are the stirrings of a very different Welsh interest in Europe, one that eventually came to focus primarily not on the classic liberal aspects of contemporary developments but on their relevance to growing Welsh aspirations for greater political, as well as cultural, recognition. The late 1880s onwards saw the beginnings of a national awakening in the country. This eventually crystallised into the Cymru Fydd movement, and one of the most arresting harbingers of this movement's new approach to European affairs was the electrifying polemicist Emrys ap Iwan. He opened his essay for *Y Geninen* (IV/3) in July 1886 with a robust salvo of criticism of the English:

> Nid oes un Llywodraeth mor ddiofal a Llywodraeth Lloegr am hawliau y cenhedloedd sydd ddarostyngedig iddi; ac yn sicr, nid oes un genedl wareiddiedig mor ddiofal â'r Cymry am ei hiawnderau ei hun.[10]

> (There is no government more heedless than the English government of the rights of nations subordinate to herself; and to a certainty, there is no civilised nation so heedless as the Welsh for her own rights.)

By contrast, he points to the tiny kingdom of Belgium, home to several different nationalities and languages. While French may be the official language of government there, care is also taken to publish all official documents additionally in Flemish and in German. A similar situation obtains in the civilised republic of Switzerland, where every official whose native language is German is expected in addition to be fluent in French, and vice versa, while native speakers of Italian are required to master both French and German. The failure of England to have any regard for the Welsh and their language prompts Emrys ap Iwan to recommend the example of the Irish to his compatriots, because they, in his opinion, have already advanced far down the road leading to self-government. Praising the leadership of Parnell in this matter, ap Iwan pours scorn on the bigoted anti-Catholic prejudices of the Nonconformist Welsh who contemptuously regard the Irish as no better than an ignorant peasantry. His own preferred model of government for Britain is that of a federal structure such as already exists in the USA, Switzerland, Germany, Austria, Australia and Canada (161). And how is it, he asks, that the English can profess great sympathy for the Poles and Alsatians, smarting under the heel of their oppressors, while they prove totally incapable of like sympathy with the similar plight of their next-door neighbours, the Welsh? (160)

Robert Ambrose Jones – to give Emrys ap Iwan his baptismal names – was a socially and theologically enlightened Nonconformist minister. Although ordained by the Welsh Calvinistic Methodist Church (in the teeth of considerable resistance from some senior clergymen of rigidly conservative bent), he mocked the sectarian wars by which his Wales was riven. Such bitter squabbling, he protested, not only seriously hampered the promotion of spiritual harmony but also prevented the Welsh people from developing the sense of collective identity essential for the survival of any mature nation. And never, in his opinion, had such national self-awareness been more sorely needed than in his time, when Wales and its language were very much at risk from the crass materialistic arrogance of an English middle class whose acquisition of a global empire had made it ineffably self-satisfied and self-assertive. What particularly troubled ap Iwan was the steady colonisation of the Welsh mind by the English language. It was evident everywhere as regions hastened to abandon Welsh in favour of a tongue that for them represented progress and modernity. This development was strongly reinforced by the confinement of teaching in the new system of state schools in Wales to the medium of English. While the population at large was ready to accept this, supposing that the future of Welsh was safeguarded by its continued use at home and in the chapels, Emrys ap Iwan was perceptive enough to realise otherwise, and accordingly campaigned (presciently but in vain) for its use in all schools throughout Wales.

Ap Iwan anticipated socio-linguists of the twentieth century in his key recognition that language was not simply a neutral tool of communication but rather a rich repository of social history and a subtle carrier of moral and cultural values. Although it was produced by the human mind it was also a fashioner of the human mind. In a sense, every language created the minds of its speakers in its own distinctive image. For English to replace Welsh as the language of the Welsh people could mean only one thing: the fatal weakening of all such markers of difference – habits, values, mores – that had traditionally constituted a Welsh identity.

In an effort to prevent what seemed to be the inexorable advance of English, Emrys ap Iwan adopted several initiatives. In his astute analysis, the Welsh language was being steadily weakened from within as its speakers unconsciously adopted constructions, phrases and words imported from the foreign tongue. Accordingly their spoken and their written Welsh became circumlocutory and pompously inflated. He therefore recommended to their attention the elegant texts of Welsh prose produced in the seventeenth and eighteenth centuries by Morgan Llwyd, Ellis Wynne and Theophilus Evans. To the same end, he urged his compatriots to study the classically restrained style of great French writers from Blaise Pascal to Paul Courier – the latter being a crusading contemporary pamphleteer on whom Emrys ap Iwan modelled his own writing. And as an author he himself strove to ensure his Welsh always exemplified the swiftness, plainness and directness of expression he so admired in others.

Ap Iwan also recognised that the parlous state of the language was an acute symptom of a larger malaise. The Welsh had become so overawed by the English as to lose all self-esteem and become cravenly anxious to ape them. Although in part the consequence of England's world domination at this time, such embarrassing servility on the part of his compatriots was exacerbated, in his opinion, by their inability to look beyond their looming neighbour to catch a liberating glimpse of the nations of Europe and so to realise that England did not after all represent the be-all and end-all of human achievement. He was therefore one of the first Welsh thinkers to realise that Wales might benefit socially and culturally from seeing itself mirrored in the glass not of England but rather of other European nations. Particularly revealing, in his opinion, were the examples offered by Belgium, Switzerland, Germany and, above all, France. He had himself learnt both French and German as a young man, before teaching for some years in schools in both France and Germany, and his attachment to the former was greatly reinforced by his proud awareness that one of his great-grandmothers had been French.

One of his favourite ploys as a writer was to adopt the persona of a citizen of France or Belgium in order to expose the unfairness of England's domination of Wales. Here he is, for example, writing as a Frenchman about an imaginary French occupation of England:

In the name of all that is reasonable what more do you want? You have more than thirty members representing your bit of a country in the Lower House in Paris, and they are free to speak their mind on any subject on earth, in the sea, or in the air, so long as they do so in the language of the Republic. We have been generous enough to establish French schools all over your country to teach your children to speak, to think, and to feel like Frenchmen . . . You have had a share in the development of the Republic, so you should be proud of it . . . We are ready to be friendly, but on our own terms. But if you persist in stirring up your naive fellow-countrymen by maintaining that England has a right to its own government, that English should be the first language in your schools and public offices, and that the French should not hold the most remunerative posts without a knowledge of English, I shall throw aside all French courtesy, and hurl on your head a sackful of your own writers' adjectives, and call you a petty, extreme, narrow, bigoted, prejudiced, foolish, crazy, hot-headed coterie.[11]

The adult life of Emrys ap Iwan spanned the period that saw the Cymru Fydd movement in the ascendancy, led by such brilliant talents as T. E. Ellis and David Lloyd George, and in many ways his own social, cultural and political aspirations chimed with theirs. But he felt little but scorn for a movement whose members he regarded as no more than an ineffectual pressure group within English Liberalism. It was another sad case, he acidly remarked, of 'Welsh wind in the sails and an English hand on the helm'.[12]

Michael D. Jones, another of the most arresting leaders of Nonconformist opinion, matched Emrys ap Iwan in the ferocity of his attacks on the anglicisation of the Welsh mind and in his alertness to the relevance of contemporary European affairs to the situation of Wales, although he is chiefly remembered today as the prime mover in the establishing of the Welsh colony in Patagonia. As fiery in character as he was compact of body, and as outspoken in his polemics as he was bold in his actions, Jones campaigned tirelessly in favour of a government for Wales. And he regularly looked to the continent to supply examples of national minorities agitating for greater social and political freedom.

While there was sympathy enough in mainstream Nonconformist Wales for the heroics of romantic leaders such as Garibaldi – indeed by the end of the nineteenth century some young men entering the ministry gloried in such names as J. Garibaldi Phillips and D. Garibaldi Thomas – it tended to be no more than a local variant of

English enthusiasm for a supposed champion of classic Liberal values. But Jones's reading of events was different. For him the Risorgimento furnished Wales with an inspiring example of successful agitation for national self-determination. And he readily looked further afield for further evidence of his conviction that no people, however small, ever voluntarily relinquished control over their own affairs, and that no determined struggle by suppressed nationalities for self-government – such as those of the Swiss and the Belgians – had ever ended in failure.

In 1875 his attention was drawn to the revolt of national minorities in eastern Europe against oppressive Turkish rule. England and Russia were ready enough, he sardonically noted, to support these revolts while they resolutely ignored their own equally unjust practices[13] (*Y Celt*, 3 Mai 1875, 10). He then extended his attention to the parallel cases of Romania, Herzegovina, Bulgaria, Serbia, Thessaly, Montenegro and Crete, and foresaw the ongoing struggles there as inspiring the Irish, the Polish, and the many millions in India. Finally he homed in on Crete, quickly sketching the island's geography and history. Condemning the foreign policy of Prime Minister Disraeli (Lord Beaconsfield) as lacking in sympathy for such cases, he predicted it could result only in driving eastern minorities into the welcoming embrace of Russia.

It was, however, the death of the legendary Hungarian patriot Kossuth in 1890 that moved the ageing Michael D. Jones to the most impassioned statement of his commitment to the principle of self-determination.[14] The irony of English lionising of the Hungarian was not lost on him: it was in blatant contrast with their treatment of the Irish, the Scots and the Welsh. Reverting to the old myths about the coming of Hengist and Horsa and the perfidy of the Saxons, he styled the conquest of the island by the English as no better than naked piracy and a clear prefiguration of their future actions in America, both North and South, in the West Indies and Africa, and across large tracts of Asia. For him, the armies that had achieved such 'victories' were never more than the mere stooges and mercenaries of the English ruling class. And he concluded by calling for the establishing of a senate for the Welsh people to be based in Aberystwyth.[15]

Attitudes in general towards Europe began to change, and to become more politically charged, in the wake of the development of the Cymru Fydd/Young Wales movement. Originally established in the late 1880s by a cadre of young intellectuals as primarily a cultural movement of national reawakening, by the middle of the last decade of the nineteenth century it had begun cautiously to develop a political consciousness, in the wake of the prominent success of such brilliant young politicians as T. E. Ellis and Lloyd George. And so, when the Liberal and Cymru Fydd MP, J. Hugh Edwards, launched a new English-language journal in 1895 under the title *Young Wales*, it was not long before he began to outline his clear social and political aims.

The first of these, he announced in a powerful editorial, was to 'preach the gospel of the national unity of Wales'.[16] As for the second, while it was couched in conventionally vague Cymru Fydd terms as 'to foster that spirit of national awakening which now has touched this little country of ours', it was also for the first time given a political edge by Edwards's open, enthusiastic commendation of the efforts of Thomas Davis and the leaders of the Young Ireland Movement of the mid-nineteenth century. 'We do not hesitate', wrote Edwards, to preach 'the same gospel of Nationalism as did Thomas Davis and the other Young Irelanders in the pages of their periodical.' And indeed, *Young Wales* was to allude many times over the coming years to the efforts and pronouncements of Thomas Davis – who was on record as having been proud of his Welsh descent. Moreover, in the editorial which fronted the first, launch, edition of *Young Wales*, Edwards had already pointed to the model example set by the movements of Young Italy, Young Ireland, and Young Switzerland, all of which had passionately advocated the regeneration of their respective nations. It was his intention, he implied, to follow those inspiring European examples.[17]

No sooner, however, had some sections of Cymru Fydd begun to entertain timid political aspirations than these were terminally crushed at an infamous meeting in Newport. There the whole course of modern Welsh history was altered when self-styled 'cosmopolitans' – powerful south-east industrialists and politicians who found a spokesman in an incomer from Bristol – vociferously objected to any move towards a degree of self-government, as championed at that point by Lloyd George and his north Wales followers. Consequently, all subsequent attempts by *Young Wales* to make some connections between the Welsh situation and those of small nations in Europe were darkly shadowed by this fateful development. And by the conclusion of the nineteenth century, the fight of the Boers in South

Africa against imperial English bullying, beginning at the time of the notorious Jameson raid (sponsored by Rhodes) and culminating in the Second Boer War, became another factor in the equation. Welsh feeling on the issue was, of course, reinforced by awareness of the core Calvinism of Boer culture.

In the early numbers of *Young Wales*, however, John Hugh Edwards devoted some cautious space to advancing a vision of Wales more alive and open to continental examples. In the matter of memorialising national heroes (*sic*) he observed: 'it is becoming more and more patent that small nations can resist the absorbing tendencies and aims of the more powerful nationalities only by jealously guarding and preserving their own special characterisation.'[18] By way of example he pointed to Hungary's recent celebrations of a thousand years of remarkable Magyar history, viewing it as a lesson for Wales, whose history had fortunately been far less bloody and tragic. 'But there are other dangers which now menace the existence of small nationalities', he perceptively continued. 'They are veiled in that subtle force of absorption which is so largely practised by the larger states. It is that silent elimination of national features that is to be feared and guarded against' (203).

As usual, by far the most rousing and visionary of European models for a Welsh future came in the form of an essay on 'The National Unity of Wales' by the young MP Tom Ellis. It is trenchant and succinct enough to warrant extensive quotation:

> Ireland has given a new significance to all schemes of local self-government by struggling and suffering for the principle of nationality, which in other countries has exercised a controlling and fertilizing influence upon human destiny. Throughout the course of this century, the best traditions of the foreign politics of England are connected with British help and sympathy with rising nationalities. The resurrection of Greece and Italy found its staunchest friends in England. The Magyars of Hungary, the Teutons of Holland, the Catholic Celts of Belgium, the Slavs of South Eastern Europe have secured the sympathy of England in the assertion of their national existence. Nationality is now become a factor in English domestic politics. Catholic Ireland, Nonconformist Wales, and Presbyterian Scotland have emphasised their national existence in worship and even in religious policy in face of pitiless persecution and of the strenuous opposition of a large section of English opinion. In Wales the aspirations for national unity and the need of an instrument for the good government of Wales will react on each other.[19]

In the very same number, a contributor named John Jones set out to paint a somewhat unconvincing portrait of Lloyd George, that other young Welsh luminary at Westminster, as an 'Apostle of Welsh Nationalism' who was as alive to European examples as Ellis.[20] Written in the immediate aftermath of the debacle in Newport, this piece was an attempt to demonstrate the viability of a Young Wales movement that was underwritten by history and ordained by God. To demonstrate this, Jones relied heavily on the previous examples offered by Young Ireland and Young Italy of national campaigns that ultimately triumphed over seemingly insurmountable difficulties. 'Did not Mazzini', he rhetorically inquired, 'establish an association of Young Italy, as a society of young men, in which the regeneration of their country was not only made a cardinal point of its creed, but also an object of religious enthusiasm?' (197). That dedicated little cadre of activists eventually 'shook the whole of Europe to its very foundations. They sowed the seed which found its harvest in the revolutions of 1848. They ensured the political resurrection of the national unity of Italy. They breathed a new and a living spirit into small nationalities.' 'The reverberations of their passionate declamations', he continued with all the fervour that was beginning at this very time to be diverted away from traditional Nonconformity into the new secular religion of Welsh nationalism, 'as to the sacred rights and the divinely-appointed mission of nations are ringing as clearly today as ever' (197–8).

Finally, and again very much with an eye on Newport, Jones offered what turned out to be a prophetic warning. If Young Wales retreated into defending those cultural matters (or cultivating those 'poetic sentiments', as Jones chose to put it) that had characterised its early years, it would wither away. Its ultimate success could be ensured only by a sustained 'united effort on the part of young Welshmen to conserve the national individuality of Wales and to inspire its regeneration in every direction' (198). It was the fate of a merely cultural movement to fail, as was, for him, conclusively proved by the brief history of the Young England movement of 1841–6. By contrast, the Young Italy movement, committed to political action, had proved totally successful, and the Young Ireland movement, which had after all been modelled on the Italian example, was also on the brink of success.

Mazzini was also Hugh Edwards's great continental hero at this time, and as well as sprinkling rather tiresome little pearls of wisdom by the great man throughout many issues of *Young Wales*, he devoted several pages, over two issues, to a lengthy portrait of the Italian. He begins by drawing a distinction between the great established nations of Europe and the smaller peoples. The latter 'have to struggle hard lest they become altogether absorbed by the more powerful nations'.

They realize that great as has been their loss of territory and of sovereignty by the conquest of the more powerful nations, their loss will be infinitely greater if they suffer the conqueror to disintegrate their national traditions and customs, or extirpate their language and characteristics.[21]

By way of example of such struggles he refers to the Czechs of Bohemia, the Slavs, and the Magyars of Hungary. Then there are the cases of Bulgaria, Serbia and Romania, and 'the little isle of Crete', all of which are striving for release from the Ottoman Empire. Additionally, Finland is fighting to maintain its nationality, while Portugal is resisting assimilation by Spain, and Norway is claiming 'equal rights and privileges with Sweden'. An analogous case much nearer home, of course, is that of contemporary Ireland (135). Finally, there is 'gallant little Wales', who clings to her language and culture despite 'the alternate ruthless opposition and disdainful scorn of the great John Bull (135).

Mazzini, Edwards confidently announces – conveniently overlooking the Italian's indifference, and indeed outright hostility, to the rights of the inconveniently clamorous smaller nationalities of Europe (including the Irish) – 'is chief among the order of the prophets of nationalism'. Tellingly, he presents him as the first 'to infuse patriotism with religious fervour'. He had travelled the length and breadth of Europe preaching the 'glorious evangel of nationalism [and] teaching men that it was their prime duty to love and to reverence their native-land as the home where God himself had placed them' (136). Then, briefly switching to a scientific model to justify his vision, Edwards claims that the new late nineteenth-century classification of nationalities is as grounded in scientific fact as is the celebrated taxonomy of Linnaeus. But it is the argument from religion that is, Edwards well knows, best suited to the Welsh Nonconformist mind. Therefore, in the second part of his portrait, he notes how Italian unification had been treated by Young Italy as 'a religious mission', grounded as it was in divine purpose.[22] Mazzini had devoted his life to the service of this 'sacred idea of nationality', and it was this idea that should be embodied in Welsh action. Trusted to, it would 'arrest the baneful influences that are disintegrating our national energies', being most evident in 'denominational strife, political bickerings, and in the perpetuation of the hateful feud between North and South Wales' (277).

Elsewhere, other like-minded contributors to *Young Wales* also ventured to look further afield than neighbouring continental countries. In 1897, the editor was sharply critical of English opposition to Cretan wishes to be freed from the malign grip of the decaying Ottoman empire and to be united with Greece. 'In no part of the country', he resoundingly if unconvincingly claimed, 'is there a deeper note of indignation and of righteous wrath at the action of the Continental Powers in seeking to crush by brute force the passionate sufferings of a long-suffering and oppressed people than there is in Wales.'[23] In other numbers extensive attention was paid by contributors to Bishop Grundtvig's model work in establishing a national system of education in Denmark, culminating in the proposal to create a 'popular university in which national subjects should occupy the most prominent place'.[24] A number of well-informed reports were also published on the state of contemporary education in such countries as France, Germany and Italy, as well as other articles highlighting the progressive work in commercial education being pioneered elsewhere.

Another continental thinker much favoured by *Young Wales* was Ernest Renan. A Breton, he had, of course, deeply influenced Matthew Arnold and inspired his very influential, but highly damaging, prattling about Celtic magic and the poetic temperament of the Celt. The enthusiasm for Renan – who ultimately identified as French at least as readily as he did as Breton – was very much in keeping with the fashionable pan-Celticism that gripped Ireland, Wales, Scotland and Brittany alike during the 1890s. *Young Wales* carried several extensive reports from various pan-Celtic gatherings, but it was the contemporary state of Brittany that received the most sustained attention. Recording his 'Impressions of the Breton eisteddfod at Vannes', Dr J. Llewellyn Treharne loftily opined that while the Bretons had sensibly disregarded 'the nonsense of Home Rule', they aspired, like the Welsh, 'to be recognized as ancient nations and [to be] awarded limited powers accordingly'. In the case of Wales, Treharne the loyal Briton tellingly concluded, such powers should be 'pro rata to her population and her contribution to the Imperial Exchequer'.[25]

Welsh visitors to Brittany were particularly taken with the colourfulness of the native costumes and the quaintness of the region's

surviving Celtic customs and legends. After visiting a Breton 'pardon'
(religious festival), A. H. Withers waxed lyrical about such features.
Much more considered and penetrating was the analysis by J.
Arthur Price of the role of the Catholic Church in Brittany as a national
Church, a unifying body of which he, a Welsh nationalist but also a
devoted Anglican – a highly unusual combination at the time – very
much felt the want in Wales. In Price's stimulatingly unorthodox version of Welsh history, the sad process of alienation from the Church
had begun in Wales even before the Reformation, after which it had
steadily become nothing but a foreign, occupying, body wholly alien
to the Welsh people. The state Church's 'continuous resistance to
Welsh national sentiment' had, in Price's opinion, been little short of
a tragedy. It had enabled the growth of an equally alien phenomenon,
the pernicious cult of individualism that lay at the very heart of Welsh
Nonconformity. Brittany, by contrast, had enjoyed an unbroken connection with the Catholic Church dating right back to late Celtic
times. Its devotion was, Price rejoiced to note, nowhere more evident
than in its memorable *pardons*, the local festivals celebrating saints'
days filled with all the colour of medieval times. These rituals and
beliefs were, he added, proof positive 'of the manner in which Breton
Catholicism has taken over the mystic inheritance of Celtic paganism
and Celtic Christianity'.[26]

In the late Victorian era, however, Welsh Europeanism was
doomed never to be more than a peripheral affair. It could not compete with craven Welsh devotion to the British empire, in the eyes of
Welshmen a wondrously providential machine for civilising the world,
and one capacious enough to allow safe haven for such cautious,
harmless aspirations as their own for a degree of self-government.
Some of the declarations of loyalty to the British empire in the pages
of *Young Wales* can seem embarrassing and pitiful to modern readers.
'Let Welsh thought be brought into closer sympathy with the general
thought of the Empire', proclaimed J. Young Evans, 'for only thereby
can Wales fulfil that intellectual, moral, and religious work which we
all agree it is destined to perform.'[27] In like manner, Professor Edward
Anwyl drew attention to the consciousness aroused throughout Wales
by the contemporary Boer War that 'the Briton's outlook has come
to embrace habitually the Empire as a whole, and not the British isles
only'. The Welsh, he added, were proud to belong to such an empire
and any merely 'local and provincial patriotism' should be dedicated
to its service.[28]

There is indeed a tragi-comic aspect to the convictions of contributors like Evans and Anwyl that tiny insignificant little Wales – even
though routinely, if bitterly, acknowledged elsewhere in the periodical to be contemptuously overlooked by the English, who had eyes
only for the Scots and the Irish – had a special, divinely appointed
and world-changing mission to perform under the benevolent auspices of the empire. Witness the pathetically splendid assertion by the
Rev. Price Hughes on the opening page of the millennial number of
Young Wales. 'It has increasingly seemed to me', wrote Price, addressing the subject of 'The Twentieth Century: Its Message to Wales',
'that our Providential task as the nearest and closest neighbour of
mighty England is to encourage our great neighbour in substituting
a spiritual for a materialistic ideal.'[29] Warming to his task, he continued: 'The romantic and intensely religious tendency of the Celtic race
seems to be the necessary counterpoise, if we must not say antidote,
for some of the excessively commercial and materialistic tendencies
of our gifted and imperialistic Teutonic neighbour.' Intoxicated by his
vision he went on to compare Wales to Greece in its civilising influence relative to the great crude Roman power of England. Wales, he
crowed, could even surpass Greece, because it stood not for beauty
but for goodness. And that was the only quality that could save the
British empire from eventual catastrophic decline. Hughes went on
to ground his impassioned argument for the speedy disestablish-
ment of the Welsh Church, and the full empowerment of the Welsh
Nonconformist sects, on such convictions as these.

'It seems clear', wrote the Rev. Richard Hughes, reflecting on the
'Conditions of a National Progress', 'that we can enter into [the]
rivalry of nations only as part of the great British Empire. We must
identify ourselves with its commerce and its imperial policy.'[30] There
was, however, one obvious snag. At the very time when Hughes was
writing, the empire was in the process of altering tack and changing
the whole temper of its outlook and actions. It was the era of the
new imperialism, fiercely championed by Joseph Chamberlain, whose
unsavoury qualities were embodied in the remarkable character of
Cecil Rhodes and were shortly to find expression in the notorious
Jameson raid that prepared the way for the Boer War. The more
progressive Welsh Liberals sensed uneasily that under the auspices
of this new, predatory, opportunistic and unscrupulous empire the
pieties of Welsh Nonconformity were likely to be given very short
shrift indeed.

True, when the Boer War eventually materialised, there were those in Welsh Liberal ranks who enthusiastically supported it. Such were satirised in an entertaining anecdote the editor included in *Young Wales* in 1900. Two solemn, self-important bards, Gwilym Cowlyd and Penfro, he reported, had valiantly ventured to ascend Snowdon in a 'blinding storm of wind and rain'.[31] Arrived there, attired in their full bardic gear, they began to process around a circle of white stones. Coming to a standstill, Cowlyd gripped his grand Gorsedd sword and roared 'A Oes Heddwch' ('Is there Peace?'). To which his sidekick Penfro mournfully replied 'Nac Oes' ('No, there is not'). With this Cowlyd dramatically unsheathed 'the mystic sword of truth, peace, and justice', and again perambulated the circle of stones, this time striking the earth outside the circle with the naked blade thrice at each stone. As the editor drily noted, 'It seems that the sword will remain unsheathed until the present war is brought to a triumphant conclusion – a piece of intelligence which would surely strike terror and dismay into the heart of President Kruger if reported to him.' In retrospect, this whole incident cannot fail to seem to us to be a perfect emblem of late Victorian Wales's pitiful delusions of grandeur about its imperial role.

There were many in Welsh Liberal ranks, however, who were totally opposed to the Boer War, and these found an incomparable spokesman and leader in Lloyd George. Recognising Rudyard Kipling to be the poet laureate of the new imperialism, 'Elphin' wrote a deft parody of his poetry at its most jingoistic, under the title 'Kipling-Mad':

> When you've Kitchenered the Dervishes and Bullered all the Boers,
>   When the warrior-hosts are whitening on the plains,
> When you've civilised the Zulus with the poisons from your shores,
>   When you've branded them and riveted their chains,
> When you're sick of all the slaughter, when you've plundered all you need,
>   When you see not even an island unannexed,
> When your admirals and generals are running all to seed,
>   When your soldiers are but Hooligans unsexed . . .[32]

He ended by grieving for what England had become, rallying the shades of the mighty liberators Milton, Cromwell and Shakespeare to bear witness to their nation's degradation, and he appealed to the Almighty for consolation and redress for this vile parody of 'how things divine should be' (261).

At the beginning of the twentieth century, then, the nascent Welsh Europeanism cautiously explored by *Young Wales* could not hope to compete with contemporary Welsh infatuation with the empire. And this preference for an alternative orientation to pan-Europeanism, based on a fearful wish to belong to a powerful collective, continued thereafter to characterise the popular mind in Wales and to be reflected in the productions of her writers and intellectuals. As the empire was first dismantled piecemeal before mutating into the sentimental fiction of the Commonwealth, so Wales happily and quietly subsided into passive acquiescence. But in reality it opted, like the rest of the British Isles, to belong to the new powerful Saxon 'empire' of Anglo-American culture worldwide, even while continuing to yearn, just like England, for the glory days when British influence had enjoyed a global reach. The Brexit vote was therefore, in a way, nothing but the inevitable outcome of such a long-settled outlook, although exacerbated of course by the chronic social deprivation experienced by the remnants of a long-neglected and casually abandoned post-industrial region.

Notes

1   See R. J. W. Evans and Hartmut Pogge von Strandmann (eds), *The Revolutions in Europe, 1848–1849* (Oxford: Oxford University Press, 2000), particularly Chapter 1, '1848–1849: A European Revolution?', pp. 1–8. See also Richard Evans, *The Pursuit of Power* (Milton Keynes: Penguin, 2016), particularly Chapter 5, 'The 1848 Revolutions,' pp. 198–231.
2   See D. Densil Morgan, *Lewis Edwards* (Cardiff: University of Wales Press, 2009).
3   *Y Traethodydd* (Ebrill 1848), 261.
4   Gregory Claeys, 'Mazzini, Kossuth, and British Radicalism, 1848–1854', *Journal of British Studies*, 28/3 (July 1989), 225–61; 232; Denis Mack Smith, *Mazzini* (New Haven and London: Yale University Press, 1994); D. Ben Rees, *Parchedig William Rees, Gwilym Hiraethog 1802–1883* (Liverpool: Cyhoeddiadau Modern Cymraeg, 2002).
5   Quoted in T. Roberts and D. Roberts, *Cofiant y Parch W. Rees, DD (Hiraethog)* (Dolgellau; W. Hughes, n.d.), p. 284.
6   Quoted in *Cofiant*, pp. 289–92.
7   *Y Traethodydd* (Ionawr 1849), 5.
8   'Chwyldroadau y flwyddyn 1848', *Y Traethodydd*, V (1949), 270–85; 270.
9   *Y Traethodydd*, VI (Ionawr 1850), 90–107.
10   *Y Geninen*, IV/3 (July 1886), 156.
11   D. Myrddin Lloyd, *Emrys ap Iwan* (Cardiff: University of Wales Press, 1979), p. 31.

[12] Lloyd, *Emrys ap Iwan*, p. 42.
[13] *Y Celt*, 3 May 1875, 10.
[14] Jones was much influenced by a Welsh-language study of Kossuth, *Hanes Louis Kossuth, Llywydd Hwngari*, by E. Davies and G. Humphreys, published in Bala in 1852.
[15] *Y Celt*, 7 March 1890, 1.
[16] *Young Wales*, II (January 1896), 299–300.
[17] *Young Wales*, I (1895), 2.
[18] *Young Wales*, II (1896), 202.
[19] *Young Wales*, II (1896), 153.
[20] *Young Wales*, II (1896), 196–7.
[21] *Young Wales*, III (1897), 134–6; 134.
[22] *Young Wales*, III (1897), 273–7.
[23] *Young Wales*, III (1897), 95.
[24] *Young Wales*, II (1896), 39.
[25] *Young Wales*, V (1899), 213–16; 214.
[26] *Young Wales,* IV (1898), 'The National Church of Celtic France', 241–5; 243.
[27] *Young Wales*, II (1896), 152.
[28] *Young Wales*, VI (1900), 3.
[29] *Young Wales*, VI (1900), 1.
[30] *Young Wales*, II (1896), 51.
[31] *Young Wales*, VI (1900), 24.
[32] *Young Wales*, V (1899), 260–1; 260.

2

THE WELSH WHIG VERSION OF EUROPE

O. M. Edwards (knighted late in life) has acquired a legendary status in the annals of Welsh-language culture. Deservedly so, although he was no paragon. His shortcomings are evident enough, closely connected as they mostly are to the limitations of his outlook. His was a Victorian, paternalistic attitude to his readers. A countryman born and bred, he failed to grasp the vital fact that in industrial south Wales a brand-new social formation had emerged, one capable in due course of producing its own, distinctive, version of Welsh identity. His only response to this new Wales was to attempt to incorporate it into the pre-existent Wales with which he was so fondly familiar. Culturally speaking, his was a narrow, 'sectional' view of Welsh society. And, typical of most enlightened Liberals of his day, he was blind to the condition of the working class, and unsympathetic to any militant proletarian action to remedy manifest social, economic and political injustices. Indeed, he was deeply averse to politics, believing that they inevitably resulted in nationally divisive party factionalism.

Nevertheless, when his career is considered in the round, it is undeniably evident that no other single individual rendered that section of Welsh society and culture of which he was a product more varied or more prodigious service than 'O.M.' And it could have been so very different. Edwards could have opted for a comfortable berth at Oxford, where he was early established as a respected Fellow of Lincoln with a stellar academic record, and there he could have subsided into the calm untroubled life of a don. But even then he was possessed by an almost demonic determination to serve his native country and its culture according to his lights. He was driven by this to establish a series of widely popular pioneering journals and to take

on the immensely onerous task of overseeing their every detail himself. Later in his career he abandoned even this distant place of refuge
to plunge into the fray in Wales, accepting a challenging appointment
as His Majesty's Chief Inspector of Schools. This, he believed, would
enable him to reform the existing educational system radically, but
from within. No wonder he came to a relatively early end.

His was a classic Victorian tale of giddy ascent from very lowly
beginnings. He was born in Llanuwchllyn, Bala, to a small ten-
ant farmer, who had been oppressed by his landlord, and his wife.
Eventually he went on to complete his education at the newly established University College of Wales Aberystwyth before proceeding to
Oxford, where at Balliol he came under the influence of the renowned
Benjamin Jowett and was influenced by the work of John Ruskin.
With a few kindred spirits he also established the Dafydd ap Gwilym
Society, devoted to a study of Wales past and present, and out of
this came some of the seeds for the Cymru Fydd movement. Hidden
behind such brilliant and prominent academic success was a different
story, though: one of cultural trauma. And it was this hidden wound
that Edwards sought to staunch and heal for the remainder of his life.

He had first attended the little local church school in Llanuwchllyn.
The teaching there, the little boy had been stunned to discover, was
wholly through the medium of English, a language totally unintelligible to him, as to all the other children. Llanuwchllyn and
neighbouring Bala were at the very centre of the Welsh-language
heartland.[1] Bewildered, he had made little progress and was accordingly branded stupid. After he had eventually found his feet and made
spectacular progress, he clearly determined to ensure such humiliation
would not be visited on Welsh children of future generations. His
main crusading purpose in publishing his many books and journals
was therefore to ensure that Welsh readers were provided with the
knowledge of their own country's history and culture that was still
being denied them in the state schools, and to supply this information
through the medium not of English but of Welsh.

Ancillary to this primary mission was a wish to open Welsh eyes
to the world at large, beginning by introducing them to Europe.
Accordingly, at the very outset of his career he published a trilogy of
travelogues during the short course of a year, all written not with the
rigour of an academic but in the relaxed, unbuttoned and informal
style of a genial Victorian essayist. Such texts were new in Welsh
literature, and so entitle Edwards to be considered the father of the

travelogue genre in Wales. An account of his pilgrimage from his native Bala to Geneva (*O'r Bala i Geneva*, 1889) was quickly followed by reports on his trip to Italy and then to Brittany (*Tro i'r Eidal*, 1889; *Tro i Lydaw*, 1890).[2] They constitute the first Baedekers, so to speak, to have appeared in Welsh. There were several prominent threads linking the three volumes, including Edwards's devotion to Nonconformity, his related suspicion of Catholicism and his passionate embrace of the Whig version of modern history as a divinely ordained progress towards mature constitutional government with (limited) popular voting rights.

Edwards's gifts as a popular essayist were deployed to extensive, complex effect in these volumes, and are what make them still appealing period pieces for a general reader. He had a sharp, frequently amused eye for the details of dress, conduct, gestures, manners and mores of ordinary everyday life, the revealing incidentals and accidentals of a bygone age so intriguingly different and distant from our own. And his 'thick descriptions' also served the serious contemporary purpose of familiarising his stay-at-home Welsh readers with the captivatingly strange ordinary life of neighbouring peoples, thus strengthening the important bonds common to all humanity. His observations can, however, sometimes be alienating in their effect – uncomfortably memorable examples being his depiction of Catholicism and his infamous treatment of the Jews.

One oddity to which he repeatedly returns in *O'r Bala i Geneva* is that of dog carts, where the animals actually ran beneath the carts and thus did the work normally done by wheels. Before adjusting to the sight, he had been astonished to see one cart that seemed to be magically self-propelled, until he eventually glimpsed the great St Bernard labouring away underneath it (*OBG*, 37). Being a seasoned countryman, he was vastly entertained by the sight of two of these dogs, hampered as they were by the heavy carts on their backs, resolutely attempting to square up to each other, but managing only to smash their carts to smithereens. Given Edwards's familiarity with the rhetorical devices of the Welsh pulpit, there may be the merest hint of a parabolic meaning in such a reminiscence. It is after all suggestive not only of the law of unintended consequences but also of the need for the eyes of travellers visiting foreign parts to become thoroughly acclimatised before being able to recognise what is being seen.

Elsewhere Edwards recalled travelling on a train with an unaccompanied little boy who alarmed his fellow passengers by leaning so far out of the window that he seemed in imminent danger of falling out completely. And when he was holed up in a Heidelberg hotel for several months, he had plenty of time to observe the quiddities and oddities of the other guests. There was the daughter of the British consul in Smyrna with first-hand experience of the Middle East, who could expatiate on the culture of the Orient, the character of the Turk, the state of the seven Churches and so on. Two resident Americans were medical specialists, one in mental illness the other in healing fractures (*OBG*, 40). Another American, a grandson of Jonathan Edwards, the famous eighteenth-century American divine, was intimately familiar with all the details of the American Civil War and regaled Edwards with accounts of Lincoln and Grant, Jefferson Davis and Stonewall Jackson, General Robert E. Lee and John C. Calhoun, Sherman's devastating march through Georgia and the freeing of the slaves (*OBG*, 41). There was a virtuous young woman who was unfortunately a little slow of mind, and another young lady from London, who could sing a little and paint decent pictures. Taken as a whole these details constituted a snapshot of a Europe that was now becoming a pleasure ground not, as of old, for the aristocrats of the eighteenth-century Grand Tour, but for the moneyed professional travellers of the new middle class, to which Edwards himself obviously belonged.

Whenever he arrived in a new town he found himself besieged by a rabble of noisy, brawling petitioners, each trying to entice – or rather bully – him into staying at the hostelry whose paid lackey the pest was and whose name was prominently blazoned on his colourful headgear. There then followed the solemn carnival procession from station to hotel. His bags were seized by one, his umbrella by another, his coat proudly claimed by a third, and a fourth reverently carried his hat, while a fifth guarded his papers with ostentatious ceremony. For them, these garments and objects were simply the spoils of an unseemly struggle for the bounty expected in the form of a tip at the short journey's end – and a much more hefty tip, Edwards feelingly complained, than was customary in England.

He liberally spiced his narrative with uninhibited comments on his fellow travellers, those from the US, the UK and many of the countries of Europe he encountered on his journeys. He was a great believer in national types, and therefore liberal with his cavalier generalisations.

A native of Belgium, he informed his readers, could be reliably identified by the shoes he wore, wooden clogs that could be put to multiple use: a clunking clog could usefully be turned into a mug for beer or into a weapon to be hurled at some offending servant (*OBG*, 35). A German invariably favoured a great big high boot – Edwards even claimed to have seen a *Hausfrau* washing her husband's clothes in one, secure in the knowledge that her toddler had been safely imprisoned in another (*OBG*, 35). Germans, he added, also loved tall hats, while the French preferred flat caps with peaks. But then German men were invariably ugly, and this, Edwards uncharitably believed, was due to their inordinate consumption of beer, although he did concede he had never actually ever seen a single one drunk. Never, he authoritatively pronounced, had he seen more unsightly men than when in Germany: they were enormously stout, unhealthy, short-sighted and mentally dim, their faces scarred. The country, he added, seemed populated by dwarfs and hunchbacks (*OBG*, 36). Germans moreover were incessant smokers, so that, rather like the Israelites of old, they were preceded by a pillar of cloud by day and a pillar of fire by night.

As for the women . . . here Edwards went into loving, fascinated detail. The ladies of all countries invariably dressed appallingly, in his opinion, sporting unnatural flowers on their heads instead of proper hats, with every manner of lurid designs below. So compressed had their waists become as almost to turn women into wasps. Country girls, Edwards added, with the hearty prejudice of the born countryman, were altogether more appetising. They actually resembled girls, their calico dresses of blue or pale blue, a petticoat of the same colour, and nothing on their heads but their own plaited yellow hair. How superior was their natural look to the fashionable dresses of the women who drank tea fastidiously holding the handles of their china cups between two delicate fingers.

It may be tempting to dismiss Edwards's travelogues as lightweight, as mere gossip and trivia. But that would be a mistake. Very few indeed of his original readers could have entertained even the faintest hope of visiting the Continent. O.M. it was who first provided them with a vivid sense of ordinary day-to-day living in distant European locations. He thereby created in them a new sense of immediate human connection and even warm solidarity with other human beings who were living in what at the time must have seemed 'remote' and 'exotic' places. His gift for sensuous evocation likewise ensured that for those same readers he was able to conjure up the sensation of

entering an intriguingly strange world. These were not only important
gifts of his as a writer, they were also a means of making the idea of
Europe real to ordinary Welsh people for the very first time.

When it came to recording memorable aspects of his trip to Italy,
Edwards's tone was somewhat different from the one he had adopted
in *O'r Bala i Geneva*. He responded readily to those seductive aspects
of the country that clearly spoke to the suppressed, sensuous and
aesthetic sides of his nature. So, even though it was midwinter when
he visited, he gloried in the rich colours he saw everywhere:

> Between the mountains there, that stretch along the sea's edge towards
> the west, there is many a magical haven, where the palm-tree shoots up
> beneath a crown of white blossoms, as if it were newly risen from the
> suds of foam below it, where the lemons are so golden because the ocean
> below is so azure, and the olives so green above. (*TI*, 29)

It was an idyllic landscape and Edwards's sympathies began to
broaden cautiously into generosity in the warmth of this southern
environment. He was stunned by the divine images of Sassoferrato,
transfixed by the astonishing verisimilitude of Caravaggio and sensu-
ously awakened by Veronese's paintings, 'where flesh seems warm on
the canvas' (*IT*, 124). As for Titian, Edwards somewhat guiltily registered the Venetian master's astonishing ability to capture 'cryniadau
cynnes cnawd pechadurus' ('the warm shivers of sinful flesh') – that
last adjective was no doubt a sop to conscience – and he uneasily
admitted that the great painter's mortal women could seem more
beautiful than even the angels of Luini (Edwards's favourite painter)
and the saints of Andrea del Sarto.

The hallmark geniality and amiability of Edwards's writing persona is, however, sadly shattered in the notorious chapter in *O'r Bala
i Geneva* where he discusses the plight of European Jews. Here the
negative, repellent side of his Welsh Nonconformity surfaces strongly
at the end of a lengthy discussion, the guarded structure and judicious
tone of which only serve, in the end, to make its conclusions all the
more repugnant. Conscientiously expatiating, with all the apparent
scrupulousness of a genuinely dispassionate historian, on the sufferings of European Jewry, he seems to promise genuine understanding
and sympathy. Jews, he graciously concedes, have indeed been subjected to inhumane treatment. But then his tone alters to that already
ominously set several chapters earlier. There he had complained that

the Jews were busily multiplying in Worms as the native population declined, spreading like poisonous weeds in a garden gone to seed (*OBG*, 53):

> Gweli Iddew yn sefyll wrth ddrws ei siop fel pryf copyn, neu a'i hanner allan o'i ffenestr yn rhythu ar dy ôl – y mae lliw ei lygaid a maint ei drwyn yn ei fradychu. Er cased ydynt gan bawb, yr oedd eu henwau cynefin – Abraham a Jacob a Levi a Joseph – yn gwneyd i mi deimlo yn rhyw gynnes atynt. (*OBG*, 53)

> (You see a Jew standing in the doorway of his shop like a spider, or half of him hanging out of the window staring after you – the colour of his eyes and size of his nose betray him. But hated as they are by everyone, their familiar names – Abraham and Jacob, and Levi and Joseph – made me feel quite warm towards them.)

This frightened reaction, it is clear, is a reflex of the cultural shock he had experienced when first he had recognized in those Jewish names a sinister distortion – subsequently expressed in the physical, visceral terms of literal visual disfigurement – of the familiar world of his Welsh chapel. He had been totally unprepared for the *gross familiarity* of those names in what he had expected to be a totally alien culture.

Edwards's implicit awareness of the inevitability of viewing Europe through the lens of his own particular presuppositions and preoccupations is neatly encapsulated in an amusing story, told typically at his own expense. Scarcely had he set foot on the continent than he had a *contretemps* with the natives. Strolling along the banks of the Scheldt in Antwerp, he was accosted by a rough-looking Fleming who blocked his way, rubbing his thumb threateningly along the edge of his knife. Annoyed and alarmed in equal measure, the burly Edwards tried to push past him, only to end up grappling with the stranger, whom he succeeded in pushing over the edge of the quay into the water. Only when the man had struggled ashore did the truth emerge: all he had wanted was a light for his pipe.

In this volume, as also in the other two travelogues, the ruling passion of Edwards's mind becomes abundantly apparent. It is, after all, specifically advertised in the book's very title *O'r Bala i Geneva*, and is then further underlined in the brief Preface. His journey, Edwards grandly announces, is 'rhwng hen gartref meddwl Cymru a hen gartref meddwl Ewrob' ('between the old intellectual home of Wales and the old intellectual home of Europe'). What has he in mind? Well, he is thinking of late nineteenth-century Wales, and therefore viewing his own home town of Bala, with its colleges for training ministers, as the powerhouse of the Nonconformist nation. As for Geneva, it is the cradle of Reformed Protestantism, and the legendary site of John Calvin's sixteenth-century experiments in establishing a truly godly, theocratic civic society. Edwards, the sophisticated young Oxford don, may have become far removed from the Calvinistic Methodism of Bala, but that Methodism had certainly not been expelled from his mind, nor eradicated from his soul. In his travel books he repeatedly reverts to his root beliefs and consequently experiences real difficulty both in confronting contemporary Catholicism and in accounting for its continued hold on so many regions of the continent.

If Edwards had been unnerved when he found himself confronted by uncanny resemblances between European Jewry and Welsh Nonconformity, his experience of Brittany was analogous, except in reverse. In the case of the Jews he had found himself profoundly nonplussed by the similarities of Jewish names to those so common in his own culture. But having crossed to Brittany expecting to find nothing there but strong family resemblances with Wales, he had actually found the region to be strangely disorientating and rather uncanny. Everything was indeed in one sense very familiar, but it was disconcertingly strange and foreign at the same time.

In essence, Brittany was for Edwards Wales minus its religious revivals, its Nonconformist faith, its moral integrity and its popular democracy. It was pre-Nonconformist Wales as it used to be around the beginning of the eighteenth century. To travel there was to travel back in time. And because of this arrested historical development, Brittany was seriously at risk – at risk of being swamped by the cold irreligious rationality of an aggressively secular France. All it had to protect it was the complacent, corrupt, ignorant, immoral and exploitative Catholic clergy. Edwards's anti-Catholic bigotry was given full rein in this volume, to an extent that is difficult for us to stomach today, unless one appreciates its unintentional sardonic irony – today's Wales is, after all, almost as distant from the chapels and their faith as was Brittany from Welsh Nonconformity at the time that Edwards visited it. And the Bible is much more of a closed book to the bulk of the contemporary Welsh than ever it was to the devoutly Catholic Bretons of the late nineteenth century. The whirligig of time has indeed brought in its sweet revenges on Edwards's complacent, patronising opinions.

As the volume unfolds, so do other important aspects of Edwards's governing ideology loom ever larger. Some of these are neatly encapsulated in the little vignette he offers us of his travelling companions at an early stage of his train journey along the Welsh border. He and his sidekick Ifor Bowen share a carriage with three others who begin to engross Edwards's attention. Two are women – one jocosely plump and agreeably silent, the other sharp-featured and voluble. The latter lady is conspicuously well-heeled and has connections with Liverpool, where she has apparently inherited some property. Lost in her own loquacity, she has turned to face her female friend, in the process turning her back on her male travelling companion – a timidly querulous, shrinkingly frail Welsh country-man, dressed in somewhat worn and tattered homespun cloth. The class and ethnic differences between him and the others are visually very evident. His occasional stumbling efforts to break into his well-dressed companion's monologue are wholly ineffectual. That is, until she mangles the name Llangollen. This prompts him to angry protest at the atrocity being committed by her English tongue before he once more relapses into passive silence.

For Edwards, the countryman represents the poor Welsh 'peasant' tenantry, staunchly chapel-going. These are the rural 'gwerin', long oppressed by alien landlords, who have at long last begun to find their voice and the political means of using it to powerful effect, thanks to the new, brilliant generation of Liberal politicians risen from the same background. And it is through the lens of such Welsh 'progress' that he patronisingly views the condition of the poor Breton peasantry. They are deprived of the benefits of Nonconformity with its progressive Liberalism and remain in thrall to the priests who jealously guard their ignorance.

But if that is the unmistakable dominant thesis of *Tro yn Llydaw*, it is accompanied by a *sotto voce* subtext registering feelings that are somewhat more mixed and accordingly more interesting. For example, Edwards rather envies the Bretons the visceral anger at their exploitative foreign landlords who had prompted them to rise up in raw, violent reaction during the Revolutionary era. This very same violence had dramatically secured for the Breton peasantry a measure of freedom that the pacific, eminently respectable, long-suffering and law-abiding Nonconformist Welsh tenantry were still patiently

seeking through the established political process and by carefully law-
ful means.

Similar to this grudging, half-suppressed admiration of Breton
aggression is Edwards's ambivalent reaction to the region's colourful
folk customs. While deploring the riotous aspects of peasant life and
tut-tutting at all the Dionysiac drink and dance, he cannot help reluctantly appreciating its *joie de vivre*. And even his virulent, not to say
rabid, anti-Catholicism is tempered from time to time by a fascination with the simple dignity of the ritual of the Mass, the sensuous
beauty of the music and the religious images at their best. He is, though,
always quick to suggest that, compared to those simpler forms of Welsh
Nonconformist worship solidly grounded in familiarity with the Bible
and safely underpinned by stern Calvinist theology, these Catholic practices may be superficially attractive but are in reality totally lacking in
true spiritual substance. They are no more than gaudy window dressing.

Particularly embarrassing is Edwards's habit of subjecting hapless
young ordinary Bretons to an unsparing inquisition concerning their
familiarity with the scriptures and their understanding of the sacraments. A thesis to which he regularly returns is that the Welsh have
both an opportunity and a missionary duty so to educate their fellow
Celts as to lead them from the pagan darkness and superstition of the
Catholic Church into the light of Welsh Calvinistic Methodism. It is
this process of education alone that can save Brittany from becoming
completely overwhelmed by the irreligion of the French, a people for
whom Edwards can barely spare a single approving word.

Edwards's version of Brittany is a highly selective one, largely
limited to those coastal areas where distinctive Breton culture was to
some (diminishing) degree still alive. He resolutely overlooks the fact
that Brittany, like late nineteenth-century Wales, was a country with
a clear linguistic and cultural division, in the case of Brittany between
a residually Breton fringe and a dominantly French area. He fails
even to distinguish between Lower Brittany and Upper Brittany, and
studiously overlooks the Gallo dialect spoken along with standard
French in the latter. And when discussing the fate of Breton he pays
no attention whatsoever to the deliberate Jacobin policy of weakening
'regional' minority languages that had been implemented by successive centralist governments of the republican French state throughout
the nineteenth century

Edwards's account is essentially constructed to emphasise
exclusively the country's affinities with Celtic Wales. He is for ever

exclaiming over the 'Welsh' faces he sees at every turn, the strains of Welsh music he believes he hears, and he is fascinated by the uncanny similarity between Breton (whose common use was already fairly limited) and Welsh. It never occurs to him that it is the very process of industrialisation that elsewhere so horrifies him that is actually saving Welsh, and with it his Wales, from going the way of rapidly waning Breton. His is the typical belief of his times that the 'true' chapel-going and Welsh-speaking Wales is the Wales of the countryside. As for industrialism, all he can see is that it is threatening to strangle Welsh piety, just as French irreligion is threatening to strangle Breton piety (benighted and misguided though that may be in his eyes).

An arrival at one small place in particular triggers his strong anti-industrial bias. As 'Daoulas' is called he briefly mishears it as 'Dowlais', a visit to which he recalls with a rural mid-Walian's shiver of horror. Deafened by the roar of machinery and hypnotised by the showers of fire and ash from the great ironworks there, he had supposed he could hear a voice reciting lines from Longfellow's ominous poem 'Prelude' (from *Voices of the Night*, 1839):

> 'Learn that henceforth thy song shall be,
>   Not mountains capped with snow,
> Nor forests sounding like the sea,
> Nor rivers flowing ceaselessly,
> Where the woodlands bend to see
>   The bending heavens below.
>
> 'There is a forest where the din
>   Of iron branches sounds!
> A mighty river roars between,
> And whatsoever looks therein
> Sees the heavens all black with sin, –
>   Sees not its depths nor bounds.' (*TL*, 164)

While grudgingly admitting that industrialisation has brought wealth to the Welsh people, he regards it as no compensation for the moral degradation that follows in its wake, and he predictably concludes that the poverty of a rural Brittany still dependent on its small potato patches is preferable to the klondyke of the new south Wales.

The hostility of France to any manifestation of Breton distinctiveness is noted (but not analysed or explained), with Edwards remarking that it greatly resembles England's treatment of Wales a few years earlier, when every effort had been made to extinguish Welsh-speaking Wales and to turn the Welsh into English men and women (*TL*, 189). He also learns that contemporary Bretons have failed to develop the proper pride in their language and culture, and the national self-consciousness, that Nonconformist Wales has so successfully nurtured (*TL*, 174). His Protestant informer further assures him that the Catholic Church has played an influential role in suppressing Breton feeling. The parallel with the role played by the Church of England in nineteenth-century Wales is left implicit.

It is shocking for us today to discover that Wales was at this time busily sending Calvinistic Welsh Methodist missionaries to Brittany, and Edwards meets several of them, including a former contemporary of his at Aberystwyth (*OBG*, 170). Long settled in Quimper, W. Jenkyn Jones is convinced that so rotten is the Catholic Church there that it is already tottering, and that Welsh Calvinism is therefore sure to prevail. The anti-Catholic bigotry intermittently evident throughout the volume seems to intensify following this particular distasteful encounter. Thus, when he arrives at the home of the Protestant minister, Le Groignec (*TL*, 195), Edwards extols its neatness and cleanliness, contrasting it with the dirt and slovenliness of the interiors of Catholic dwellings with a censorious gusto worthy of the Anglican commissioners who in 1847 had produced the notorious Blue Books Report on education in Wales that so outraged Welsh Nonconformity.

But Edwards is also capable of occasionally tempering his vulgar prejudices with some degree of sympathetic understanding. Particularly noteworthy is his defence of the worship of the Virgin Mary – totally unscriptural though he hastens to emphasise it is (*TL*, 182). He spins an intriguing theory. Whereas the emphasis in Catholicism is on sympathetic recognition of the sinner, that of Protestantism is on total, uncompromising condemnation of sin. The latter, he remarks in what initially seems to be a self-contradiction, is a religion for the Teuton, the former a religion for the Celt. So why, he inquires, are the Welsh not Catholics? That, he argues, is because Ann Griffiths rapturously hymned the praises of the Church as the bride of Christ, thus feminising Welsh Nonconformist theology at a crucial juncture of its development in a way roughly corresponding to – but in its scriptural orthodoxy contrasting with – the Catholic Church's exaltation of the figure of the Virgin Mary. Edwards also finds himself somewhat uneasily enchanted by some of the traditional

Breton ballads, legends and tales – the relics of a Celtic culture that Nonconformity had zealously eliminated in Wales. He even tries to justify some of them (*TL*, 203–5), converting them into improving allegories of impeccable Nonconformist morality.

A similar dichotomy of response is evident in *Tro yn yr Eidal*. Edwards is ready enough there to parade his puritan prejudices, virtuously renouncing all sensuous delights, however seductive (*TE*, 152). The fine arts – to which he was himself clearly very attracted – can flourish, he sternly instructs his readers, only in those periods when two factors coincide: loss of freedom and decline in morality. So that disposes neatly of Renaissance Italy. It also explains to his considerable self-satisfaction why virtuous, progressive countries like Wales (whose freedom Edwards, the confirmed champion of British Liberal as well as Welsh Nonconformist values, chooses to believe has been retained) are not exactly renowned for their rich visual culture.

The rot sets in when towns and communities experience a decline in civic pride, placing their trust in princes who are autocratic as well as aristocratic, and tolerating a laxity in moral conduct. It is only under such decadent conditions, he adds, that artists and sculptors feel compelled to image the values that have already been lost as embodied in the great figures of the past. Thus, having begun by seeming ready to indict artists for their complicity in tyrannical, immoral regimes, he ends by representing them as custodians of conscience and preservers of best practice. It is an attempt to reconcile his culturally inherited puritan mistrust of the fine arts with his instinctive personal love and admiration of their productions.

He is on much more comfortable ground once he begins to narrate the history of Savonarola, whom he predictably views as a crypto-puritan, a great cleanser of the moral filth of Florence and, as a virtuous populist, a harbinger of late Victorian Welsh 'democratic' politics. Wasn't he, after all, a mesmerising preacher, and wasn't he thus obviously the precursor of the giants of the Welsh pulpit? And to clinch it all, Savonarola was even a Calvinist *avant la lettre*. He viewed the field of religion as an uncompromising battleground between God and the devil, the legions of light and of dark. There was no choice but to enlist under the banner of one or the other (*TE*, 155). As for the eventual downfall of Savonarola, that allows Edwards to give full, unbridled, rein to his anti-Catholic antipathies. Pope Alexander is denounced as one of the most evil men ever to tread the earth. And proof of divine approval of Savonarola's mission conveniently followed, when Martin Luther began his spiritual and moral crusade in Germany.

Such anti-Catholic venom recurs periodically throughout *Tro yn yr Eidal*. Thus Edwards loses no opportunity to mock the religious orders contemptuously. Grave and stately though the bearing of Dominican and Franciscan monks may be, clad as they piously are in their white and black and brown, he is not so easily fooled. They seem, he sarcastically comments, to be comfortably at home in what they self-servingly depict as the barren wilderness of this world, and 'chwery gân foddhaus ddichellgar ar eu gwynebau tewion' ('a sly, self-satisfied smile plays on their fat features'). It is a caricature worthy of the celebrated 'Gothic' novels of 'Monk' Lewis or Mrs Radcliffe at their most sinister. Edwards views the monks of both of these orders as renegade puritans, contrasting their pure beginnings, as preaching itinerants and mendicants, with their decadent, worldly present condition.

But Edwards's response to Catholicism can sometimes surprise us with its multi-layered complexity. One such moment occurs when he attends Mass with the townspeople of Lannion on a Sunday morning. His initial reaction is his customary one of scepticism and so, even while honestly registering the fervour of the worshippers, he cannot resist concluding:

> Yr oedd rhith crefydd yma, heb ei grym; ei llawenydd, heb ddylanwad ar fywyd; yr oedd gorchudd ar bethau mawrion Duw; a chyda gweddi'r Llydawiaid, esgynnai gweddi dieithriaid – perthynasau ar ymweliad . . . (*TE*, 101)

> (There was but the illusion of religion here, without its power; its joy, but unconnected to life; the great things of God were concealed; and with the prayers of the Bretons there rose the prayer of strangers – [we] relatives on a visit . . .)

And yet . . . With his customary honesty he feels compelled to admit that some sense of divine presence, and an answer to prayer, is palpably evident in the service. The people bend like grass before the wind. And once they begin to sing, he finds himself transported back to a chapel service in Wales, the congregation caught up in the ecstasy of one of Ann Griffiths's great hymns. An idea strikes him: Welsh chapel service is nothing but the Mass brought into the open air and reconsecrated to the service of Christ in the original simplicity of the gospel.

He thus unexpectedly discovers an intimate link between the Church of Rome and the Calvinistic chapels of Wales. There still linger in the latter echoes of the old Welsh fidelity to the Catholic Church, and it is these that temper the austerities of puritan worship, providing it with its beauty (*TL*, 103).

Recognising the undoubted majesty of Catholic services, he nevertheless misses in all the pomp of the liturgies and the gorgeousness of the garments the simple spiritual directness and moral integrity of familiar Nonconformist worship. But he still feels, now more intensely than ever, that there is a profound underlying connection between the two religions. Pondering it, he comes to an interesting conclusion. Traditional religious Dissent had been altogether too coldly cerebral ever to have appealed to the Welsh people in general: it was alien to their emotional Celtic natures. It was only when the great late eighteenth-century Methodist hymn writers William Williams Pantycelyn and Ann Griffiths embarked on their inspired work and produced their powerfully moving hymns that the Welsh had at last begun to take to the new Nonconformity *en masse*. And in that the Welsh were like the Catholic Bretons after all. Both peoples required a faith that appealed to the emotions as much as to the intelligence. And that was why the Welsh could never again become attached to the tepid religion of mainstream Anglicanism, any more than they could be satisfied with the new High Church Anglicanism that was, in Edwards's opinion, nothing but a weak and watered-down version of authentic Catholicism.

Paradoxically, Edwards is not as obsessed with Catholicism in Italy as he is with it in Brittany. But what does emerge instead is his other major ideological preoccupation, his preoccupation with the Whig version of history as a steady progress towards the kind of democratic political order already supposedly achieved by contemporary Britain. In *Tro yn yr Eidal* he is repeatedly moved to lyrical evocations of both the bustling present and the romantic past of the many towns and villages he visits. And since the Catholicism of Italy is so evident a settled fact, he largely takes it for granted and ignores it, save for occasional pious outbursts and homilies. He even manages to single out in Milan some meagre signs of Protestantism on which to pin his forlorn Whiggish hopes. But it is the proud mercantile history of the sometime self-governing Italian towns, and the romance of the recent unification of Italy, that prompt him most often to reconnect with his own ingrained political and social ideology. It is in this aspect of medieval Italian history that he finds compelling evidence to support his Welsh Nonconformist, and above all Whiggish, view of history as an irresistible human advance towards enlightenment.

But even this vision has its decidedly ugly aspects. Enthusiastically summarising the story of Pisa's heroic 'defence of Europe' during the eleventh century against the powerful invading forces of Islam, he contemptuously dismisses the 'Mahomedans' as nothing but 'a barbaric nation [*sic*] that had appeared, unexpectedly, out of the heat of the sandy Arabian wastes' (7). Fortunately, he has the gift to spice his particular version of the past with lively, attractive anecdotes. He recalls the familiar story of the great Galileo on his knees before the Inquisition agreeing that the earth did not, after all, rotate around the sun. Only to murmur under his breath as he rose to his feet, 'E pur si muove' ('And yet it *does* move'). And this reminds him of the reeling drunk he'd seen being mocked in Italy who'd replied 'You see, children, Galileo was right after all. The earth does indeed move' (*TI*, 88). Another story sees him in such a great hurry to catch a train that he disdains all assistance, only to have a servant from the hotel appear before him just as he is making himself comfortable in his carriage and smugly present him with the watch he'd left behind in his haste.

Bearing in mind the nostalgic view of pre-Reformation Europe later to be elaborated by Saunders Lewis and Ambrose Bebb, in which the spiritual power of the medieval Catholic Church is depicted as the great unifying force of the whole continent, Edwards paints a very different picture. The forging of a single nation out of the diverse civic regions of Italy has long been hampered, he argues, not only by the natural geography of the country (and here no doubt he had the history of Wales in mind) but also by the fact that papal Rome had for centuries insisted on being seen as the centre of the whole Catholic world rather than as simply the capital of Italy. Moreover, far from having presided over a unified Europe, Rome had for bitter centuries been embroiled in a power struggle with the Holy Roman Empire, whose headquarters had been not in Italy but in Germany. Only with the Risorgimento, and thanks to the various promptings of Mazzini, Cavour and Garibaldi – of whom Edwards was avowedly a great admirer – had Italy finally succeeded in becoming a single, unified nation.

But, as one would expect, it is in *O'r Bala i Geneva* that Edwards's Whiggism comes overwhelmingly to the fore. The Preface promises a brief survey of several of the main towns to be visited. Antwerp, Aachen, Cologne, Mainz, Frankfurt, Strasbourg, Basel, Lausanne, Geneva – these and many more are in his itinerary. And to Edwards the confirmed progressive Liberal they represent the nodal points of growth of modern commercial trade and representative democracy. A whole chapter is therefore devoted to a reverent narration of the representative contributions of these burgher towns to the creation of the kind of society to be found in late nineteenth-century Wales: a society, according to Edwards, governed in essence by 'y werin', the bulk of ordinary people from whom he was himself, as the son of a poor tenant farmer, so proud to have sprung.

Edwards was an accomplished professional historian. He was also a born educationalist, highly conscious of the need to familiarise his general readers with the history of Europe. Accordingly, there is scarcely a town – or even a street – that he visits that is not viewed in the perspective of the past, albeit a past recalled very selectively, even tendentiously, and painted with a broad brush and in decidedly bold colours. He loves, in particular, to indulge his progressive view of European history. So he reels off the names of the celebrated burgher towns of Protestant northern Europe as if telling a rosary, enumerating their splendid respective contributions to the advance of human society. A whole chapter is devoted to the history of Antwerp, Utrecht, Ghent, Brussels, Liège and the like (22ff.), as also to Lübeck, Bremen, Hamburg, Cologne, Mainz, Frankfurt and Nuremberg.

As he explains to the reader of his euphoric secular epistles:

Gwyddost mai dyna oedd ymdrech fawr y canoloesoedd – ymdrech y dref yn erbyn y castell; ymdrech rhyddid yn erbyn caethiwed; ymdrech y gweithiwr am fwynhau ffrwyth ei lafur; ymdrech am fasnach rydd yn erbyn gorthrwm arglwydd ac offeiriad; ymdrech Masnach, seiliedig ar allu llaw gelfydd a bywyd diwyd, yn erbyn y *Feudal System*, seiliedig ar waed a gwahaniaeth sefyllfa mewn cymdeithas. (*OBG*, 22)

(You know that that was the great effort of the Middle Ages – the struggle of the town against the castle; the struggle of freedom against slavery; the struggle of the labourer to enjoy the fruits of his labour; the struggle of free trade against the oppression of lord and priest; the struggle of Trade, dependent on a cunning hand and industrious life, against the Feudal system that was dependent on blood and status within society.)

The lowlands, he adds, belonged to the forces of progress while the uplands and the mountains remained the strongholds of aristocratic privilege. Nor did the former find it easy to maintain their way of life. After all, the forces of reaction had the might of monarchies and empires on their side, and it was the struggle against imperial Catholic Spain that had produced in the Low Countries legendary resisters such as Egmont and Horn (*OBG*, 23). He even finds a distant echo of such struggles in the courageous stand of John Penry, the orig inal Welsh puritan, against the tyranny of the Church in Elizabethan England, an act of moral and spiritual bravery that in Edwards's opinion deserves to be commemorated and celebrated much more than the physical bravery displayed by General Picton on the field of Waterloo.

For a reputable professional historian, O. M. Edwards's view of the continental countries he visited is, then, strikingly narrow, seeming at times to be almost wilfully ignorant. His blinkered approach can be accounted for only by his ideology, the dominant features of which have already been identified. How else to account for what he overlooks, including republican France's disgraceful treatment of such of its country's minority languages and cultures as those of Brittany? In Milan, he averts his gaze even from the important role that the great Welsh Catholic humanist Gruffydd Robert, author of the first Welsh grammar, had played in that city during the Counter-Reformation, as one of Cardinal Borromeo's right-hand men. As for Switzerland, and indeed Geneva, we learn absolutely nothing of their history apart from the glory years of Calvin and the other Protestant reformers. Curiouser and curiouser, as Alice might have said.

But if his travelogues are certainly unreliable as guides to the labyrinthine history of the European continent, and though they are sadly far from free of bigotry and even rank anti-Semitism, they still have the power to disarm us at times, and even to beguile us. And they are indisputably valuable evidence of the step change in the view taken of Europe by the ordinary readers of late Victorian Wales. They are all classic, indispensable documents of a crucial phase in the evolution of a modern Welsh Europeanism.

'Yr wyf yn treulio y rhan fwyaf o'm bywyd ar grwydr' ('I spend most of my time wandering'), wrote O. M. Edwards in January 1895, 'and if I could, I would spend my entire time doing so . . . there is many a cranny in the Alps and the Apennines as familiar to me by now as the mountain valley which is still my home . . . I know well of many a haven on the eastern coast of the Atlantic, and I have several times marvelled at the blue hills of the Mediterranean and on a quiet beach of the Adriatic sea.'[3]

A mere ten years earlier it is doubtful whether such a passage could have been written. But by the end of the nineteenth century, continental travel was becoming much easier for educated, prosperous middle-class Welshmen (women were still another matter). Edwards's purpose in launching and editing his immensely popular and influential journal *Cymru* in 1891 had been to remedy the deficiencies of the current, relentlessly anglocentric education system that deprived readers of any acquaintance with their own history and culture. An allied purpose was to offer a synoptic, pan-Welsh overview that promoted a sense of national unity and counteracted the baleful influence of sectarian conflict and parochial obsession. But the Edwards who had already published three popular travelogues also consciously aspired to widen Welsh horizons. To that end he included a section on other countries in every issue of *Cymru*, along with relaxed, informative and entertaining bulletins of his own extensive adventures abroad.

Nor did he confine himself to reporting on European matters and excursions. He serialised the Rev. John Owen's vivid accounts of his travels across the United States, reported on the Rev. Griffith John's remarkable missionary work in China, carried an account of a visit to the West Indies, and another about Arabia, printed a highly romantic adventure story based in Patagonia by John Ceredig Davies and a personal reminiscence by 'JL' of the Wladfa , included a survey of the high peaks of the Andes, and featured an essay from Constantinople by Samuel Evans about his experience of travelling to Baghdad in the company of a Persian pilgrim, as well as an account of an earthquake in the Khasi hills of northern India, where Welsh missionaries were busily at work. Most ambitious of all, perhaps, was the 'Notes from Egypt' he published in December 1896 by Edward Davis Bryan, the remarkable Welsh entrepreneur who, along with his brother, had established an emporium in Cairo that was eventually to prove a magnet right across the Middle East.[4]

In comparison, the coverage of Europe was – particularly bearing the earlier trilogy of travelogues in mind – very disappointingly restricted. Indeed, it was virtually confined, very much in the spirit of *Tro yn Llydaw*, to attempts to situate Welsh-speaking Wales in the context of its Celtic 'cousin', Brittany. There were thus some incipient signs in these articles of the Welsh beginning to register the arguments of Emrys ap Iwan, that situations cognate to their own were to be found not by examining England but by opening their eyes to the European continent. Since pan-Celtic fervour was at its height in the later 1890s, it is not surprising that Brittany was given particular attention. In its perceived 'backwardness' it sometimes served as a useful foil to a 'progressive' Nonconformist Wales that had long since resolutely turned its back on the Catholic religion.

By the end of the nineteenth century, however, sectarian concerns in Wales were just beginning to give way to secular matters. And of particular interest to the educated Welsh were such belated efforts as Brittany was making not only to revive the Breton language but also to record and thus perpetuate its rich history of legend, folk tale, and song. A collection of Breton proverbs appeared in the September 1896 issue, accompanied by pithy Welsh translations.[5] Some three years earlier, W. Jenkyn Jones, the Welsh Protestant missionary already mentioned in *Tro yn Llydaw*, had approvingly reviewed *La Chanson de la Bretagne*, a collection of patriotic songs by the prominent poet and folklorist Anatole Le Braz (subsequently awarded a prize by the Académie Française) while sadly noting that (although Breton was Le Braz's native language) they had been written in French. Jones's melancholy comments on this very precisely anticipate sentiments to be expressed by another Jones, the eminent Welsh philosopher and patriot J. R. Jones, some seventy years later: '

> Trist yw canu cân alltud, pan y gorfyddir gwneyd hynny, nid am fod y bardd yn gadael ei wlad, ond am fod ei wlad yn ei adael ef, er bod ei bryniau a'i dyffrynnoedd eto o dan ei draed.[6]

> (It is sad to sing a song of exile when compelled to do so not because the poet is forced to leave his country, but because his country is leaving him, even though its hills and vales are still beneath his feet.)

By the 1890s, a generation of gifted young scholars, mostly trained at Oxford, had begun the task of seriously excavating the Celtic past of Wales that had been conspicuously overlooked by the Victorians. After all, the Celts had suffered the fatal disadvantage of not being Nonconformists, and so the chapels had closed their doors against such an unsavoury period of the country's past. For them, serious Welsh history had begun only with the Protestant Reformation and with such heroes of early Dissent as the Elizabethan puritan martyr John Penry. But Edwards, himself at this juncture a young Oxford don, shared the enthusiasm of the new generation for things Celtic, and so several issues of *Cymru* reviewed the state of the various Celtic languages in the contemporary world.

An overview of the history of the Celts and their languages was offered by D. Lloyd Jones in 1898.[7] The first essay traced their origins back to the closing centuries of the pre-Christian era, and, probably with a disapproving eye on Arnold's feminisation of the Celts and condescending treatment of their supposed otherworldliness, stressed in contrast their virile vigour, boldness and courage. This essay particularly emphasised the major stature of Celtic languages at that time. The second addressed the issue of their continuing strength in the late nineteenth century, beginning with an assessment of the condition of Gaelic in Ireland. It singled out the steep decline recorded in census data between 1871 and 1881, sadly suggesting that the death of the language seemed as inevitable as it was imminent. The regions in which it hitherto remained most stubbornly resistant were Munster and Connaught: over half the population of Mayo continued to be able to speak Irish. Some evidence of its persistence could also be found among the almost two million Irish immigrants to the United States and when these were combined with estimates of speakers in the far-flung Irish diaspora, it seemed safe to assume that some million and a quarter Gaelic-speakers remained.

The situation of Manx was even more dire.[8] This branch of the Goidelic language had flourished right down to the eighteenth century, but then English immigration had steadily intensified. By 1869 Manx had become little more than a distant memory, save in some country districts, and by the end of the century it was questionable whether out of some 50,000 islanders even as few as a thousand Manx- speakers could now be discovered on the Isle of Man. Cornish was long dead, as pretty well were most of the languages of Scotland (Highland Gaelic was spoken by fewer than 6 per cent), as separate articles of the same period dolefully confirmed.[9] But as a kind of mournful memorial to Cornish, the opening chapter of Genesis in that language was published with parallel Welsh text in the March 1898 issue of *Cymru*, drawing attention to the striking linguistic similarity between the two versions.[10]

As recently as 1881, figures had reliably recorded over a million Breton speakers in Brittany, and a similar number (out of a total Breton population of more than three million) was reported to be still living in the region of Finistère and parts of the Côtes du Nord and Morbihan, with some signs of a revival elsewhere.[11] All in all, the article concluded, Breton seemed to be even more flourishing than Welsh at the end of the nineteenth century.

The fascination with Brittany that was a feature of *Cymru* during this period owed something, no doubt, to O. M. Edwards's own earlier travels around the country. February 1898, saw the publication of a compilation of the songs of Brittany in Welsh translation by 'Gwylllt Walia'.[12] These sample poems were taken from the celebrated 1838 anthology *Barzaz Breiz*, edited by the Breton philologist and man of letters Théodore, Vicomte de La Villemarqué, who drew on work done by his mother and others. This compilation is still regarded as a seminal text in the history of modern Breton patriotism. It consists of folk poems and tunes that had been assiduously collected, and the original edition was printed as a dual text, French translations alongside the original Breton. The whole was prefaced by a history of the collection and an ethnographic report on the traditional culture of Brittany, and it concluded with a reflective essay. Augmented editions of the work appeared over the next few years and thereafter it continued to attract the approving attention of such fashionable Parisian figures as George Sand, as well as to appeal to writers, artists and musicians.

Controversy remains as to the authenticity of the materials – some have argued that Villemarqué had a significant creative hand in the fashioning of them and have compared him with the Macpherson of *Ossian* – but consensus tends towards viewing the work as similar to that of the brothers Grimm, whose friend the Vicomte was, in being a nineteenth-century reworking of traditional sources. Such Welsh interest in it as these translations indicate was very much a consequence of the late nineteenth-century pan-Celticism that involved not only Wales, Ireland, and Scotland but also France. In the aftermath of the Romantic movement in France, and the enduring passion there for Macpherson's *Ossian*, interest remained in the Celtic substratum of the French nation, supposed to be still outcropping in such primitive marginal regions as Brittany, as evidenced in its 'folk' Catholicism. Further translations of Breton songs were included in later issues of *Cymru*.[13]

This intense Welsh interest in Brittany was reciprocated in the case of the nineteen-year-old Breton patriot François Jaffrennou, who in 1898 published a flattering essay in *Cymru* comparing the mid-Victorian doggerel of Mynyddog favourably with the poetry of Byron and Hugo, proof, he pointedly asserted, that small nations were perfectly capable of producing great poets. Such a passion for sentimental patriotic poetry was natural for a Breton who was just embarking on a lifetime of dedication to the cause of Breton nationalism. A year after the appearance of the article he visited the Eisteddfod in Cardiff, where he was given the bardic name of Taldir ab Hernin by the gorsedd, and he subsequently went on to establish a corresponding gorsedd in Brittany. Around the same time he translated the Welsh national anthem 'Hen Wlad fy Nhadau' into Breton, and that has been generally accepted ever since as the national anthem of Brittany. Sadly his later years were clouded by accusations of collaboration during the Nazi occupation of France, although his reputation was eventually rehabilitated.[14]

Already proudly styling himself 'Taldir,' Jaffrennou contributed a short article to the January 1900 issue of *Cymru* (41) on a Breton's view of Llanberis and Beddgelert, in which he commented wistfully on the Welshness of the primary school in Caernarfon. As if by way of reply, O. M. Edwards published a recollection of his departure from Wales on a visit to Brittany in the same issue. This, Edwards guiltily admits, was partly by way of escaping into memory and the past from the press of the current worrying situation in South Africa and other painful matters. It is a rare psychological confession, that would perhaps bear further exploration by anyone interested in Edwards's manic passion for travel and his obsessive concern throughout his lifetime with the Welsh past, careful though he always was to connect it to the concerns of contemporary Wales. Was one of the drivers, one wonders, a need to seek refuge from so many dispiriting aspects of the Welsh present in which he nevertheless remained resolutely and bravely active?

Nonconformist preoccupations still remained very evident in the pages of *Cymru*. Their lopsided nature was nowhere more noticeable than when the periodical printed a lengthy history of France's Protestant reformers while completely ignoring the sequence of turbulent events in France from the time of the French Revolution down to the end of the nineteenth century.[15] The great state funeral of the eminent Breton Ernest Renan was covered in detail in January 1893, but he was revered by the correspondent not, as he often is today, for his illuminating analysis of national ideology in the discourse *Qu'est-ce qu'une nation?* (1882), but as a biblical scholar, author of *Histoire des Origines de Christianisme* (1863–81) and the five-volume *Histoire du Peuple d'Israël* (1887–93). Both works continue to enjoy a high scholarly reputation today and provide the foundation for Renan's reputation as an outstanding expert in Semitic languages. No mention was however made in this obituary report of Renan's controversial *Vie de Jésus* (1863), in which he had argued for the humanity rather than the divinity of Christ, although there is some suggestion of the Nonconformist author's particular approval for the Breton's disavowal of mainstream Catholicism.

To the October issue of *Cymru*, Edwards contributed a typically lively essay on his visit to Italy, in the form of snapshot impressions of Turin, Florence and Rome, finding everywhere evidence of the potential for Italy to become a great nation again once it abandoned Catholicism for Protestantism and granted political freedom to its people. He was particularly scandalised by the Italian celebrations of Easter, which featured chocolate lambs, doves of white sugar and oranges with red spots to denote Christ's blood spilt on the cross.[16] But this was a rare continental excursion for *Cymru* to undertake beyond the narrow confines of coastal Brittany. For evidence of some awareness of Europe's rich multiculturalism one needs to turn to the translations from several European languages featured in its pages. Almost invariably, the author of these was the remarkable Robert Bryan, who was as productive as he was obviously a talented multi-linguist.

Over three issues of the periodical between July and December 1899 he published lists of Italian proverbs with Welsh translations.[17] These were but a footnote, however, to his previous efforts, which featured translations of the fifteenth century 'Verslets à mon premier né,' as well as poems by Petrarch, Tommaso Grossi, Giovanni Battista Niccolini, François Coppée, Victor Hugo, Jean Reboul, Goethe, Müller's *Winterreise*, Schmidt von Lübeck, Heine, Schiller, along with half a dozen Spanish folk songs (*canciones populares españolas*).

No doubt stimulated by Bryan's efforts, Edwards announced in February 1893 an intention to publish a sample of the best of poetry from other countries every month, so that Welsh poetry could be compared against the highest international standards.[18] Sadly, little came of this ambition, but in the January 1892 number there appeared seven singularly accomplished translations of lyrics by Heine by the young John Morris-Jones that were to presage the flowering of Welsh poetry anew at the beginning of the twentieth century.[19] If a little stiff and formal, as if on their best behaviour, these graceful lyrics were a great advance on the constipated poems of a late Victorian Wales, bloated as they invariably were with sentiment, patriotism and piety and liberally laced with cliché.

These slight translations by Bryan and Morris-Jones were the harbingers of the remarkable cultural revolution that was to follow as a new, highly gifted, generation of Welsh writers began to connect with European literature in ways that helped release, and refine, their own innate talents. This process, along with the cultural renaissance that it helped enable, will be studied in detail in the following chapters.

Notes

1 For a useful introduction to O. M. Edwards, see Hazel Davies, *O. M. Edwards*, Writers of Wales (Cardiff: University of Wales Press, 1988).
2 *O'r Bala i Geneva* (Bala: Davies and Evans, 1889); *Tro yn yr Eidal* (Dolgellau: E. W. Evans, 1889); *Tro i Lydaw* (Dolgellau: E. W. Evans, 1890). The last two were the first in a series of popular classics launched under Edwards's editorship, while *Tro yn yr Eidal* was also dedicated to Edwards's distinguished mentor, Benjamin Jowett, Master of Balliol. Hereafter these three volumes will be respectively cited as *OBG*, *TE* and *TL*.
3 *Cymru*, 8–9 (January 1895), 37.
4 *Cymru*, 11 (July–December 1896), 253.
5 *Cymru*, 11 (September 1896), 130–1.
6 *Cymru*, 4 (January–June 1893); (May), 257.
7 *Cymru*, 14 (March 1898), 101–3 and May (1898), 235–8.
8 *Cymru*, 14 (June 1898), 271–3.
9 *Cymru*, 15 (July–December 1898), 67–70, 29–36.
10 *Cymru*, 14 (1898), 128–30.
11 *Cymru*, 14 (1898), 114–20.
12 *Cymru*, 14 (1898), 97–8.
13 *Cymru*, 15 (July–December 1898), 62, 157, 281.
14 Further, see Gwenno Piette, 'Breton literature during the German Occupation (1940–4): Reflections of collaboration', conference paper on the theme of Celtic Literature in the Twentieth Century, presented in 2000 at the University of Ulster, Coleraine.
15 *Cymru*, 2 (1892), 34, 89, 120, 235, 278.
16 *Cymru*, 18 (1900), 119, 149.
17 *Cymru*, 17 (1899), 17, 73–5, 121–3, 256–8.
18 *Cymru*, 4 (1893), 86.
19 *Cymru*, 2 (1892), 150.

3

The Little Five-Foot-Five Nations

On 19 September 1914, barely a month into the war, Lloyd George addressed a huge crowd, largely consisting of the London Welsh, in the Queen's Hall in London, an auditorium noted for its acoustic. Privately, Lloyd George had a fairly low opinion of his audience, recording that addressing the serried ranks of the affluent, self-satisfied Anglo-Welsh of London was like cutting through 'layers of fat'. But political expediency prompted him to do so. It was his great opportunity to shed the anti-war reputation that had clung to him ever since his courageous and principled opposition to the Boer War – indeed a recent historian has dubbed the speech '[Lloyd George's] personal declaration of war'.[1] And with the country now facing the serious and urgent challenge of recruitment, following the Cabinet's very recent vote against the bellicose Churchill's proposed bill to introduce compulsory conscription, Lloyd George saw, and seized, the opportunity to mobilise his countrymen with the aim of establishing – in the teeth of opposition from Kitchener – a Wales Army Corps, clad in plain Welsh woollen flannel.

The result was a triumphant performance, in the form of an address so electrifying that the text was soon circulating around the world, becoming 'Britain's first great propaganda success' (*DLG*, 120). At the heart of it lay Lloyd George's contrast between the bullying Great Powers of the continent – Prussian Germany he characterised as one of the 'road hogs' of Europe – and the 'five-foot-five nations', as he put it, the small fry like Belgium, Serbia and of course his own beloved Wales, whose rights were in need of courageous protection. Warming to his subject, he winningly alluded to his own short stature before ecstatically hymning the bravery of a 'race that faced the

Normans for hundreds of years in a struggle for freedom, the race
that helped to win Crécy, the race that fought for a generation under
Glendower against the greatest captain in Europe'. It was the little
nations, he added, that had produced some of the greatest art in the
world; it was even a little nation that had been home to the Messiah
himself. It was irresistible flattery, and the London Welsh lapped it
up, as were those back home also to do (*DLG*, 119).

While admiring Lloyd George's rhetoric and marvelling at his political adroitness, modern historians view his version of events, both
contemporary and ancient, with very considerable scepticism. The fate
of Belgium, they point out, was never really the key issue – indeed the
British government even made a secret offer to Germany at this time
to allow Belgium to be overrun provided the security of France (the
real cause of concern) was guaranteed. But Lloyd George had come up
with a wonderful cover story that allowed politicians opposed to war
to cross the bridge with a good conscience, and join a wartime alliance.
And of course, his inspired fiction went down a treat in Wales. It spoke
to the masses in the very terms of morality and principle to which
almost a century of Nonconformist indoctrination had conditioned
them, guaranteeing that most of the ministers, who were still by and
large chapel society's leaders, would vigorously support, and even assist,
recruitment. And it also spoke to the small, but influential, elite of
motley Welsh academics and intellectuals one of whose most important organs was the heavyweight new periodical *The Welsh Outlook*.

The coverage of the continent afforded by the *Outlook* over the next
half-dozen years – and under several editors of varying political outlook, including Thomas Jones, Edgar Chappell and T. Huws Davies
– is fascinating to examine, consistently based as it is on the supposition of Wales being exactly what Lloyd George had resoundingly
announced it to be: one of the proud little five-foot-five nations of
Europe deserving of the right to self-determination. But, understandably, it is specifically the plight of Belgium that looms large at the
beginning. Already, in the editorial notes prefacing the September 1914
issue, we find the *Outlook* admitting that 'perhaps, as Mr Shaw has
told us, the violation of the neutrality of Belgium made no difference;
it is probable that we should have joined with France in any case.' But,
it then proceeds to add, '[it is the case of Belgium] that has made all
the difference to the feelings behind the government in the country'.[2]

And whereas a photograph of Rodin's statue *The Genius of War* graces the frontispiece of the September 1914 issue, as if to emphasise the centrality of the threat to France to British war efforts, the frontispiece of the October issue is a reproduction of a *Punch* cartoon in which the buxom warrior figure of Britannia, complete with familiar gear, urges the demure, maidenly figure of Belgium, who stands at her side clutching spear and shield, to 'Trust Me', before adding, this time as the unabashed personification of 'England': 'Let us hope that they won't trouble you, dear friend. *But if they do . . .*'.[3]

This is prelude to an editorial note drawing attention to the 'many thousands of persons in Belgium whose homes have been destroyed and for whom the Belgian Government . . . are unable to provide'.[4] There follows a clarion call to councils and churches across Wales, hitherto laggard in their response, to rally to this cause, because as 'Welshmen . . . whatever duties the war has laid upon us, this of opening our homes to the Belgians is one of the simplest and most urgent. The Belgians are fighting our battles. They have helped to keep our homes secure' (420). Special commendation then goes to the various initiatives – though disappointing in number – that have already been launched at listed sites across Wales to address this crisis. For many months to come, the *Outlook* would feature regular updates on the Welsh response to the Belgian refugee crisis.

Throughout the war years, the *Outlook*'s perspective on Europe was every bit as much cultural as practical or political, and as a foretaste of this, the October issue included the first of two astute articles (the second followed in the November issue) on the poetry of Émile Verhaeren by the young P. Mansell Jones, who was later to become professor of French first at Bangor and then at Manchester University. Verhaeren (born near Antwerp in 1855) is presented as a writer of 'world-wide significance and utmost originality', who should be of particular interest to 'Welshmen who are witnessing a reawakening of our national life and a revival of our national literature'.[5] The Belgian revival is illustrated by reference to 'the novels of the late Camille Lemonnier, the poetry of Verhaeren, the dramas of Maurice Maeterlinck, and the sculpture of Constantin Meunier'. As for Verhaeren himself, he is praised for having developed into a social visionary, a 'prophet-poet' who has perceived and celebrated the utopian potential of currently degrading modern urban and industrial life, and who accepts, even as he laments, the inevitable decline of rural life. A pioneer of crowd psychology, who 'voices the turmoil, tragedy and aspirations of modern city life,' the 'Visionary of Flanders'[6] is implicitly presented as a poet of particular relevance to the new and largely anglophone Wales of the industrial south.

Although Flemish by birth and upbringing, Verhaeren wrote in the French of the Walloon culture he had embraced. His case is thus broadly analogous to that of the Welsh-speaker of that day who had enthusiastically adopted anglicised south Wales as his culture of choice. It is interesting and appropriate, therefore, that the article on Verhaeren is followed by a study of 'National Movements in Belgium' that introduces the Welsh reader to the bilingual and bicultural character of the country. At the heart of this careful, thoughtful study by Fabrice Polderman is an appreciation of Belgium's move towards a genuinely bicultural structure, in which 'the principle of the *equality of languages*' is not only recognised but fully implemented. The parallels with the case of a newly bilingual Wales are obvious, as are the concluding remarks emphasising that 'from the point of view of general civilisation it is to be desired that each community should keep its own language and develop through it'.[7]

Although the November issue includes reproductions of four paintings by Eugène Laermans (including *The Strike*, with its obvious interest for industrial Wales[8]), even in these early numbers Belgium is not the only continental country to be considered by the highly Europe-conscious *Outlook*. The case of the Slavs begins already to receive attention, with reference not only to the obvious case of Serbia but also to the wider constellation of Slavic countries, most prominently, of course, including still Tsarist Russia, whose glittering galaxy of great nineteenth-century writers in particular begins to receive close critical examination in the wake of a sudden surge of interest in a country now viewed as a key ally. So even as 'an Italian', contributing to the October issue, expresses misgivings about the possible emergence of an aggressive pan-Slavic nationalism,[9] the review section for that month includes a review of a collection of 'Russian sketches' translated by Beatrix L. Tollemache – the forerunner of many more such reviews of Russian authors to follow.[10]

The June 1915 issue of the *Outlook* contained an appreciative assessment of Constance Garnett's translation of Dostoevsky's *House of the Dead*, while its pages also featured an article on 'Some Aspects of Russia' by Lilian Winstanley. Beginning by disparaging the decline into barbarism and bestiality of the Germany whose culture had for decades been the envy of both Welsh and English intellectuals, it

proceeds to offer an overview of Russian history that includes the
bizarre claim that 'Russia is, in some ways, the most democratic country in Europe' – a claim based on the supposedly 'classless' character
of peasant society.[11] It proceeds to conclude condescendingly that
'Russia is exceedingly grateful for our friendship', and that 'No countries have more to give each other than Russia and England [*sic*].' A
few pages later sees Rosa Newmarch embarking on her two-part study
of 'Russian Music and Painting'[12] that is duly concluded in the next
issue of the *Outlook*.

It was the poet and short-story writer Sologub (Feodor Kuzmich
Teternikov) whose work, recently translated into English by John
Cournos, was praised by Ernest Rhys in October for interpreting
'the great and troubled spirit of Russia', as that had been revealed
for the first time to the West through the travails of the Great War.[13]
For Rhys, some of the tales recalled passages from the grotesque folk
tales of Wales, while others could easily be transferred, and translated, into a 'Welsh or English milieu'. And while rendered a little
uneasy by Sologub's treatment of the 'morbid' aspects of human
psychology, Rhys is perceptive enough to recognise that in this he
resembles Dostoevksy, and that to 'the more complex spirit of life
that has grown up in Cymru, Sologub's artistic stimulus should be of
much account'. After all, there are strong affinities, in Rhys's opinion,
between the Slav and Celtic temperament. As if in confirmation of
this, in October 1916, the *Outlook* carried John Cournos's translation of Sologub's story 'Dreams',[14] while the review section for that
month noticed Kropotkin's work on *Russian Literature – Ideals and
Realities*,[15] and the editorial notes at the beginning of the November
issue praised the anthology, entitled *The Soul of Russia*, recently produced to raise money for Russian refugees.

Particularly interesting, from a literary point of view, is the
review of Constance Garnett's translation of *The Tales of Anton
Tchehov*.[16] Still a relatively unknown figure, Checkhov intrigued and
puzzled early readers because his stories – and his plays – seemed so
unfocused, vaguely suggestive, inconclusive – 'there is no sense of construction or climax, no massing or co-ordination of material', as the
reviewer put it. But, intelligently resisting the temptation to dismiss
such work as random, arbitrary and pointless, the reviewer shrewdly
concludes that in fact it cunningly suggests some new kind of 'form
and meaning which perpetually mock[s] and elud[es] the mind'.

*

But it was Belgium that for some considerable time received star bill-
ing in the *Outlook*, with the November 1914 issue carrying an essay
by 'A Refugee' on 'The Germans in Brussels', culminating with a reference to the calamitous fall of Antwerp.[17] In December the *Outlook*
published, in addition to a tame, conventional lyric by Alafon on
the terrible contemporary fate of Flemish Louvain, a translation by
Eilian Hughes of Verhaeren's 'Aéroplanes sur Bruxelles', while the
review section opened by assessing a portfolio of studies of Verhaeren,
including one by Stefan Zweig, a translation by Arthur Symons and
a number of *Aberystwyth Studies* that included a pioneering essay by
P. Mansell Jones on Verhaeren's debts to his acknowledged American
'master', Walt Whitman.[18] Then, to round off this Belgian 'fest', there
was a letter from H. Hubert, 'Professor at the University of Liège',
attacking the preceding article on Belgian nationality as unpatriotic,
because at the time that Belgian unity was paramount it had foregrounded the history of internal dissension and conflict that had long
plagued the country. In truth, the letter is written from a Francophile
position. While grudgingly admitting the right of Flemish to exist, it
praises those Flemish artists who have deliberately chosen to write in
French because 'they wished to give to their noble thoughts a wider
public'.[19] Once more, the parallels with some attitudes highly influential in early twentieth-century Wales are very obvious.

Having reaffirmed in its March 1915 number its firm commitment to the rights of small nations 'like ours' (the claims of Belgium
were clear, it asserted, but difficulties would arise at war's end with
'the maze of Hungary and the Balkans'[20]), it included in May an
article on the Flemish sculptor George Minne that emphasises the
'sublimity' of work increasingly calculated to capture the physical
lineaments of the human soul – a subject guaranteed to be of interest to religiose Welsh readers still heavily influenced by the culture
of the chapels.[21] But Verhaeren continued to be the *Outlook*'s star
Belgian exhibit, so his brief visit to Wales – he was photographed
alongside the equally eminent exile figures of the socialist politician
Émile Vandervelde, who in 1914 had been named Belgian minister
of state, and the Flemish painter Émile Claus, who was the father of
Belgian luminism[22] – received reverential notice, as did the translation of his poems by Alma Strettel in a review that has some shrewd
observations to make about Verhaeren's indebtedness to the French
Symbolists, and his skilful deployment of *vers libre* (the term 'free
verse' had yet to establish itself in the English dictionary).[23] Finally,

when Verhaeren unexpectedly died in November 1916 after falling under a train in Rouen station, the *Outlook* mourned him as 'of all Europeans, the champion of small nationalities' such as those of Belgium and of Wales.[24]

There is again much talk of the soul in the *Outlook* of September 1915, this time in an essay by Raphael Petrucci, 'Professor of the History of the Fine Arts' in Brussels, on 'The Soul of Belgium'.[25] It is addressed specifically to 'the Welsh nation' who have been 'so hospitable to our fugitives'. The author seems to be particularly concerned about the bad reputation the Belgians may have had in Britain following the revelations, as recently as the 1890s, about the atrocious conditions that had prevailed in the Congo Free State. This was, Petrucci emphasises, very much the responsibility of the late King Leopold II, the last twenty years of whose reign had been 'infamous'. Also aware of the reputation the Belgians might have for being plagued by civil strife between Flemings and Walloons, he takes pains to explain the historical background to the situation, including the distinction between the industrialised French region with its preference for Liberal politics and the agrarian Flemish region partial to socialism. The German invasion, Petrucci concludes, brought an end to this internal dissension, uniting the Belgians as one nation and rekindling the people's historical reputation as staunch champions of independence and liberty. 'A nation that wills to live', he finishes with a fine flourish, 'and to live free may be oppressed but the instant the conqueror determines to destroy it, he seals his own sentence of death.'

In August 1915 the *Outlook* rekindled its interest in the 'Slav imagination' with a brief essay by John Henderson on 'Ivan Mestrovic: Sculptor and Patriot' – during the course of which it is asserted that

> the mighty war we are engaged in teaches us to see many things we ought to have seen long ago, and one is that the Slav element in Europe has more of the divine impetus to create than the Teutonic has ever had or can ever have, except, possibly, in music. And again it is worth saying that this is Celticism, this impulse to create out of uncreated dream rather than manufacture from tangible material.[26]

As if to prove this point, the *Outlook* then prints reproductions of two pieces by Mestrovic, *The Widows*, and *The Deposition from the Cross*.[27]

Although a Croat, Mestrovic – whom Rodin had once declared to be a greater sculptor than himself – was by 1915 an admirer of Serbian culture and, now known as 'the Prophet of Yugoslavism', a strong promoter of the pan-Slavic model that Henderson himself also advocated as a post-war ideal.

Henderson returned to his Slav theme in the next issue of the *Outlook*, this time with a highly romantic and magniloquent essay on 'Songs of Serbia', described, in a manner obviously calculated to appeal to the Welsh, as a 'light shining from a cottage dwarfed by the houses of larger nations, but the larger nations, by comparison, too often dim their illumination by the use of ornament'.[28] In the next (October) issue the essay was continued, and concluded with the confident assertion that, while Serbia might look to Russia, as an 'elder brother,' for guidance and support, she must 'like every nation, like every individual . . . find her own way, and will find it'.[29] For Serbia here read Wales, and for Russia, England.

Then, in July, 1916, the periodical featured an essay by E. Chivers Davies on 'The Serb as an Artist', that repeatedly drew parallels between Serbia and Wales, ending with the pious assurance that 'Wales, which has struggled long and hard for the preservation of her national entity will understand, will sympathise with that intrepid little nation in the far-away Balkans'.[30] The similarities actually noted between the two nationalities are, however, disappointingly vague and highly romantic, with emphasis being placed on the supposed natural musicality of both peoples, and on the role of preserving cultural memory traditionally assigned in both societies to national bards, usually in the service of powerful, glamorised warlords. And a contrast is insisted on between the supposedly advanced character of modern Welsh society and the charmingly primitive state of the Serbian peoples.

The Slavic theme was resumed by the *Outlook* in March 1916, when the number for that month included an admiring article on 'The Southern Slavs,' whose long heroic struggle against a succession of occupying powers, including Turks, Venetians and Austrians, is eloquently extolled, with the palm going to a Serbia that already in the Middle Ages was moving towards the creation of a consolidated Jugo-Slavic state until the process was arrested by Turkish conquest.[31] In another article, Poland is described as a 'country which has vanished from the maps, but which lives in the hearts of twenty million Slavs, today condemned to serve under one or other of the three powers who carved their nation like a piece of cardboard'.[32] This vision of the tragic plight of the Poles is reinforced in the painting by the Polish patriot Artur Grottger, entitled *Come with me through the Vale of Weeping*, that features as frontispiece to the May 1916 number of the *Outlook*, and in the same month the periodical published a review of a collection of patriotic Polish poems under the heading 'Poland hath not Perished'.[33] Nor did the periodical limit its Slavic focus to Poland and the Balkans. The review section for May opened with a notice of a recent Russian study, in English translation, of the 'very strange and wonderful' personality of Dostoevsky, and of the peculiar 'psychopathology' of his fictions.[34] The work of the great novelist was again noticed in August 1916, this time in the form of a review of the Constance Garnett translation of *A Raw Youth*, understood as a masterly study of the disturbing extremes of human nature.[35]

At the end of months of exaltation and celebration of the rights and virtues of small nations, in September 1915 an anonymous correspondent struck a welcome note of realism. Referring to 'the chorus of laudation of the little nation, and . . . the acknowledgement of the world's "debt" to them' that had swollen to a grand climax in the pages of the *Outlook* over the previous months, he sceptically observes that 'before the war we heard very little of the small nations unless to suppress them and annex their territory'.[36] Referring to the hugely powerful and influential nineteenth-century cultivation of the myth of 'the "superior" Anglo-Saxon race', the writer bitterly notes that

> nothing is more remarkable than the change in the mentality of the English people since the German eagle has come and inserted his carefully concealed talons in the innocent flesh of the people of Belgium, and so disclosed the true Teuton character, as tradition has handed it down to us from the days of the Brad y Cyllyll Hirion.

Further interesting light on the subject of small nations is thrown by an outstanding article in April 1916 on 'Nationality and Patriotism' by a contributor tantalisingly identified only by the letter 'G'. An avowed Welsh nationalist, the writer nevertheless adopts a splendidly caustic view of the traditional 'heroes' of the Welsh past. The famous princes of the Middle Ages, the essay notes, were in honest truth no

better than warlords, who had no conception of a modern inclusive
national community. Whatever their claims to occasional idealism
and magnanimity, they were in essence merely defenders of their own
elite class interests and intent only on territory and power. As for
the vaunted Welsh bards, they were simply the eloquent toadies of
their masters. Similarly, all great contemporary nation states were at
bottom motivated by nothing more noble than a determination to suppress, oppress and dominate, and these were also the motives that had
always been conspicuously present in Empire-building. Similarly, 'in
the Western European State-Cult, Christianity has been japanned with
ancestor-worship.'[37] Therefore, whereas Émile Verhaeren had declared
that 'this war had cured him of his internationalism', for the writer it
had instead 'cured me of my nationalism'. Affection remained only
for the valuable distinctive peculiarities of 'smaller cultural groups',
generally referred to as 'nationalities', as distinct from 'the powerful governmental organisations [that] call themselves nations'. 'In a
way', the writer concludes, 'this war is the revenge of the submerged
"nationalities"', the previously despised small fry such as the Welsh.
This article thus first sounds a note that will recur throughout the
twentieth century in the writings of those (such as Gwynfor Evans)
who continued to believe that small peoples, if given their head, would
prove far more pacific, civilised and collaborative in outlook and in
practice than the old traditional nation states have been.

By this stage in 1916, the early unbridled enthusiasm for things
Belgian had begun to fade. An editorial note of February 1916 recalls
the early days of being 'stormed at' over the phone by secretaries of
Belgian committees. 'In those far-off days all Belgians were heroes
and refugees, they were all novel and picturesque and good, and for a
few weeks the brotherhood of two nations was no more dream but a
reality. But familiarity has brought classification and criticism.'[38] Not
all Belgians had turned out to be the paragons of industry and virtue
that had been supposed, and a small minority had even 'been trouble-
some'. Nevertheless, sympathy for the refugees remained, and the
Outlook drew attention to the affirmative chapter on south Wales in a
recently published book recording Belgium's gratitude to the UK, as
well as to the 'painting of Valerius de Saedeleer *Le Pays de Galles*, and
the reminiscences of Verhaeren, Dumont-Wilden, and Souguenet'.

The *Outlook*'s identification of Wales as one of the small nations
of Europe didn't, however, preclude sympathy with such of the 'great
powers' as were under threat. In 'A Note on Patriotism', Richard

Roberts quoted from a letter by a Welshman to a French friend that began:

> Please do not suppose that I do not understand your feeling; I think I know what it feels like to have the Germans on French territory. I belong to a little nation which has gone through all that you are suffering, and more. We have had our land invaded, and the enemy took it all except a few mountains. For centuries they oppressed us; it is only comparatively lately that they have desisted from the endeavour to suppress our language and have permitted it to be taught in schools.

Such outspoken comments are, of course, hastily offset by assurances that nowadays Wales and England are good friends united in a single, grand cause. But the article concludes with Roberts deploring the contemporary cult of 'Empire', as 'the inversion of the process by which peoples seem to gain their souls'.[39]

It was another small European nation, though, that was beginning increasingly to interest the *Outlook* in 1916, and that nation was Ireland. The 1916 St David's Day issue was devoted to celebrating 'patriotism' – and it interestingly included a predictably scathing review by Principal Ivor John of that most unpatriotic of recent Welsh texts, Caradoc Evans's notorious short-story collection *My People*. The issue featured a set of photographs, accompanied by appropriate quotations, of several of Europe's most prominent 'nation-builders' with the tag 'The Road to Internationalism through Nationalism'.[40] The first photograph was that of the old favourite of nineteenth-century Nonconformist Wales, Giuseppe Mazzini – conveniently overlooking Mazzini's hostility to small nations. After all, the unification of Italy had taken the form of the more or less forced unification of a clutch of previously independent 'statelets', and so it was natural for Mazzini to suppose, in line with the most 'advanced' European thinkers of his time, that the progress of human history itself dictated the assimilation of the small by the big. But following Mazzini, there are photographs of Thomas Davis – another of the darlings of nineteenth-century Welsh Nonconformity – and of the future Unionist Horace Plunkett, greatly admired because of his success in persuading Westminster to allow Ireland its own Department of Agriculture and Art – a long-standing unrealised dream of Welsh Liberals.

Reinforcing these two photographs was an essay on 'The New Ireland and A.E.,' by T. Huws Davies, and the first of two articles on Thomas Davis by the always splendid J. Arthur Price. The former includes a shrewd summary of the mainstream Irish nationalist movements of the nineteenth century, including the literary renaissance two of whose luminaries were Yeats and George Russell (A.E.), although few today would agree with his estimate that the latter was the greater writer and visionary of the two. This estimate is based on Huws Davies's admiration for A.E.'s 'communal conception of nationalism':

> The true aim of all national art and literature and politics should be the creation of some powerful, overmastering tradition that will impress itself upon the work of every worker and become a kind of mysterious signature upon it, enabling the whole world to discern the source of its inspiration.[41]

And Huws Davies couples this with Plunkett's project of the collectivisation of the rural economy of Ireland. By 1916, A.E. had become an employee of the Agriculture Ministry that Plunkett had been so instrumental in establishing.

As for Thomas Davis, Price, himself an old Cymru Fydd hand of the 1890s, continued to admire him as 'the first of the Pan-Celticists', and as one who, for all his love of Ireland, had never forgotten the Wales from which his family had originated. Recalling that Mazzini and Davis had been the twin idols of Tom Ellis, Price noted:

> in the great war which is raging today much is heard of the rights of the little nations, and there is probably no statesman in Europe, today, who does not in his heart realise that only by a recognition of the rights of nationalities can a durable peace be established.

Was it not Davis, Price asked, who had presciently noted of the 'Cymric nation' that 'Edward's castles are in ruins / [but] still his empire stands'? And had not Davis, when pleading the case of Irish home rule within the empire, explained to the Duke of Wellington, no less: 'were I an Englishman, I should ask [the same] for England . . . so I would for Wales, were I a Welshman, and for Scotland, were I a Scotchman.' Elsewhere he had argued for the union of Welsh and Irish to wrest more self-control from the imperial headquarters at

Westminster, and had insisted that 'A million of the Kymri – have as good a right to a local senate as the 700,000 of Greece, or the half-million of Cassel or Mecklenberg have to independence, or as each of the States of America has to a local congress.'[42]

Finally, as if to clinch its intense interest in the Irish connection, the *Outlook* published the text of T. Gwynn Jones's important recent *awdl*, 'Tir na n-Óg', based as it is on an old Irish legend tragic in its outlines. It features a young prince, Osian, whose passionate love for Nia Ben-Aur, daughter of the king of the magical eternal world of youth, Tir na n-Óg, leads him to desert his earthly life in 'Erin' to dwell at her side, eternally young. As time passes, however, he is overcome by a yearning to revisit his native land, but the instant he does so he is afflicted with old age and struck down by a mortal sickness. The work of a pacifist ruminating on the state of the world at a point when carnage was reaching its peak on the Western Front, the *awdl* is resonant with implications, not least for a small people like the Welsh who cannot escape their grim contemporary fate of wholesale slaughter in the trenches.

A month after the Easter Rising in Dublin, the *Outlook* began tentatively to engage with the new situation in Ireland. As was repeatedly to happen over the coming years, blame for the eruption of violence was in part attributed not to the rebels but to Sir Edward Carson, with the Sinn Feiners having been prompted by 'the evil fashion set by Belfast' to forsake 'their ancient peaceful ways'.[43] The editorial notes looked back approvingly to the efforts that had been made in the columns of the *United Irishman* from the late 1890s onwards to encourage the Irish to ignore London and Westminster and engage in self-help activities, both political and social. Such attempts at self-reliance, the *Outlook* noted, chimed perfectly with the very name *Sinn Fein* ('ourselves alone'), and it obviously saw in these Irish initiatives a blueprint for the actions the Welsh likewise would need to take if they were ever to be serious about securing a degree of self-determination. Two books on Ireland – one a personal memoir of an attempt to establish a small farm in the unpromising landscape of Mayo, the other a compendium of Irish poetry of 'the last generation' – are featured in the review section for May 1916.[44]

Immediately preceding these two reviews, the *Outlook* prints a review essay on 'The Soul of Brittany' – a national region with which the

Welsh could sympathise but to which they could also condescend. And condescend they duly do, with the ardent Breton nationalists patronisingly advised to tone down their shrill criticisms of Paris, and to 'work out their own salvation patiently and prudently'.[45] The description of the Bretons as a 'fine, stern, tenacious race' whose simple religious beliefs are tainted with 'superstition' reeks of Nonconformist Welsh prejudice against continental Catholicism. Brittany is sagely advised to produce its own enlightened, progressive educationalists, such as Sir Hugh Owen, and to engage in the kind of 'silent, hopeful toil' that has brought such success to Wales: 'We are well ahead in the race: they are only starting, greatly handicapped.'

Like Brittany, the various constituent nationalities of Spain had hitherto received no attention from the *Outlook*, but it remedied this deficiency in October, 1916, when it published an interesting piece on 'Spanish Nationalist Problems' by Salvador de Madariaga. Then a young man, he was to go on to enjoy a highly distinguished career as diplomat, writer and internationalist, culminating in nominations both for the Nobel Prize for Literature and the Nobel Peace Prize.

Having clarified the strong regional and indeed multinational character of the Spanish state, Madariaga concentrated in his essay on the highly distinctive case of Catalonia, where the nationalist movement was undoubtedly most powerful. While recognising the superficial resemblance between this case and that of 'other nationalist cases known in Europe', such as those of 'Ireland or Italia Irredenta or Poland or the Austrian Slavs', Madariaga points out that in all those instances the peoples had been subjected to economic oppression by the dominant nation. The reverse was true of Catalonia, which had benefited substantially from Castilian Spanish support and investment. Having unfairly blamed centralist Spaniards for the decline of Spanish power and influence during the nineteenth century, Madariaga argues, Catalan nationalist leaders began to campaign for a measure of self-government and active support for the Catalan language. Latterly, this seemingly moderate programme of demands had escalated, in Madariaga's concerned opinion, to a form of 'nationalism on the Irish Home Rule lines', arguing for regional sovereignty similar to that allowed under the federal structure of the German confederate state.[46]

As if anxious not to be forgotten, Belgium reappeared in the September issue in the form of an essay on 'The Belgium of Tomorrow' by Richard Dupierreux, writing from the address of the

Légation de Belgique, Rome. Anticipating the need for the country to reconstruct itself as part of the rebuilding of Europe at war's end, the author emphasised the importance of no resumption of the dangerous pre-war conflict between Flemings and Walloons. A stronger, unified, confident affirmation of Belgian patriotism would need to replace the sullen indifference and passivity that had afflicted the nation in the pre-war years, and an end would have to be put to the 'neutering' of Belgium that had been bred of its studied pre-war neutrality. The country would have to resume, after decades of abeyance, its important role as a 'barrier state' that had been assumed in 1830.[47]

Related to this aim was the need to resolve issues such as the exact status and orientation of Luxembourg, the question of Limbourg and control of the mouth of the Escaut river upon which access to Antwerp depended, which would involve reaching an agreement with Holland. Finally, to safeguard any encroachments by Prussia in future, Belgium should be allowed to recover 'the ten cantons between Liège and Cologne, which were taken from her in 1815'. Much more contentious, the article conceded, was the determination of the future state of 'Rhenish Prussia, that is, of that portion of Germany which lies between the Rhine and the Belgian frontier'. In total, the article served as an important reality check for enthusiasts of a new Europe of the post-war period who wished to see the rights of small nations fully and triumphantly affirmed both in principle and in practice. It clearly showed what a minefield such an exercise would inevitably turn out to be.

The difference between theory and practice in this matter is neatly illustrated in the difference between the Belgian essay and an essay in October 1916 on 'State, Nationalism and Conscience' by J. Arthur Price, which opens with the assertion that the Welsh continue to be enthusiastic for war, understood in the terms Lloyd George had trumpeted in his historic Queen's Hall address, 'as a fight for liberty and nationalism'. But this reading of the conflict is, in Price's opinion, in process of being supplanted by a vision advanced by 'Prussianising Englishmen', of the post-war might of a centralised English state. Signs of implementation of such a vision are, for Price, visible in contemporary response to the Irish national rising, a response at odds with the professed war aim of liberating small nationalities such as Belgians, Serbs, Poles and Czechs, and the respecting of the rights of such regions as Alsace and Lorraine. Dismayingly for Price, this state worship has found a powerful Welsh advocate in the distinguished figure of Sir Henry Jones, whose Hegelianism has led him to the conclusion that 'the nationalities and individuals in the British Empire are mere chattels of the State, and as against the State, have no rights at all'.[48]

Anticipating his disciple Saunders Lewis, Price blames the emergence of the powerful modern nation state on the Reformation, and most specifically on Germany, which exported the idea to other countries, including eventually Napoleonic France, as well as facilitating Prussianising tendencies within Germany itself, beginning with the iron centralised rule of Frederick the Great. Though a reluctant late convert to the cause of 'the omnipotent State', England had increasingly succumbed to it during the nineteenth century. Welsh Nonconformity had within it the seeds of resistance, in the name of individual conscience, to such state tyranny, and so had Welsh Nationalism. In his Queen's Hall speech, Lloyd George had even partly justified the war in the name of the latter, and therefore 'unless the War is waged on false pretences by the Allies, Wales has the same right to a recognition of its nationhood as Bohemia or Poland', a recognition that, in Price's opinion, would require the granting to Wales of its own national parliament.

The early months of 1917 saw a marked decline in the attention the *Outlook* paid to the state of European nations, large and small. There were no substantial articles on the subject for several months, only a scatter of reviews – of the Belgian poems of Émile Cammaerts,[49] a translation of Dmitry Grigorovich's novel *The Fishermen*,[50] a study of Scriabin,[51] and two books on Poland, one on the country's art, the other on its partitioned condition.[52] A brief, troubled note in April did, however, record the revolution in Russia, and a conventional lyric poem by Eifion Wyn protesting against the violent invasion of Belgium was included in the same number,[53] while the following month saw the appearance of a brief article by 'Balkanensis'. This emphasised the historical calamity of western connivance in the 'Russian settlement of the Balkans' and the crushing of the aspirations of Bulgaria and Serbia. 'We pay the cost' of such desertion of the little nations 'in blood', the writer asserts.[54]

The number for May 1917 included an essay by 'GLD' reviewing a book that advocated the formation of a League of Nations. This piece turned out to herald a departure in the *Outlook*'s treatment of nationalities. For the next few years, the whole issue of nationhood

and national rights in the post-war period became increasingly sub-
sumed under an argument in favour of the creation of a League of
Nations that would be the safeguard and guarantor of all nations, of
whatever size. This important shift in direction owed a great deal, no
doubt, to the passionate commitment of the *Outlook*'s owner, David
Davies (later to become Lord Davies of Llandinam), to the cause
of international peace – throughout the inter-war years he was to
remain one of the most active and ardent supporters of the League.
Moreover, for months after the *Outlook* launched its campaign, it was
to cling, with slowly decreasing conviction, to the hope that Lloyd
George, now that he was Prime Minister of Great Britain, would
ensure that the case for Welsh home rule would be acknowledged
and advantaged in whatever settlement eventually concluded the war.

As such hope slowly faded, however, the *Outlook* attempted to
organise a Welsh campaign to persuade a post-war Parliament to
grant the country self-determination in keeping with that commitment to respect the rights of Europe's small nations that had been
repeatedly proclaimed during the War. Yet, even as it was running
its campaign, the periodical was forced also to recognise that the war
had seen a shift of political power in Wales away from the Liberal
party (several of whose prominent figures readily supported the campaign) and towards a Labour movement that threatened to dominate
the post-war political scene in the industrial Valleys. And while the
Independent Labour Party might remain unenthusiastically willing
to support a measure of home rule, such a development was of no
interest to a Labour Party increasingly dominated by trade union
representatives and concerned only with the rights of the working
class.

The review article that appeared in May 1917 fervently supported
the proposal that a League of Nations be created in the belief that it
could avoid any reversion to the 'armed peace which preceded and
led up to the war'. It noted that, even before the US had entered
the war, President Wilson had made clear he would not support any
settlement 'which was based on the coercion of any State'.[55] What
the essay clearly brought out, however, was the difference of opinion
there was likely to be between those who favoured, say, the granting of independence to all the small Slavic nations, and those who
were disinclined to go to such 'extremes'. As if in line with this latter
approach, the *Outlook* at this point chose to re-emphasise the case
of some of Europe's larger nations, such as Poland, for post-war

recognition. Thus an article on 'Some Polish Questions' by H. J. Fleure appeared in its pages in September 1917.[56]

By July 1917 the *Outlook* was already supporting the proposal to create a League of Nations through its editorial notes of the month, on this occasion praising President Wilson for the lead he had already taken in the matter and adding its own gloss on the subject.[57] It did not yet, however, link its campaign to the cause of Welsh home rule. Instead, in an article in the same number, J. Arthur Price was left to hope that a national parliament might come as part of a post-war reconstruction of the empire along federalist lines (247–9).

In October 1917 the *Outlook* devoted many pages to the situation of Serbia, beginning by printing the address delivered by Lloyd George in London before the Serbian Society in which he once more hymned the glories of small nations: 'I am a believer in small nations', the Prime Minister asserted. 'I have the honour to belong to one myself.' 'I believe in the nation which can sing about its defeats', he declared, adding that both the Serbs and the Welsh shared that indomitable spirit.[58] This notion that 'both [nations] are countries which fought for generations against the invader' was again touted in the following article on the war in the Balkans by Shenkyn ap Morgan, while in a portrait of Nikola Pashitch, prime minister of Serbia, 'Miles' emphasised 'the debt which civilization owes to the small nations of the world', such as Serbia, Scotland, Ireland and Wales.[59] On the same theme, A. F. Whyte, reflecting on the structure of a post-war Europe, warned against the reinstatement of the dominant power of the continent's great nations, noting that the rights of small peoples would need to be clearly recognised by a League of Nations, whatever its final form.[60]

The editorial notes for November 1917 frankly acknowledged that 'the nationalism of Welsh Members of Parliament has well-nigh evaporated in the House of Commons' and that 'Mr Lloyd George has outgrown the nation that gave him birth'.[61] It was the *Outlook*'s first tentative step towards advocating the formation of a new political party dedicated to advancing a Welsh nationalist agenda, in keeping, it vainly hoped, with the kind of post-war European settlement recognising the rights of small nations that would draw the war to a conclusion.

As the *Outlook* began to intensify its campaign in favour of a League of Nations early in 1918, a very brief history of the origin and eventual outcome of such a proposal may be of some use. In the light of the experiences of World War One, the ramshackle nineteenth-century international order dependent on the system of intermittent Conferences, Congresses and national alliances that treated national sovereignties as sacrosanct came to seem a totally unsatisfactory means of ensuring a settled, permanent peace. Similarly bankrupt was the 'balance of power' approach to international affairs. From 1914 onwards, therefore, influential figures in Britain began to search for an alternative, while a parallel initiative was started in the USA, where, in May 1916, President Woodrow Wilson became 'the first world statesman to give the idea of a League of Nations after the war his official approval.'[62] By January 1917, the Entente powers had committed themselves to supporting Wilson's idea in principle. But the various national committees that were convened to consider possible models were quickly divided between minimalism (Britain favoured informal agreements) and the maximal option (France strongly recommending the establishing of an international force to enforce compliance). Wilson was dissatisfied with both options, and laid out his own blueprint in the Fourteen Points address delivered before Congress on 8 January 1918. Thereafter several further blueprints were circulated before the victorious powers agreed in February 1919 that a commitment to establish a League would be an integral part of the peace treaty. By April 1919, a Covenant of the League of Nations, essentially voluntarist in character, had been unanimously approved.

The *Outlook* for January 1918 devoted a substantial leader article by David Davies to the subject of a League of Nations, a fundamental tenet of which, he argued, should be 'the free self-determination of nationalities, carried out under international guarantees', and reinforced by a league with the military muscle to implement them. Wales, Davies concluded, should become an active participant in the construction of such an organisation that would have particular care for 'the cause of small and struggling nationalities'. It would be the country's 'first step towards any claim by Welshmen to their full share in not only British but European citizenship'.[63]

Much the same argument was continued in another essay by Davies in the following month. His recognition that it might take the emergence of a specifically Welsh political party to effect this was reinforced by the *Outlook* in its editorial notes for February 1918.[64] It was a theme it was repeatedly to return to with ever-increasing vigour and insistence over the following months, as it expressed its deep dissatisfaction with the moribund state of affairs within the old guard of Welsh Liberal MPs, and in an article for the March number, on the need to restructure the post-war Parliament in the wake of radical wartime developments, David Davies specifically pressed once more the claims of small nations such as Wales for a place in the new order. That issue also devoted five full pages to the (typically lukewarm) comments of leading politicians and intellectuals on proposed changes to the status quo. Undaunted and forthright as ever, J. Arthur Price still trenchantly insisted in April that

> either Welsh Nationalism must follow the light with the other little nationalities of Europe and secure political self-expression within the Empire or it must accept the view . . . that there is no such thing as Welsh Nationality, only an amiable county sentiment.[65]

The *Outlook*'s interest in Serbia resurfaced in both the May and June numbers. In the former, M. Curcin, warming to the theme of affinities between Slav and Celt, drew attention to a poem by Jovan Jovanović Zmaj about the legend of the massacre of the Welsh bards, having 'borrowed the subject' from the Magyar poet J. Arany's much better-known poem.[66] A month later, and disappointed that his earlier appeal had fallen on deaf Welsh ears, Curcin addressed a poem to Lloyd George that finished by asserting that

> Like Wales we want to be at peace at last
> We fought to our last man to prove the right.
> Oh don't restore us to the bitter past!
> Help us to save our land – bid us unite![67]

James Emsley Wood wrote in similarly impassioned tones of 'The Russian Tragedy and the Young Serbia',[68] which served as prelude to the *Outlook*'s appeal in July to Wales to respond to the need to supply young Serbian refugees with educational opportunities.[69] Then in August the periodical published translations from the Serbian by L. F. Waring.[70]

Tiring of all the talk about the rights of small European nations that excluded the case of Wales itself, J. Arthur Price, in a powerful attack on a recent speech by Lloyd George, pointed out that 'no promise is made to Wales that she shall receive after the War the limited amount of autonomy that the Czech-Slovaks in Bohemia enjoyed in theory before the War commenced'. And this, Price asserted, although 'I would venture to affirm that, historically, Wales can make out as good a claim to nationhood as can any country in Europe'.[71] As if to confirm Price's claims, neither Sir Henry Jones – the most august and influential Welsh academic of the day – nor David Davies made any reference to Wales when arguing, in a special supplement to the September issue, the case for a 'League for Peace'.

The endowment by David Davies and his sisters of the world's first chair in international politics at the University College of Wales, Aberystwyth, prompted the *Outlook* to emphasise at the beginning of 1919 the relevance to Wales of the fact that 'the League of Nations, when it is established, will not be merely a League of Big Nations'.[72] It further warmed to this theme when, in February 1919, it responded to the opening of the Peace Conference at Versailles:

> As a small nation whose whole history for centuries has been one of endeavour to save and establish a national inheritance, Wales is above all interested . . . in securing for all struggling nations – Irish, Poles, Czechs, Jugo-Slavs, Czecho-Slovaks, yes even Masurians and Silesians – full justice and free development under conditions which will reduce to a minimum the temptation to the freed to forget his chains and to essay the enslavement of others.

Following this, it pointed to the contradiction between British commitment to respecting the rights of small nations to self-determination and its current conduct in Ireland.[73]

The peace negotiations in Paris were viewed by E. T. John, in a strong article on 'Wales and its Programme' in March, 1919, as providing an ideal opportunity for pressing the rights of Wales to self-government. Taking the case of Ireland as being in most urgent need of resolution, John argued for the creation of a Federation of Celtic nations, partly under the wider international auspices of a federalised British empire.[74] The demands of the Celtic peoples were, he emphasised, 'no more . . . legitimately [to be] resisted than those of Poland or of Bohemia . . . the interest and convenience of England', he pointedly added, 'being no more sacrosanct than those of Germany or of Austria'. (As a supplement to this issue, the *Outlook* printed the full text of the bill intended to enable Wales to establish its own government, sponsored by John among other prominent Welsh Liberals.) Fittingly enough, in a neighbouring article T. Huws Davies examined the career of Henry Richard, the 'Apostle of Peace' and 'Good European' whose tireless work on behalf of an international system of diplomacy had paved the way for the formation of the League of Nations.[75]

With the final details of a peace settlement still to be agreed in Paris, the *Outlook* continued to advertise the cause of the little peoples of Europe, with articles in April both on Grundtvig's role in consolidating a Danish sense of nationality in the nineteenth century and on the revival of Czecho-Slovak nationality during the same period.[76] 'A Plea for Hungary' was published in the same number, including an obligatory invocation of Kossuth and the claim that Wales had in common with Hungary an intense attachment to and talent for music.[77] The situation in Ireland was examined in May, with the *Outlook* urging a 'return to the policy of Tom Ellis and . . . the immediate grant of autonomy to Scotland, Wales and Ireland',[78] but an ominous shot across the bows came in June from William Harris, secretary of the South Wales Labour Federation, in an essay that emphasised a commitment to the formation of an international proletariat and included a scornful dismissal of the *Outlook*'s tendency to 'speak of Wales as if no change had taken place during the last 25 years'.[79] It was similarly misguided, Harrison added, 'to speak of Wales as being analogous to Ireland'. Undaunted, the *Outlook* for that month still featured an essay on 'The Swiss Democracy'.[80]

Meanwhile the periodical continued faithfully, of course, to track the different stages in the formation of a League of Nations, publishing an editorial article in June forcefully supporting the actions of President Wilson[81] and another in August along much the same lines.[82] That the situation of Wales was never far from the *Outlook*'s mind whenever the Versailles conference was mentioned was again confirmed in July, when the hostility of William George to the movement for Welsh home rule was sarcastically contrasted with his brother's 'conceding absolute independence to Bohemia and Poland. On the principles of the Paris Conference Wales can safely claim autonomy.'[83] Then in August an editorial article on 'the fame of the Prime Minister' concluded by noting: 'he has given freedom to Bohemia, he has given freedom to Poland . . . but his own country remains one of the few historical nations of Europe, that is still refused national self-government.'[84]

In July the *Outlook* printed an address by Alfred Zimmern, by then first holder of the world's inaugural chair of International Politics at Aberystwyth, on 'The International Settlement and Small Nationalities'. With his customary acumen, Zimmern recognised what a driving force in current affairs nationalism had become right across Europe, but emphasised that the ideal of a stand-alone nation had proved to be wholly illusory, as what characterised the age was a 'sense of the unity of the modern world and of the essentially international character of modern civilization'. International organisation, such as was most ambitiously represented by the experiment of a League of Nations, was therefore of paramount importance, and the British Commonwealth and the United States furnished older models of the same tendency. However, he ended by stressing, this in no way diminished Wales's urgent need for 'nationally-minded men and women'.[85] Reference to Zimmern's piece was made in August by Stephen Gwynn, who offered 'An Irish View of Welsh Nationalism' and urged the Welsh to join the Irish and the Scots in demanding self-government, but only within a British federation of peoples.[86]

By the end of 1919, the kind of relatively conservative settlement being agreed in Paris was evident for all to see, prompting J. Arthur Price, in his shrewd, jaundiced analysis of developments from the point of view of a Welsh nationalist in November, to conclude pithily that the cynicism of Clemenceau and the pragmatism of Lloyd George had won out over the idealism of President Wilson, so that the will of the large, powerful established nation states was sure to prevail, and that the international organisation emerging from the consultations would more closely resemble a 'League of Empires' than a League of Nationalities.[87] In recognition of this emerging political reality, from the beginning of 1920 onwards the *Outlook*'s reporting of the progress of the League of Nations made no more reference to Wales and the cause of small nationalities and even when in March J. Arthur Price reviewed 'some national rebirths of today' it was only frankly to admit that there were only 'three nations whose re-birth has been one of the miracles of the war – Finland, Poland, and Czecho-Slovakia'.[88]

That retreat was a prudent one. The naivety of the Welsh supposition that its proper place was alongside that of the other small, previously submerged nations, several of which had been granted their independence at Versailles, was cruelly exposed over the coming decades. What had been consistently overlooked in Wales throughout

the First World War was that the 'small nations' that elicited such
sympathy in the nation were not socially and politically homogeneous
entities at all. They, too, consisted of any number of subnational ethnic minorities; and the truth of the matter was that if the Welsh case
mirrored any aspect of the post-war European scene it was insofar
as the people of Wales, too, were no more than one of several minor
ethnicities within the British state. As the highly varied, and increasingly conflicted, plight of the new Europe's submerged ethnicities
became apparent, for reasons glaringly apparent in the comparative
situations of the Jews in Germany, the Germans in the Sudetenland,
the Basques and Catalans in Spain, the Bretons in France, and so on
and so on, a 'European Nationality Congress' was established in 1925.
Consisting of representatives of many different substate ethnicities, it
was plagued from the outset by deep differences of political condition
and radical divisions of outlook.[89]

Welsh identification with the 'small peoples' of Europe, then, was
a naive and doomed affair from the very start. And then, as if administering the *coup de grâce* to the *Outlook*'s presentation of Wales in
such terms over the last couple of years, Alfred Zimmern, in a penetrating lecture delivered at Llandrindod Wells in August, scoffed at
the supposition that 'Wales is a small nation'. This was, he argued, a
defensive posture assumed by a servile Wales whose life was poisoned
by 'a sense of inferiority, of . . . dependence, of . . . inner bondage or
slavery'. The national characteristics assumed by the Welsh, he dev-
astatingly added, were 'the mark, not of a great free people, but of a
small and subject people'. And yet Wales had given much to the world
and had as much still to give. His message to the Welsh therefore was
for them to '*straighten your back*. Stand erect and four-square to the
world. Stand up, for instance, to England.'[90]

It is instructive to compare the treatment of Europe in the *Welsh
Outlook* during the war with that in the other influential Welsh
heavyweight periodical of the day, O. M. Edwards's *Cymru*. Ever the
conscientious pedagogue, Edwards took the opportunity to introduce
his compatriots to a potted history of each of 'Gwledydd y Rhyfel'
(the Nations of the War) in turn. His accounts of Poland, 'Prussia'
and Russia from their foundation to the present were routine enough
for their day. It was only when he came to Bosnia that Edwards began
to display his own particular Welsh bias. Recognising that Bosnia,
like both Wales and the other Slavic countries in Yugoslavia, was
a small country, Edwards homed approvingly in on the supposedly

'puritan' character of the Christian faith in Bosnia from the very earliest centuries of its existence. It was this strain in their worship, he argued, that made the Bosnians so admirably reluctant to toe the 'Popish' line and to begin a 'Protestant' movement in the late Middle Ages. And it was the same instincts that caused some Bosnians later to convert to Islam, because they found in that religion a purity of belief and practice consonant with their own preference. But then, once the Turks had turned to bloody suppression of Bosnian uprisings, Edwards suggested, the only accounts adequate to the intensity of the suffering that resulted were those images of hell in Ellis Wynne's early eighteenth-century Welsh classic, *Gweledigaetheu y Bardd Cwsc*.

Edwards's reading of Bosnian history from the point of view of a confirmed nineteenth-century Welsh Nonconformist anticipates his subsequent reading of Italy along exactly the same lines. Having already elsewhere attributed the beginnings of an enlightened modern liberal democratic politics to the fiercely independent, self-governing, anti-'papist' and proto-Protestant mercantile Flemish towns of the later Middle Ages, Edwards proceeded to lay similar emphasis on the role of the famous mercantile towns and tiny principalities of medieval Italy in resisting the tyrannical power of a Church of Rome that was clearly the successor to the Roman empire – which had notoriously been an enemy of smaller nationalities across the Europe of the day. He then interpreted the process of Italy's nineteenth-century unification along exactly the same, prejudiced anti-Catholic lines, as involving the struggle of the people, led by the likes of Mazzini – to whose links with Gwilym Hiraethog and importance for Tom Ellis he duly alluded – against the papacy.

To compare the treatment of the issue of Welsh nationhood during the First World War in *Cymru* with that in the *Welsh Outlook* is an instructive experience.

O. M. Edwards is clearly still viewing Europe from the perspective of a Welsh Nonconformist culture that had already begun to lose its grip on the mind of the new, largely industrialised Wales even before the outbreak of the War. The categories he therefore deploys in his discussion are still the old staples of nineteenth-century denominationalism. In the many pages devoted by *The Welsh Outlook* to the subject on the other hand one finds a new awareness of the direct relevance to Wales of the cases of similarly small 'subordinated' nationalities right across the continent, along with a real, sustained effort to determine how, and how far, Wales might benefit from following their examples. This new kind of Welsh Europeanism was to find very little purchase in the Wales of the inter-war years, when the terrible crises afflicting the heavy industries sustaining the core modern society of the country naturally inclined most intellectuals to deploy a class language in an attempt to analyse and address a crisis situation. But as Wales began to enter its post-industrial economy, so the kind of Euro-Welshness pioneered by the *Outlook* began to interest Welsh intellectuals anew. While, even during the intervening period, when industrial south Wales had understandably become preoccupied with class politics and with advancing a British socialist agenda, leading writers and intellectuals of the Welsh-language community had found in the Welsh European outlook first trialled in the *Outlook* inspiring opportunities for an electrifying cultural renaissance. Such developments will be the subject of the next few chapters.

Notes

[1] Bentley Brinkerhoff Gilbert, *David Lloyd George: A Political Life* (London: Batsford, 1992), 117. Hereafter *DLG*.
[2] *Welsh Outlook* (September 1914), 375. For *The Welsh Outlook* see Gwyn Jenkins, 'The Welsh Outlook', *National Library of Wales Journal* 24:1 (1986), 463–86; E. L. Ellis, *T. J: A Life of Thomas Jones CH* (Cardiff: University of Wales Press, 1992).
[3] *Welsh Outlook* (September 1914), 414.
[4] *Welsh Outlook* (September 1914), 419.
[5] *Welsh Outlook* (October 1914), 423.
[6] *Welsh Outlook* (November 1914), 465.
[7] *Welsh Outlook* (October 1914), 428.
[8] *Welsh Outlook* (November 1914), 468.
[9] *Welsh Outlook* (October 1914), 439.
[10] *Welsh Outlook* (October 1914), 448.
[11] *Welsh Outlook* (June 1915), 217.
[12] *Welsh Outlook* (June 1915), 223–4.
[13] *Welsh Outlook* (October 1915), 342.
[14] *Welsh Outlook* (October 1916), 328.
[15] *Welsh Outlook* (October 1916), 333.
[16] *Welsh Outlook* (December 1916), 397.
[17] *Welsh Outlook* (November 1914), 485.
[18] *Welsh Outlook* (December 1914), 526.
[19] *Welsh Outlook* (December 1914), 531.
[20] *Welsh Outlook* (March 1915), 83.
[21] *Welsh Outlook* (May 1915), 195–7.
[22] *Welsh Outlook* (July 1915), 265.
[23] *Welsh Outlook* (July 1915), 283–4.

24 *Welsh Outlook* (January 1917), 7.
25 *Welsh Outlook* (September 1915), 354.
26 *Welsh Outlook* (August 1915), 297.
27 *Welsh Outlook* (August 1915), after 304.
28 *Welsh Outlook* (September, 1915), 340–2.
29 *Welsh Outlook* (October 1915), 379–82.
30 *Welsh Outlook* (July 1916), 229.
31 *Welsh Outlook* (March 1916), 99–100.
32 *Welsh Outlook* (March 1915), 101.
33 *Welsh Outlook* (May 1916), 148.
34 *Welsh Outlook* (May 1916), 102.
35 *Welsh Outlook* (August 1916), 270.
36 *Welsh Outlook* (September 1915), 368.
37 *Welsh Outlook* (April 1916), 113–14.
38 *Welsh Outlook* (February 1916), 44–5.
39 *Welsh Outlook* (February 1916), 82.
40 *Welsh Outlook* (March 1916), 89.
41 *Welsh Outlook* (March 1916), 86-7.
42 *Welsh Outlook* (March 1916), 89–91.
43 *Welsh Outlook* (April 1916), 142.
44 *Welsh Outlook* (May 1916), 169–70.
45 *Welsh Outlook* (May 1916), 166.
46 *Welsh Outlook* (October 1916), 289–91.
47 *Welsh Outlook* (October 1916), 292–4.
48 *Welsh Outlook* (October 1916), 311.
49 *Welsh Outlook* (January 1917), 37–8.
50 *Welsh Outlook* (February 1917), 74–5.
51 *Welsh Outlook* (February 1917), 77–8.
52 *Welsh Outlook* (April 1917), 137.
53 *Welsh Outlook* (April 1917), 122, 144.
54 *Welsh Outlook* (May 1917), 190–1,
55 *Welsh Outlook* (May 1917), 191.
56 *Welsh Outlook* (September 1917), 303–5.
57 *Welsh Outlook* (July 1917), 232–4.
58 *Welsh Outlook* (October 1917), 337–8.
59 *Welsh Outlook* (October 1917), 342.
60 *Welsh Outlook* (October 1917), 346–7.
61 *Welsh Outlook* (November 1917), 375.
62 F. S. Northedge, *The League of Nation: Its Life and Times, 1920–1946* (Leicester: Leicester University Press, 1986), 27.
63 *Welsh Outlook* (January 1918), 10–12.
64 *Welsh Outlook* (February 1918), 36.
65 *Welsh Outlook* (April 1918), 119.
66 *Welsh Outlook* (May 1918), 167.
67 *Welsh Outlook* (June 1918), 226.
68 *Welsh Outlook* (June 1918), 182–3.
69 *Welsh Outlook* (July 1918), 212.
70 *Welsh Outlook* (August 1918), 261.

71 *Welsh Outlook* (August 1918), 275.
72 *Welsh Outlook* (January 1919), 4.
73 *Welsh Outlook* (February 1919), 27–8.
74 *Welsh Outlook* (March 1919), 57.
75 *Welsh Outlook* (March 1919), 61–3.
76 *Welsh Outlook* (April 1919), 94–7, 101–2.
77 *Welsh Outlook* (April 1919), 127.
78 *Welsh Outlook* (May 1919), 119.
79 *Welsh Outlook* (May 1919), 145.
80 *Welsh Outlook* (May 1919), 152–4.
81 *Welsh Outlook* (June 1919), 144–5.
82 *Welsh Outlook* (August 1919), 189–90.
83 *Welsh Outlook* (July 1919), 168.
84 *Welsh Outlook* (August 1919), 193.
85 *Welsh Outlook* (July 1919), 173–4.
86 *Welsh Outlook* (August 1919), 195–7.
87 *Welsh Outlook* (November 1919), 271.
88 *Welsh Outlook* (March 1920), 71.
89 U. v. Hirschhausen, 'From Minority Protection to Border Revisionism: The European National Congress (1925–38)', in Martin Conway and Kiran Klaus Patel (eds), *Europeanization in the Twentieth Century* (London: Palgrave Macmillan, 2010), 87–109.
90 *Welsh Outlook* (August 1920), 213–14.

4

THE EUROPE OF THE CULTURAL
RIGHT IN WALES

The ideal of a single European community, united in membership of a single Christian Church, has long haunted the minds of intellectuals across the continent, most particularly, of course, those of a Catholic persuasion. It was given eloquent expression for example by Novalis at the end of the eighteenth century:

> Those were the bright, glorious times, when Europe formed but one Christian land; when one Christianity dwelt throughout the civilized part of the world, and one great mutual interest bound together the most remote provinces of this wide spiritual empire.[1]

At much the same time, the Anglican Edmund Burke was memorably declaring that 'no citizen of Europe could be altogether an exile in any part of it' (*EL*, 65). The whole culture of Europe, he powerfully insisted, was deeply rooted in Christian values.

Such beliefs and aspirations naturally took on an urgent new life during the increasingly ominous inter-war period. One carnivorous war between powerful nations had newly ended only for another to loom darkly on the near horizon. It was a period that spawned many ameliorative models of pan-European structures and institutions, most prominently instanced by the League of Nations. These were expressly intended to tame the unbridled, destructive actions of rampant national and nationalist states. Many of these models were pragmatic and secular in character, but a few were explicitly constructed on a broadly Christian or even an expressly Catholic basis.

The latter in particular appealed to a highly talented group of Catholic writers and intellectuals, including G. K. Chesterton, Hilaire Belloc and Christopher Dawson. One common factor in their otherwise diverse forms of pan-Europeanism was the intense interest they showed in the pre-Reformation Europe of the later Middle Ages, a period to which they turned in fascinated imagination because, at least in their highly selective reading of it, it seemed to epitomise a deeply spiritual form of advanced civilisation. Examples of a challengingly radical conservatism of social, and indeed political, outlook, all these British models were also, in a way, products both of the Catholic revival that had steadily gained ground in Victorian England and of the Romantic medievalism of the same period.[2]

The intellectual roots of the English Catholic revival, a sort of belated insular Counter-Reformation, can be traced back to the Tractarian Movement within the Church of England of the 1830s, whose guiding spirit, John Henry Newman, became the highest-profile conversion to Catholicism a decade or so later (and who was duly canonised in 2019). But the real impetus for the revival came not from the direction of the intellectuals but from the vast numbers of Irish labourers who flooded into all parts of Britain in the wake of the catastrophic famine. By the end of the nineteenth century, the organisation of a Catholic Church that was no longer proscribed by the Protestant state had become thoroughly regularised and firmly established. Then, from the beginning of the twentieth century, several prominent writers and intellectuals, many of whom were converts, became well known for their Catholic faith. In addition to the likes of Chesterton, Belloc and Dawson these included David Jones, Graham Greene, Edward Elgar and Evelyn Waugh. Additionally there were several eminent fellow travellers, such as the High Anglican T. S. Eliot.[3]

Such momentous developments in England had very little impact on a Wales that, by the end of the nineteenth century, seemed wedded to the Nonconformist beliefs and practices of its innumerable chapels. Catholicism still seemed to be the preserve of Irish immigrants in their various enclaves across the south Wales coalfield.[4] Imagine, therefore, the consternation when in 1932 Saunders Lewis, one of the brightest of young intellectual luminaries, startlingly announced his conversion to Roman Catholicism. The announcement astonished and scandalised Nonconformist Wales in equal measure, and embarrassed even his closest colleagues in Plaid Cymru, the new political party dedicated to the service of Wales that Lewis himself had co-founded in 1925 with a handful of others, all of whom were staunch Nonconformists. By 1926 Lewis was President of Plaid Cymru and acknowledged as its pre-eminent strategic thinker. Moreover, he came from the most distinguished Nonconformist stock, two of his forebears having been prominent Calvinistic Methodist ministers.[5]

Lewis remains one of the most singular, compelling, controversial and complex figures to have dominated the cultural and political scene in twentieth-century Wales. A creative writer sufficiently talented to be eventually nominated for a Nobel Prize in Literature, he was an innovative analyst of Welsh cultural history and an incisive polit-ical polemicist. Above all, he was the boldest of political activists on behalf of his convictions, who spent a period in prison follow-ing the burning in 1936 of the training centre for aerial bombers the government, overriding unanimous Welsh public opinion, had established on a site of Welsh cultural importance on the Llŷn pen-insula.[6] His European vision was as strikingly bold and original as it was politically unrealisable, its proper constituency being really that of culture and most specifically literature. What has been said about Eliot applies directly to him:

> His interest in such matters, and in the wider question of what constituted a 'good' or 'just' society, was not primarily that of a political, economic, or social theorist at all. Rather it was that of a poet and critic, trying to conjure up a picture of all the social relations most conducive to the flour-ishing of a cohesive and creative culture among human beings. (*ETC*, 54)

There were no doubt several secondary, ancillary reasons for Lewis's conversion to Catholicism, including his huge admiration for the boldness of the Catholic Irish in challenging the seemingly indestructible might of the British empire in the rising of Easter 1916, his similar admiration for such luminaries of the modern Irish liter-ary renaissance as Yeats, Synge and O'Casey, and his marriage to an Irish Liverpudlian who was herself a Catholic convert. But there can be no doubt that his primary motive was deeply and authentically spiritual in character. Lewis came to believe with all his soul in the majestic tradition and spiritual authority of the Catholic Church, and to find great sustenance and solace in the sacraments and the rituals attendant upon it. For him, his new faith had also one other minor, yet significant, dimension: it had always recognised, valued and deliberately satisfied the aesthetic side of human nature. Lewis was a man naturally endowed with an acute sensibility as well as a powerful, trenchant and original intellect.

The case of Saunders Lewis has always been dogged by one great, persistent irony. He has come to be known – and variously praised and condemned – for his supposedly 'extremist' dedication to Welsh nationalism.[7] The irony is that Lewis was never a nationalist, nor was Plaid Cymru ever the 'nationalist' party of Wales. In fact, he was the very antithesis of a nationalist; he was an avowed anti-nationalist, a dedicated enemy of the arrogant nationalism of the mighty states which had so devastated Europe in the Great War (in which he had served as an officer) and an implacable opponent of the resurgent nationalisms of Germany, France, Britain and Russia that threatened further catastrophic conflict during the inter-war period. Lewis was a strong believer in a confederation of nationalities, small as well as large. It would be both a folly and a sin, he repeatedly announced, for Wales to think of going it alone. While he fervently wished for self-government, that self-government was to be tempered by due subjection to some appropriate transnational, or international, order. There were two such orders existent to which he was attracted: one was the British Empire, at that time beginning its evolution into a Commonwealth of free nations that were voluntarily entering into loose association, and the League of Nations. And if ever it came to a choice between those two international collectives, Lewis made it clear he would not hesitate:

> If a choice must be made, as Chamberlain insists, between the Empire and the League of Nations, there can be no doubt as to which way Wales will tend. To her, always, and to the greatest of her sons [*sic*] in thought and learning, contact with Europe has meant a renaissance and an inspiration. To her, the Empire was never anything but a name and an empty noise. (*PSL*, 33)

Wishful thinking, unfortunately, as the recent past of Wales at that juncture amply confirmed and future history was shortly and cruelly to demonstrate. But if Lewis is placed in a wider context, then at this formative juncture in his career he could be viewed as a fringe member of the informal community of 'intellectual dissidents' who were between the wars 'both dreamers and activists in the Europeanisation of Europe'. Heinrich Mann, one of the most famous of such intellectuals, insisted in 1923, as Lewis was to do, that 'it is in the minds of thinkers that Europe is most alive, and they transmit this inheritance from generation to generation, even at times when most Europeans have almost forgotten the name of Europe.'[8]

This vision of Lewis's can be understood only if it is realised that it was anchored in the crucial, core view of individual being that, he believed, the Catholic Church had always taken, and that was everywhere embodied in its teaching and practices. This view was the very antithesis of the view taken by the various denominations of the Nonconformist Wales of which he was a distinguished, if dramatically dissident, product. Whereas the latter gave primacy to the sole, solitary individual, in the name of honouring the dignity, integrity, and attendant spiritual and social responsibilities of every human soul, the former had always stressed that an individual could find true fulfilment only by participating in a common life and in collective endeavours. It was furthermore the claim of the Church that its own majestic traditions were themselves in all their aspects – from the theological and liturgical to the practical, social and political – the tried and tested products of an ancient, majestic, ongoing collective endeavour. The wisdom of the Church was indeed the wisdom of the ages, the accumulated fruit of vast human experience guided and enlightened, of course, by divine providence. Hence the sacred authority of tradition – a key concept and value for Saunders Lewis, as it was for his fellow Catholic David Jones and the fellow-travelling Anglo-Catholic T. S. Eliot.

Saunders Lewis's magisterially holistic outlook, incorporating as it did social, economic, political and cultural philosophies, owed much, not least in its European leanings, to the key encyclicals of two popes, Leo XIII and Paul XI.[9] *Rerum Novarum* ('Of new things') by the former (1891) has been described as a foundational text of modern Catholic social thinking, and it was clearly equally fundamental to the thinking of Saunders Lewis. Abjuring the idea of class conflict, it argued for better worker–employer relations in the agreed best interests of both and in the spirit of mutual recognition of duties. To this end, it proposed worker involvement in the running of industries and local collectivised models of production. Most important of all, from Lewis's point of view, it advanced the principle of subsidiarity, understood to mean recognising the primacy of parents, families and communities over the claims of the state, claims of which the encyclical was very deeply suspicious because of their tendency to compromise the freedom of conscience and action of individuals and to encroach on the sacred unity of the family.

Lewis likewise was a strong opponent of state intervention in human affairs, an opposition he actually owed as much to the Liberal individualism of the Nonconformist tradition in which he had been raised as to Catholic teaching. What the encyclical – which in turn was based on the authoritative theological edifice constructed by St Thomas Aquinas – offered Lewis, however, was a clear vision of human relationships as consisting of a series of concentric circles, beginning with the family and then extending out to the whole 'community' of Christian Europe.

The central tenets of Pope Leo's encyclical were reaffirmed, in the context of the various totalitarian threats and in the face of the rampant capitalism of the period, by Pope Pius XI in his encyclical *Quadragesimo Anno*, issued to mark, as its title indicated, the fortieth anniversary of Leo's encyclical. This of course means that it appeared at the very time that Lewis was finalising his own thinking on socio-economic and political matters. The encyclical's emphasis on respect for property and on the need to ensure that it was fairly distributed was welcomed by thinkers of Belloc's persuasion, as it was by Lewis, whose own ideas approximated closely to those of the English Catholic Distributists of the same period.

For Lewis, modern nationalism was nothing but a deeply destructive example of Protestant individualism operative at a grand, state level. Each nation viewed itself as complete and sufficient unto itself and therefore as authorised to pursue its own particular interests even at the expense of every other national state. Like many conservative thinkers throughout human history, Saunders Lewis was very partial to theories of the Fall; that is to the view that everything had begun to go disastrously awry at some specific, identifiable point in the past. For him, the history of Wales pivoted around the Reformation that had enabled Henry VIII to defy the Europe-wide authority of the papacy and to establish the apparatus of a separate, Protestant, national state of England. One of the very first actions of that new English state had, predictably, been an aggressive and predatory one: it had peremptorily annexed Wales to itself and begun the steady, inexorable process of assimilation. Thereafter, or so the Act of Union of 1536 had unambiguously decreed, Wales was to be regarded, and governed, as nothing but an extension of England.[10]

Viewing the history of indigenous Welsh and Welsh-language culture from this perspective, Lewis saw it as reaching the very zenith of its achievement in the great body of strict-metre poetry produced in the fourteenth and fifteenth centuries. One of the glories of the European civilisation of the late Middle Ages, as unprecedented in quantity as it was in quality, this was a poetry that had been made possible only by the socio-spiritual order whose primary character-istics it both reflected in its very forms and structures and made the subject of its praise. Infused by the spiritual and ethical values of a medieval Church that embraced the whole of Europe, this polity was strictly hierarchical in character, allotting a place and a function within the organic body of society at large to every individual. Thus, in praising the princes and leaders, both secular and spiritual, of the late medieval world in Wales, the poets were not being shrewdly sycophantic opportunists. They were playing their crucial role in iden-tifying and maintaining the core values of their unique society by treating the princes and the gentry (however flawed they may very probably have been in historical reality) as if they were the impeccable embodiments, custodians, and transmitters of those values.

For Lewis, the great literary productions of the late Middle Ages were made possible by a socio-economic order he believed was char-acterised by 'perchentyaeth', by which he broadly meant a society of small owners of land and property, a kind of incipient *petite bour-geoisie*. It was an order that had naturally resulted from the end of the feudal world which, in Wales, had also more or less coincided with the demise of the indigenous princes with their powerful courts. And it was an order that at that juncture prevailed across the whole of Western Christendom. This was a valorisation of the post-feudal late medieval order very closely paralleling that of Hilaire Belloc in the *Servile State*. That 'excellent consummation of human society', he argued, was characterised by an order 'in which the determinant mass of families were owners of capital and of land . . . production was regulated by self-governing corporations of small owners . . . and . . . the misery and insecurity of a proletariat was unknown' (*SS*, 52). Like Lewis, Belloc regarded this order as one that spanned the whole of Catholic Europe and that was underpinned by the Church. It came to an end in England with the Tudor Reformation, whose immediate result was the seizure of monastic lands to the immense enrichment of the king and his powerful aristocratic associates. This destabilisa-tion of society prepared the way for the advent of a predatory and exploitative pre-industrial capitalist society in England (and in Wales, Lewis would of course have added).

*

Placed in the context of Welsh cultural history, Saunders Lewis's extraordinary valuation of the late medieval poetic culture of Wales can be seen as the culmination of a long, slow process of cultural reclamation, dating back to the heroic work of London-Welsh anti-quarians of the later eighteenth century.[11] In that first period, the process had involved the preliminary task of actually finding such forgotten and abandoned remnants of authentic Welsh 'bardic' poetry as were mouldering in the attics of many of Wales's great country houses. Later stages in the process involved the deciphering, transcrib-ing and editing of these manuscript remains, a task first undertaken by enthusiastic amateurs but eventually performed by a talented cadre of professional academic scholars. Finally came the work of interpret-ing and authoritatively evaluating this rich body of work, and it was in this task that Saunders Lewis, more of a remarkably gifted critic than an erudite and meticulous scholar, so influentially excelled.

Background to all this labour was the stateless condition of a Wales that was accordingly denied the crucial advantages of a sophis-ticated infrastructure – conspicuously evidenced in the educational field by Oxford and Cambridge – that enabled a nation state's work of cultural preservation and transmission. And another vital driver of the process from its eighteenth-century beginnings was the need felt by intellectuals from Wales to gain British and international rec-ognition and respect for the cultural inheritance of their country. In the late eighteenth century this need had taken the form of the search for highly prized evidence that the Welsh had indubitably been the very first Britons. Moreover, while they might never have produced the great epic regarded by classicists as the supreme production of an advanced civilization, the Welsh could be shown to have certainly produced a body of 'ancient' poetry worthy of British respect. What is more, the samples of ancient poetry the scholars managed to pro-duce were undeniably authentic, unlike the fake poems of Ossian, for which there was at the time a crazy vogue that had gripped the whole of Europe.

By the late nineteenth century, however, this work of cultural reclamation was beginning to be put to a different use. It was now being utilised to instil in the Welsh people a pride of national being compatible with the aspirations of the Cymru Fydd movement, one of which was limited self-government.[12] Growing to maturity during the period that saw both the heyday of Cymru Fydd and its effective demise, Saunders Lewis had astutely recognised that the patriotic movement's failure had been due to its refusal to countenance any aggressively political initiatives, such as those so successfully adopted by the Irish, to agitate seriously for Welsh 'independence'. Hence the formation of Plaid Cymru in 1925. And Lewis also realised that a parallel initiative was needed in the cultural field to reflect and advance Plaid Cymru's political agenda. Hence his brilliant redirection of the historic process of cultural reclamation to unambiguously political ends: he refashioned the whole history of Welsh culture to mirror his political belief that, in order to muster self-confidence sufficient for it to begin placing itself on the political map, a long-suppressed Wales needed to reconnect with its past at its most glorious. In so doing, it would also note that that glory had necessarily coincided with the very last period when Wales could claim to have retained some degree of independence – but independence only as part of a Europe-wide order.

For Saunders Lewis, therefore, the political and the cultural dimensions of national being were intimately intertwined. A decisive European turn was necessary in order to free the Welsh mind from that long subservience to England that had been the inevitable outcome of four hundred years of Wales being treated as no more than a minor, remote extension of the English state. While independence of government was a necessary political ideal, independence of outlook, a prerequisite if such self-government was to be meaningful, meant freeing the Welsh mentality as soon as possible from its long exclusive preoccupation with English affairs.

His vision of historic Welsh Europeanism did not begin and end, however, with his particular version of the holistic Catholic culture of medieval Europe. It extended much further back, to the time when the Britons/Brythons, forerunners of the Welsh, were beneficiaries of the *pax Romana* of the mighty empire of Rome to which they belonged. According to the foundation myth favoured by Lewis, the 'Welsh' were a people who could trace their origins back to Roman times, when they had been one of the constituent peoples of the Roman empire. They were therefore the original Europeans, unlike the English, who were descended from the barbarian peoples, such as the Saxons, who had laid siege to the empire until eventually they had laid waste to it completely. For Lewis, there was a direct continuity perceptible in Welsh history from Roman times, through the Middle Ages, and right down – although now manifest only as potential – to modern Wales. It was this potentiality he attempted to activate in his own writings and in his own political actions. For him, the recovery by the modern Welsh of some meaningful, active sense of nationhood would necessarily involve their recovery of an awareness of their inherent Europeanness, an invaluable feature that set them apart from all the other peoples of the British Isles

This European vision informed not only the political thinking of Lewis but also his creative imagination as a major artist. It was given compelling, stately expression in the majestic elegy he wrote on the death of his friend Sir J. E. Lloyd, the great historian of medieval Wales who had, in 1911, published his authoritative study of the history of Wales down to 1282. The poem opens with Lewis reliving in imagination the visit of Aeneas to the underworld in Virgil's *Aeneid*:

> I read how, long ago, Aeneas went
> Through the cavern with the Sybil, and to the land
> Of Dis and the shades, like a man wayfaring
> In a wood by night beneath the inconstant moon[.][13]

And having thus implicitly asserted at the outset the legitimacy of Wales's claims to be the product of Roman civilisation and heir to its values, Lewis ends his stately poem by reprising Dante's celebrated visit to Hades in the *Inferno*, with the aim of thus placing Wales within the ambit of the Christendom of the medieval Catholic Church. Except that in Lewis's Welsh version, the place of Virgil as guide in Dante's poem is taken by Owain Glyndŵr, the would-be redeemer of Wales who had supposedly reappeared in ghostly form to the abbot of the monastery of Glyn y Groes, only to be sadly told that his return had been premature, as Wales was not yet ready to follow him:

> Then near Glyn y Groes
> A second Tiresias in the dawn of Berwyn gave
> The verdict of fate's oracle, and there was an end.
> His shade melted in the mist that covered him.

In the frustrated, bitterly disappointed ghost of Owain Glyndŵr, Saunders Lewis is here clearly discerning his own *alter ego*. Like the great rebel reader, he too came gradually to feel that his rebellion had likewise come to nothing. He saw his vision of a self-governing Wales in Europe receding into the gloom, just like Glyndŵr, and just like his recently departed old friend J. E. Lloyd, the eminent historian who had himself once been 'an ancient seer':

> . . . he, the lantern-bearer of lost centuries,
> He was there no longer, neither his lamp nor his word.

Given Saunders Lewis's pronounced Europhilia, it is hardly surprising that his political and cultural thinking should have been significantly influenced by Catholic Europe's writers and intellectuals. Much has already been written on this subject, and so it will be touched on only briefly here. One of the greatest influences on Lewis, by his own admission, was that of Maurice Barrès (1862–1923), a writer, journalist and politician given to anti-Semitic outbursts and situated well to the right on the political spectrum in France. While Barrès was less extreme than his close associate Charles Maurras, the dominant figure behind the infamous *Action Française* movement, many of his seminal ideas were decidedly authoritarian and militantly (even at times militaristically) nationalist in character. When Lewis was charged in 1927 by a close friend, the highly combustible W. J. Gruffydd, a peppery Nonconformist, with having come under Maurras's influence, he vehemently denied it in a letter written in the viperish prose at which he excelled: elegantly short, assertive, sentences flicker out to deadly effect in rapid order. In that letter, he also gave two fundamental reasons why the accusation could not be true: Maurras's philosophy was statist, while all of Lewis's thinking had consistently favoured policies designed to minimise the interference of the state in the life of the individual; and Maurras opposed the interests of France to those of Europe, whereas the whole thrust of Lewis's thinking was that Wales could not fully exist save as part of Europe.[14] Anyone interested in tracing the influence of French Catholic intellectuals on his work, Lewis added, should look not to Maurras and his school but to the dramatist Paul Claudel, the novelist François Mauriac, the literary critic Jacques Rivière and the historian Étienne Gilson.

As for Maurice Barrès, he began as a devotee of late Romanticism, aestheticism, Symbolism and exquisite self-cultivation, but he later forswore individualism to promote the cause of a grand ethnic national community, rooted in the soil, centrist in organisation, but grounded in respect for a plethora of local and regional differences. He began to develop this nationalist ideology only after 1897, and in the aftermath of the Dreyfus affair, in which he eventually chose to side with the army's version of events, despite growing evidence of Dreyfus's innocence. Starkly polarising public opinion, the Dreyfus controversy both exposed the anti-Semitism underlying much of French life and also clearly demonstrated the schismatic state of French society. Barrès's nationalism was therefore specifically intended to envisage and promote a reintegrated, unified vision of national life. As for his Catholicism, while he declared himself to be a Catholic in the later phases of life, his Catholicism was always a curious, somewhat idiosyncratic affair, and decidedly dubious in the eyes of the orthodox. It took the form of a vague religiosity, powered by a mystical belief in the divine mission of the French nation as, supposedly, the 'first born' of the Catholic faith.[15]

It was those aspects of his thinking in which the interests of the individual were viewed as best served by participation in the national collective, and key aspects of modernity were roundly repudiated, that attracted the attention of Saunders Lewis at the time when he was a young officer serving in the First World War. However, Lewis was never remotely a slavish disciple of Barrès, and so caution needs to be taken when considering the exact nature of his mature intelligence's eventual indebtedness to the Frenchman. It is, though, worth noting in passing that just as the nationalism of Barrès – a form of authoritarian republicanism rather than the monarchist model preferred by Maurras – was an attempt to hijack for the right the cult of nationalism that had been the preserve of the republican left in France ever since the time of the Revolution, so Lewis's nationalism, likewise inclining somewhat to the radical right, was an attempt to 'rescue' Welsh nationalism from the palsied grip of the Nonconformists and Liberals of the failed Cymru Fydd movement.

It is also interesting to note the part played by an acute sense of national humiliation in the thinking of both Lewis and Barrès. The latter, like Maurras, was determined to avenge decisive French defeat in the Franco-Prussian war. Wales, of course, had no such appalling catastrophe to fuel its resurgent nationalism. But in fashioning his account of the early Tudor era as a calamitous chapter in Welsh history, Saunders Lewis was, in fact, preparing the ground for his appeal for a much more assertive and politically active form of contemporary Welsh nationhood designed to halt and reverse the humiliating post-Reformation process of progressive assimilation by England. Another interesting factor was the initial feeling of rootlessness that in the case of both Barrès and Lewis so strongly inclined them to place the constructed ideal of a powerful national community at the centre of their respective nationalisms. In his early years Barrès had wandered the continent in search of a spiritual home. As for Lewis, he had been raised outside Wales, among the large Welsh expatriate community of the Birkenhead–Liverpool conurbation, but he hankered after a self-authenticating – if largely imaginary – 'heartland' in several senses of that word.

Such parallels between the two thinkers having been noted, however, it is important immediately to emphasise the profound difference between the ways in which they sought to translate national humiliation into political action. In Barrès's case, a seething sense of national grievance was mobilised in the form of the Union Sacrée, the form of sanctified nationalism that helped propel France into the carnage of the Great War. By contrast, Saunders Lewis had no such militaristic intentions. His interest was in promoting not bloody conflict but mental strife; the struggle of the Welsh mind to free itself from English hegemony. And his important precursor in this effort was not Maurice Barrès but Emrys ap Iwan, to whose ideas some attention has already been paid earlier in this volume. Likewise influential was the writing of the interesting maverick J. Arthur Price, an Anglican and a Shrewsbury-born Welsh nationalist since the Cymru Fydd days. Price it was who cogently, even trenchantly, argued that the cause of Welsh nationalism should by rights be the preserve of Welsh conservatives and not radical Welsh Liberals and Nonconformists. The whole ideology of the latter, he correctly pointed out, was predicated on the radical individualism of their religious and social outlook and not on the respect for cultural tradition, historical precedent and the organic character of society that, ever since the time of Burke, had consistently concerned thinkers of a conservative persuasion and leaders of the Church of England.[16]

Another figure whose ideas roughly paralleled those of Lewis was the freelance historian A. W. Wade-Evans, who was an Anglican clergyman. In his collection of essays *Papers for Thinking Welshmen* he asserted baldly that 'we can only be good Welshmen [*sic*] by aiming to be good Europeans and good Men as well' – the cleric being obviously apparent in the final phrase.[17] Like Lewis, he traced the origins of the Welsh people back to the period of the Roman occupation of Britain and the early centuries following the departure of the imperial legions. But unlike Lewis, he did not build elaborate cultural claims on that basis, or explicitly argue that Welsh Europeanism was therefore an ancient feature of the country's history that needed to be rediscovered and exploited by the modern nation.

While Lewis himself was happy enough to admit the relevance of the thinking of Price and Wade-Evans, and particularly of Emrys ap Iwan, to whom he declared himself profoundly indebted, he was noticeably reluctant to comment on the striking parallels between aspects of his religio-cultural Europeanism and those of two major contemporary figures of English culture, T. S. Eliot and David Jones. While the similarities to Eliot are obvious enough to have been thoroughly canvassed already, little attention has as yet been given to the links with Jones.

Following the publication of *In Parenthesis* in 1937, Lewis and Jones formed a very close friendship, based not only on their shared faith as Catholic converts, their pronounced intellectual affinities, and their high regard for each other's creative work, but on the fact that both of them were immensely proud to be old sweats – whenever they met they immediately lapsed comfortably into military slang. Both had experienced while serving in the First World War an intense camaraderie they were to miss for the rest of their lives. It was an experience Jones attempted to convey in *In Parenthesis* through his stylised, but lovingly respectful, recreation of the mixed lexicon and register of the troops with whom he served. In the Preface to *In Parenthesis* Jones honestly lamented the convention that had required him to bowdlerise the eloquently colourful language of his beloved comrades. In context, he pointed out, the ritual use of obscenities seemed to assume an exalted, liturgical form.[18] Lewis would most certainly have agreed. Both had additionally appreciated the fact that the camaraderie of the front existed within, and was even enabled by, an authoritatively ordered military structure that fulfilled their deepest personal needs. For both, too, such camaraderie, coexisting with such discipline, had come to seem a late, twentieth-century manifestation of the kind of pan-European solidarities that had existed within the framework of the Roman empire at its most mature and powerful, and that had continued to be nurtured throughout the Middle Ages by the Catholic Church.

In some ways, their respective, overlapping, political views, religious philosophies and powerful creative writings were an attempt to replicate their military experience in civilian life. Moreover, both had grown up outside Wales, so that their Welshness had been an elective affinity rather than one given by the circumstances of their upbringing. In the Preface to *Epoch and Artist* Jones identified himself frankly as 'an English monoglot, and a Londoner' (*EA*, 16) who felt a strong attraction to his father's native country of Wales. Like Lewis, he had accordingly constructed highly distinctive and markedly selective versions of a Welshness which was a complex historical fiction, more a product of the mind than of lived engagement with the (uncongenial) established realities of contemporary Wales. In both their cases, their respective versions of a Welsh Europeanism was one important facet of their idiosyncratic imaginative project of self-fashioning.

Invited in 1973 to contribute to an authoritative tribute volume entitled *Presenting Saunders Lewis*, Jones responded with typically brief and pungent reflections on their friendship. He referred to Lewis archaically (and misguidedly) as a 'Venedotian' Welshman – that is as the latter-day descendant of the Celtic tribe that had originally occupied what later became Gwynedd, the Snowdonia region of north-west Wales centred on the powerful Roman legionary fortress of Segontium (Caernarfon). Praising Lewis's greatness, Jones pointed to 'his width of appreciation of the arts of man, especially of Western man and the whole tradition of Europe'. This was a matter which, he sadly added, 'for historical reasons, is not all that common to most Welshmen' (*PSL*, xvii).

While Jones was a highly sympathetic supporter of Lewis's nationalism, his own preferred vision was of a Britain that, contrary to the narrowly anglocentric Britain of the British Empire, gloried in its hybrid nature, according an honoured place to the various constituent peoples and cultures, present and past, of the British Isles. It was a Britain that was thus a microcosm of the pluralistic *unitas* of the Roman empire and of the medieval Church. That is why he constructed a masterpiece that was a cultural palimpsest, a remarkable monument to the mix of peoples, cultures and languages in the British battalions of the First World War – what he called 'that hotch-potch that is ourselves' (*EA*, 36). His remarkable work, hugely admired by T. S. Eliot, also compressed different historical epochs in the history of the evolution of modern Britain into a single time frame. Jones regarded this modern vision of Britain, 'catholic' both in the religious and secular senses of that work, as being very much in the spirit of the Roman empire which, at its greatest, had, just like the later medieval

Church, spanned much of Europe, hospitably accommodating a wide
diversity of peoples.

The tribute volume to Saunders Lewis, Jones went on shrewdly to
hope in his brief prefatory essay, would

> help to dissipate the idea that Welshmen who show a concern for the
> things of Wales are necessarily of narrow outlook and the more the image
> of them is one of restriction to some form of "nationalism", so much
> the more are they imaged as unrealistic, fanatical and removed from the
> actual in our twentieth-century world. (*PSL*, xviii)

Further to emphasise the pan-European character of Lewis's outlook,
Jones pointed to his familiarity with both French and Italian literature, his love of Dante and his suggestive comparison of the glowing
splendours of Welsh bardic poetry of the great age of the fourteenth
and fifteenth centuries with the astonishing achievements in stone and
glass still visible in Chartres cathedral.

As it pertained to the ancient 'matter of Wales', Jones's
Europeanism 'hark[ed] back, through the factual and governmental
unity of Roman Britannia, to the true history, quasi-history, and genuine myth of a Celtic and pre-Celtic "Britannia" of pre-history' (*EA*,
45). This was, he added, 'partly because the beginnings of specifically
Welsh history were tied up with the ends of a Romanic Britannia'
(*EA*, 45). The similarity with Saunders Lewis's version of the circumstances that produced Wales is too obvious to need labouring.
And like Lewis, Jones emphasised that it was these origins that made
the case of the Welsh fundamentally different from that of their near
neighbours, the Scots, the English and the Irish.

But Jones also recognised that modern Ireland had an advantage
when it came to connecting with Europe, because it had remained a
Catholic country. He obliquely addressed his own sense of cultural
positioning as a writer when he set out to explain the *desiderata*, as
he called them, of James Joyce's astonishing accomplishments as a
modernist novelist. 'For the Joycean achievement', he wrote,

> his medium had to be English, because that language is the *lingua franca*
> of today . . . But if the medium had to be English the cultural and mytho-
> logical content had to be European, and West European at that; which
> means that nothing less than a proper understanding of the Catholic
> mind, would serve. (*EA*, 304)

*

In the Preface to *The Anathémata* David Jones singled out for thanks those who, 'by some work of theirs have, however obliquely, aided us to make our artefacts'. The first such unwitting assistant he names is 'Mr Christopher Dawson, to whose writings and conversation I feel especially indebted' (*EA*, 131). A major, arrestingly original Catholic historian of the age, Dawson was the author of several singular studies, including the classic *The Making of Europe*. It is a work whose vision of the Catholic civilization of the Middle Ages, and whose understanding of its relevance to the present, is well worth comparing with the Europhile work of Saunders Lewis, for purposes of identifying both striking resemblances and illuminating differences.[19]

Both Dawson and Lewis traced the origins of European unity back to the period of the Roman empire, with Dawson then proceeding to define that traditional unity as tripartite in structure. To the political unity accomplished by the empire he added the spiritual unity that subsequently came with the growth of Catholicism and the intellectual unity that was the legacy of the Classical tradition. But when he came to consider Britain's place in that unified Europe Dawson differed sharply, and very significantly, from Lewis, because he expressly denied that the Celtic peoples had been the heirs of the Roman empire (*ME*, 90). This, he claimed, became clear on a proper inspection of 'Celtic' Christianity, which showed it was never a true, insular branch of the Catholic Christendom of Europe but rather 'a new creation due to the grafting of Christianity on to the Celtic tribal culture' (*ME*, 91).

For him, true integration with Europe came therefore only following the arrival of Augustine as a missionary from Rome, first to the Saxons and then to the Celts. The crucial consequent event was the Synod of Whitby, which had enabled the flowering of the great religious tradition of Northern England. Such a reading of early Christian history thus allowed Dawson to see England, rather than Wales, as providing Britain with its strongest initial link to Europe. While expressly acknowledging the invaluable work performed by the wandering Celtic 'saints' – from great Welsh monastic centres such as Llanilltud Fawr (modern Llantwit Major) as well as from Ireland – in Christianising a variety of European peoples, Dawson sees the 'conversion of the Saxons' as a 'reasserting of the old cultural tradition [of the empire] after the temporary victory of barbarism. It was the return of Britain to Europe and to her past' (*ME*, 209). What is more, it was the Church that 'embodied the whole inheritance of Roman culture as compared with the weak and barbarous tribal states' (*ME*, 209).

In this way, the Church had prepared the way for the political unification of what became the English state. It 'led the way to national unity through its common organisation, its annual synods and its tradition of administration' (*ME*, 210). Moreover, it was the work of Anglo-Saxon monks and missionaries in key posts and at key moments in Europe that had 'produced the conditions that made Europe-wide Christian culture possible'. 'It was the Anglo-Saxon monks and, above all, St Boniface, who first realised that union of Teutonic initiative and Latin order which is the source of the whole medieval development of culture' (*ME*, 213). According to Dawson's master narrative, therefore, the medieval English actually played a formative role in the sustaining and developing of a European unity. He emphasises, for instance, the important part played by the Northumbrian cleric Alcuin of York as adviser to the mighty Charlemagne.

To read Dawson alongside Lewis is to view the latter's Welsh Europhilia in a totally different, fascinating new light. It becomes apparent that it is, in part, an attempt, exactly parallel to Lewis's cultural and political endeavours and explicitly opposite to Dawson's thesis, to prevent Wales from being once more relegated to a bit part in the history of England. Because that, according to Dawson's model of the development of European unity, is the only, very modest, role Wales can claim, since it is England whose history, according to Dawson, demonstrates it to have been in its day one of the powerhouses of the development of a spiritual culture embracing the whole of Europe.

Lewis's religio-cultural Europeanism is as interesting for what it is intended to oppose as for what it asserts. Broadly speaking, it is constructed to contrast with many aspects of the modern industrialised world which, as Lewis emphasises, is in his view the highly pernicious product of an aggressive individualistic capitalism. Such a belligerently competitive socio-economic model is, he insists, inimical to the nurturing of that respect for the collective and the communal on which true nationalism depends. The mammoth and monstrous growth of the huge conglomerates of the iron, steel and coal industries provides proof that capital, and with it power, inevitably ends up accumulating in the hands of a few. He favours small units in the areas of both the rural and the industrial economy, and strongly advocates worker representation on the management bodies of business and industry.[20] Proving that his passionate pro-Europeanism is not merely medieval in character but that it stimulates him to address contemporary affairs, he writes enthusiastically and at length about the pioneering work done in Belgium from 1860 onwards to nurture a cooperative ethos in the sectors of finance, business and industry. Successful examples of this philosophy in practical action, he continues, have included the establishment of a Cooperative Bank for local authority use in 1860, a similar initiative in the field of industrial development, subsequently copied in France and Italy, a cooperative programme to create a railroad network for Belgium (1885), a Cooperative Water Board (1891), and a cooperative scheme to furnish workers with houses (1921)[21] (*CA*, 90).

In 1934, Lewis took advantage of a holiday in Ghent to fashion a remarkable address to be delivered back home to his fellow Catholics in Wales (*AWI*, 8–13). He began by noting resemblances between the Belgium he styled a small Latin country and Wales, mentioning their common experience of industrialisation and the presence in both of two distinct linguistic communities. Presuming on these similarities, he then proceeded to urge an audience he imagined as being primarily made up of Welsh descendants of Irish immigrants, to imagine how very different their history would have been had they settled in Belgium. Since it was a Catholic country, they would quickly and happily have been assimilated into society, becoming thoroughly Belgian; instead, having settled in Nonconformist Wales, they had defensively distanced themselves from the Welsh nation and confined themselves to their own separate religious and ethnic enclaves. This, he added, was utterly understandable; but its consequences had been highly regrettable, because it had prevented the incomers from ever identifying with Welsh life or supporting the distinctive national culture of Wales. They had thus remained stubbornly ignorant of Welsh history and Welsh traditions.

The golden age of the industrial Wales to which the Irish had flocked was now passing, Lewis acutely noted, and he forecast it would be sure to be followed by a flight from the south Wales Valleys back to the rural lands of the west. Should the Irish Catholics of Wales wish to benefit from these developments, it would be necessary for them first to make peace with the Welsh-language culture that was

still native to the rural regions. And it would likewise be necessary for
them to embrace Welsh identity fully. To assist them in this transition,
and to equip them for it, he proceeded to reassure them that there was,
indeed, within that seemingly hostile Welsh culture an ancient tradition, now hidden and latent, of Catholic worship. It pertained to that
long period of a thousand years during which Wales had been a part
of Catholic Europe, the very period during which Welsh-language
culture had been at its most flourishing. Far from moving into the
west as foreign colonisers, therefore, the Irish were ideally placed to
serve Wales by reconnecting her with that great tradition of which she
had sadly entirely lost sight. They could thus be the means of saving
the Welsh nation from that absorption into England that otherwise
would be its inevitable fate.

Ever since the Reformation, and the Act of Union that had been
one of its very earliest products, Wales had been governed as a mere
region of the English state. All that had saved it had been its culture,
whose commitment to religion – the lone survival from the Catholic
ages – had ensured its distinctiveness. But modern, anglicised Wales
had abandoned religion altogether and had in effect become thoroughly secular in character, after the usual English fashion. This
development had already been partly anticipated and facilitated by
Welsh puritanism. It had steadily narrowed awareness of the sacred
and thus abandoned much of the world of human society to secularism. Only at the beginning of the twentieth century had Welsh writers
begun to rebel against these tendencies and to make attempts to rein-
vigorate Welsh culture by re-establishing a much more generous sense
of sacred presence. But their attempts in this direction had inevitably
failed, for want of the necessary resources. Those were available only
in the form of that rich vocabulary of Symbolism that was uniquely
available in Catholic sacramentalism.

If the Irish Catholics of Wales could only come to view their role in
the context of these cultural circumstances, they would understand that
they had an opportunity and a spiritual vocation to act as the saviours
of the very Welsh nation from which they had hitherto held their distance. Saunders Lewis's largely neglected address is, therefore, a striking
example of the highly unexpected and deeply original uses to which he
could put his Welsh Europeanism. It also exposes the intimate connection between it and his felt needs as a modern Welsh creative writer.

Just as Lewis was interested in contemporary developments
in Belgium, so did events in central Europe attract his approving

attention. In the spring of 1930, Thomas Masaryk, the revered president of Czechoslovakia, celebrated his eightieth birthday, an event
Lewis marked by publishing an admiring essay about his extraordinary life. It is obvious enough, upon reading it, that Lewis is highly
conscious of the parallels between Masaryk's struggles for Czech self-
determination and his own on behalf of Wales, but with the obvious
difference of course that, whereas the Czech had proved successful, he
had not. The cases of the Czech and the Welshman were specifically
advertised in tandem by Iorwerth H. Jones in *Y Ddraig Goch* after
Lewis had been sentenced to a term of imprisonment in Wormwood
Scrubs for his part in the Penyberth episode. The point this time made
was that whereas Masaryk had been treated as a hero by his own
people, Lewis had been treated as an outcast.[22]

Rather like Lewis, Masaryk had started out as a cultural nationalist, whose awakening to the subordinate condition of his nation had
come with the growing realisation that neither the Czech language nor
the history of Czechoslovakia was taught in schools or acknowledged
by the dominant Germanic culture of the Austro-Hungarian empire.
It was only later that circumstances conspired to bring Masaryk to the
realisation that the survival of a distinctive Czech nationhood would
be possible only if his country freed itself from the claustrophobic
grip of that oppressive empire. He refused, however, to contemplate
any resort to violence to secure his aims, preferring instead to work
at introducing his people to their rich cultural heritage, awareness
of which they were being denied – another important aspect of
Lewis's own mission. Masaryk's efforts in this educational direction
involved first taking steps himself to acquire an understanding of
the very best that Western civilisation had to offer from the Classical
period onwards, just as Lewis had familiarised himself with the culture of seventeenth-century France. And while the Czech's studies
were invariably informed by a passion for his native culture, he never
allowed that passion to compromise in any way his commitment to
a rigorously dispassionate mode of inquiry, consistent with the very
highest standards of international scholarship. Again, the parallel
between him and Lewis, who was renowned for his unflinching intellectual integrity, is evident.

Lewis is sharply critical, however, of what he calls Masaryk's political naivety and immaturity. At this point it is obvious that he regards
the contrast between the Czech and himself as being a highly salient
one; but rather than say as much, he refers instead to the career of

the great Irish leader Arthur Griffith (*CA*, 133). What the politically astute Griffith and his comrades had eventually achieved by way of self-government for Ireland was far less the mere result of good luck (or Providence) than was the self-government that had come the way of the Czech people as an almost incidental, or accidental, part of the Versailles peace settlement. But Lewis nevertheless finds some consolation in the latter unlikely turn of events, because it is from some such future accident of history, he adds, the Welsh too might one day hope to benefit, provided Plaid Cymru was well positioned, at the critical time, to take full advantage of it.

Returning to consider the pre-war condition of Czechoslovakia, Lewis critically notes that at that juncture Masaryk's political work for his nation had been strictly limited to a thoroughly misguided attempt to win it a more favourable place within the Austro-Hungarian empire – precisely, of course, what all the 'mainstream' politicians of Wales, from the Cymru Fydd period of Liberal domination to the new Labour hegemony of the inter-war period, had contented their consciences by doing within the established confines of the British empire. Plaid Cymru had come into being as a result of the realisation that any such attempt at a conciliatory politics was inevitably doomed to prove futile.

Developments in contemporary Europe, most particularly in Soviet Russia, also influence another key aspect of Lewis's Europhilia. He is implacably opposed to systematic governmental management of what he regards as those aspects of human relationships – in particular as they operate within the structure of the nuclear family – that are sacred and should exclusively belong to the realm of private personal interactions. So he objects to the state schooling of children from an early age, to state control of public health initiatives, and even to legislation declaring man and woman to be equal in status and to have equal rights in law. In this latter connection, he harbours markedly reactionary notions of the male as the proper head of the family.[23]

Accordingly, Lewis repeatedly displays alarm at the breakdown of what he regards as the hallowed internal hierarchy of the supposedly traditional Christian nuclear family. Radical developments in that direction under the communist regime in Russia he regards as deeply ominous and outrageous, as likewise he does the analogous 'unnatural' case of the new, liberated young woman which he associates with the scandalous flapper generation in the United States. In due course, he proceeded to explore his deeply ambivalent fascination with the New Woman in several creative masterworks of the inter-war period, most notably the verse dramas *Blodeuwedd* and *Siwan*, and his daring novella *Monica*. In all three cases the right of women to complete self-fulfilment, including in the sexual sphere, is pitted against the moral obligation to respect and consistently honour in practice the vital conventional ties of society, marriage and kinship.[24]

Along with Soviet Russia, Lewis regarded the United States as the breeding ground of the New Woman. In the case of the States, her appearance was just one more dangerous manifestation of the disruptive energies of a vulgar, brash, culture that exemplified to the full all the evils of an unbridled capitalist system. Such a culture was the malign, purely materialistic, 'other' of the ancient, civilized world of Europe he so idolised. Interestingly enough, though, he did eventually admit that he had first been awakened to the integrated character of European culture when, as a pre-war undergraduate in English at the University of Liverpool, he had read the work of the great expatriate American Henry James. Writing in 1949, he offered a shrewd assessment of James's depiction of Europe.

James's Europe, he accurately noted, was a Europe without national borders and therefore a Europe that could be regarded as a single entity. This was a view that could be adopted, so Lewis argued, only by members of a nineteenth-century bourgeois elite of sophis-ticated cosmopolitans, and James had been the last great chronicler of their lost world of gilded privilege. His Europe was an endlessly subtle Europe of high civilisation and exquisite manners, and its cul-ture could best be viewed as the illuminating counterpoint of that of James's youthful United States. They were the opposing and balanc-ing poles of the single world of the West: both were the products of a single civilisation. And by the end of the nineteenth century, it was the States, for all their naivety and crassness, that had actually assumed the responsibility of acting as custodians of the core moral values of that civilisation, values that old Europe had quietly allowed to be eroded. Hence, in James's novels, the Americans arrive in Europe as innocents to be gulled, exploited and seduced by the subtle serpents of the old world. But in the process, they act as salutary reminders, for Europe, of the code of ethics on which Western civilisation as a whole has been built, and upon which it remains entirely dependent.[25] In recording all this in the most complex and powerful of terms, James the novelist had proved himself to be one of the last great artistic masters of the Western world.

The Great War had put an end to that European world so beloved of Henry James, as Lewis demonstrated by contrasting his fiction with the post-war poetry of his fellow American expatriate, T. S. Eliot. In *The Waste Land*, Eliot had a made a heap of the detritus of the great European cultural catastrophe. The poem was a bitter lament for a lost civilisation. Moreover, wrote Lewis, writing from a vantage point after the Second World War, after many talented young American writers of the 1920s had continued for a while to be attracted to a ravaged Europe, a disillusioned reaction had set in that had sharply reversed the process. Europe itself, too, in its turn, had actually begun to look to the States for cultural models that could assist it in its reconstruction, so that an equivalent emerged in the cultural sphere of the practical and financial support that the USA had provided to post-war Europe in the form of the Marshall Plan. Written as it was some twenty years after Lewis's original, highly influential accounts of Europe in the 1920s and early 1930s, his essay is a reminder of how alive he remained to the ethos of contemporary affairs and how willing he was to revisit, and to revise, his earlier views of Europe in the light of his experience of a profoundly different period.

But Saunders Lewis was far from having it all his own way in European matters. He was faced with spirited dissent from the ranks of the Welsh-language scholars, critics and writers who were his closest associates. Some of the sharpest criticism came from W. J. Gruffydd, who was always eager to fight fire with fire. And it appeared in the pages of *Y Llenor*, the hugely influential inter-war literary journal of which Gruffydd was the editor. He began to print snide asides about the kind of militant Catholic revival apparent not only in Wales but throughout Britain for which, in his opinion, Lewis had begun to act as an advocate, and even as a secret agent.

Lewis was not slow to respond to this provocation, and in 1927 a magisterial, elegantly worded letter on the subject of Catholicism appeared in *Y Llenor* in which he took Gruffydd to task for his assertions and insinuations.[26] In particular, Lewis objected to Gruffydd's damaging implication that he was a disciple of the highly controversial French reactionary, Charles Maurras. As has already been noted above, Lewis adamantly insisted that he was not, and pointed instead to other French intellectuals and writers, most particularly to Barrès, who, he claimed, had truly influenced his thinking. He went on to suggest that the tragedy of Wales was not so much that it had no religious intellectuals of the quality of such as he admired in France, but that it lacked intellectuals who were openly and uncompromisingly anti-religious in their convictions. Only such – and he singled out André Gide as an example – could provoke the complacent Nonconformists of early twentieth-century Wales into a searching reassessment, rigorous analysis and reasoned defence of the essentials of their faith, a faith that had, during the twentieth century, been allowed to veer dangerously away from its core theological beliefs and towards a comfortable acceptance of a mawkish, vaguely religiose humanism. What had been lost in the process was that precious awareness of human sinfulness that had been the passionate concern of such great figures of the Methodist revival as William Williams Pantycelyn, and that had, in addition, ensured for a time that at its best the creative writing of Nonconformist Wales had been stiffened and immeasurably strengthened by a willingness to confront the realities of the human condition. Modern Welsh literature, he added, had been fatally weakened by its loss of this fearful respect for human sin.

This letter brought into the open the very issue that Gruffydd had long been angling to address. His response to Lewis was fierce, and exposed the deep misgivings he had begun to feel.[27] However, he was quick to insist that his was not at all a blanket prejudice against all things Catholic. Rather, it was a particular, strong, objection to any attempt to impose the Catholic point of view on an unwilling culture. One key instance of this attempt, in his opinion, was Lewis's dismissal of the claims of Welsh Nonconformity to represent what was best in Welsh national culture, and his assertion that, to the contrary, the true 'native' religious and cultural tradition of Wales was that rooted in the wider international culture of the Catholic Church.

Gruffydd was particularly incensed by Lewis's dismissal of one of his own prime cultural heroes, O. M. Edwards, as nothing but a provincial whose mind had been in thrall to the values of the bourgeois England of his time and whose writing was therefore inevitably derivative in character and second-class in quality. For Gruffydd, Edwards had been the supreme product and champion of the culture of the nineteenth-century 'gwerin', the ordinary, devout people of rural Wales who had been the true transmitters of all that was best, and authentic, in the Welsh cultural tradition. And, as Gruffydd clearly understood, Lewis had nothing but contempt for the powerful cult of this gwerin.

As for Lewis's enthusiasm for European culture, Gruffydd readily admitted that it contrasted with his own exclusive interest in the literature of Wales itself, but added that Lewis's passion for Europe was almost exclusively confined to a passion for the culture of Italy, and most particularly of France. Gruffydd proceeded to point to those innumerable nations of Europe in whose culture Lewis had never shown the slightest interest. And then, for good measure, he went on to suggest that there was a fair amount of preciosity and snobbish attitudinising in Lewis's whole approach to things French. Their dispute was, then, an arresting example of what is often euphemistically termed an 'open and frank discussion', and the issue of Europe was to remain a bone of contention between them for the rest of their remarkable lives.

In his editorial notes for *Y Llenor* in June 1928, Gruffydd placed his misgivings about the Catholic Church in a wider context. His objections, he emphasised, were not to the theological doctrine of the Church, but rather to its deployment of its considerable and very rapidly growing political influence. Evident on the international stage from the number of Catholics prominently active in Westminster and as ambassadors across the world, it caused Gruffydd to become alarmed at the growing Catholic presence across Wales, instanced by the remarkable number of new churches under construction.[28]

A somewhat gentler, but no less incisive, critic of Lewis was R. T. Jenkins who, although best known as an eminent historian of Wales, seems to have been not one whit less knowledgeable about French literature than Lewis himself. But Jenkins, although he too harboured a very deep love for France, took a much more detached view of the country than did Lewis, and accordingly seems to have viewed the latter's raging Francophilia with some bemusement, and amusement. It was that detachment, born of his historian's training in carefully weighing events in the round, that enabled Jenkins to provide such a cogent analysis of the origins of that conservative, not to say reactionary, form of French political and cultural opinion that Lewis found so irresistibly attractive.[29]

He placed this phenomenon in its historical context, showing it to be the outcome of a number of important developments in recent French history, and demonstrating how the Dreyfus affair had been both the focal point of a growing conservative respect for Church, army and state and a stimulus for subsequent developments in the same spirit. And he also made clear how the catastrophic defeat of French troops during the Franco-Prussian war had provoked a delayed reaction in the humiliated French nation that had taken the form of a new belligerence and found an outlet in the ugly Dreyfus controversy in which the Jews had been scapegoated and branded traitors to the nation. The incident had also been used by right-wingers to attack the anticlerical republicanism that had been the mainstream ideology of France ever since the French Revolution and to promote the idea of the national Church as the traditional mainstay of proud French nationality. Needless to add, Jenkins had no patience with any of those interrelated reactionary tendencies he believed had so possessed Lewis's imagination as to render him incapable of seeing contemporary France, and contemporary Europe, for what they really were.

At the same time, Jenkins went out of his way to demonstrate his admiration for the extraordinary richness and vitality of contemporary French literature and to indicate, without any suggestion of cultural self-satisfaction or superiority, his impressive familiarity with a whole spectrum of French writing. But he also had a shrewd scholarly awareness of the regrettable tendency among contemporary patriots to reshape the Welsh past so as to make it consistent with their own ardent wishes. An avowed patriot himself, Jenkins was nevertheless unsparing in his exposure of all such examples of deception, rooted as they inevitably were in self-deception.

Thus, reviewing in *Y Llenor* a new history of Wales during the time of the French Revolution, he is quick to point out that it makes altogether too much of that tiny group of Welsh intellectuals whose radical politics had naturally made them eager supporters of the Revolution.[30] However distinguished a major radical thinker the Welsh Dissenter Richard Price, for example, may undoubtedly have been, and however fascinating the tracts, pamphlets and underground activities of such mavericks as Jac Glan-y-Gors, Morgan John Rhys and Iolo Morganwg undoubtedly were, they were clearly unrepresentative of majority Welsh opinion, which was staunchly pro-British and strongly supportive of the reactionary and repressive politics of Pitt. The radicalism that was to give rise to the Liberal politics of late nineteenth-century Wales, and that had produced a great tradition of popular reform to which Jenkins himself felt proud to belong, had not put in an appearance, according to the level-headed Jenkins, until the Chartist protests of the 1830s, which were actually a foreign import brought into industrial Wales from England. And clearly, Jenkins

believed that Saunders Lewis's beguiling version of Welsh medievalism, and of the great European tradition to which Lewis felt modern
Wales should be heir, was but another example of this tendency to
glamorise the Welsh past with the intention of instilling a sense of
patriotic pride in the modern Welsh.

Jenkins also gave short shrift to what he obviously thought were
the snobbish and pretentious aspects of Lewis's Francophilia. While
he was himself entranced by the long, distinguished history of French
society, he was disinclined to make a cult of its culture, or to regard
it as representing the very zenith of human civilisation. The *politesse*
of high French society, its wines and cuisine and elaborate genteel
courtesies – in short, everything Lewis believed was of the essence
– all leave him cold. Good manners, he knew, did not make perfect.
Accordingly, his accounts of the numerous visits he paid to France
failed to meet with Lewis's approval. Indeed, the latter went so far as
to imply that Jenkins had demonstrated but a superficial acquaintance with the country and that he lacked the discrimination and the
experience needed to appreciate the 'true France'. He said as much in
his otherwise highly respectful review of Jenkins's engaging historical
travelogue *Ffrainc a'i Phobl*.[31] The strength and weakness of Lewis
was his great love of constructing a grand narrative of history. This
was precisely what he proceeded to do in the case both of his beloved
Wales and his equally beloved France. Jenkins was prey to no such
inclinations. He was ever content to potter about in the higgledy-
piggledy of history, always ready to take things exactly as they came
and to exclaim at the wonder of it all. That is the great, endearing
charm of his writing.

Never the belligerent controversialist that Gruffydd was, with
his instinct for the jugular, Jenkins responded to Lewis's criticism of
Ffrainc a'i Phobl in typically genial and urbane fashion. Pretending to
have taken the comments to heart, and to have been duly chastened,
he returns to France, this time to visit Tours and the Loire valley,
precisely the kind of region Lewis clearly had in mind as representing the very heartland of majestic French civilisation.[32] But, quite
deliberately, Jenkins in no way mends his ways when wandering in
these culturally hallowed regions, and so once more his account would
have been much too preoccupied for Lewis's taste with a clubbable
narration of French history and altogether too disregarding, and too
disrespectful, of deep culture. No better implicit critique could have
been imagined of Lewis's grand Francophilia.

Telling criticism of Lewis of a very different kind was given oblique expression by Iorwerth C. Peate in an essay in *Y Llenor* warning of the sinister rise of authoritarian regimes right across the continent of Europe.[33] To read it can serve as a welcome reality check if one has been long immured in the somewhat claustrophobic cultural world of *Y Llenor*. The periodical served a Welsh middle class that seemed insulated against, and to be culpably ignorant of, the situation of the Welsh industrial working class, and to blithely disregard the crises mounting on all sides. These ranged from the great strike in the south Wales coalfield and the heroic struggle of the miners for fair treatment, to the ominous contemporary developments on the international stage. It is the latter that concern Peate, who draws attention to the totalitarian regimes that have strangled the popular democracies of Europe, from Germany, Italy and Spain to Yugoslavia and Soviet Russia. Nowhere does Peate mention Saunders Lewis, but what he does do is make clear his own convictions as a fervent champion of his beloved common people, the rural 'gwerin'. What alone can protect Wales from absorption into a powerful, centralised and authoritarian state, in his view, is its proud Nonconformist and Liberal tradition of a principled individualism combined with a strong social conscience. And this, of course, as Peate very well knows, is the very tradition Saunders Lewis is so anxious to belittle and dismiss in the interests of advocating his own alternative vision of a fanciful 'European' model of Welsh society based on examples taken from his equally fanciful version of Catholic medieval Europe.

When he was taxed with being a follower of Charles Maurras, Saunders Lewis not only vehemently denied it, as we have seen; he pointed the finger at a colleague, Ambrose Bebb. Evidence of this was clear, he argued, in Bebb's work, although his most recent articles had suggested an even deeper indebtedness to the *Revue Universelle* and to the conservative philosopher and historian Jacques Bainville. It is far less evident, we might add, in Bebb's popular travel writings.

To read the European travelogues of some of the young, or youngish, Welsh writers of this period, such as Bebb, is to become enthralled with the enthusiasm, bordering at times on euphoria, that pulses through the texts. Theirs, after all, was one of the first generations (after that of O. M. Edwards) to be granted the privilege and luxury of easy continental travel. Most had been lifted by the education system out of ordinary, usually rural backgrounds, and their parents, grandparents – and even the common run of their friends, acquaintances and contemporaries – could scarcely have conceived of the freedom they were experiencing. Their book-learning had ensured they were already excitedly steeped in European history, and this prepared them to view the historical locations of the continent as a perpetual romance and adventure: they were sights as much as they were sites in their dazzled eyes, and travelling from one to another was like enjoying the unrolling of some great, rich tapestry.

And they were all men – few women were admitted to the very highest echelons of the education system, and fewer yet were granted all the liberties of travel. Nowhere is the boyish nature of European travel more clearly expressed than in the opening pages of Ambrose Bebb's popular classic *Crwydro'r Cyfandir*.[34] The very word 'crwydro' – to wander rather than to travel – communicates the leisurely, unstructured and unbuttoned nature of the whole experience. It was an experience Bebb shared with two young male companions, and between them they formed a kind of cosy homosocial society central to which was the experience of male bonding. There is no need to resort to heavy Freudian analysis, for example, to appreciate the implications of travelling pillion, as Bebb did, on the back seat of a powerful bike piloted by his friend. Or to reflect at tedious analytical length on all the textual strategies suggestive of an intensely 'bachelor' relationship, expressed, for example, through mutual, twinkle-eyed teasing about the 'female attractions' of various attractive women encountered along the way. There is, of course, never anything that is in the slightest improper, not even by way of sexual innuendo, because these were all still good, hearty chapel boys at heart.

This advertised maleness is not, then, merely incidental to the writing. It is integral to it, and determines the kind of experience of Europe that they together share. Equally important is another dimension of the text that likewise may, at the outset, seem merely peripheral, even irritatingly digressive. Bebb devotes several early pages to an enchantingly lyrical description of rural Tregaron in the vicinity of the farm on which he grew up. To read it is to weep – not only with pleasure at the idyll portrayed, but in pain, because he is clearly elegising a dying world, and is doing so with a richness of local, idiomatic language that is likewise destined to disappear. Rarely has the remarkable palette of the Welsh language been on more sumptuous display. And this elegiac passage may have a significant bearing on the reason European travel was proving so seductive to Welsh-language writers at this time

Bebb makes clear the choice he has to make at the very outset of his travels: does he stay close to home, in imagination if not necessarily in everyday fact, or does he venture to embrace that brave new world, excitingly unknown, encounter with which, he well knows, will further distance him from his origins? In some ways, all his efforts throughout his extensive encounters with Europe constituted an attempt at compromise between these two alternatives – that is, at seeking continuities and connections between the old culture from which he came and the new culture(s) into which he ventured.

Having spent five years studying at the Sorbonne under distinguished Celtic scholars such as Vendryes and Loth, and attending lectures by such luminaries as Étienne Gilson, Bebb had reason enough to feel he was an authority on the French and their way of life.[35] During that time he had also travelled the length and breadth of the country, and had done so in a state of perpetual mental excitement, it would seem, as he manically collected information about France's history and culture to assuage his insatiable curiosity. He was thoroughly in thrall to France's grand, exceptionalist view of its national history and destiny, as the cradle and bulwark of Western civilisation. No wonder he ended up feeling scornful of those of his compatriots who ventured words of wisdom about the French on the basis of occasional excursions over the Channel.

But if his two travelling companions are anything to go by, it was these other timid and cautious travellers who most faithfully represented the outlook of the Welsh-speaking Welsh, a people who, for all that Bebb and Lewis loved to lord it over their English neighbours in their ardent Europeanism, were every bit as suspicious of 'foreigners' as were the English. Thus when one of his travelling companions, Owen, gets accidentally separated from Bebb, upon whom, as a non-French-speaker, he is entirely dependent, panic ensues for the perilous plight of this poor hapless soul cut adrift in a foreign land whose language, it is evident, he has made not the slightest effort to understand. Suddenly, Bebb's darling France assumes a positively sinister and threatening aspect! The whole scene unconsciously exposes Welsh Europeanism as the fiction that it actually is, particularly when it takes the fanciful – if intellectually fascinating – form it does in the writings of Lewis and Bebb.

Crwydro'r Cyfandir is a letter of unbridled love addressed to France by one who had become thoroughly besotted with French history and culture and who was ardently convinced it represented the pinnacle of human civilisation. Over several touchingly naive pages in the very middle of the travelogue Bebb elaborates his infatuated vision. At the centre of it is his love of the elaborate code of courtesies and fastidious concern for good taste he sees as lying at the very core of French life and in which he believes he discerns traces of what, like Saunders Lewis, he imagined to have been the high, aristocratic culture of the late Middle Ages both in Provence and in Wales. Equally fantastical is his paean of praise for an enlightened France whose manifestly superior qualities are loved and embraced even by its colonised African subjects. All who have come into close contact with the French, he assures his Welsh readers, invariably end up desiring to be French themselves. The same, he sniffily adds, could scarcely be claimed for the English and their imperial subjects. Fortunately – or unfortunately – for a Bebb whose French nationalism in this period rivalled even the later version of General de Gaulle, the bloody Algerian experience still lay decades ahead.

The allusions to the medieval world alert us to that love of tradition Bebb also attributes to a France he regards as historically committed to a vision of the essentially unchanging character of human nature. He clearly finds such a vision deeply reassuring, and a moment's reflection on this will enable us to understand that *Crwydro'r Cyfandir*, not least in its fierce opposition to modernity, is every bit as much elegy as love letter. In a particularly revealing passage Bebb confesses he loves France not least because it was during one sleepless night in Paris, after he had read an essay by a Welsh scholar advocating the cause of a bilingual Wales, and despairingly feeling that his Wales lay in ruined fragments around him, that he resolved to dedicate his life to the service of Welsh-language culture (*CC*, 200–1). To register this is to have important aspects of *Crwydro'r Cyfandir* suddenly come into focus, such as those many passages during their travel through the Breton countryside when a landscape triggered Bebb's nostalgic memories of boyhood and youth in the idyllic rural setting of Tregaron, with its rich Welsh-language culture, now increasingly at risk.

This later episode also recalls the earlier occasion when Bebb, spending a night en route at an English inn, is upset to hear one of his friends gloomily predicting the death of Welsh-language Wales.

In reacting so angrily to this prophecy of doom, he inadvertently acknowledges that he recognises in it a voicing of his own deepest fears (*CC*, 46). When, therefore, he embarks upon his continental travels, the presence of his two companions allows him to journey cocooned in his own little comforting capsule of Welshness. Wherever he goes he eagerly looks for similarities with, or contrasts to, Wales, and even more importantly he is able to share with his friends random snippets of Welsh classical poetry, popular verses and folk songs. These are the invaluable cultural fragments that he busily shores against his, and their, ruin.

As in the case of O. M. Edwards, therefore, Bebb's continentalism was in part an escape from the press of what for him were the many urgently threatening aspects of modern Welsh society. This displaced cultural anxiety may even partly account for the frenetic energy with which he travelled. He idealised France as an obvious, highly preferable alternative to England, whose stifling, overpowering presence and destructive, ominously advancing culture so very deeply worried him. In France he found a powerful, deeply traditional national culture that could afford him solace and psychological refuge. And in some of the key contemporary productions of French thinkers he found expressed an ongoing sense of national humiliation, following comprehensive defeat in the 1870 Franco-Prussian war, that chimed with his own fury at the condition of a subjugated Wales.

It was this consuming, and largely uncritical, passion for all things French that led Bebb, during his callow years, to become infatuated with the sinister if beguiling Charles Maurras and his *Action Française* movement, born over twenty years earlier as a conservative nationalist reaction against the liberals, democratic republicans and progressivists who had rallied to the defence of Dreyfus.[36] The journal kept by Bebb when a naively impressionable and headstrong young student in Paris in the early 1920s records the excitement he felt at attending meetings addressed by the charismatic anti-Dreyfusard Maurras, who was an arch-royalist, would-be violent insurrectionist and militant reactionary, originally from Provence, with pronounced anti-Semitic prejudices. Addicted to an anti-republican vision of a deeply traditional French state in which due order, discipline and authority would be maintained under a constitutional monarchy subject to the oversight of the Catholic Church, Maurras was a thinker

and activist fatally attractive to the taste of a young Bebb alarmed
and dejected at what he believed to be the imminent disintegration
of his traditional Wales. He did not, however, subscribe to any of
the most extreme aspects of Barrès's ideology, never demonstrating
any inclination towards anti-Semitism or any love for either royalism
or militarism.[37] That he remained thereafter an avid reader of the
Action Française periodical is hardly surprising as during that period
the *brio* of the daring ideas regularly expressed in its pages attracted
the attention of a very wide constituency of such leading writers and
intellectuals of the day as Marcel Proust, André Gide, Auguste Rodin,
Guillaume Apollinaire, André Malraux, Henry de Montherlant,
François Mauriac and Maurice Maeterlinck (*Ll*, 292).

The France of the early twenties was riven by disagreements over
the policy of reparation and other post-war measures designed in
part to weaken Germany, with the belligerently nationalistic *Action
Française* taking a hard-line stance on the matter. A corollary of such
issues was increasing French hostility to Britain – a hostility, focused
in reality on England, that one suspects would have been much to
Bebb's taste. He would, though, have been very much at odds with the
accompanying extreme hostility to President Wilson as the architect
of the Versailles agreement, and to the League of Nations, of which
the president, like Bebb, was an ardent champion.

Bebb was in Paris when, in July 1925, street riots that overthrew
the government marked the high-water mark of *Action Française* as
a political force. The anti-communist and anti-socialist propaganda
of *Action Française*, accompanied by its support for authoritarian
government even of the strong-arm variety, made its outlook very
attractive to the fascist movement emerging under Mussolini in the
early 1920s, and the young Bebb seems not to have been entirely
immune to such developments.[38] By the thirties, however, he had
become a vociferous critic of both German and Italian fascism, and
was eventually firmly committed to the British struggle during the
Second World War.

Bebb also undoubtedly registered the important point of difference between fascist ideology and the ultra-nationalist platform of
Action Française. Whereas fascism was militantly anticlerical and
secular, Maurras was, of course, an impassioned Catholic polemicist. And whereas the former was ruthlessly and uncompromisingly
centralist in its thrust, the latter preached a decentralist and regionalist philosophy – France was subdivided into 10 different zones or

composite regions – very much to the taste of a young Welsh nationalist. Indeed during much of the time he spent in France Bebb, who
had taught himself Breton, participated enthusiastically in the activities of the emergent Breton nationalist movement, most particularly
contributing articles to its periodical *Breiz Atao*. A decade later, this
movement also swung decisively rightward in its outlook, culminating
during the Second World War in what turned out to be a disastrous
policy of appeasement and collaboration with the occupying Nazis.
But in the early 1920s it was still oscillating between a regionalist
position that was compatible with Maurras's political philosophy
and a claim to recognition of a specific Breton national identity. Of
particular concern to Bebb, for obvious reasons, was the place of the
Breton language in this ideology.

After his return to Wales in 1925 to take up an academic post,
Bebb soon associated himself with the newly formed *Plaid Cymru*, a
party for which he had helped prepare the way. By the 1930s he was
a regular columnist for the party's weekly, *Y Ddraig Goch*, contributing a typically outspoken commentary on contemporary political
affairs on the continent. In these columns, his continuing attachment
to France surfaces from time to time. It is this for example that sen-
sitises him in 1933 to Hitler's threatening rise to power, even though
his nationalism inclines him at times to sympathise with a Germany
still smarting from comprehensive defeat in World War One with its
consequent loss of territories.[39] Six years later, he warns of Hitler's
baleful designs on such French acquisitions as Alsace, Nice, Tunis and
Corsica.[40] Noting the growing tensions in 1933 between France and
Germany, he pins his hopes on the 'Little Entente' under construction between a number of the smaller peoples of eastern Europe, an
incipient federation that as well as already involving the Czechs and
Romanians promises to include the Austrians, Hungarians and Slavic
peoples.[41] By the late 1930s he is pragmatically inclined to accept
both the Anschluss and German reclamation of the Sudetenland: the
Treaty of Versailles, he explained, had left Austria a mere rump of
what once had been a great empire and it accordingly yearned for unification with Germany, while Czechoslovakia, a country of 15 million
people, included within its borders three and a half million Germans,
two million Slovaks and one million Hungarians, which made calls
for the Sudetenland's union with Germany perfectly understandable.[42]

While Bebb's Franco-centred Europeanism sometimes closely
parallels that of Saunders Lewis, the viewpoints of the two are never

really identical. Indeed in places – most obviously in their attitudes
to the Catholic Church – they diverge quite decisively. But between
them they do evolve an outlook on Europe that is rooted in their
conviction that in political as much as cultural matters their Wales
should take its bearings from Europe and not from England. Their
Welsh Europeanism, rooted as it was in their exclusive allegiance
to a Welsh-language Wales, may seem to us unrelated to the actual
circumstances obtaining in the mainstream industrial society of the
anglophone Wales of their time, and correspondingly irrelevant. But
it nevertheless remains a bold, intriguing, and intellectually compelling attempt to fashion a distinctively Welsh view of European
affairs.

As for their respective claims to be the leading Welsh Europeans
of the inter-war period, Pennar Davies ventured, in a lecture delivered to a Plaid Cymru Conference in 1951, to compare and contrast
their credentials. Impressed though he was by the scope and authority of Lewis's visionary Welsh Europeanism, Davies adjudged it to
be ultimately sterile in its effects, as Lewis's emphasis on a Europe
united by a single, magisterial, Catholic faith had no hope of ever
finding favour with a modern Wales that had essentially been born
of Nonconformity. Bebb, by contrast, presented his Europeanism as
a natural outgrowth of that Nonconformist tradition, as it envisaged
a Europe of free peoples and of transnational cultural sympathies
and solidarities. It was Bebb, therefore, Davies concluded, who was in
the end the greater and more pertinent Welsh European of the two.[43]

It is difficult to read the pro-European writings of some of the figures
discussed in this chapter nowadays without ruefully concluding that,
for all their intelligence and cultural passion, they were in essence
exercises in nostalgia, and quite moving exercises of that kind in
many ways. In her influential study, *The Future of Nostalgia*, Svetlana
Boym distinguishes between two fundamental forms of a condition
she terms a 'hypochondria of the heart'.[44] There is, she argues, a
'restorative nostalgia', and there is a 'reflective nostalgia', and both
are 'tendencies, ways of giving shape to longing' (*FN*, 41):

> [Restorative nostalgia] characterizes national and nationalist revivals all
> over the world, which engage in the antimodern myth-making of his-
> tory by means of a return to national symbols and myths . . . reflective

nostalgia lingers on ruins, the patina of time and history, in the dreams
of another place and another time. (*FN*, 41)

There is much of the former in the Welsh Europeanist ideology and
writings of both Saunders Lewis and Ambrose Bebb. To read these
two highly talented intellectuals of a past time is therefore an experience both stimulating and melancholy. It is to witness the rearguard
action of a particular form of 'traditional' Welshness that found
itself, between the wars, confronted by massive annihilating forces
of change. It is also to register inventive local forms of resistance to
'modernity,' a reaction which, in its turn, can be variously construed
as both a renunciation of modernism and a variant of it.[45]

Notes

1 Luisa Passerini, *Europe in Love: Love in Europe* (London/New York: Tauris,
1999), 64. Hereafter *EL*.
2 Particularly interesting, and of direct relevance to Lewis's thinking, is Hilaire
Belloc, *The Servile State*, third edition (London: Constable, 1927), hereafter
SS. Belloc's distributist conception of 'proprietorship' corresponds closely to
Lewis's seminal term 'perchentyaeth'.
3 For an outstanding summary of Eliot's vision of Europe, see Jose Harris,
'"A Struggle for Civilization": T. S. Eliot and British Conceptions of Europe
during and after the Second World War', in Martin Conway and Kiran Klaus
Patel (eds), *Europeanization in the Twentieth Century: Historical Approaches*,
Transnational History Series (London: Palgrave Macmillan, 2010), pp. 44–63,
and particularly 52ff. (Hereafter *ETC*.) Much of the discussion here could be
applied directly to Saunders Lewis.
4 Trystan Owain Hughes, 'Anti-Catholicism in Wales, 1900–1960', *The Journal
of Ecclesiastical History*, 53/2 (2002), 312–25; Trystan Owain Hughes, *Winds
of Change: Roman Catholic Church and Society in Wales 1916–62* (Cardiff:
University of Wales Press, 1999).
5 For an authoritative overview of Lewis's life and career in politics and the
arts, see Alun R. Jones and Gwyn Thomas (eds), *Presenting Saunders Lewis*
(Cardiff: University of Wales Press, 1973). Hereafter *PSL*. The definitive biography is T. Robin Chapman, *Un Bywyd Ymhlith Llawer* (Llandysul: Gwasg
Gomer, 2006).
6 See Dafydd Jenkins, *Tân yn Llŷn* (second edition, Cardiff: Plaid Cymru, 1975).
7 Lewis has also been dogged by an unfair accusation of fascism, a charge
which is definitively disposed of by Richard Wyn Jones in *The Fascist Party
in Wales? Plaid Cymru, Welsh Nationalism and the Accusation of Fascism*
(Cardiff: University of Wales Press, 2014).
8 Jessica Wardhaugh, Ruth Leiserowitz and Christian Bailey, 'Intellectual
Dissidents and the Construction of European Spaces, 1918–1988', in *ETC*,
pp. 21–43; 22, 24.

9   This was intelligently noted by D. Tecwyn Lloyd, 'Saunders Lewis', in Derec Llwyd Morgan (ed.), *Adnabod Deg* (Denbigh: Gwasg Gee, 1977), 9–30 (hereafter *AD*).

10 For an outstanding assessment of Lewis's politics, including his version of Welsh Europeanism, see Dafydd Glyn Jones, 'His Politics', in *PSL*, pp. 23–78; Richard Wyn Jones, *Rhoi Cymru'n Gyntaf* (Cardiff: University of Wales Press, 2007), passim (hereafter *RCG*).

11 Prys Morgan, *The Eighteenth Century Renaissance* (Llandybïe: Christopher Davies, 1981).

12 For a treatment of the cultural impact of the Cymru Fydd movement, see M. Wynn Thomas, *The Nations of Wales, 1890–1914* (Cardiff: University of Wales, 2016).

13 Joseph P. Clancy (trans.), *Selected Poems of Saunders Lewis* (Cardiff: University of Wales Press, 1993), p. 31. The two following quotations are from p. 33.

14 Marged Dafydd (ed.), Saunders Lewis, *Ati Wŷr Ifainc* (Cardiff: University of Wales Press, 1986), pp. 4–5. Hereafter *AWI*.

15 See Eugen Weber, *The Nationalist Revival in France, 1905–1914* (Berkeley and Los Angeles: University of California Press, 1968); Richard Griffiths, *The Reactionary Revolution: The Catholic Revival in French Literature, 1870–1914* (London: Constable, 1966); Stewart Dory, *From Cultural Rebellion to Counterrevolution: The Politics of Maurice Barrès* (Athens: Ohio University Press, 1986).

16 For a discussion of Price, see M. Wynn Thomas, *The Nations of Wales 1890–1914* (Cardiff: University of Wales Press, 2017).

17 A. W. Wade-Evans, *Papers for Thinking Welshmen* (London: T. Fisher Unwin, 1909), p. 41. See also A. W. Wade-Evans, *The Emergence of England and Wales* (Wetteren, Belgium: De Meester, 1956).

18 David Jones, *Epoch and Artist* (London: Faber, 1959), p. 35. Hereafter *EA*. The volume is dedicated to Saunders Lewis, 'gŵr celfydd a gâr ei wlad a phob ceinder' ('a cultivated man who loves his country and all things beautiful').

19 Christopher Dawson, *The Making of Europe: An Introduction to the History of European Unity* (London: Sheed and Ward, 1932). Hereafter *ME*.

20 Lewis was heavily indebted to the economic theories of D. J. Davies when elaborating his own views on the Welsh economy. Davies's views, themselves derived from contemporary European sources, are considered in detail in the following chapter.

21 Saunders Lewis, *Canlyn Arthur*, p. 90 (hereafter *CA*).

22 Iorwerth H. Jones, 'Masaryk a Saunders Lewis', *Y Ddraig Goch*, XI/12 (Rhagfyr 1937), 5.

23 This is strictly in line with the Catholic teaching outlined in the two papal encyclicals considered earlier.

24 I discuss this strand of Lewis's Europhilia further in 'Ewtopia: cyfandir dychymyg y Cymry', in M. Wynn Thomas, *Cyfan-dir Cymru* (Cardiff: University of Wales Press, 2017), pp. 149–70.

25 Gwynn ap Gwilym (ed.), *Meistri a'u Crefft* (Cardiff: University of Wales Press, 1981), pp. 216–20.

26 'Llythyr Ynghylch Catholigiaeth'. Originally in *Y Llenor*, 6 (1927), 72–7. It is conveniently reprinted in *AWI*, 4–7.

THE EUROPE OF THE CULTURAL RIGHT

147

27 'Atebiad y Golygydd', *Y Llenor*, 6 (1927), 78–95.
28 'Nodiadau'r Golygydd', *Y Llenor*, 8 (March 1928), 65–6.
29 R. T. Jenkins, 'Yr Adwaith yn Llenyddiaeth Ffrainc yn yr Oes Bresennol', *Y Llenor*, 1 (1922), 102–21.
30 Jenkins, review of J. J. Evans, *Dylanwad y Chwyldro ar Lenyddiaeth Cymru*, *Y Llenor*, 8 (1929), 126–8.
31 *Y Llenor*, 8 (1930), 110–13.
32 'Ar Lannau Loire', *Y Llenor*, 11 (1932), 28–41.
33 'Awdurdod a Thraddodiad', *Y Llenor*, 13 (1934), 205–12.
34 Ambrose Bebb, *Crwydro'r Cyfandir: Anturiaethau Tri o Gymry drwy Ffrainc, yr Eidal a Swistir* (Wrexham: Hughes a'i Fab, 1936). Hereafter *CC*.
35 See his journals of this period, edited by Robin Humphreys. *Lloffion o Ddyddiaduron Ambrose Bebb, 1920–1926* (Cardiff: University of Wales Press, 1996). Hereafter *Ll*.
36 See the sketch he draws of Maurras in 'Trithro Gydag Athrylith', *Y Llenor*, 2 (1923), 177–80.
37 See the excellent, eminently fair-minded treatment of Ambrose Bebb by Gareth Meils in his outstanding essay in *Adnabod Deg*, pp. 77–95. Also the article by the same author in *Planet*, 37/38 (May 1977), 70–9.
38 See Meils, *Adnabod Deg*, for a balanced account of Bebb's brief interest in Mussolini.
39 *Y Ddraig Goch* (July, 1933), 5–8.
40 *Y Ddraig Goch* (January 1939), 7, 6.
41 *Y Ddraig Goch* (December 1933), 11. He makes no mention, however, of the influence of that extraordinary character Dimitrje Mitrinovic on these proceedings. See *EL*, Chapter 3.
42 *Y Ddraig Goch* (April 1938), 7.
43 Pennar Davies, 'Yr Ewropead Mwyaf yn ein Llên', *Y Ddraig Goch,* XXV/9 (Medi 1951), 3.
44 Svetlana Boym, *The Future of Nostalgia* (New York: Basic Books, 2001), Hereafter *FN*.
45 There is a vast literature on this vexed subject. For the direct relevance of the issue to Wales and to Saunders Lewis, see Grahame Davies, *Sefyll yn y Bwlch: Cymru a'r Mudiad gwrth-fodern* (Cardiff: University of Wales Press, 1999).

5

FROM SPAIN TO SCANDINAVIA

1936 was an important date in the calendar of the Welsh cultural
and political nationalists whose views of Europe were examined in
the last chapter. Not only was it in their opinion the pivotal year
of the entire decade; it promised to be a transformative year in the
annals of modern Wales. Its inflated significance for them related to
the bold, non-violent action taken in 1936 by a group of three well-
known writers and intellectuals at the culturally important site of
Penyberth on the Llŷn peninsula. There the government had insisted,
in the face of Wales-wide cross-party opposition, on building a facil-
ity to provide RAF pilots with training in aerial bombardment.
In protest, the group –which included Saunders Lewis – set fire to
huts and materials on the building site. A jury at Caernarfon having
failed on two separate occasions to secure a conviction, the case was
moved to the Old Bailey, where the defendants were each sentenced
to nine months' imprisonment. The action of the three had, in part,
been intended to prompt Wales to rediscover and assert its nationhood, and as such it was very much in keeping with the outlook of
Lewis and his colleagues and associates on Wales's relationship to
Europe.

Viewed however in the light of the experience of the industrial
south, the heartland of modern and largely anglophone Wales,
Penyberth seemed an event as exotic as it was geographically and
culturally remote. For them, 1936 proved memorable for very different reasons. Their own industrial experience also gave rise to a species
of Welsh Europeanism, but it was a version wholly unlike that of
Lewis and Bebb, and one that reflected the beleaguered circumstances
of the proletariat. In the south Wales Valleys, where unemployment

remained sky-high and undernourished children suffered from
rickets, 1936 saw fifty-three men and three women imprisoned for
the 'Taff Merthyr riots', a fourth Hunger March to London, and
seven people imprisoned for taking part in anti-fascist protests in
Tonypandy. Working-class hopes arising from the February victory of the Popular Front in the Spanish election were dashed when
it was followed in July by a fascist military rising against the new
government in Spain, an event ominously replicating fascist Italy's
annexation of Abyssinia (Ethiopia) that year and the seizure of the
Rhineland by Hitler's Germany. In September the British government
took the fateful step of establishing a Non-intervention Committee,
to prevent 'war goods entering Spain'. This initiative was to ham-
string republican forces as they were left virtually unarmed in the
face of royalist troops supplied with the latest lethal weaponry from
Germany and Italy.

This was the situation that prompted the Communist International
in October of that year to form International Brigades to fight in
Spain. As many as 174 young Welshmen volunteered to serve, the
largest 'regional' group in the British contingent, drawn mostly from
the industrial Valleys of the south.[1] Their Welsh Europeanism took
the form of an international working-class solidarity, reinforced in
many cases by strong communist sympathies. As for the people of the
coalfield, they identified most strongly with the workers of Asturias
and the Basque country, those areas of Spain that were heavily industrialised like the Rhondda and its neighbouring valleys. Syndicalism
had been an active factor in the politics of the cosmopolitan south
Wales coalfield since before the First World War, and so some affinity was naturally felt with the anarcho-syndicalist component of the
forces arrayed against Franco.

'Parts of South Wales in 1935', Hywel Francis has written, 'had
more in common with parts of France and Spain than with the rest
of Britain' – or with other parts of Wales, such as those represented
by Lewis and Bebb, one might add (*MAF*, 68). Francis goes on to
draw a specific comparison between 'the social and political unrest
in South Wales in 1935' and 'the Asturian miners' rising in Spain the
previous year: both were primarily working class rebellions against
an authoritarian central government, even though the one was a
full-scale military rising and the other was a largely peaceful "demonstration" of resistance' (*MAF*, 68). On Sunday 3 February 1935,
300,000 people took to the streets across south Wales to call for 'an

adequate livelihood for the unemployed' (*MAF*, 69). Increasingly, coalfield militants drew comparisons between the workers' plight and that of the working class in Germany under the fascists. The Welsh miners, too, they concluded, would need now to use underground tactics like their German counterparts, and to deploy extra-legal methods to achieve their aims, rather than seeking open confrontation, direct but futile, with powerful repressive authority.

It was in April 1937 that an event occurred in the Spanish Civil War that aroused outrage across the Western world. Guernica was a small town of 7,000 people in the Basque country, of negligible importance save that for the republicans it played a crucial role in the defence of the important industrial city of Bilbao, which was some twenty-five miles to the east. It was also the site of a major arms manufacturer. Guernica was accordingly singled out for aerial assault by Göring's Condor Legion, aided and abetted by Mussolini's air force. Since the raid had been deliberately planned for market day, when the town square would be packed with people, there were 1,664 civilian casualties.[2]

There was an obvious comparison to be made between the assault from the air at Guernica and the protest action taken a year earlier at Penyberth against Westminster's decision to sanction the building of a training centre for aerial bombing. But the leaders of Plaid Cymru seemed to have no interest in making it, perhaps because of ingrained misgivings about the infiltration of Spanish republican ranks by members of the Communist International and a variety of other groups on the far left. It was left to a young Welsh socialist named Cyril P. Cule to express dismay at such apparent indifference, and to add that it was all the more surprising since Guernica was no ordinary little Spanish town. It was the spiritual capital of the Basque people, historic seat of the parliament of the province of Boscay, the home of their ancient liberties, and the site of the old oak tree that symbolised those traditional freedoms.

Cyril P. Cule is a very interesting figure of the Welsh left. An accomplished linguist, who passed away in 2002 some six months short of his hundredth birthday, he was widely travelled, having spent periods of his life teaching in schools in Armenia, the Lebanon, France and Spain.[3] His early upbringing in Llantrisant, where his father was a Baptist minister, although the family had previously

spent a short period living in New Zealand, naturally attuned him
to the values and concerns of industrial south Wales and also made
him very sceptical of the capitalist world, with its strong imperialist
leanings. This outlook is very evident in the little volume about his
travels, *Cymro ar Grwydr*, published in 1941, a year of so after the
fall of France.[4] The first section of that book deals with his time as
teacher at an English school near Beirut, Lebanon being at that time
part of a Syria that was a French protectorate. Having originally
accepted the argument of the great European powers of France and
Britain that theirs was a presence in the Middle East necessary for
keeping order between the different feuding peoples of the area, he
gradually came to view the situation otherwise, as one where Europe
was intent on meddling in order to maintain its imperial overview of
a region vital to its interests. He also realised his own agency, as a
teacher of English, in this process.

Since he was teaching in the French zone of the Middle East
between the summer of 1925 and January 1927, it was natural for
him to concentrate his attention on the involvement of France in the
area. But by the mid-1930s he had returned home, and at this time it
was Britain's meddling in Palestine that he mentioned repeatedly in
the occasional pieces he published in various Welsh periodicals, particularly those that appeared in *Heddiw* under the title 'Cwrs y Byd'.
The relationship between the Palestinians and the incoming Jewish
population would become much more amicable, he was convinced,
were Britain simply to withdraw from 'the Holy Land'.

As he explains in *Cymro ar Grwydr* (*CG*, 33), he was exclusively
concerned in that little volume with 'the social and political problems'
of his age. And as he also went out of his way to emphasise on the
opening page, he was no educated man of leisure (contrast Bebb, for
example) with a love of travel in his blood and a romantic passion
for the past wherever traces of it could be discerned. No, he was an
ordinary graduate of the University of Wales, a qualified teacher
who could find no employment at home, or anywhere else in Britain,
after he had left university. He had then gone abroad as one of the
great contemporary army of the unemployed and as a needy migrant
worker. In that respect, we might add, he was well placed to sympathise with the plight of the unemployed wherever he encountered it,
as with that of the refugees and other scattered peoples. And it was
also natural for him to seek out the social, economic and political
causes of a situation such as his own, as it was for him to reach the

conclusion that the most satisfactory explanation – and attendant remedy – was that proposed by the thinkers and activists well on the left of the political spectrum.

Forced to move abroad again in search of work, Cule ended up (after much difficulty in securing a visa) in Paris, only to find, not long after his arrival, that the devastating effects of the great Wall Street crash of 1929 were beginning to affect the French economy a year or so later. He fell victim to 'la crise', and found himself wandering the streets, hanging out with artists, writers and intellectuals in the Parisian cafés. This both opened his eyes to the boom-and-bust cycle that was the natural rhythm of a capitalist economy, and allowed him to see French society from the bottom up. He therefore soon detected the strong xenophobic streak in the French character (*CG*, 37) and took note of the mad lurch from one extreme to the other in popular consumer spending. He was given penetrating lessons in Marxist-Leninist philosophy by a former White Russian now turned fanatical communist (*CG*, 38), and learned to sympathise with another refugee friend, a Hungarian who had fled to Paris to escape persecution at home only to discover he was ineligible for unemployment benefit because France had signed no agreement with Hungary to cover such cases. (*CG*, 40–1). Last heard of, he had entered the limbo world of the stateless refugee (*CG*, 42).

Meanwhile Hitler had risen to power in Germany, and Cule, already aghast that fascism had escaped the bounds of Mussolini's Italy, began to attend meetings and rallies. Uncertain initially what exactly to make of Hitler's philosophy, he soon underwent a crash course in its underlying principles and their grim practical consequences as he mixed with the refugees, many of them Jewish, fleeing the fledgling Nazism of Germany (*CG*, 43). It became clear to Cule that the choice facing Europe was to side either with Hitler's Berlin or with Stalin's Moscow, and his regret that Germany had chosen to identify with the former was all the greater because a Russo-German socialist alliance would, in his opinion, have guaranteed the rapid and painless collapse of the capitalist order across the Western world (*CG*, 44–5). Fascism, he came to believe, was an inevitable by-product of capitalism, and a symptom of its inherently morbid nature; and so he became a supporter of the Popular Front in France (*CG*, 45). This was the alliance of left-wing movements that eventually came to power in May 1936, under the leadership of Léon Blum, the first Jew to become prime minister of France.

One of the most sensational events in France during Cule's period there was that of the Stavisky affair (*l'affaire Stavisky*), one of the most significant and dramatic political events of the inter-war period in France, which came to public attention after the mysterious death of the embezzler and confidence man in January 1934. The official verdict of suicide was met with general disbelief, and with the cynical question 'So who committed his suicide?' Many saw in it a govern-ment cover-up for corrupt entanglements by powerful public figures in Stavisky's murky dealings.

Widespread public unrest precipitated a massive anti-government demonstration in the Place de la Concorde (near the parliament build-ing) on 6 February 1934 by right-wing groups, amongst which *Action Française* supporters were highly active, and this in turn provoked left-wingers to attempt an anti-Fascist counter-demonstration at the same venue the following day. Cule was present as a left-wing witness of the former demonstration, but his attempt to attend the second was thwarted when, upon leaving the tube station, he found himself threateningly confronted by a thuggish policeman and was forced to flee the scene (*CG*, 50).The episode served to confirm him in his anti-fascist, pro-left sympathies, while the turmoil in France effectively put paid to his hopes of finding work there, setting him on the road to Spain in May 1934, where he embarked upon the seminal period of his life to which he devoted two-thirds of the pages of *Cwrs y Byd*.

Not long after his arrival in Madrid, the coalminers of Asturias – 'the Rhondda of Spain' in Cule's designation of the region – rose up in protest against the appointment of members of a deeply reaction-ary Catholic party with fascist tendencies to posts in the supposedly moderate, centrist Spanish government. The response of the author-ities was to summon a young, little-known general named Franco back from Morocco to suppress the rising. He brought his Moorish Moroccan troops with him, and they set about their bloody business with noted brutality, not even scrupling to use human shields and sanctioning the aerial bombing of food queues. An Englishman sym-pathetic to the miners, who had been trapped in Asturias for a brief period during the turmoil, did, however, draw Cule's attention to the many different factions that constituted the forces of the left, drawing attention to the bitter divisions between them, divisions that were, of course, to spell disaster for the republican forces during the Civil War.

Having spent a brief period towards the end of 1935 in Barcelona – a city whose progressive sophisticated cosmopolitanism he found

attractive, although he warns against any comparison with Wales
(*CG*, 68–70) – Cule returned to Madrid just in time to witness the
historic election of February 1936. He was accordingly caught up
in the euphoria that followed the triumph of the Spanish Popular
Front, whose victory was based on a compromise programme notably
moderate in character. Victory was all the more welcome given the
ominous threat that had been posed during the run-up to the election
by Gil Robles and his fascistic followers. Speedy release of political
prisoners was now eagerly anticipated. And as a teacher, Cule himself
looked forward to the promised development of the education system.
However, the machinations of Mussolini were, he sadly notes, to shat-
ter his hopes very quickly.

Fascist forces quickly initiated actions designed to demonstrate
the inability of the new government to guarantee social order, and
Cule, who had developed strong prejudices against the malign role
of cunningly scheming Jesuits in Spanish life, believed he detected
the hand of this powerful order in various schemes, such as currency
smuggling, to destabilise the *peseta* (*CG*, 75). Franco's violent seizure
of control over the military in Morocco heralded the carnage that
was to come, and followers of the left began to arm themselves for
conflict. Soon Cule found himself caught in the midst of popular
hysteria as first he, as a foreigner, was suspected of being a spy and
then his ground-floor flat was turned upside down as militia searched
for the fascist who had been sniping from an upstairs window (*CG*,
80–1). As disturbances increased, his building was caught in the
midst of an exchange of gunfire (*CG*, 82–3). Gradually it dawned on
him that what he was witnessing was class war, involving a struggle
between the mass of working people and the entrenched forces of
capitalism, strongly supported by unscrupulous international arms
manufacturers.

Later he witnessed with disgust the formation of the Non-
intervention Committee in Britain and bitterly deplored the policy
it implemented, along with a France desperate to avoid its own civil
war, of denying the forces of the republican government any military
equipment. It was a revelation that confirmed him in his passionate
belief that the armies of a state were no more than the enforcers of
the bourgeoisie, and the servants of the ruling class (*CG*, 90). And
it sensitised him to the way that the British government began early
to demonise the 'Red threat' that lurked behind the struggles of the
republicans in Spain. Conversely the government later took every

precaution to distance itself from the fate of the Britons who had volunteered to serve with the International Brigade. What Cule had not
registered was that British capitalists had a vested interest in thwart-
ing the advance of the left in Spain. British finance was what had
effectively enabled the creation of a modern Spanish economy from
the middle of the nineteenth century onwards, and British business-
men had proved the most successful and influential of entrepreneurs.
By the time of the Civil War, 'British companies owned the greatest
share of Spanish business with nearly 20 per cent of all foreign capital
investment. The United Kingdom was also the largest importer of
Spanish goods', not least including iron ore (Beevor, 114).

Little did Cule think in the autumn of 1935, however, that the
struggle would descend into a protracted, blood-soaked Civil War
that would last for years. He left Spain, via Valencia, in a great hurry
in the autumn of 1935, following the urgent advice of the British
Embassy in Madrid that all British citizens should leave immediately. Only later did he become convinced the assistance he had been
given by the Embassy to make his 'escape' was motivated by the
British government's determination to ensure that the local British
residents would not become 'infected' by republican propaganda.
He reproached himself for being so innocent as to allow himself to
be effectively deported from Spain in order to suit the interests of
London financiers (*CG*, 95), and he even briefly considered enlist-
ing with the International Brigade. He had, he suggests, been made
aware that the struggle in Spain was of direct consequence to Wales,
a realisation, he emphasises in 1941, that had now been confirmed by
present circumstances, when young Welsh men were being required to
serve in the armed forces and Wales was being required to provide a
refuge for English evacuees. He considered himself fortunate when,
following his return home, he was enabled to act as a teacher of
English to fifty children from Bilbao. Indeed he felt a particular affinity, as a Welshman, with the small country of Euskadi, its population
smaller even than that of Wales, and he felt a corresponding pride in
the key role played by the Basques in resisting Franco.[5] The Basque
government that had been allowed to assemble by the republican
government had adopted policies strikingly similar, he noted, to those
of Plaid Cymru. All the greater, therefore, had been his astonishment
and dismay when, even following the incident at Penyberth, nationalists had shown no interest in, or sympathy with, the sufferings of the
Basques in Guernica.

He contrasted this indifference with the bold action of 'Potato Jones,' a legendary old salt from Ammanford who, commanding the ship the *Marie Llewellyn* and sailing out of Swansea, was reported (mistakenly) to have defied the instructions of the British government in order to deliver a consignment of potatoes to a starving Bilbao, and was reputed also to have supplied the city with a consignment of guns that had been secreted amongst the potatoes. What is certain is that several ship owners from south Wales did send ships to run the blockade, motivated in part by the financial incentives being offered by the republican government in Spain.

Although Bilbao fell to the royalists, Cule was relieved that Britain had at least enabled the evacuation of a small group of Basque and Spanish children to Britain. The effects of war trauma were evident to him in those he taught at Caerphilly (*CG*, 103), where he acted as director. They were naturally highly suspicious of all adults and accordingly inclined to unruliness and worse. He was also glad to see that other similar centres were established in Old Colwyn, Sketty Hall, Swansea and, briefly, in Brechfa. From Caerphilly, Cule watched in dismay as Santander fell to the royalists, effectively bringing the resistance of the Popular Front government to an end along the northern coast of Spain, save for Asturias. Conversely, he was gladdened by the support shown for the republican cause by the South Wales Miners Federation. It was the Welsh working class, he came to feel, and not the Welsh bourgeoisie, who were most sympathetic to the plight of the suffering of the ordinary people of Spain, as evidenced in that of the children at Caerphilly. As for the middle class in England, their class interests were manifest for Cule in the movement that arose in favour of repatriation of the Basque refugees – although Cule does concede that in some cases the parents were also genuinely requesting their return, a fact corroborated by recent historians. Some of the children he had taught at Caerphilly were duly condemned to return, to his deep distress.

The fall of Barcelona in January 1939, following a famous heroic resistance, effectively brought the Civil War to an end – apart from a rearguard action in Madrid – leaving Franco's royalist forces jubilantly victorious. Government troops fled in their hundreds of thousands across the Pyrenees to France, where they were first interned before, in many cases, they were 'persuaded' to return to Spain and abandoned to the tender mercies of Franco. That the Second World War started in September of the same year came as no surprise to Cule, who had foreseen in the fall of Spain the aggressive advance of a juggernaut fascism.

Events in Spain had for him been an education in disappointment and disillusionment, but also a revelation of the conditions of hope. The Second World War he saw as a struggle between two kinds of imperialism – the fascist and the capitalist (*CG*, 129). Wales, he was certain, would be made to pay for the failure of republican popular government in Spain. His social and political values had always been rooted, he realised, in his Welsh Nonconformist origins. Now he fell back on the firm belief that God's will in the world was sure in the end to prevail. And he continued to believe that capitalism would inevitably decline and wither way, just as had happened to the feudal system. He also placed his faith in the industrial proletariat, of Wales as well as in Spain and elsewhere, to act as the vanguard of a new and fairer order (*CG*, 119). He therefore took immense pride in, and hope from, the huge crowd that had flocked into the pavilion at Mountain Ash to welcome home the local boys who had served in the International Brigades (*CG*, 116). There he had seen the contingent proudly march in, bearing the flags both of the Spanish republic and of Wales. And he ends his book by dedicating it to the glorious future of socialism, just as he had opened his brief Foreword by recommending it as a handbook to assist Wales to advance towards that future.

Cymro ar Grwydr was first published in March 1941, with a second edition following in August that year. It is therefore a retrospective record, and to some extent inescapably shaped as such, with future events implicitly anticipated in the accounts offered of earlier ones. For first-hand accounts by Cule, hot from the press of immediate circumstance, one needs to turn to the many columns he contributed throughout the thirties to a number of Welsh-language weeklies and periodicals. These included *Y Ddraig Goch*, *Y Cymro*, *Y Ford Gron*, *Y Fflam* and *Heddiw*. The first of these was the official bulletin of Plaid Cymru, while the last was launched by Aneirin Talfan Davies and Dafydd Jenkins partly as a riposte and counterweight to the right-wing bias of those prominent Welsh-language intellectuals, such as Ambrose Bebb and Saunders Lewis, who were the leading lights of the nationalist movement and whose most powerful organ was *Y Llenor*.

Cule's construction of Europe was, in turn, fashioned in part with the *Llenor*'s version of current European affairs in mind. Whereas the

latter favoured a European outlook that reflected middle-class values
and the historical experiences of a traditional, largely non-industrial
and anti-urban Wales, central to which was the Welsh language, Cule
always positioned himself as a Welsh-speaking product of the south
Wales Valleys who felt a natural solidarity with the Welsh proletariat and viewed contemporary Europe through the eyes of their
experience.

In an article on India, Spain and Wales he contributed to *Heddiw*
in May 1937 he plainly distinguished between two kinds of nationalism in Wales. One kind readily acknowledged the class war that was
ongoing in the country, the other chose to turn a blind eye to it. He
also made it perfectly clear that he identified with the former. By way
of example he quoted at length from a powerful speech Jawaharlal
Nehru delivered to the Indian National Congress in December 1936,
where he drew attention to the struggle against the different kinds
of imperialism that was ongoing in Europe and accused the British
government of pursuing policies that, fashioned to reflect the interests
of the middle class, were silently favouring the governments of Nazi
Germany and fascist Italy. Those nationalists who were forever proclaiming that Wales belonged to Europe and not to England should,
Cule emphasised, lift their eyes to look as far as India if they wanted
to clarify their understanding of what was really happening on the
continent.[6]

In a note published later in the same number of *Heddiw*, the editor commends Cyril Cule for his whole approach to the European
crisis. Quoting from a private letter from Cule in which he identified
himself as a Welsh nationalist, the article praises in particular his
devotion to the cause of the Basques, a people not unlike the Welsh
in their circumstances. Indeed, it is not at all out of the question, it
adds, that Wales might shortly find itself in the same dire situation as
the Basques. Pointedly, and with no doubt more than half an eye on
Saunders Lewis, it quotes a passage from a pamphlet by the Basque
Nationalist Catholic Youth in which the movement presents itself
as dedicated to the cause of democratic rights and political liberties,
as being therefore implacably opposed to imperialism, and pledged
to respect the values of the Christian religion. Is this declaration, it
asks, not strikingly similar to the court statements made by the three
Welsh nationalists following their arrest for their action at Penyberth?[7]
A year or so later, the editor returned to the same theme, again mentioning Cule approvingly in order to regret the ditherings of Plaid

Cymru over the Basque issue. The central committee of the party had, it seems, opposed a motion to send a letter of sympathy and support to the Basque people on the grounds that the situation in Spain was too complex to unravel with any certainty. Even though the motion had in the end been carried, that letter had nevertheless, it seemed, never actually been sent.[8]

Cule himself drew a similar comparison in the brief profile he published in *Heddiw* of the situation in Euskadi in April, 1938. Again, with more than a glance, obviously, at the leaders of Plaid Cymru, he deliberately omitted to mention the munitions powerhouse that was Bilbao while depicting the Basques instead as being deeply pious, traditional, even conservative people who inhabited a mountainous country like Wales and were mostly farmers and fisherman, although the country did indeed include 'some heavy industries'. As for the propaganda of the nationalists, he added, it was very similar to that of Welsh nationalism, with its emphasis on the interests of the small capitalists, the revival of the rural economy, and the protection and strengthening of the Basque language.[9]

Cule was not the only Welsh-language writer to spend time in Spain during the Civil War. Another was J. Williams Hughes, Marianglas, Anglesey, who broadcast Welsh-language bulletins for the BBC from Madrid aimed not only at listeners in the UK, but also at the Welsh-speaking community in the United States. Hughes was a journalist by profession, and 'a classic example of a child of relatively well-to-do liberal Calvinist parents'. He was one of the first to raise money locally in Gwynedd to support the republicans, an effort that benefited from awareness of the Basque refugee children at Old Colwyn. And he acted as joint secretary of the North Wales Medical Aid Committee. This gathered funds enough to fill two trucks with supplies and sent them to the beleaguered fighters in the capital city.[10] While he was there, Hughes offered medical assistance to several hospitals. His talks avoided engagement with the complicated politics of the situation, preferring instead, in keeping with his humanitarian mission, to lament the destruction being wrought by the royalist forces, and they were subsequently printed in *Heddiw*. Thus the report that appeared in that periodical in the autumn of 1937 opened with an account of the indiscriminate bombing of Madrid hospitals that had driven Hughes to seek refuge in caves nearby, and continued by surveying the ruins of the city.[11] A letter from a young reader in a subsequent number of *Heddiw* favourably contrasted the even tone of Hughes's reports with what the correspondent claimed was the strident polemical bias of Cule's writings.

As well as providing vivid first-hand, eyewitness accounts of crucial European developments, Cule's numerous columns also trace the stages of his political education, as he struggled to find his bearings amongst the turmoil of contemporary affairs.

A short article he published in *Y Ford Gron* captures the optimism and enthusiasm of his first visit to Berlin in 1931–2. He had experienced at first hand the welcoming warmth of the German people, he reported, a people that, contrary to accounts in the demonising imperialist British press, were not in any way hostile or belligerent towards foreigners. While warily acknowledging the popular support being attracted by Hitler, he explained that he found this at least perfectly understandable, given the sufferings the German people had had to endure since the war. It was high time, he ended by arguing, for the British to ditch those impressions of Germany and of Germans that were but the relics of 1914–18.[12]

As we have already seen, Cule's political outlook was hardened and sharpened by his experience of living in France, where he witnessed the ominous rise in support for right-wing movements such as Action Française. His move to Spain more or less coincided with the beginning of the Civil War, and from the very beginning he was clear about where the sympathies of the Welsh should lie, because he understood the struggle to be a war not only between the upper and middle classes and the working class but also between two kinds of fascism – that represented by fascism itself and that concealed under the mantle of imperialism. While supportive of the brave volunteers of the International Brigade, he was realist enough to understand that their romantic heroism would do little to determine the outcome of the war. What was needed was arms supplies sufficient to counteract the flow of weaponry and the decisive military interventions that came from Germany and Italy.[13] As it stood, the war was a hopelessly uneven contest between men and machines, but the French and British – where a Tory government led by Chamberlain even briefly considered recognising the legitimacy of Franco – were totally resistant to any kind of involvement.[14] He found himself watching in despair as the republican government and the people of Spain were thrown to the wolves.[15] The Welsh people at large, he stressed, should understand that if Franco prevailed, the Welsh could eventually suffer the fate of the Jews in Germany, the Germans of the Tyrol and the Basques in Spain.[16]

For the first years of the Civil War, Cule sustained his hopes by believing he detected signs of republican victory in Spain and of a swell of anti-fascist feelings rising in Italy, and even in Germany. The fall of Barcelona, and the start of the Second World War some nine months later, left him thoroughly disillusioned, however. And towards the end of the war, such pieces of his for the Welsh press were filled not just with anger, like the earlier ones, but with an increasingly bitter outrage tinged with a degree of cynicism. He had come to take a dark view of the relations of Wales to Europe, while never wavering in his conviction that eventually the tide would turn, when capitalism, and the imperialist policies that supported it, would collapse, as Marx had predicted, under its own contradictions.

That Cule saw himself as a Welsh class warrior is evident enough from the foregoing, as it is that he regarded the working class as constituting the very core of modern Welsh identity and as carrying the best hope for a better Welsh future. His whole outlook on Europe was informed by these strong commitments. What is a little surprising, given the Welsh tradition to which he consciously belonged, is that nowhere does he make mention of those key events in Welsh history – the Rebecca Riots, the Chartist demonstrations, the Merthyr Rising – that have come to assume an iconic significance in the version of Welsh history favoured by the Welsh left. It is in this omission, perhaps, that we best see that, while Cule identified himself with the working class of Wales, and while he had been largely raised on the edge of the south Wales coalfield, he was actually the son of a Baptist minister. He was not therefore a product of the working class, and his naturally affinity – as both a Welsh-speaker raised in a largely English-speaking setting and as one of middle-class background – was with the Nonconformist, chapel tradition of progressive, radical dissent. And so, when he so proudly attended that huge popular rally in Mountain Ash to welcome home eleven local members of the International Brigade, what came to his mind was how disgraceful it should be that the country of 'Henry Richard and S.R.' should tolerate the presence in Cardiff of an emissary of Franco.[17]

Another Welsh commentator on the Spanish scene at this time was Gwilym Davies who was, as has already been noted in Chapter 2, a close associate of Lord Davies of Llandinam in the Welsh League of Nations movement between the two wars. The article he published in

Y Traethodydd in 1937 on the 'House Divided' of Spain arose from his experience of attending an annual conference held at Gregynog on education and world Peace.[18] Back in 1930 the conference had been addressed by Madariaga, professor of Spanish at Oxford, architect of the Spanish democratic constitution, sometime ambassador in Washington and Paris, and at the time chief Spanish representative at the League of Nations in Geneva.

Davies recalls how Madariaga, in concert with Professor Castillejo, had expounded enthusiastically on the past cultural greatness of Spain but had been most enthused by the prospect of the new, democratic Spain that at that optimistic time seemed in process of forming. Surveying the sequence of events in the country from the time of the dictatorship of Primo de Rivera onwards, Davies emphasises that the 1931 constitution had been highly idealistic and correspondingly impractical, featuring as it did an intention to end Catholic control of the state, to redistribute the vast swathes of land owned by the great feudal landowners, and to grant strong regional self-government to Catalonia. The result was a right-wing backlash that in turn prompted uprisings in Catalonia and Asturias. Discussing the establishment of the Popular Front, Davies astutely notes the many rival factions of which it is composed, concluding by recording Franco's seizure of power on 19 July 1936, and reporting how it was underpinned by the fascists and enforced by a brutal government police force. Also mentioning the involvement of Hitler and Mussolini, Davies points out that France refused to intervene for fear of the French fascists, while Britain remained determinedly neutral. And he ends by sadly quoting the hopeful message of peace that had been officially sent by the Spanish parliament on 18 May 1932 to the Children of Wales in response to the latter's message of peace broadcast that year to the children of the whole world.

Davies's article was reprinted in *Y Byd – Ddoe a Heddiw*, a collection of essays he published in 1938.[19] His tireless work on behalf of peace and in the name of the League of Nations took Davies, a staunch internationalist, to every corner of Europe during the inter-war years (which he termed 'the era of change'), and these essays include what he considered 'interim', first-hand journalistic sketches of Czechoslovakia, Germany and Italy as well as Spain, and reflections on the state of play in Russia, Ethiopia and Japan. In his report on Masaryk's Czechoslovakia he highlights the dangerous divisions in the country between Czechs and Slovaks, and between both and

the Sudeten Germans, also noticing unrest among the Hungarian segment of the population, the growing hostility between Czechoslovakia
and Poland and the presence in the country of a restless Ruthenian
minority. He ends by pinning his hope on Czechoslovakia's resolute
commitment to peace and, writing as he does in September 1937, he
trusts the country will somehow manage to survive intact, despite the
ominous signs of Hitler's evil designs on it.

March 1936 is the date of Davies's report on the state of play in
Germany, and it is by now clear to him that Hitler, who has already
turned the whole country into one vast garrison, harbours the intention of total elimination of the Jewish race, and is beginning by
scapegoating them as the source of all the country's ills. He succinctly
summarises the regime's main aims as including the restoration of a
humiliated Germany to Great Power status, recovery of lands lost
by the Treaty of Versailles, reclamation of the 'expatriate' Germans
living in neighbouring countries, extension of Germany's eastward
reach (the *Drang nach Osten*), and the creation of strong alliances to
buttress all these gains. Davies then expands at length on each of these
aims, in the process making the sinister turn of events abundantly
clear. His detailed mastery of the whole scene is most impressive. He
clearly foresees the Anschluss and also forecasts an eventual German
onslaught on Russia, while he punctuates his analysis with reminiscences of revealing personal encounters during his visits to Germany
and neighbouring countries. And while he retains a desperate glimmer
of hope for peace, Davies the shrewd realist obviously fears the worst
that was indeed to come.

His lively sketch of Mussolini's malign rise to power in Italy, written in 1929, concludes on a similarly sombre, ominous note, and it
demonstrates Davies's mastery of the current state of affairs across
the Western world, firmly underpinned as his analyses were by first-
hand experience. That his outlook is consistently influenced by his
awareness of Wales's precarious situation as one of the 'little nations'
in a world in which the Great Powers are increasingly strutting their
aggressive stuff is made explicitly clear at the end of his succinct
summary of bully-boy Italy's increasingly belligerent relationship to
a vulnerable Ethiopia. His article ends by observing that if Mussolini
gets his way, the ability of the League of Nations to defend the rights
of small nations will have been fatally compromised.

Another of his articles, dated July 1939, is devoted entirely to
praise of the League of Nations as the indispensable guardian and

champion of the rights of small nations. As such, the League is a new experiment in safeguarding popular democratic government on a worldwide scale. Out of the original fourteen or fifteen members of the annual parliament, eight or nine represented small countries (*BDH*, 185) and Davies lists the names of individuals and their countries who significantly influenced the League's policies: Smuts and Hertzog from South Africa, Branting from Sweden, Hymans from Belgium, Nansen from Norway, Motta from Switzerland, Beneš from Czechoslovakia, Madariaga from Spain, Munch from Denmark and De Valera from Ireland (*BDH*, 186). Then in 1934 there had been a threatened radical shift in the League's outlook, when Mussolini proposed a so-called 'Four Power Pact' (UK, France, Germany, Italy) that would serve as a kind of international 'Peace Club'. That proposal was eventually rejected, but in the end Great Power might won the day, when Mussolini's claims on Ethiopia were grudgingly recognised by both France and the UK.

Davies's own convictions as a Methodist minister surface when he accuses the Great Powers of having failed in this crucial instance to rise to the challenge of setting self-interest aside in the interest of a higher good: that of universal justice and fair play. He then proceeds to relate the decidedly mixed history of the United Kingdom's involvement with the League, beginning by noting Ramsay MacDonald's enlightened approval of the 1924 Geneva Protocol and the subsequent rejection of the Protocol by Stanley Baldwin's government, which was slightly offset by its support for the Locarno Agreement of October 1925, that bound the UK to support France if attacked by Germany and Germany if attacked by France. This was followed by a fleeting suggestion that Europe be subdivided into five regions of influence, each of which consisted of a number of small countries along with one or two of the Big Boys.

Davies sees the central differences between the powers of Europe as deriving from two contrasting philosophies; the sacred statism of Hegel on the one hand and the sacred individualism of Kant on the other, the second being of course the cornerstone of every popular democracy. In the final pages of his article he surveys several possible constructive adjustments to the League's guiding principles and policies while sadly admitting that national self-interest has grown to sinister and dangerous proportions in the contemporary European world. It could be, he adds, that the human race is for ever condemned to be attracted to violence, like moths to a flame, or it could be that the human race will eventually opt for cooperation rather than mutual destruction. And if so, then perhaps the League might one day develop into a true single society inclusive of the whole of humanity.

These are themes developed further by Davies in an article on democracy and peace dated July 1927. There he predicts that in the immediate future the main threat is less likely to be an all-out Europe-wide conflict but rather a series of internal wars within many countries on the pattern of the Spanish Civil War, between the forces of democracy and of dictatorship (*BHD*, 223). The ensuing turmoil will, he suggests, far exceed that of 1848, the year of revolutions. And to offset such a gloomy picture all he has to offer is his Christian belief in the eventual triumph of human fellowship over human discord. In a radio broadcast, Davies elaborates on this stubbornly hopeful vision, setting it against the dark background of what he freely admits has been the deeply worrying decline in international cooperation and the maintenance of social harmony during 1937. Sadly, he proved a somewhat mistaken political prophet, but that should not be allowed to detract from his impressive achievements as a concerned, well-informed and eminently fair-minded political analyst and as an activist totally dedicated to the cause of international peace. Davies is undoubtedly one of the most distinguished modern Welsh Europeans, and it is sad that his achievements should have been allowed to fade from memory in his native country.

France, Germany, Italy and Spain were not the only countries to attract the particular attention of Welsh writers and intellectuals of the inter-war period, however. J. Clement from Llanelli, for example, contributed a series of articles to *Y Ddraig Goch* on the many small or smaller peoples of Europe who had recently emerged into modern nationhood. These included Finland, Estonia, Romania, Czechoslovakia and Hungary. And then there was the substantial contingent of Plaid Cymru activists who looked to the Scandinavian countries, and most particularly Denmark, for inspiration and example. Foremost among these was the economist D. J. Davies and his Irish wife, Noëlle.

Davies had a degree and a doctorate in economics from the University College of Wales, Aberystwyth, but his had been a far from conventional academic career. Indeed, he had enjoyed a notably adventurous and colourful life, and his early background, every bit as much as his educational qualifications, predisposed him to take a deep interest in the economic nuts and bolts of the current economic system, particularly with regard to its impact on the ordinary working people of the south Wales coalfield. Accordingly, no sooner had Davies joined Plaid Cymru than he began to criticise its neglect of the plight of the Welsh proletariat, and to point out that it would have no chance of making effective political progress until it stopped acting primarily as a lobby group in defence of the Welsh language.[20] Moreover, he was already in his mid-thirties before he joined the party, and therefore already a highly experienced and a mature thinker.

Davies's working-class sympathies sprang directly from his own background and early life experiences. Whereas the leaders and founders of Plaid were all of impeccable middle-class background, whatever the origins of many in the yeomanry of rural Wales or the working society of the north Wales quarrying district, Davies was a son of the anthracite region of the great south Wales coalfield. He was born in 1893 in Carmel, near Cross Hands, the third of nine children in a working-class family.[21] At the age of twelve he went to work underground, gradually developing an interest in unionism and the ILP, before, at the age of nineteen, he took ship for the USA, where he stayed for seven years, working in the mining industry in most of the States and wandering as far as Canada and Mexico. He travelled on the trains, in risky hobo fashion, and found work at the coalmines from Pennsylvania and Illinois to Colorado and Washington State, venturing as far north as British Columbia. As an assistant to surveyors, he even visited Alaska and the Yukon, accompanying them also to China and Japan. Having himself discovered a seam of coal in Colorado, he established his own company, the North-Western Coal and Coke Co., Steamboat Springs, with the intention of mining there, but he somehow lost control of the unprofitable venture. While working underground he had also found himself trapped, with a fellow Welshman, for ten worrying hours behind a roof fall. Coming from the south Wales coalfield, he was naturally a convinced trade unionist, and so was frequently targeted by management as a troublemaker. His experience of working in a multi-ethnic and highly cosmopolitan coalfield environment, where many of his fellow miners knew no English, confirmed him at this stage in his Marxist analysis of class solidarity and class conflict.

When the States belatedly decided to enter World War One, Davies volunteered to serve in the navy, choosing selflessly to take the place

of a Welsh friend of his, who was married with children. He then
spent a year visiting several of the world's great ports, including
Ostia, the ancient port that served Rome. Somehow, during his brief
trip ashore there, he contrived to get himself presented to the pope.
Maintaining his chapel sobriety even in the midst of the notorious
company of a ship's crew, he was able to arrange passes that enabled
him, while docked in some of the great European ports, to secure
cheap tickets at many of the leading theatres and opera houses of
the era. Davies had trained from his youth to ensure peak physical
fitness, and once he tried his hand at boxing and ended up taking part
in forty professional fights, of which he won all but one.

Being so widely travelled and vastly experienced, Davies was naturally a wonderful raconteur. He would regale his listeners at Plaid
events by recalling the Grand Canyon, Yellowstone National Park and
the Arizona desert; the heavy-scented Chinook winds of springtime
blowing on the shores of the Mediterranean (*sic*); the inhabitants of
East St Louis, fat from inhaling the air from the corned beef factories;
his wandering lost on the slopes of Mount Rainier for two days and
two nights, and his terror at venturing into a fishing warehouse in San
Francisco where huge conger eels were kept that wrapped themselves
around all the pillars while the fisherman walked amongst them una-
fraid, nonchalantly striking away their waving, weaving heads with
their sticks (*AD*, 144).

At his own request, Davies was set ashore in Wales at the end of his
period of service in the US navy. He then returned to working underground, until he was trapped for a second time by a roof fall, and this
time sufficiently injured to be rendered unfit for further employment.
His unionism was reinforced by the indignation he felt at the way
injured miners like him were treated by the coal board officials, and in
Ammanford he became active in a discussion group of young ILP and
Labour Party members, one of whom was Jim Griffiths, who went
on to become a long-standing MP for Llanelli, UK Commonwealth
secretary, and the first secretary of state for Wales. He campaigned
vigorously for Labour in elections, while gradually coming to register,
and deplore, its anti-Welsh attitudes and policies.

The turning-point in his life came in 1924 when, at the age of
thirty-one, he spent a period of study at the International People's
College at Elsinore, in Denmark, where he met his future Anglo-Irish
wife, who was at that time Noëlle Ffrench.[22] Together they determined
to start an International College of their own in Ireland, but the

project having miscarried, Davies returned to Denmark, this time to attend an International People's College at Vestbirk, Jutland. Of interest to him later was the book *Denmark: A Cooperative Commonwealth* published in New York in 1921 by a Senator from Ohio, Frederic Clemson Howe. Howe was also president of the League for Small and Subject Nationalities formed during the First World War, and he found in Denmark a model of socio-economic development he recommended to the attention not only of post-war and war-torn Europe but also of his own turbulent country, the USA. 'Denmark', he wrote in the Preface,

> seems to me to be quite the most valuable political exhibit in the modern world . . . Denmark is one of the few countries in the world that is using its political agencies in an intelligent, conscious way for the promotion of the economic well being, the comfort and the cultural life of the people.[23]

The country's socially progressive economic structure appealed to Howe partly because it seemed to him to be developed along the enlightened lines advocated by the influential US 'populist' economist, Henry George, whose disciple he was.

George's powerful reformist book *Progress and Poverty* (1879) – still one of the best-selling non-fiction books in America – had had a huge impact not only on the United States of the late nineteenth and early twentieth centuries but on many of the advanced, industrial nations of the world, including Wales.[24] At the time D. J. Davies was active, first in the labour movement in the States and subsequently in the ILP, George's theories would have been very widely known and often highly admired. And since he had emerged from this background of working-class intellectuals, it is hardly surprising that Davies went on to become deeply committed to the 'Georgist' experiments he found in Denmark in the early 1920s. Moreover, the intermingling of the rural and the industrial in the Amman valley– Gwendraeth valley region from which he came, meant that he could quite easily envisage that (re)turn to the land that Saunders Lewis, for example, was in effect urging and that was also a central plank in the political philosophy both of Henry George in the States and of the founders of the Danish experiment.

Further evidence of the widespread interest shown in the US of the twenties in these Danish 'peasant' schools is afforded by Olive Campbell's lyrical study of *The Danish Folk School*. Published in 1928,

it is another text specifically recommended by Davies to the attention
of his Welsh readers. Campbell had spent an extended period studying the schools in Denmark, and the immediate impetus for her work
was the admiration she felt for her husband, John C. Campbell, who
had embarked on 'an adventure in adapting the principles underlying
the Danish schools to the conditions of rural life in the Southern
Highland', at Brasstown, Southern Carolina.[25] The Campbells were
convinced that such schools could assist in the strengthening of rural
cultures and economies across the world. It is therefore easy to see why
both Davies and Saunders Lewis became fascinated with such projects
of agrarian revival from a Welsh perspective, particularly when one
notes the characteristics of the school as summarised by Peter Monroe
in the Foreword he supplied for Campbell's volume. He praised 'their
individualism, their high idealism, their devotion to culture and to a
national spirit, their revelation of strong personalities, their independence of government control' (*The Danish Folk School*, p. v).

The time D. J. Davies spent studying in Denmark was therefore
for him an experience every bit as formative as that he had spent
at University of Wales, Aberystwyth. The People's College (or Folk
School) movement had been established by Dr Peter Manniche in
1921 with a view to promoting better international understanding
and the fostering of world peace in the wake of the First World War.
But Manniche was building on the work of the renowned Danish
Bishop N. F. S. Grundtvig (1783–1872). He it was who had advocated
a new, unconventional, type of academic institution, one that prepared students to be active in their society by making them aware of
the history, traditions and culture of their people, and by providing
them with the practical skills to be of service. Central to this system
was an emphasis on respecting and encouraging individual creativity
as well as inculcating a patriotic spirit. Grundtvig thus did much to
foster a national consciousness, within an internationalist context,
in the Danish people, and his example accordingly proved of great
interest to some Welsh thinkers, aware as they were that Denmark was
a relatively small country, very roughly comparable in size to Wales.[26]

His time in Denmark exposed D. J. Davies therefore to this stimulating educational environment, and predisposed him and his wife
to examine in detail some of the innovative practices of the Danish
economy. In particular, it seems to have opened his eyes to the cultural
shortcomings of Labour policy in Wales and to have thus predisposed
him to turn to Plaid Cymru when he did. He never, however, lost his

focus on the living and working conditions of the Welsh proletariat, or his passion for improving their lot, albeit by the implementation of economic instruments and projects that were often modelled on those in Denmark, and thus seemed alien to the resolutely anglocentric and increasingly statist Welsh Labour Party of the day. Above all, he seems to have learned from his Danish experience the supreme value of collaboration as opposed to conflict, and thus to have resolved to promote correspondingly cooperative ventures in Wales. These ventures were bound by their very nature to be relatively small-scale and local rather than large and centralist in character, and were the antithesis of the giant nationalised industries favoured by conventional British socialists.

There can be no doubt that the periods he spent in Denmark had a decisive influence on Davies's thinking thereafter. Above all, perhaps, it suggested to him the means of integrating his economic analysis with his cultural commitments. But there is also no doubt that his mature thinking owed much, too, to his early exposure to the range of ideologies and social models that characterised the socialist thinking of this fluid period. There are signs, for example, of William Morris's Guild Socialism in his policies, as of the Distributist economics popular among some middle-class artists and intellectuals in the 1920s. He also admitted to having been influenced by the distinguished 'libertarian Socialist' G. D. H. Cole (an admirer of Morris), who could later boast of both Hugh Gaitskell and Harold Wilson as having been his pupils. Like Davies, Cole was not an advocate of state socialism, preferring instead to champion local cooperative ventures.[27]

Davies's economic theories also bore some similarity to those of the Syndicalist movement whose pre-war influence in the south Wales coalfield had resulted in that memorable, groundbreaking publication, *The Miners' Next Step*. The core aim of Syndicalism was the revolutionary overthrow – by violent means if necessary – of the established system of industrial production, and its replacement by a network of local, worker-owned and worker-run industries. One of the sources of thinking along these lines was the Central Labour College, a highly influential body supported by several of the most powerful unions of the day and situated (after a brief original sojourn at Oxford) in London. Several of the leading 'organic intellectuals' of the early twentieth century in Wales, Jim Griffiths among them, were trained at this institution. But even before his participation in that discussion group in Ammanford, Davies would have become familiar with Syndicalism

during his period of activity with American unionism. The thinking
and the practice of the Wobblies,[28] for example, was certainly influenced by Syndicalism, a form of voluntarist cooperation that well
suited the mainstream, highly individualistic and broadly liberal
sociopolitical culture of the US, as, indeed, it sat well with the corresponding culture of nineteenth-century Liberal and Nonconformist
Wales. It is easy enough to see how Syndicalism, albeit shorn of its
insurrectionist tendencies, would have appealed to products of chapel
culture, such as Jim Griffiths – and D. J. Davies, for that matter.

All this said, what is noteworthy about Davies is that in his
thinking, perhaps partly under the influence of Saunders Lewis's
'distributist' ideology, he began to concentrate on the means of tran-
sitioning from the industrial society that, in the inter-war period,
seemed so immovably entrenched in south Wales, to a post-industrial
order, which involved imagining the emergence of smaller units of
wide geographical spread. And there is no doubt that his Danish
experiences proved invaluable to him in this context. His background
in the western anthracite region of the south Wales coalfield had, I
believe, greatly facilitated his belief that it was possible to adopt a
holistic approach to the crisis of the Welsh economy. That region
was characterised by the widespread use of the Welsh language in the
mining industry, contrasting sharply, of course, with the decisively
anglophone character of the steam-coal region of the coalfield in the
south-eastern Valleys.

Accordingly, it was possible for Davies – mistakenly – to believe
that there was a cultural continuity to be discerned between Wales's
rural parts and rural past and the industrial societies of the new Wales.
He found it difficult to realise that the latter was, in fact, the product
of the cultural schism consequent upon irreversible language shift.
And this, coupled with the radically disruptive and transformative
late nineteenth-century shift in south Wales towards monocultural
large-scale industrial production, had resulted in the emergence of
a diverse, inchoate, multinational and proletarian society. This new
Wales was a world away therefore both from the old pre-industrial
Wales, vestiges of which could still be discerned in Davies's native
district, and from that 'homogeneous' national population Davies had
discovered in Denmark, which he recognised had been a necessary
prerequisite of the kind of modern society that had been built there.

This is not in any way to slight the fact that, down to the end
of the nineteenth century, Aberdare had been a powerhouse of

Welsh-language culture as well as a major industrial centre, or that
Welsh lingered on well into the twentieth century in the Merthyr–
Dowlais region, or that it maintained a presence, too, as far east as
the Rhymney valley. But by the thirties the remnants of the culture
were a sign that it had become residual, and indeed the trend was not
to be reversed until the later part of the twentieth century. Therefore
for Davies to assume a commonalty of cultural values and cultural
outlook right across the south Wales coalfield, let alone across the
whole of Wales, was, sadly, wishful thinking to say the least.[29]

That this was the case is a little surprising, given that, from his
earliest association with Plaid Cymru, he had urged the party to
make extensive use of English in pursuit of its goals, because that
was an obvious prerequisite for gaining a foothold in the industrial
south-east. Commenting in a powerful letter to *Y Ddraig Goch* on an
observation made by Saunders Lewis that Plaid needed to become
fluent in the 'language of facts, figures and economic terms' since that
was the language of the working class in Wales, Davies shrewdly noted
that 'we have to remember that the language of a great number – the
majority of these industrial workers – is not merely "facts and figures
and economic terms" but *English*'.[30]

And it was this flawed presumption of continuity that made it possible for Davies to believe that the cooperative ethos nurtured by the
Folk Colleges of Denmark and apparent in the country's collaborative
economic practices could be replicated in a Wales he imagined to be, in
essence, a single, unified whole. Saunders Lewis inadvertently exposed
this presumptive vision when, in reviewing Davies's seminal work on
The Economics of Welsh Self-Government (1931), he noted that whereas
he had asked Davies solely for an analysis of the economic crisis of
industrial Wales, Davies had refused, insisting instead that the plight
of coalfield society was inseparable from the plight of the agricultural industry in Wales, and that therefore his analysis had to adopt a
comprehensive, holistic approach.[31] Lewis then refers to examples to
be found in Holland and Belgium of the kind of remedies Davies was
proposing. He also clearly points up the important point of conver-
gence between his own thinking and that of Davies when he states:

> A nation, in Dr Davies' understanding of the term, is a people who dis-
> cover in themselves and in their past and in their natural circumstance,
> reasons for co-operating and wishing both well-being for themselves and
> respect for each other.

Lewis also approvingly emphasised that, contrary to the outlook
of Marxist socialists, that of Davies did not regard class war as the
inevitable outcome of imperialist capitalism and laissez-faire economics. He then proceeded to restate Davies's philosophy in the distinctive
terms of his own commitments:

> The aim of the National Party of Wales is to de-proletariatise the people
> of Wales, to turn Wales once again into that which it once was, a coun-
> try of independent men [*sic*], strong in character because they were all
> owners of property and masters of themselves rather than being merely
> wage slaves.

Lewis warmed very enthusiastically to the crucial emphasis Davies
put in an important early article he contributed to *Y Ddraig Goch*
on the cultural preconditions of the economic remedies he was proposing. This was a direct reflection of the principles and practices
he had encountered in the Danish Folk Colleges he had attended.
His statement on this matter is so powerful and so important that
it deserves to be quoted in full, emphasising as it does that the collaborative enterprises he had admired in Denmark had depended on
the previous cultivation of a strong sense of national identity. Where
such exists, he explains, an individual

> can experience the presence of the nation in and around himself [*sic*], the
> customs and traditions of his locality, his beliefs and manner of think-
> ing, and he can feel, in the natural atmosphere of his country or town,
> the historical connections of his community. And this awareness of his
> relationship to his nation will awaken the very best in his nature. He has
> experienced in his nation a concrete character greater than himself, a
> spiritual entity that has its roots in the past and that will last for ages to
> come, and it is a character to which he can himself make a contribution
> commensurate with the enrichment of his own personality. It is particu-
> larly easy for a member of a small nation to experience all this, as the
> efforts of an individual are more readily evident in the context of such
> a national context.[32]

He then refers to Denmark as affording the best example of this.
Given this outlook, it was obviously important for Davies to seek to
demonstrate that there would be a natural continuity between Welsh
sociocultural tradition and his own recommended models of socio-
economic collaboration, and so he took particular pride in noting that

Robert Owen, the acknowledged British founder of the cooperative movement, was a Welshman.

One natural corollary of Davies's philosophy was that, just as economic practice in Wales should be a reflection of that which was distinctive in national life, so that in England had long proved such. In support of this claim, he summoned Spengler, a highly influential thinker of the day, to witness: 'Spengler states that every form of economic life is an expression of the life of a [national] soul. In England that expression has taken the form of Imperialism.'[33] Wales, Davies added, could escape the tyranny of such an outlook and such a practice only by establishing its own government that would implement the collaborative economic practices that were consonant with the historical values of the Welsh nation.[34]

It was on this very note that he opened the pamphlet in which he succinctly summarised his proposals, *The Economics of Self-Government*.[35] Wales, he argued, had hitherto been treated by England as merely a subordinate region within the imperial economy, and had accordingly fallen victim to the laissez-faire policies that had inevitably resulted in a grossly uneven social distribution of wealth. 'While other countries, such as Denmark', he continued,

> have, under the direction and with the assistance of their National Government, been working out a well-balanced and well-organised system of industry and agriculture, Wales has been left as a field for exploitation by capitalist enterprise, unchecked by any consideration of national welfare. (*ESG*, 4)

The whole thrust of his pamphlet, therefore, was that Wales badly and urgently needed to follow Denmark's example. In *Y Ddraig Goch* he had already quoted a passage from a contemporary study of Denmark in support of his arguments: 'In Denmark work and government are a single undertaking. The economic and the political state are merged.'[36] He was particularly admiring of the resoluteness of a government that had refused to support the opening of a Ford factory in Denmark.[37]

Under the existing regime, he pointed out, the Welsh monocultural industrial economy was in a desperate plight, the rural areas had been fatally weakened by depopulation, and public health was a national disgrace. Imperialist policies had dictated that the economy be geared to maximise exports rather than to the cultivation and

supply of internal markets. Wales, in his opinion, was ideally suited
to adopt Danish practices, because it, too, was a small country where
'people know one another . . . and are willing to make experiments'
(*ESG*, 13). He therefore advocated the implementation of an agricultural policy 'along the lines of co-operation, thus maintaining the
principle of voluntary efforts and individual initiative while securing
the benefits of collective organisation' (*ESG*, 14). [38]

In order to ensure a proper transition to such a system and to
provide its development with the appropriate impetus and support,
practical and financial innovations would be necessary, sometimes
involving an initial injection of money from government. It would
be important, for example, to establish agricultural banks and credit
unions, as had already happened in Denmark, and also to legislate
for state-aided schemes of land purchase (*ESG*, 14–15). Cooperatives
were in his opinion 'the ideal form of ownership and management . . .
since this is the form which permits of the fullest human development
of the worker and encourages individual initiative together with the
sense of responsibility and solidarity' (*ESG*, 18).

As for the mining industry, a corresponding economic system
should be introduced there, with the creation of local cooperative
ventures that involved worker ownership and control of individual mines. These should then be linked up into district federations
(*ESG*, 19). Works councils, he pointed out, had long been introduced
in Holland, Belgium and Czecho-Slovakia (*ESG*, 20). Davies also
admired the way in which Denmark had established a technologi-
cal institute in Copenhagen to provide workers with training in the
newest developments 'in industrial mechanism and technique' (*ESG*,
320). And the Welsh industrial economy, he emphasised, should be
expected to prioritise cooperation with the rural areas. Moreover
Wales would need to develop a transport infrastructure appropriate
to its own internal needs. 'A co-operative commonwealth such as we
have foreshadowed', he concluded, 'is not a fantastic dream. It has
already been achieved in great measure in Denmark for more than
a generation: it is being gradually worked out in many of the little
countries that have now their independence since the war' (*ESG*, 32).
Among these, he added, were Denmark, New Zealand, Eire, Latvia,
Estonia and Finland. (*ESG*, 67–76)

So enamoured was D. J. Davies of the International Folk Colleges
of Denmark that he and his wife largely retired from active participation in Plaid Cymru from the early 1930s onwards in order to attempt

to establish their own Welsh International College in Pantybeiliau, a large house on the outskirts of Gilwern near Brynmawr, a venture the launch of which was timed to coincide with the summer school held by Plaid Cymru in Brynmawr in 1932. Consequent on his embryonic college's proximity to Monmouthshire, Davies also became increasingly involved in a campaign to get that county legally recognised as being Welsh, since it had ever historically been a part of Wales. As for Pantybeiliau, it would be interesting to compare and contrast the Daviesses' project with the 'Brynmawr Experiment' (1929–40) that was established in the town at much the same time. It was largely run by Quakers from Worthing with the laudable aim of providing some thousand and more miners rendered unemployed during the Great Depression with fulfilling work on allotments and community projects, and enabling some to craft their own 'Brynmawr furniture' for sale, frequently in prestigious outlets in London and Cardiff.

Davies's view that Wales had much to offer in the matter of the socio-economic innovations that would benefit a small country was closely mirrored in the thinking of Moses Gruffydd, another significant figure in the nationalist movement of the 1930s. His study of Wales's rural economy, published, in 1941, was predicated on the belief that 'the Welsh nation is a nation with its roots in the countryside and the land'. [39] He agreed with Davies that the Welsh economy had been allowed to develop in a lopsided fashion, owing to the phenomenal growth of the industrial areas. As a result, where once 90 per cent of the population had been employed on the land, the percentage had now dropped to a mere 7 per cent, resulting in the devastation, and virtual eradication, of rural culture. Gandhi's India, he argued, had already come to realise the folly of over-industrialisation and was reverting to development of small-scale initiatives, designed to satisfy not external markets but the needs of the local economy. Many of the leading nations of Europe, he added, had also ensured a better balance between agriculture and industry than had Britain. Thus in Belgium, 19 per cent of the population were employed in agriculture, 20.6 per cent in Holland, 30.5 per cent in Germany, 34.8 per cent in Denmark, and 38.3 per cent in France (*AC*, 8).

Gruffydd followed Davies's lead in recommending not that the clock be turned back but only that a healthy balance be restored to the Welsh economy, and again like Davies, he strongly advocated the adoption of a system based, as in Denmark, on principles of cooperation. These would become operational through the establishment

of a series of measures along the Danish model, beginning with the
conversion of towns to dependence on the produce of local, small-
scale allotments, and proceeding through the creation of larger
communities based on cooperative ventures to a network of farms
that collaborated to establish factories, marketing boards and the like.
The transition to such a scheme would be financed by cooperative
agricultural credit banks, as already found in most of the progressive
nations of Europe. And the whole system would be underpinned by
an education system designed, as were the International Folk Schools
and Colleges of Denmark, to make young people aware of the invaluable, distinctive, social, cultural and economic inheritance they had
derived from their nation's agricultural past (*AC*, 21). The outcome
of this programme of radical change, he predicted, would be a robust
self-sufficiency for a Welsh economy currently crippled by its dependence on an industrial monoculture, on international markets and on
the financial world's ruthlessly exploitative credit systems.

Another important figure of the period eager to look to Scandinavia
for enlightened instances of national development was Iorwerth C.
Peate, who came to national prominence in Wales in 1948, when
he became the founding director of the National Folk Museum of
Wales at St Fagans, an institution which was the culmination of all
his scholarly efforts over a decade and longer to raise the profile of
'popular ethnography'.[40] The 'folk traditions' of Wales – which Peate
primarily associated with the class of rural artisans and craftsmen
from which he had himself very proudly originated in Llanbryn-mair,
Montgomeryshire – were, he had long argued, in serious danger of
being totally lost to an industrial society.[41] This meant that there
would be no proper record of the wealth of distinctive artefacts, skills,
buildings, music, tales, superstitions, customs and festivals that had
constituted the traditional rural culture of Wales. He therefore set out
to ensure that the remaining physical and other traces of this culture
would be appropriately described, analysed, memorialised and valued,
and in order to advance the ends of this 'salvage ethnography' he took
his inspiration from the innovative practices he had encountered in
Norway and Sweden.

Peate had completed both his undergraduate and postgraduate
studies in the celebrated geography department of the University
of Wales, Aberystwyth, under the overall direction of the renowned

scholar of human geography and anthropology, H. J. Fleure. Having studied directly under Fleure, and specialised in Celtic anthropology, he spent some time in the practice, academically fashionable at the time, of measuring human skulls in an attempt to identify evidence in the inhabitants of modern Wales of their earliest racial origins. But he then gravitated gradually to an intensive study of the traditional social characteristics of rural Wales. In so doing, he was in some part consciously reverting to his own roots – throughout his life he took immense pride in being a product of what he called 'the Llanbryn-mair tradition', by which he meant the values and practices of the skilled yeoman class in which he had grown up and which he passionately believed had for centuries provided the very backbone of the social life of Wales as a whole. But he was also choosing to be a Welsh pioneer in a field of academic research that had steadily grown in importance across Europe in the wake of the folk culture enthusiasms of the late eighteenth century, enthusiasms which, throughout the nineteenth century, had contributed substantially to the awakening of peoples and nations across the continent. It was a movement that had impacted powerfully on Welsh culture at the end of the nineteenth century, when the Cymru Fydd movement highlighted the cult of 'y werin', a cult that found its most distinctive and influential expression in O. M. Edwards's immensely popular little volume *Cartrefi Cymru*.[42]

Peate was first made aware of the important developments in his field in Scandinavia as an undergraduate, through his close friendship with a 'young Norwegian scholar of Celtic, Alf Sommerfelt, from the University of Oslo' (*IP*, 14). But it was Sweden that provided him with the inspirational vision of what a 'folk museum' should be and of what it could accomplish. In his informative little bilingual volume *Amgueddfeydd Gwerin/Folk Museums* he acknowledged the originator of such institutions to have been the nineteenth-century Swedish language teacher Artur Hazelius, founder first of a Northern Museum (*Nordiska Museet*) in Stockholm in 1873 and subsequently of the seminal Skansen Museum, near Stockholm, in 1891.[43]

In their aims and achievements Hazelius's museums conformed, Peate approvingly noted, to the purposes proper to such important national institutions, namely 'to awaken the best in the national spirit' (*FM*, 11). Far from merely exhibiting the mummified remains of an irrelevant past, they aimed to 'afford the firmest foundation for the national life of the future' (*FM*, 13). They were concentrations of 'the self-knowledge of the nation', and from them breathed 'the inspiration of a truer patriotism' (*FM*, 13).[44] In other words, the museums were a product of the larger movement characteristic of nineteenth-century Europe, 'which aimed at strengthening the national culture' (*FM*, 17). Peate, who had become resolutely apolitical in outlook as he grew older, hoped that his own museum would become the means of safeguarding, advertising and thus advancing that which was distinctive in 'the national culture' of Wales. In that way, it would 'afford the firmest foundation for the national life of the future' (*FM*, 13). That is why he was at pains to explain that he intended the term 'folk museum' to stand 'for the whole community or nation and not merely a part of it' (*FM*, 13). 'Its purpose is to present a concise picture of a nation's life and culture – the traditional culture, the native way of life' (*FM*, 23). Sadly, implicit in such a conclusion, however, was Peate's conviction that industrial south Wales was a foreign phenomenon, the result of an invasion and consequently alien to 'the native way of life' he nostalgically associated exclusively with the rural life of the Welsh countryside, particularly the more inaccessible inland and upland areas of the country.

Peate then proceeded to trace the spread of the Folk Museum movement to other Scandinavian countries. Norway established one in Lillehammer in 1904, thanks to Anders Sandvig, and the National Folk Museum of Norway, established a short distance from Oslo in 1894, was also the creation of a single determined visionary, in this case Dr Hans Aall (*FM*, 25–7). Peate's poetic nature had been stirred, he reported, by the visit he had paid in 1946 to the museums in Sweden and Norway:

> I felt that I had consciously conquered Time and had returned to a distant past to find revealed to me the spirit of far-off ages whose mystery I had never expected to penetrate. At Skansen . . . the past took complete possession of me; at Maihaungen I came to know the spirit and nature of the Gudbrandsdal in a way which would have been impossible had I contented myself with merely a tour of the region itself; at Bygdoy I had completely forgotten that I was within half-an-hour's distance of Oslo, and had just as completely lost all feeling of being in a museum. The *living* past of Norway took shape before me and I felt that I understood its traditions and the very foundations of its society. It is indeed difficult to imagine the effect of such a museum upon the members of the nation which it serves. It is certain – and many Scandinavians so testify – that it is incalculable. To quote one of them: 'It is a deep well of living waters invigorating the soul of the nation.' (*FM*, 29)

This is an important autobiographical and confessional passage that lays bare the fusion of poetry and scholarship in Peate and in the museum he created, with the invaluable assistance of Francis G. Payne, whose part in the process tends to be overlooked. In Peate's loving view it was what later came to be termed 'a museum without walls'. It afforded privileged access to the very quintessence of national life, the very soul of a people. And it was Scandinavia that had been the Muse benignly and providentially guiding all his efforts. What has been insufficiently understood by Peate's interpreters is that the connection between his poetry and his ethnographical work was a deeply intimate one; a mystic bond tied the one to the other. They were the alternative expressions of a single, complex, integrated sensibility. Peate was in reality the scholar-poet of Matthew Arnold's dreams.

From Sweden and Norway, Peate proceeded to consider Denmark, which developed its folk museum on a basis laid by Peter Holm at Aarhus in 1909 (*FM*, 29) along the new lines of a 'town museum'. From that time onwards there was a positive outbreak of museum-creation across Scandinavia, and Peate approvingly noted the dynamic contribution they made to contemporary society, serving as 'living community-centres not memorials of a dead culture. Each is the fountainhead of a new cultural energy' (*FM*, 33). In establishing St Fagans, Peate was therefore hoping to launch a (deeply conservative) project of national revival in Wales parallel in purpose to the reconstruction of the Welsh industrial economy along agrarian lines envisaged by Davies and Gruffydd, although he did wryly note that the Folk Museum at Trondheim had played host to meetings held by all sorts of political parties, including the communists (*FM*, 35). By 1948, Peate confidently noted, Folk Museums had spread, via Finland, to many of the countries of continental Europe.

He then turned his attention to a summary of the movement to establish Folk Museums first in England and subsequently in Wales, and paid generous tribute to the role of Dr W. Evans Hoyle (first director of the National Museum of Wales) and others in the latter process that first bore fruit in a 'Welsh Bygones' exhibition held in the National Museum in 1917 (*FM*, 1939). It was a visit paid to Sweden in 1930 by two members of the museum's council that had provided the crucial impetus to proceed further, an impetus supported by the third director of the museum, Sir Cyril Fox. Peate concluded his volume with an account of the generous grant of a building and vast

acreage at St Fagans, on the outskirts of Cardiff and at the gateway
to the Vale of Glamorgan, by the Earl of Plymouth in 1946. He then
proceeded to detail the work in progress there, and outlined the plans
for ambitious future developments. Tellingly he insisted that 'every
member of the Welsh Folk Museum staff . . . will be a Welsh-speaking
Welshman [*sic*]. For without this key to our tradition, he cannot be
competent to carry out his duties' (*FM*, 59). And through St Fagans,
he ended, 'we may attain new standards in our life and culture and
serve civilization yet again for long centuries to come as a small nation
which is conscious of its part in a larger world' (*FM*, 63).

After the Second World War, the tradition of Europhilia that had
been established by many of the writers and intellectuals of the pre-
war period was continued by leading figures within Plaid Cymru,
most prominently Gwynfor Evans. Having been a conscientious
objector during the war, he succeeded Saunders Lewis as president
of the party in 1945 and remained in post until 1981.[45] During that
period he became in 1966 the first Plaid Cymru candidate to be elected
to Westminster, and was again returned to Parliament in 1974, after
losing his seat in 1970. Avowedly influenced in his thinking by both
Saunders Lewis and D. J. Davies, Evans steadily promoted the concept of a Welsh nation within Europe. He followed Lewis in viewing
the history of the Welsh as beginning within the Europe-wide empire
of Rome, and also as constituting the modern continuation of the
pre-Roman, Europe-wide civilisation of the Celts. According to this
national historiography, the Welsh could claim to be one of the oldest
of Europe's nations, and their history accordingly contrasted strikingly with that of England, where the formation of an English nation
had occurred much later and had not been rooted in a European
past.[46] And Evans also followed the Lewis line in arguing that 'there
was a far stronger relationship between Wales and Europe before we
were incorporated into England in later centuries'.[47]

After the war, therefore, Evans elaborated a future for an independent Wales within a developing Europe. Britain he regarded as
being, in its established state, no more than a euphemistic term for
a Greater England, although he also tentatively supported the idea
of a federation of nations within a future, radically reconstructed
British state.[48] But once a European community actually began to
take shape, he became increasingly dissatisfied with the direction of

its development. Consequently he declined to support Britain's entry in 1973 on the grounds that the European Community as it existed was no more than a powerful club of the great traditional nation states. His own preference was, again consistent with the vision of Saunders Lewis, for a very vaguely conceived and constitutionally imprecise form of European federation of nations. This would include the smaller peoples of Europe such as the Welsh, whose progress towards independence, he believed, should eventually entitle them to their own place in such an assembly.

Viewed from a British perspective, Evans's post-war version of pan-Europeanism could be regarded as a distinct Welsh inflection of the plethora of pro-European trends in the Britain of that period. These have been outlined in masterly fashion and in all their bewildering variety and complexity by Jose Harris.[49] The ground had been prepared during the war, she points out, by a number of individuals, prominently including Cyril Connolly, whose influential periodical *Horizon* consistently featured leading continental writers and thinkers. Also of significance was the number of distinguished and original European intellectuals, both of Marxist persuasion and otherwise, who had sought refuge in Britain during the 1930s and were beginning to impact powerfully on the intellectual scene after the war.

As Harris points out, many politicians and thinkers during the war itself had been primarily interested in safeguarding British interests both at home and across the empire, and pro-Europeans of that time were very wary of advancing any model that might even remotely resemble the infamous 'new European order' advocated by Hitler. Direct experience of Europe was at a premium amongst ordinary Britons during the conflict, and, after the countries of the Empire, it was the Soviet Union that commanded general respect once Stalin had entered the war. After 1945 many preferred to view Britain's future not as involving closer union with Europe, but rather as acting the role of 'benevolent guide, neighbour and friend' to a revitalised Europe (*ETC*, 47):

> Even among those who were unequivocally committed to Europe not just as a strategic gambit but as an imaginative ideal, there was clearly a world of difference between those who saw the continent as the historic site of culture, liberty, classicism and Christianity, and those who viewed it in much more bureaucratic and functional terms as ripe for various models of institutional 'reconstruction' and 'modernization'. (*ETC*, 46–7)[50]

Gwynfor Evans, like his mentor and model Saunders Lewis, is clearly to be aligned with those of this period who strongly inclined to view Europe as the traditional home of 'culture, liberty, classicism and Christianity'.[51] Decades later, when he came to commit his vision of Welsh Europeanism to paper, this was the vision he consistently articulated, to what today can seem a rather unfortunate and counterproductive degree, given its markedly pious character, although in person Evans was the most gentle, principled and ardently ecumenical of persons.

Notes

[1] Hywel Francis, *Miners Against Fascism* (London: Lawrence and Wishart, 1984) (hereafter *MAF*); Robert Stradling, *Wales and the Spanish Civil War, 1936–39* (Cardiff: University of Wales Press, 2004); Antony Beevor, *The Spanish Civil War* (London: Orbis, 1982). An interesting first-hand account by a Brigader from Aberdare of his service in Spain is Edwin Greening, *From Aberdare to Albacete: A Welsh International Brigader's Memoirs of His Life* (Torfaen: Warren & Dell Publishing, 2006).

[2] Contrary to popular belief, however, this was not the first instance of aerial bombardment. Ten years earlier, for example, when Primo de Rivera was military dictator in Spain, the Spanish air force had bombed the Berbers in the Rif (coastal Morocco), who had staged an uprising against both French and Spanish colonial rule. Chemical weapons were also deployed in what was a brutal conflict that brought Franco, then a lowly army officer, to prominence.

[3] D. Ben Rees, obituary in *The Guardian*, 2 April 2002; entry in Meic Stephens, *The New Companion to Welsh Literature* (Cardiff: University of Wales Press, 1998).

[4] Cyril P. Cule, *Cymro ar Grwydr* (Llandysul: Gomer, 1941). Hereafter *CG*.

[5] For a comprehensive account of the attitude both of Cule and of Plaid Cymru to the Basque nationalist movement in this period, see Ander Delgado, 'Building Bridges? The Welsh and Basque Nationalist Parties During the Spanish Civil War', *International Journal of Regional and Local History*, 9/1 (June 2014), 63–78; Richard Wyn Jones, 'From Utopia to Reality: Plaid Cymru and Europe', *Nations and Nationalism*, 15/1 (2009), 129–47.

[6] 'India, Sbaen a Chymru', *Heddiw*, 2/4 (May 1937), 123–7. During the final year of the war in Europe, Cule published a piece in which he deeply regretted the failure of Plaid Cymru to understand that Wales was involved in a class war, both at home and abroad. The party had no chance of attracting the support of anglophone industrial Wales, he argued, unless it faced up to this truth and then worked to form a Popular Front with the existing movements of the left in Wales. At that stage of his career Cule also made clear his admiration for what had been achieved in the Soviet Union: 'Cenedlaetholwyr', *Y Llenor*, 24 (1945), 35–7.

7 'Dyddiadur Cymro,' *Heddiw*, 2/4 (May 1937), 147–50. In a later number of *Heddiw*, 4/4 (December 1938), 124–5, Cule published a letter replying to an accusation by an earlier correspondent that he was a supporter of communism. Far from it, he insisted. Although recognising that freedom and justice had come to Russia through the rough ministrations of the Communist Party, he did not believe that Britain, or other European countries, would benefit from following the Russian example. He himself was inclined to identify with the position of 'Urdd y Deyrnas', who, while acknowledging the accuracy of Marxist analysis, then proceeded to say that its conclusions could be improved through an injection of sound Christian moral principles.

8 'Dyddiadur Cymro', *Heddiw*, 3/7 (February 1938), 262.

9 'Trychineb Euskadi', *Heddiw*, 3/9 (April 1938), 249–52. He repeatedly turned to the fate of the Basques at this time, always drawing a clear parallel with Wales. See, for example, *Heddiw*, 3/7 (February 1938), 259–62.

10 This information is gathered from 'Gwynedd Museum's Guernica Story', an item posted on the North-West Wales website of BBC News on 19 October 2009. The report movingly includes a child's drawing, acquired by Williams, of the carnage at Guernica.

11 'Yn yr Ysbaen, 1937', *Heddiw*, 3/3 (October 1937), 88–91.

12 *Y Ford Gron*, 3 (January 1932), 1966.

13 See 'Cwrs y Byd', *Heddiw*, 3/4 (November 1937), 130–2.

14 'Cwrs y Byd', *Heddiw*, 3/6 (January 1938), 212–13.

15 'Cwrs y Byd', *Heddiw*, 4/1 (September 1938), 32–4.

16 'Cwrs y Byd', *Heddiw* (October 1938), 3/3, 49–51.

17 'Cwrs y Byd', *Heddiw*, 3/12 (July/August 1938), 369–72.

18 Gwilym Davies, 'Sbaen: Myfyrdod ar Dŷ wedi ymrannu yn erbyn ei hun', *Y Traethodydd*, XCII/VI (1937), 43ff.

19 Gwilym Davies, *Y Byd – Ddoe a Heddiw* (Denbigh: Gwasg Gee, 1938). Hereafter *BDH*.

20 *Y Ddraig Goch*, 6/4 (September 1930), 5ff. His first contribution, on 'The Economic Aspect of Welsh Self-Government', to *Y Ddraig Goch* was in 1927.

21 For these biographical facts I am heavily indebted to the excellent essay on D. J. Davies by Ceinwen H. Thomas, in Morgan (ed.), *AD*, 140–53. For an excellent, illuminating account of Davies as one of a talented group of Welsh 'organic intellectuals' that included Noah Ablett and W. J. Mainwaring, see Emyr Wyn Williams, 'D. J. Davies – A Working-Class Intellectual Within Plaid Genedlaethol Cymru, 1927–32', *Llafur*, 4 (1987), 46–57 (hereafter *WCI*); see also the relevant pages of Richard Wyn Jones, *Rhoi Cymru'n Gyntaf: Syniadaeth Plaid Cymru*, Cyfrol 1 (Cardiff: University of Wales Press, 2007), particularly 92ff., and of D. Hywel Davies, *The Welsh Nationalist Party, 1925–1945: A Call to Nationhood* (Cardiff: University of Wales Press, 1983), passim.

22 D. J. Davies is still listed as one of three distinguished alumni of Elsinore on the college's current website. Another is Jomo Kenyatta, prime minister and first president of Kenya.

23 Frederic Clemson Howe, *Denmark: A Cooperative Commonwealth* (New York: Harcourt, Brace and Co., 1921), pp. iii–iv.

24 The thrust of George's powerful polemic has been well captured by Eric Goldman, in his classic study *Rendezvous with Destiny: History of Modern*

American Reform (New York: Knopf, 1952), p. 27: '. . . the United States had used up much of its public domain. With industrialization helping to speed up the concentration of wealth and power, the New World was beginning to repeat the Old World's dismal story. It was re-enacting the Europe experience, not only . . . by creating a corrupt ruling class; it was headed toward rigid economic and social stratification and consequent narrowing of opportunity for the masses.'

[25] Preface, in Olive Dame Campbell, *The Danish School: Its Influence in the Life of Denmark and the North* (New York: Macmillan, 1928), p. vii.

[26] Today, Denmark has a population of around 5.5 million compared to that of Wales, which is just over 3 million.

[27] In 1944 Cole published *A Century of Cooperation* and in 1951 *The British Co-operative Movement in a Socialist Society* (London: Allen and Unwin, 1951).

[28] The 'Wobblies' was the popular term in the States for the Industrial Workers of the World (IWW), founded in Chicago in 1905. Its power reached its height between 1910 and the mid-1920s, in other words the period when Davies was active in union circles in the States. Its policies, and readiness to condone direct action, contrasted with the more conservative politics of its rival, the American Federation of Labor (AFL).

[29] For an invaluable account of the Welsh culture of the coalfield, see the series of volumes in the *Cyfres y Cymoedd* edited by Hywel Teifi Edwards. Notable inter-war Plaid activists in the Rhondda, such as James Kitchener Davies, were unfortunately to be hamstrung, just like D. J. Davies, by their mistaken assumption of this kind of commonalty. See M. Wynn Thomas, *J. Kitchener Davies* (Cardiff: University of Wales Press, 2000).

[30] *Y Ddraig Goch*, 5/2 (1931), 3. He argued that in order to be proportionate with the ratio of English- to Welsh-speakers in Wales, the paper should in future be produced two-thirds in English and one-third in Welsh. But – perhaps in an attempt to pre-empt criticism – he added that once the party had gained power, it would be an easy matter to ensure through legislation that Welsh would gradually become the majority national language of a free Wales.

[31] *Y Ddraig Goch*, 5/4 (1931), 2, 3.

[32] 'Y Blaid Genedlethol a Diffyg Gwaith', *Y Ddraig Goch*, 4/9 (Chwefror 1930), 4, 5, 8.

[33] *Y Ddraig Goch*, 5/6 (Tachwedd 1931), 4.

[34] Davies also contributed many columns to *Y Ddraig Goch* (*DG*) in which he criticised the effects of English imperial economic policy on Wales. See, for example, 'Cymru a Diffyndoliaeth', *DG*, 3/9 (Mawrth 1929), 5, 7; 'Y Blaid Genedlaethol a Diffyg Gwaith', *DG*, 4/9 (Chwefror 1930), 4, 5, 8; 'Canlyniadau Llywodraeth Estron', *DG*, 4/11 (Ebrill 1930), 5–6; 'Diwydiant Glo Carreg Cymru,' *DG*, 4/7 (Rhagfyr 1930), 5, 8; 'Llywodraeth Gymreig: paham y mae yn rheidrwydd economaidd?', First Part, *DG*, 4/9 (Chwefror 1931), 4, 5; Second Part, *DG*, 4/10 (Mawrth, 1931), 4, 8; 'Ymerodraeth Economaidd', *DG*, 5/7 (Rhagfyr 1931), 1, 2.

[35] D. J. Davies, *The Economics of Self-Government* (Caernarfon: Plaid Cymru, 1931). Hereafter *ESG*.

[36] F. C. Howe, *Denmark: A Cooperative Commonwealth* (New York: Harcourt, Brace, Howe, 1921). The book was presented by the author as being 'an

attractive subject for study by the American farmer and laboring man'. Davies also referred to Olive D. Campbell, *The Danish Folk-School: Its Influence in the Life of Denmark and the North* (New York: Macmillan Co., 1928); 'Polisi Economaidd i Gymru', *Y Ddraig Goch*, 4/12 (Mai 1931), 3, 6.

37 *Y Ddraig Goch*, 4/7 (Rhagfyr 1930), 8.

38 The book that Davies published under his own name and that of his wife in 1939, *Can Wales Afford Self-Government?* (Caernarfon: Plaid Genedlaethol Cymru) was mostly only an expanded version of his 1931 pamphlet.

39 Moses Gruffydd, *Amaethyddiaeth Cymru* (Caernarfon: Plaid Genedlaethol Cymru, 1941), p. 8. Hereafter *AC*.

40 For an excellent succinct introduction see Catrin Stevens, *Iorwerth C. Peate*, Writers of Wales (Cardiff: University of Wales Press, 1986). Hereafter *IP*. Since Peate would have no truck with industrial society, it was only after his death that the museum of St Fagans was adapted to reflect the traditions of the industrial workers of Wales as well as those of the rural artisans.

41 Late in his career, his pride in the 'Llanbryn-mair tradition' was to receive a distinguished international imprimatur when the co-director of UNICEF, Maurice Pate, identified himself as belonging to a Welsh family that had emigrated to the States in the mid-nineteenth century, and acknowledged his own indebtedness to the tradition championed by Peate (*IP*, 37).

42 See Chapter 2 of M. Wynn Thomas, *The Nations of Wales, 1890–1940* (Cardiff: University of Wales Press, 2016),

43 Iorwerth C. Peate, *Amgueddfeydd Gwerin/Folk Museums* (Cardiff: University of Wales Press, 1948), p. 17 (hereafter *FM*). Peate was a prolific and highly accomplished author, primarily in Welsh, both of academic studies in his specialist fields and of personal reminiscences and poetry of a distinctly con-servative and popularly attractive character.

44 Peate was, as he carefully acknowledged, here quoting the words of F. A. Blather FRS, sometime Keeper of Geology at the British Museum.

45 Richard Wyn Jones, *Rhoi Cymru'n Gyntaf: Syniadaeth Plaid Cymru*, Cyfrol I (Cardiff: University of Wales Press, 2007). Hereafter *RCG*.

46 Richard Wyn Jones offers a trenchant and authoritative account of Evans's Europeanism in *RCG*, pp. 123–4, 153.

47 Gwynfor Evans, *Aros Mae* (Swansea: Tŷ John Penry, 1971), pp. 26, 222.

48 Gwynfor Evans, *Diwedd Prydeindod* (Talybont: Y Lolfa, 1981).

49 See '"A Struggle for European Civilization": T. S. Eliot and British Conceptions of Europe during and after the Second World War', in Martin Conway and Kiran Klaus Patel (eds), *Europeanization in the Twentieth Century: Historical Approaches*, Transnational History Series (London: Palgrave Macmillan, 2010), pp. 44–63. Hereafter *ETC*.

50 Harris, in '"A Struggle for European Civilization"', rightly regards T. S. Eliot as having been the great advocate of the former model.

51 The most sophisticated and influential advocate of this version of Europhilia was, of course, the magisterial Anglo-Catholic, T. S. Eliot, as Harris acknowledges.

6

EUROPE, WEST TO EAST

Any attempt to determine the extent, nature and quality of cultural influence is doomed to be a dark and dubious affair at best. It becomes doubly so when the subject of investigation is a creative writer. The human mind may be a receiver and a transmitter, but it is also a transformer, and never more unfathomably and mysteriously so than when it is the alembic of an author's mind. And yet the exercise must be attempted if one is to consider seriously some of the most important and most clearly fruitful instances of twentieth-century Welsh 'conversations' with Europe. It seems evident, for example, that of the nexus of 'enablers' that operated to produce the remarkable 'renaissance' of Welsh-language literature at the beginning of the twentieth century, the 'rediscovery' of Europe was one of the most significant.

That 'rediscovery' had, in turn, been made possible by a newly established education system. For the first time talented youngsters from ordinary backgrounds, some of them solely Welsh in speech, were able to attend county school and thence, given outstanding ability, to proceed to university. Their mental horizons were in consequence vastly enlarged, and the 'case of Europe', in both its past and its contemporary manifestations, naturally became a subject of interest. At the same time, Victorian Wales's anxious obsession with pleasing and aping the English began slowly to wane with the dawning of a new century. A rising generation of Welsh-language talent, the products of a monoglot English system of education, became increasingly aware that their native language was in imminent, serious danger of being not only socially displaced but actually eradicated by the English language that had been adopted by the powerful new industrial culture of south Wales as its lingua franca. Conditions were ripe, therefore, for a 'turn to Europe' both as cultural refuge and as cultural model, inspiration and escape.

As has been suggested in earlier chapters, this turn had been signalled by a few progressive thinkers and writers as early as the 1890s. Mention has already been made of Emrys ap Iwan's impassioned recommendation of elegantly concise French essayists to the corrective attention of his Welsh readership, and of the remarkably varied body of poetic translations produced by the talented loner Robert Bryan. The most important harbinger of the cultural future, however, was the young scholar-poet John Morris-Jones, whose slight but graceful translations of lyrics by Heine and other German Romantic poets marked a decisive attempt to depart from the stale, consciously genteel Victorian effusions of popular lyricists of the nineteenth century such as Ceiriog, and the vaporous abstractions of the cumbersome late-century philosopher-poets.[1]

As the eminent scholar of translation studies, Susan Bassnett, long ago pointed out, every culture has its own internal time-clock of change. It is by no means unusual therefore for a culture to find itself out of phase with developments even in a neighbouring culture. Consequently, supposedly advanced changes in the latter will be of no real interest or use to the former, since it may only be capable of what the more 'advanced' culture regards as a hopelessly belated and benighted interest in its long-past productions. This explains why some of the writers and writings of the High Romantic period, such as Heine, could come to excite belated novel attention in the Wales of the late Victorian and early modern period and how, under the peculiar straitjacketing conditions of nineteenth-century Welsh culture, even translations such as the anodyne ones of Morris-Jones could operate to startlingly liberating cultural effect.

Studiously ignoring the acerbic satire and social criticism of Heine's later poetry, he confined himself to those lyrics suffused with sentiment of the German's early work. He thereby removed entirely the spice of 'divine malice' Nietzsche so loved in Heine's best poems, including those in which he mocked his own early style. In the long term, the significance of Morris-Jones's translations lay not in themselves – there was, in fact, very little to distinguish them from the late Romantic poetry of Victorian England, as Saunders Lewis was later perceptively to realise – but in the direction to which they pointed. That, of course, was the direction of Europe.

T. Gwynn Jones, the major poetic talent of the early twentieth century, was another with a lively interest in continental poetry. Although he went on to enjoy a highly distinguished academic career and a deserved reputation as scholar as well as poet (and novelist, and playwright – Gwynn Jones was nothing if not versatile), he always retained something of the unconventional instincts of the autodidact he had originally been. Having left education early to embark on a career as a journalist, he had had his eyes opened by his journalistic colleague Emrys ap Iwan to the potential of European examples for a young Welsh writer of talent. By his own account, he first became aware of the great European masters when he came across a copy of *Don Quixote*, along with a Spanish grammar and some old French texts, while browsing, as a teenager, in the books his father had acquired from the library of some long-dead Welsh squire. This led to his teaching himself French – he subsequently acquired a familiarity with several European languages, ancient and modern, as well as with Irish.[2] Cervantes, he tartly noted, had lived at the very time when the Welsh were being persuaded by the Tudor Reformation that thereafter they needed to read only one book, the Bible, and to understand only one foreign language, English. This, he added, was a sorry belief that had survived right down to his own time.

In the early years of the twentieth century, T. Gwynn Jones con-tributed several sketches of famous European figures to the Welsh periodical *Y Traethodydd*. These figures included Leo Tolstoy, Cervantes, Garibaldi, Uhland and Maeterlinck.[3] He was impressed to discover that in 1903 Daniel Rees had produced an outstanding Welsh translation of Dante's *Divina Commedia*.[4] He himself went on to produce translations and adaptations from the works of such writers as Ada Negri and Ibsen.[5] Uhland seems to have been of par-ticular interest to Gwynn Jones because he and the German shared a passion for medievalism, and he believed that Uhland, a product of the proto-Romanticism of the later eighteenth century, with its Ossian cult, its interest in folk songs and ballads, its penchant for melancholy ruins, and its mystic Celticism, was a poet attuned to the condition of oppressed peoples. Later, Gwynn Jones was to translate Hugo von Hofmannsthal's *Jedermann* (1911) as *Pobun* (1933) and the same dramatist's *Das Salzburger grosse Welttheater* (1922) as *Llwyfan y Byd* (1936).[6]

One of the early admirers of Gwynn Jones as a translator was the young Saunders Lewis. His review of the Welsh poet's translation of

Faust is fascinating, not least because it shows Lewis warming to those aspects of Goethe's work that for him serve to highlight the deficiencies of the cultural products of a Wales still stuck in the cultural doldrums of a lacklustre Victorian and Nonconformist outlook on life.[7] The lukewarm Welsh people, he scathingly observes, know not the true nature and meaning of passion. After a year or two of tepid courting, a Welshman marries and that's the end of it. Characters of the bold, recklessly passionate calibre of Gretchen, Frederika, Lotte, Lili and Frau von Stein would be as inconceivable in Welsh life as on the Welsh stage.

That, then, is the first electrifying sign in Lewis's review of the 'shock of recognition' as the creative writer in him is awakened, excited into life by an encounter with a major European work in Welsh translation. Here we glimpse the seeds of Lewis's subsequent remarkable explorations, in play and novel, of the *terribile* of human sexual passion. Here we have the shy first emergence of that commitment to test life to the full by going to its utmost extremes upon which the mature Lewis was to base his deliberately high-risk conversion to a precariously stabilising Catholic faith.

The second sign of what is to come becomes apparent when Lewis spends some time elaborating on how indebted Goethe, the ultimate modern, was in his great play to German tradition, in the form of the many folk legends he mined on the subject of Faust: the medieval thus provides a frame for the modern and scientific. Goethe's play is understood by Lewis to exemplify a complex fusion of old and new – exactly the creatively combustive combination that he himself was shortly to attempt in his plays. Lastly, Lewis the youthful creative writer is excited by the way in which, in Gwynn Jones's translation of the play, *Faust* offers a revelation not just of the possibility but of the very necessity of turning to poetry when attempting drama dedicated to exploring human nature to its depths. Poetry is the only form of human discourse remotely adequate to such a formidable challenge, as Lewis was soon to attempt to prove in his own early work. In short, this incisive review is testimony to the power of an engagement with European literature to reorient and revivify Welsh-language literature at the beginning of the twentieth century.

Lewis demonstrates awareness of this repeatedly in several key reviews, most notably of the mature work of T. H. Parry-Williams. But before attending to them, it is important to note how Parry-Williams came, as a young man, to be caught up for a brief but highly influential period in the heady atmosphere of the early modernist revolution on the continent. Having enjoyed a stellar career as a budding philologist and phonologist first at Aberystwyth and then at Oxford, he went abroad from 1911 to 1913 to complete his pre-war studies under the renowned Celticist Rudolf Thurneysen and other scholars of like international eminence at the ancient university of Freiburg.[8] At the pioneering department of experimental psychology there he was exposed to the new 'science' of psychoanalysis, and rubbed shoulders with the likes of Heidegger and Benjamin, both of them students following a psychology course at that time. After his two-year period in Freiburg he spent some months holidaying in Switzerland (where he had the opportunity to view contemporary Expressionist art). In the wake of all this he was to write a provocative early essay welcoming the new modernist 'cult of the foul' in art as a welcome shock to the late Romantic establishment in poetry in Wales and its drearily predictable productions (*Ff*, 181–5).

April 1913 saw Parry-Williams arrive in Paris to study at the Sorbonne with Joseph Vendryes, another famous Celtic linguist, and Joseph Loth, a friend of Saussure. The star at the Collège de France, however, was the Existential phenomenologist Henri Bergson whose lectures, attended by Parry-Williams, were mesmeric exercises in thinking aloud, which was to become the signature feature of the Welshman's later remarkable *Ysgrifau* (essays). But his extra-mural 'education' proved to be at least as important. He roamed abroad to enjoy both the high life (*The Rite of Spring* with Diaghilev's *Ballets Russes*) and (however timidly) the low life of Paris, and to explore the revolution in the visual arts embodied in the sculpture of Rodin and the bewildering spectrum of artistic experimentation evident in the productions of the Fauves, the Cubists, and all the other even more astonishingly transgressive artists of the post-Impressionist generation. Parry-Williams's mature essays have been suggestively labelled instances of 'literary Cubism' (*Ff*, 259), and the work of the Cubists was featured in the *Salon d'Automne* exhibition he visited in 1913. He also spent some time in the company of Gwendoline Davies who, along with her sister Margaret, went on to assemble the notable collection of Impressionist and post-Impressionist art now available in the National Museum of Wales. Both in Freiburg and in Paris he became an avid cinema-goer, and was to remain a fan of film for the rest of his life.

On his return to Wales he contributed several prescient and highly percipient essays on European modernism to the student periodical

at the University College of Wales, Aberystwyth. A remarkably
gifted poet himself, he proceeded to incorporate some of the new
psychology he had encountered in his first great eisteddfodic success, *Y Mynydd/The Mountain*, a major winner in 1912. In 1915 this
was followed by *Eryri/Snowdonia*, an *awdl* (strict-metre ode) boldly
proclaiming itself to be chromatic in character, in the manner of
those rabid connoisseurs of colour, the Fauves. Its opening line is 'Fy
nghalon gan liw sydd mewn caethiwed' ('My heart is imprisoned by
colour').[9] It is divided into three sections, each of them an attempt
to paint Parry-Williams's beloved native region in a different colour
corresponding to the different 'moods' of weather and landscape in
those fickle mountainous parts. Grey, white, ruddy red, each in turn
sets the tone of a section.

A daringly innovative work in its day, *Eryri* can now seem little
more than an interesting curiosity. The archaic language makes it as
unintelligible as it is indigestible, and seems to doom it to dismiss-
ive classification as an interesting scholastic exercise in a rebarbative
Parnassian mode. But it has also been challengingly revalued of late
as a deliberately overwritten text, and understood as an exercise in
the kind of ironically self-reflexive and self-undercutting poetics that
characterised several major modernist productions (*Ff*, 373). There
is, I would venture to add, already a hint of the same tendency in
some sections of T. Gwynn Jones's great *awdl* of a dozen years earlier,
Ymadawiad Arthur.[10]

Parry-Williams himself soon came to recognise the shortcomings
of his eisteddfodic successes. From the 1920s onwards his writings in
both poetry and prose underwent a startlingly abrupt transformation
to which his awareness of continental modernism again made a material contribution, although one of its most immediate and important
causes was Parry-Williams's traumatic experience as an avowed pacifist in a town and college community jingoistically supportive of war.
In the short term, it wrung from him essays and poems (in English as
well as in Welsh) much more committedly 'naked' (a favourite word
of his) in their confrontation of the crises of emotion and of the
sometimes ugly realities of living. In the long term, it rendered him
permanently sceptical, wary, chronically quizzical, teasingly interroga-
tory; and out of this new temperament he fashioned the remarkable
work of his maturity, carefully calibrated to suit the ubiquitous relativism of a thoroughly disenchanted post-Einsteinian universe. His
whole sensibility had undergone an education not dissimilar to that to

which T. S. Eliot had been so thrillingly exposed when first he encountered the post-Romantic (and today we might even anachronistically
add 'postmodernist') ironies of Laforgue.

Also relevant to Parry-Williams's cultural 'conversion' might have
been his years of studying abroad and awareness of Saussure. He
had become 'estranged' from his native language of Welsh, so that
when he returned home it was briefly as if he were entering a strange
world. Language had become radically defamiliarised. Its arbitrari-
ness had been nakedly exposed. Thereafter he deployed Welsh with
a curious mixture of intuitive familiarity and a kind of detachment
that encouraged the linguistic hybridity and casual experimentation
that complemented his off-handed colloquial 'rhymes' (pointedly anti-
bardic) and the cunningly Byzantine indeterminacies of his equally
casual and artfully inconclusive ruminative 'essays'. His period of
immersion in German may also have encouraged him to adopt some
of the more unconventional features of his characteristic prose style,
such as its composite, portmanteau nouns and verbal noun forms.

Given its incorrigibly ludic quality, the work of Parry-Williams's
mature years might have been expected not to appeal to the deeply
serious and high-minded Saunders Lewis. But not so. His late reviews
of this output are unsurpassable in their critical intelligence. And typically, Lewis chooses to concentrate on the author's indebtedness to
European models, while pointedly noting Parry-Williams's reticence
on such matters – the antithesis of Lewis's own practice of course. In
the first of his two reviews, he highlights what he regards as suggestive
similarities – they are not, he implies, evidence of direct influence –
between Parry-Williams's essays and the signature features of Kafka
and Proust.[11] He resembles the former in his subtle explorations of the
workings of irrational guilt, and the latter in his fascination with the
psychological reflex of involuntary recall; those instances of sudden
mental regurgitation of long-past experiences. Lewis returns to the
same themes in the second review. Here again he notes how subtle a
psychologist Parry-Williams is, this time suggesting that he may have
learnt much about Freud and Jung during his period in Freiburg[12]

During the dying years of the nineteenth century late Victorian Wales
produced a trio of remarkable scholars who were to help transform
Welsh-language culture. These were Sir John Morris-Jones, Sir J. E.
Lloyd and Dr Thomas Hudson-Williams. Of these the last was

especially admired by Saunders Lewis as most closely approximating to his own ideal of European Welshness. He was a noted linguist, proficient not only in Latin and Greek (his own academic specialism: he spent most of his career as professor of Greek at the University College of North Wales, Bangor) but also in French, German, Italian, Spanish, Polish, Turkish, Persian and Russian. Coming late to the latter language in 1931, he proceeded to produce in short order Welsh language translations of Russian short stories (mostly by Tolstoy), poems from Russia (particularly by Pushkin), Grossman's *The People Immortal*, Pushkin's *The Captain's Daughter*, the same author's *Boris Godunov*, Turgenev's *Fathers and Sons*, Gogol's *Dead Souls* and some fourteen Russian plays, including Chekhov's farce *The Bear*. He also published *Athalia*, the only complete translation into Welsh of a play by Racine, and *Bannau Llên Pwyl* (1953), highlights of Polish literature.

That output alone would have been enough to justify Saunders Lewis's description of him as a brilliant humanist of the age; and as 'one of the giants of our literature, opening windows for Welsh writers onto worlds other than that of England. (*MC*, 11). One work in particular drew admiration from Lewis, who sadly noted that, like many another of Hudson-Williams's translations, it remained available only in the author's original typescript. The translation in question was of *La Chanson de Rolant*, the massive eleventh-century *chanson de geste* that, following its discovery and first publication in 1837 (therefore roughly coinciding with the publication of the *Mabinogion*), was adopted as the national epic of France. Lewis ended his review of Hudson-Williams's output with a brilliant and succinct reflection both on the glory of the difficult art of translation and on the impossibility of adequately transferring some of the greatest classics into any other tongue. As instances of the latter he listed the work of the dramatists he himself most highly admired: Lope de Vega, Calderón, Corneille, Racine, Marivaux (*MC*, 12). But as to the inestimable cultural value of the successful translations of Hudson-Williams, Lewis proceeded to note that 'every literature is a secret the key to which rests under the doorstep of family and village and country. To become one of the family is to be able to discover the key and to use it to open the door' (*MC*, 13). Hudson-Williams had provided Welsh readers with precisely such a key and in Lewis's authoritative opinion he was accordingly to be revered as an aristocrat of Welsh letters.

Lewis's tribute, as deserved as it was brilliant and heartfelt, came at the end of a half-century of translation work in Welsh completed by a virtual 'school' of translators, pre-eminent amongst whom was Hudson-Williams. One of the most intriguing works to appear was an anthology of short stories from Hungary, in a work jointly prepared by Tamâs Kablebô and G. M. Ashton, furnished with a brief overview of Hungarian history and short biographies of each of the ten writers whose work was featured.[13] From 1920 to 1927 more than a dozen translations appeared in the groundbreaking series Cyfres y Werin, edited by Ifor L. Evans and Henry Lewis. Scarcely could a title – 'the People's Series', a populist gesture based on nostalgic belief in 'y werin' – have been more naively inappropriate, given that among the highbrow authors featured were Ibsen, Maupassant, Daudet, Gogol, Lamennais, Molière, Descartes, Goethe, Schiller, Luther and three Czech writers: Yaroslav Vrchlicky was a leading Czech poet and translator of the late nineteenth century, Svatopluk a noted Czech satirist in poetry and prose of the Czech middle class, and Jan Neruda likewise a sardonic commentator on the bourgeoisie. When briefly revived in 1950 under the imprint of the University of Wales Press, the series was further to include works by Sophocles, La Fontaine, Boccaccio, Keller, Balzac, Giovanni Mosca (a notable Italian satirist of the inter-war period) and André Gide. In the aftermath of the Great War several Welsh translations of classics of European theatre were produced explicitly for performance by the innumerable amateur companies of the period, one of these being a translation of the play *Mair Magdalen*, by Maurice Maeterlinck.[14]

Mair Magdalen was written for performance at the National Eisteddfod at Fishguard, and the festival had long shown an interest in translations. The immediate impetus behind the translation competition held at Pontypool in 1924 was an awareness of the paucity of Welsh-language novels, as was emphasised by the main adjudicator, Professor Morgan Watkin, who had been educated at Paris and Zurich and became professor of French and Romance Philology at University College, Cardiff. He was one of the first scholars to argue (controversially) for the extensive influence of French literature on the literature of Wales. The competition winner that year was a barrister, Nathaniel Thomas, for his translation of *Pêcheur d'Islande* by Pierre Loti (Louis Marie-Julien Viaud), a popular novel set among the Breton fishing community.[15] Understandably enough, Brittany continued in this period to compel Welsh attention, as seen in Gwenda

Gruffydd's 1930 translation of stories by Anatole Le Braz.[16] Likewise, R. Silyn Roberts translated a novel by the prolific early nineteenth-century Breton novelist Émile Souvestre as *Bugail Geifr Lorraine*.[17] The short story genre naturally appealed to the country that had produced Kate Roberts, and so in 1945 R. J. Paul-Williams published an anthology of short fiction by Daudet, Flaubert, Maupassant, Anatole France and others through the Welsh press of Foyle's bookshop in London.[18]

An interest in adding to the tiny repertoire of popular Welsh novels prompted T. Ifor Rees to translate *La Terre qui Meurt* (1899) by René Bazin as *Rousille*.[19] Decades later, the same intent lay behind the admirable and enterprising efforts made by the county libraries of Ceredigion to supply their borrowers with readable Welsh fiction. In response, Rees, along with Rhiannon Davies, translated Henri Troyat's *Y Brawd*.[20] For romantic fiction, translators turned to the stories of Jacqueline Monsigny (Jacqueline Rollet), with both *Floris, mon amour* and *Floris, le cavalier de Petersbourg* appearing in quick succession.[21] Louis Hémon's novel for adolescents, *Maria Chapdelaine*, became *Ar Gwr y Goedwig* in John Edwards's 1955 edition for Ceredigion libraries,[22] Rhiannon Davies's *Mebyd* (originally *L'Écolier* by Michelle Lorraine) appeared in 1975, five years after a Welsh translation of Françoise Sagan's immensely popular *Bonjour tristesse*.[23] The classic novel *Le Grand Meaulnes* by Alain-Fournier became available in Welsh in a translation by E. T. Griffith in 1969.[24]

This strong interest in French novels was evidence of continuing Welsh fascination with the culture of the country's nearest cross-Channel neighbour. But there was also far greater variety. Although it was French in language, *Derborence* was actually written by the Swiss author C. F. Ramuz, and translated by Gwenda Thompson and T. Ifor Rees in 1968.[25] *Y Sgarff Felen* was a Welsh version by E. T. Griffiths of a number of stories by the popular Italian author Maria Tibaldi Chiesa.[26] Other Italian novels translated by Griffiths were *Calon* (*Cuores*) by Edmondo de Amicis and *Ricordi di Scuola* by Giovanni Mosca.[27] The Soviet Union was represented in W. Gareth Jones's version of a novel by Tshingiz Aitmatof.[28] And two Spanish novelists were translated: Carmen Martin Gaite, who had strong connections with Galicia, and the great 1956 Nobel Prize winner Juan Ramón Jimenez.[29]

An effort was also made to open the Welsh mind to the productions of less prominent European cultures. Particularly daring was the appearance of a Bulgarian novel of 1968 based on the late nineteenth-century revolt in Bulgaria against the Ottoman empire.[30] There was also *Tusw o Flodau*, a translation from the Greek by Eleutheria Smith of a work by C. Serracostas in 1969.[31] Two novels from Flemish literature, both by Valère Depauw, were translated, one by Dilys Price, the other – dealing with the Breton movement of *Breiz Atao* – by John Edwards from a French typescript.[32] The sole Scandinavian novel to be welcomed into Welsh was *Noson y Ddawns*, a young people's fiction from Norway.[33]

From the late 1960s onwards a plethora of fiction translations appeared, often produced with the financial support of the influential recently established Literature Committee of the Welsh Arts Council, whose literature director, Meic Stephens, had graduated in French and was the author of an important pioneering study of the minority languages of Europe.[34] Indeed, when marvelling at the richness of cultural literary translations of continental authors at this time one needs to guard against a misapprehension. The actual readership for these texts was so tiny that they would have been unprofitable to produce had it not been for the generous public subsidy received from a number of bodies such as the libraries service of Cardiganshire, the Welsh Arts Council and the Welsh Books Council.

In this period, Elin Garlick, who had spent some years living in Holland, translated *Dail Surion* by the Dutch Existentialist author Marga Minco in 1972.[35] Garlick was one of the translators of the period who was strikingly productive, with several of the Dutch novels she produced intended solely for library use. In 1968 came Hella S. Haasse's well-known children's book *Fy Ffrind Oedd Wrwg*, in 1970 *Y Ffynhonnell Gudd* (*De Verbrogen Bron*) by the same author, and in 1979 *Galarnad Annes*, by the Belgian Stoic novelist Marnix Gijsen.[36] In 1973 Garlick had published the Holocaust survivor Renata Laqueur's *Dyddiadur Belsen*, an account of the author's internment in Bergen-Belsen between March and Christmas 1944, her transportation east, the arrival of the Russians in April 1945 and her return to Holland in the summer of that year.[37]

John Elwyn Jones, the most productive of all the translators, and a figure whose wartime experiences had included highly distinguished service with the Polish underground, was almost single-handedly responsible for ensuring German literature was honourably represented. In short order he produced translations of novels by Hans Werner Richter (an important figure in the post-war literary revival in West Germany), Horst H. Tiedke, Paul Georg Kaufmann, the renowned children's writer Otfried Preussler and Eva Marianne Gowerius.[38] He also translated stories by Gerhart Hauptmann and Heinrich Böll, two novels by Horst Biernath, a Polish novel by Jerzy Andrzejewski and an anthology of Polish short stories.[39] The decision to translate Andrzejewski's *Ashes and Diamonds* was probably influenced by the release in 1958 of the film based on that book by the great Polish director Andrzej Wajda. Jones was not, though, the only one industriously at work on German texts. Thanks to the efforts of others, novels by the leading nineteenth-century German Realist Theodor Sturm, the prominent regionalist Gustav Freussen, the versatile and prolific Othmar Franz Lang, the novelist and translator Hans Nicklisch, and Barbara Noack also appeared in Welsh.[40]

Books for children received particular attention, a development foreshadowed by E. T. Griffiths's translation of the Pinocchio story from the Italian in 1938.[41] Griffiths, headmaster of Barry Boys' School, was well aware of the lack of Welsh texts for children, and he was also, as his introduction confirmed, well aware of the tragic 'break' that had occurred centuries earlier between the culture of Wales and those of the continent. A half-century after Griffiths's pioneering work came a translation of *L'Enfant et la Rivière* by the Provençal writer Henri Bosco as *Y Plentyn a'r Afon*.[42] There followed *Y Capten Bach*, a translation of the popular children's novel *De Kleini Kapitein* (1971) by the Dutch author Paul Biegel.[43] With Arts Council support, Gwasg y Dref Wen developed into a leader in this field, producing texts attractively illustrated to compete with the powerful English market. Among its publications was Elenid Jones's *Brenin Catoren*, based on Jan Terlouw's popular Dutch classic, *Koning van Katoren*, and an anonymous version (*Hanes y Nisse*) of Virginia Allen Jensen's adaptation of a Danish story by Vilhelm Bersgsoe, which had recently won the prestigious Hans Christian Andersen medal.

Centrally important both immediately preceding and following the Second World War was the commitment of R. O. F. Wynn's private, and proto-professional theatre at Garthewin, with which Saunders Lewis enjoyed an extremely close creative relationship, to the showcasing of European theatre. D. J. Thomas translated two of Molière's plays, *Cybydd/L'Impromptu de Versailles* and *Y Rhagrithiwr/ Le Tartuffe*; G. J. Evans contributed two translations of plays by Alejandro Casona, *Gofid Cudd/Los árboles mueren de pie* and *Y Cwch Heb Bysgotwr/La Barcada sin Pescador*; Luigi Pirandello's *Così è (se vi pare)*, translated by T. Gwynfor Evans and J. O. Davies, became

Fel y Tybiwch, y Mae; Ionesco's *Le Nouveau Locataire* was turned
by Ken Lloyd-Jones and John Gwilym Jones into *Y Tenant Newydd.*
A separate project of the same period was Ifor Davies's *Camddeall*,
translated from Camus's *Le Malentendu*.[44] These are all examples of
the flourishing translation culture of the post-war Welsh theatre in the
context of which Saunders Lewis's late translations and adaptations,
to be considered later, need to be set.

   That the original publications in Cyfres y Werin during the 1920s
were consciously conceived as a major attempt to open Welsh minds
to Europe is made evident in the highly approving reception that it
received at the outset in the uncompromisingly highbrow pages of *Y
Llenor*. In 1922 a review of the fledgling series by G. J. Williams was
printed, following on from a translation earlier in the same number
of a Maupassant story by Gwenda John.[45] Williams began his review
by noting how it had been the ambition of scholars from the time of
Renaissance giants such as Gruffydd Robert and Siôn Dafydd Rhys
onwards to make the Welsh aware not only of the richness of their
own history but of the wealth of advanced learning available on the
continent. The same cultural need was, Williams went on to argue,
very urgently evident in contemporary Wales. As the *Mabinogion* and
the poetry of Dafydd ap Gwilym had demonstrated, Wales had once
been part of the mainstream of European culture, but the Protestant
Reformation had put an end to that, ensuring that the iron curtain
of England had grimly fallen between the Welsh and the previously
nurturing continent.[46] The first chink in that curtain had come with
the controversial appearance of T. Gwynn Jones's translation of
Y Dychweledigion by Ibsen for Cyfres y Werin in 1920. With this
important series, Williams concluded, came the hope that the rising
generation of Welsh writers would at last be equipped to respond
fully to modern life. His optimism was shared, and if anything magnified, by the ever passionate W. J. Gruffydd when he came to review a
number of Cyfres y Werin translations in a later number of *Y Llenor*.
For him the star of the show was Gwynn Jones's miraculous Welsh
version of Goethe's *Faust*.[47]

   In singling out that translation of Ibsen's play for praise, G. J.
Williams regretted that it had provoked the predictable puritanical
accusation of its being too 'immoral' for print, let alone performance. Literature, he asserted, was not a branch of morality, and
Nonconformist Wales was proving culpably slow and reluctant
to learn that crucial lesson. His comments are a reminder of the

contribution made by a familiarity with Ibsen's plays to the emer-
gence before and after the First World War of a drama movement
in Wales, a central aim of which was to dismantle the prejudices of
Nonconformist culture. Ibsen's most insurrectionary play, *A Doll's
House* appeared in Welsh in 1926, although it had been translated by
Ifor Williams from English rather than from Norwegian.[48] In 1930,
Tom Parry and R. Hughes produced a translation of *Hedda Gabler*
specifically for acting by the Welsh Drama Society of the University
College of North Wales, Bangor.[49]

Many of the iconoclastic young dramatists of the period after the
First World War found Ibsen's exposure of the complex hypocrisy
of the claustrophobic Calvinistic culture of bourgeois Norway very
much to their taste and to their purpose. Among the most notable
of the resultant productions were *Ble Ma Fa?* (1913) by D. T. Davies,
the same author's *Ephraim Harris* (1920) and the equally challenging *Beddau'r Proffwydi* (1913) by the Young Turk W. J. Gruffydd.
Another of the luminaries of this movement was R. G. Berry, whose
play *Asgre Lân* (1916) also raised the hackles of the chapel faithful.[50] It is interesting therefore to note Berry's review for *Y Llenor* of
another of Ibsen's plays, *Yr Ymhonwyr/The Pretenders*, this time rendered into a Welsh Liverpudlian dialect by J. Glyn Davies and D. E.
Jenkins. Berry approvingly notes how the play reaffirms Ibsen's determination, already evident in this early historical drama, to emphasise
the individual's immutable responsibility to society, a heavy responsibility indeed, which might well require the dramatist to adopt the
role of unpopular truth-teller.[51]

But this enthusiasm for Ibsen was not shared by the young
Saunders Lewis, who deplored what he (rather puzzlingly, given
Ibsen's enlarging use of symbols) viewed as the Norwegian's nar-
rowing of the scope of the stage to 'realistic' representation. In
The Eve of St John – Lewis's first attempt at a play and his only
English-language stage production – he sought to reconnect drama in
Wales with what he rather fancifully believed to be its deep roots in a
pre-Nonconformist popular culture of legend, folk tale and supersti-
tion.[52] The popular late eighteenth-century stylised verse 'Interludes'
of Twm o'r Nant were later to engross his attention.

Saunders Lewis was undoubtedly the most richly complex, as he
was the most electrifyingly visionary, of all twentieth-century Welsh

Europeans. His is the most commanding example of a Europeanism born of a great creative imagination. Fortunately, his remarkable achievements in this connection have already been excellently explored elsewhere and its sociopolitical implications examined in a previous chapter. But no one has so far noted that Lewis himself was appreciatively well aware of belonging to the first important generation of modern Welsh scholars with a deep professional understanding of continental cultures. Four of these, university professors all in due course, with whom he enjoyed a particularly close and admiring association were T. Hudson Williams, Morgan Watkin,[53] John Heywood Thomas and P. Mansell Jones,[54] the last-named being a close lifelong friend with whom Lewis liked to holiday in France.

As Lewis makes very clear in the intimate tribute he paid to Mansell Jones shortly after his death in 1968, these friendships were for him important reinforcements of his European commitments, providing invaluable evidence that a substantial and meaningful Welsh Europeanism was a very real possibility (*MC*, 242–6). Indeed parts of that tribute read like a bard's celebration of his prince as the epitome of his society's desired qualities and virtues. It helped, of course, that Jones was a gourmet like Lewis, and a connoisseur of fine French wines. But it was Jones's discriminating command of French (and French-language) literary culture, as reflected first in his wartime championing of Émile Verhaeren and thereafter in a number of important scholarly studies, including the *Oxford Book of French Verse*, that prompted Lewis to the extravagant claim that his friend should be considered an Anglo-Welsh author of the first order.

So suffused with his knowledgeable love of continental culture was Lewis's mind that it was natural for him to draw casual, and usually illuminating, comparisons between it and Welsh literature. Praising Ambrose Bebb's lyrical evocation of his native district of Tregaron in *Crwydro'r Cyfandir*, Lewis is reminded of the paintings of Cézanne. And he concludes his admiring analysis of the poetry of R. Williams Parry with the typically original observation that he is at core a tragic poet like Leopardi. Most notoriously of all, he claimed, in a remarkable lecture he delivered at Newtown in 1965, that the renowned Welsh Methodist hymn writer Ann Griffith was not a mere Methodist but the heiress of the great European Catholic mystics.[55] Then, when reflecting on the profundities of the late theological works of the important philosopher J. R. Jones in the 1960s, it was to Rudolf Bultmann and, above all, Simone Weil, that he looked for the appropriate parallels.

In a coruscating late review in English of Thomas Parry's authoritative edition of the poetry of Dafydd ap Gwilym, he effortlessly
displays his mastery of late medieval European culture, referring
to the poet as a 'Welsh Minnesänger', placing him in the context
of Guido Cavalcanti and Thibaut de Champagne, mentioning the
'French cooperations or *puys*', noting how under the old, unreformed
bardic dispensation the 'Chief of Song exercised offices not dissimilar
from those of the *Roi des ministraux* of the French and Anglo-French
thirteenth century', mentioning the 'bohemian *ioculatorum turba*',
and identifying the new attempt by the bardic order to keep 'the noble
panegyrist from the miming and railing clown' with similar sentiments
expressed by Watriquet de Couvin and Jean de Condé.[56]
Thus much, one could say, might be no more than might have
been expected of an accomplished professional scholar. But then,
acknowledging H. M. and N. K Chadwick as his sources, Lewis discovers in Dafydd's embrace of Ovid 'a turning away from . . . the
tradition of the Northern Islands to the continental and classical
mode of *jongleur* and *trouveur*'. At this point Lewis's own synthetic
imagination as poet as much as interpreter suddenly seems to take
flight as he warms to the Dafydd whose close family association
with 'French-Flemish-English South Pembrokeshire' enabled him
to become an adventurously multicultural and multifaceted poet.
Saunders Lewis now revels in Dafydd's hybrid poetry, 'as compulsive
as Dylan Thomas for the English', and he wonders at how 'Dafydd's
themes seem to rise like Goethe's songs out of moments of experience,
realised with swift intensity, accidents, and occasions for incandes-
cence'. By this point Lewis has stepped out of his role as professional
scholar and has impulsively and unconsciously begun to speak 'out
of period' with the impassioned voice of a poet desperate to recover
access to the multicultural resources made available by their unforced
Europeanness to such fortunate, though unlike, souls as Dafydd ap
Gwilym and Goethe.
His own unconscious identification, as poet, with the culturally
multivalent medieval Welshman finds expression in Lewis's rendering
into English of a glinting shard of Dafydd's poetry:

> Flashing gull on the full tide,
> Hue of snow or white moon,
> Speckless in loveliness,
> Ball like a sun, fist of foam,

> Gaily-winged fish-swallower,
> There at anchor I'd have you float
> Linked hand with mine, sea lily,
> Like a paper glistening,
> A nun cresting the flowing tide.

While Lewis clearly felt that such a privilege as the hybrid multiculturalism of Dafydd ap Gwilym and Goethe could never be his, he
was determined that his own writings would nevertheless be steeped,
to the utmost of his limited modern ability, in 'the mind of Europe'.
In 'Gweddi'r Terfyn' ('Prayer at Life's End'), one of the very last
and most intense of his poems, it was to the writings of the great
European mystics of the Middle Ages that he turned for assistance
in confronting his own imminent death.[57] The individuals he named
were Meister Eckhart, Johannes Tauler, Henri Suso and John van
Ruysbroeck, while clearly disavowing any deep familiarity with their
formidable works. [58]

Nor was his continental outlook confined to literature. At the
end of the important British Academy lecture he delivered late in his
career, in 1976, on the military career of the major fifteenth-century
poet Guto'r Glyn, he reached a remarkable conclusion that has been
insufficiently remarked upon (*MC*, 107–23). Guto, he realised, had
been serving in the ranks of an army that, during the last phase of
the Hundred Years War, had changed from being a mercenary force
to being consciously the army of the newly born nation of England.
For all the boasting in subsequent centuries by the Welsh that it was
their bowmen that had won the battle of Agincourt, the truth was
that it had been a crucial victory for an English army. Confronting
this, Lewis went on to admit with characteristic disarming frankness,
led him to a remarkable conclusion. None of the great Welsh strict-
metre poets of what he himself had proudly claimed was the Golden
Age of the fifteenth century had been, as he had long supposed, a
Welsh nationalist. The sad, sobering, truth was that they were all
loyal servants of the English king and the English state. Guto'r Glyn
had only spoken truth in his poetry when he had referred to Wales
as now nothing but 'ymylon byd' ('the edges of the world'). He had
sensed the tragic truth that the true centre, even of the Welsh world,
hereafter lay in England.

It is a remarkable admission for Saunders Lewis to make at the age
of eighty-three. Because it is a repudiation of the crucial argument

upon which he had been basing the whole of his political, as well as cultural, vision since the formation of Plaid Cymru in the 1920s. No longer was Wales's severance from Europe attributed to the emergence of the Tudor dynasty and the consequent 1536 Act of Union. That tragic schism had now to be backdated to the defeat of Owain Glyndŵr and the consequent switch of allegiance during the concluding phase of the Hundred Years War by the traditional leaders of Welsh society and their bards to the service of the victorious English kings (*MC*, 123). The Tudor settlement was, it seems, no longer to blame. Nor was the Protestant Reformation. Wales, Lewis was tacitly conceding, had already become anglocentric rather than European in affiliation a century before the split with Rome. He had, though, already edged in this direction in the important essay on Tudur Aled, the great poet of late fifteenth- and early sixteenth-century Wales, he had published in 1946. Tudur Aled, he there unflinchingly demonstrated, was very much a transitional figure, one whose life culminated in the accession of the Tudors to the English throne. And his poetry was frankly admiring of the opportunism of a Welsh gentry class now largely turned adventurers keen to take every advantage of English advancement (*MC*, 98–115).

And there was even one further twist. Lewis had made it clear during the body of the 1976 lecture that he felt a personal affinity with Guto'r Glyn, because they were both old sweats who recalled their years of wartime service as being among the best years of their lives. Given that, it is tempting to conclude that in coming belatedly to view Guto's military career as having been spent in the service of England, and not Wales, Lewis was also secretly pleading guilty himself to the same cultural 'sin' during World War One.

Such a conclusion would, after all, have made sense, since it was while serving in France that Lewis had first found himself fully awakened to Welshness by reading the work of Barrès, as has been demonstrated in a previous chapter, a 'conversion' experience more or less coinciding with his first encounter, in a biography by T. Gwynn Jones, with the life and writings of that ultimate Welsh European, Emrys ap Iwan. The mature Lewis had thus been awakened to Wales and to Europe at the very same time. Each of these two crucial aspects of his mature adult identity had from the very first been inseparably entwined with the other.[59] By the same token, his development at much the same period into a Welsh-language creative writer (the earliest of his ventures had been in English) had also in a way been a reflex of his excited discovery of the wealth of Europe's literary culture. There is no major Welsh writer, in either language, remotely to be compared with Lewis in extensive indebtedness to Europe for literary inspiration and direction.

The enduring fascination of Saunders Lewis with continental theatre has been roughly outlined by Bruce Griffiths as follows:

> The influence of France has been especially great on him. He has an obvious affinity with Pierre Corneille; he has translated Molière and written a pastiche of him, *Love's the Doctor*; [60] he has translated Beckett's *En attendant Godot*[61] and adapted Balzac's *Le colonel Chabert*[62] as a moving radio play. *Amlyn and Amig*[63] is based on a French legend, and in *Siwan* constant allusions are made to Marie de France's poem about Tristan and Iseult.[64]

Furthermore, as Griffiths also notes, a recurrent theme in Lewis's treatment of the moral and religious dilemmas with which most of his main characters wrestle in Corneillean fashion is that of the famous Pascalian wager. Rather than attempt to provide rational proof of God's existence, Corneille's great Jansenist contemporary Blaise Pascal influentially pointed out in his *Pensées* that, while the existence of the divine could never be proved by reason, it would nevertheless be rationally sensible to gamble that God did exist. If he did not, then nothing more substantial than ephemeral mortal pleasures would have been lost in the gamble, whereas if he did then life eternal would have been gained and eternal suffering avoided. By the middle of the twentieth century this wager had begun to preoccupy the leading Christian Existentialist theologians whose thought, influenced by Kierkegaard and privileging as it did those critical, fateful life choices made by an individual that were the determinants of true faith, was of deep interest to Lewis.

From the outset, the theatre offered the young Lewis a forum for consolidating his nostalgic conservative vision of a regulated and graduated society, and that in turn strengthened his devotion to the classic heroic dramas produced by Racine and Corneille for the amusement and instruction of the seventeenth-century French court. The latter in particular provided Lewis with a template when writing *Gwaed yr Uchelwyr* (*The Blood of the Gentry*, although mischievously mistranslated by some reviewers as *The Blood of the Highbrows*). Set in the early nineteenth century, it celebrates the sterling qualities of an old Welsh yeoman family. Its loss of status has, it seems, in no way weakened its fierce fidelity to ancestral land now largely in the possession of English or Scottish *arrivistes*, nor lessened its sense of social obligation. It is this *noblesse oblige* that prompts the family's young daughter, Luned, to reject true love in a self-sacrificial gesture deliberately reminiscent of the Corneillean tragedy Lewis so revered.

As Lewis readily acknowledged, the play was based in outline on Maurice Barrès's *Colette Baudoche* (1909), a novella he had first read in the trenches. It is a work whose unconscionable cultural preening is perhaps just about forgivable given that it was actually Barrès's hurt and indignant response to the humiliation of losing the Alsace-Lorraine region to Germany under the terms of the Treaty of Frankfurt that had brought the Franco-Prussian war to an end. The novella is a denunciation of the German 'occupation' of the town of Metz, and a celebration of its heroic citizenry, who defy all attempts to impose the German language and the coarse, 'barbaric' culture of the 'invaders' on them. A young Prussian professor visiting from Königsberg, 'a young son of the conqueror'[65] who glories in his greased boots, is gradually charmed and civilised both by the court- liness of the ordinary people and by the young Colette Baudoche. She, too, comes to feel something for him, but at heart she resolutely remained 'a little French girl the type of Corneille's heroines, who to love, is ruled by her intelligence. She deliberated and was troubled lest her marriage might lead away from her real honour.' For Lewis, the parallels between the plight of Metz and the plight of a Wales that had been thoroughly invaded and subjugated by England were of course clear. Hence *Gwaed yr Uchelwyr*.

Lewis's mistrust of the unfettered individualism promoted by lib- eral capitalism, already implicitly criticised in *Gwaed yr Uchelwyr*, found strikingly complex creative expression in *Monica* (1930), a revolutionary novella, distantly related to *Madame Bovary*, whose frank treatment of the turbulent sexual desires of women as much as men provoked social outrage. Lewis was here consciously import- ing from French literature that bold willingness to acknowledge and openly explore the sensual, sexual aspects of human nature that he had so mocked and despised the prissy bourgeois culture of Welsh Nonconformity for so studiously ignoring.

Monica brought prostitution and syphilis directly into the respect- able bourgeois milieu of a suburban Swansea, whose underworld of lurking fantasy and frustration it thus exposed. The novella is a powerful distillation of Lewis's ambivalent feelings about the liberated New Woman, admiration and sympathy darkening into disapproval. In her headlong disregard of kinship ties, marriage vows and social bonds, Monica (a wistful fantasist like Emma Bovary) is reminiscent of Blodeuwedd. The latter is the figure from the Mabinogion out of whose socially disruptive legend (the tragically transgressive struggle for sexual fulfilment and authentic self-realisation of a woman created out of flowers to satisfy a prince) Lewis had begun in 1923 to fashion a remarkable verse drama resonant with contemporary relevance. It would not to be completed until 1948. Such texts allowed Lewis to explore the aggravated tensions in this period between women's awakening sensibility and their dependent social position.

In 1927 Saunders Lewis published a groundbreaking study of the great Welsh Methodist evangelist and hymn writer William Williams Pantycelyn.[66] Its Preface included a statement that amounted to a seminal personal manifesto. His ambition, wrote Lewis,

> is to see Welsh criticism re-established on the foundations of the European tradition that flourished and grew in Wales down to the end of the six-teenth century. Not returning to this tradition to remain in it but returning to it to develop it. Because my belief is that the criticism and philosophical principles of the Welsh literary tradition in the Middle Ages is Wales's most particular contribution to the European mind.[67]

The arresting originality of the study lay in Lewis's sensational challenge to the conventional supposition that Williams should be celebrated as one of the supreme products of the radical tradition of Welsh Nonconformity. Instead, Lewis daringly insisted, he should be regarded as instancing in his work an eighteenth-century Romantic adaptation of the 'Welsh aesthetic' that had come to perfection in the strict-metre poetry of the fifteenth century, when Wales was still firmly and securely embedded in the Europe-wide civilisation of late medieval Catholicism. To appreciate the subtlety of Pantycelyn's remarkably precise recording of spiritual conversion as a disciplined process of intellectual, rather than emotional, awakening, one therefore needed to appreciate the spiritual and intellectual rigours that characterised the great mystical tradition of the Catholic Church. 'Anti-papist' though Pantycelyn self-proclaimedly was, in Lewis's revisionary reading he appeared as an instinctive Welsh European, without his ever knowing it, and heir to a majestic Catholic culture.

But he had also been a victim of the malign culture of individualism that had been ushered in by the Protestant Reformation, and
of the social and cultural fragmentation that had been its disastrous
consequence. One positive compensatory consequence of this, however, was the intense, unremitting scrutiny of every nuance of an
individual's inner life to be memorably found in Pantycelyn's work.
So profound and unparalleled had his understanding been of the
complex manoeuvres of the psyche that it had found its counterpart
only a century later in the new continental 'science' of psychoanalysis.
In Pantycelyn's gifted hands, that key Welsh Methodist institution
the 'seiat' had come to anticipate in its workings – cunningly labyrinthine yet carefully structured – the probings of the psyche later
relentlessly conducted on the psychoanalyst's couch. It had also been
an unconscious Protestant echo of the soul-scouring confessional of
the Catholic Church.

As Densil Morgan has shrewdly (and sceptically) noted,

> By scattering across his pages names as exotic as those of Bonaventura,
> Catherine of Genoa, Teresa of Avila, John of the Cross and Jacopone da
> Todi among the dead, and Sante de Sanctis, Pierre Pourrat and Benedetto
> Croce among the living, [Lewis] created the impression of intellectual
> sophistication that was unusual in the context of Welsh literary criticism
> of that period. (*WP*, 30a)

But while subsequent scholarship has conclusively demonstrated how
almost wilfully wrong-headed Lewis's interpretation of Pantycelyn
actually was, his study remains a classic example of how the bril-
liance of many of the greatest works of literary criticism is often
laced with, and indeed energised by, a sheer perversity of approach
and of conclusion. As Lewis emphasised in his Introduction, quoting the words of T. S. Eliot, 'The important critic is the person
who is absorbed in the present problems of art, and who wishes
to bring the forces of the past to bear upon the solution of these
problems' (*WP*, ix). As a creative writer, Lewis felt he had been
called to re-Europeanise the Welsh mind. One important corollary
of this realisation, as he was to state almost forty years later, was
that 'our religious literature and our theological disputes' do not
divorce Wales from Europe. 'Wholly to the contrary, it is they that
prove that we are part of the civilization of Racine and Pascal and
Milton and Dante.'[68]

For Lewis, the seventeenth century (most particularly in his beloved France) had seen the Christian faith of Europe reach its zenith. In his incisive study of *Y Ffydd-Ddiffuant* (1667/71), the classic devotional work by the Welsh Anglican Charles Edwards, Lewis therefore found it natural to point for comparison to the works of Bishop Bossuet. But he also summoned up the unlikely example of Molière, because for Lewis his comedies represented a renunciation of the pernicious doctrine of the perfectibility of man that had arrived with the humanism of the Renaissance. The mysterious reality of human sin, albeit in its absurd aspects, Lewis argued, was as much the subject of the Frenchman's plays as it was of the great book of the Calvinist Welshman (*MC*, 169). Further proof of the sophisticated European scope of Welsh religious writing in the golden age of the seventeenth century for Lewis was a translation of Thomas à Kempis's *Imitatio Christi* into Welsh by an anonymous Anglican priest (identified only by the initials W.A.M.B) that appeared in 1723 but had been completed in the previous century (*MC*, 189–205). There was also the famous case of Ellis Wynne's supreme visionary classic *Gweledigaetheu y Bardd Cwsc* (1703), that openly acknowledged its heavy debts to Sir Roger L'Estrange's English translation of Francisco de Quevedo's satiric dream-visions *Sueños y discursos* (1627) (*MC*, 206–24).

But if Ellis Wynne's work was in this respect the culminating Welsh product of the great Europe-wide religious culture of the seventeenth century, it was also significantly influenced, through the mediating influence of L'Estrange's translation, by the popular writings of the 'Cockney' school of the late seventeenth century. In these, London, with its fashionable street slang, became the social and cultural centre not only of the world of England but also of what remained of the world of Wales. This made Wynne, in Lewis's estimation, the first 'modern' Welsh author, modern in the sense that with him Welsh-language culture effectively turned its back on Europe and firmly placed itself under the governing auspices of English culture. The eighteenth century thus saw the culmination of the inexorable process of assimilation that had been steadily distancing Wales from Europe from the age of the Tudors onwards. This didn't prevent Lewis, however, from discovering in the 'Interludes' of Twm o'r Nant, those highly popular 'folk' entertainments of the late eighteenth century, traces of the homely sermons of St Francis of Assisi and of the grandeur of Dante's cosmic vision (*MC*, 280–98).

Lewis's reading of Welsh cultural history, which dated its modern decline to the Tudor ascendancy and the consequent death of the great medieval bardic tradition, was not, of course, one that convinced professional Welsh historians. One of the most eminent of them, Glanmor Williams, argued that the Welsh humanists' sixteenth-century dream of forging a new literature for Wales had come to naught not because of English treachery, nor of the bad faith of the Welsh gentry, nor of the unreconstructed bardic order, nor of the cowardice of the populace, but because literary ambition had outpaced the laggard progress of Welsh society. Needless to say, Lewis did not agree. These were specious rationalisations, he argued. In truth it was the economic, political and cultural bandwagon set in motion by the Tudors that had proved fatal in the long term to the mature development of a distinctive Welsh culture and polity (*MC*, 400).

Given the high value Lewis placed on the profound spirituality and subtle cultural classicism of the seventeenth century in Europe, it is not surprising that as a dramatist he repeatedly returned throughout his career for inspiration and example to the great writers of his favourite period. The stately aristocratic dramas of Racine and Corneille, with their restrained treatment of the conflict between love and duty, and their key off-stage actions reported on-stage in classically approved fashion, continued to provide him with the ruling conventions of such important plays of his maturity as *Blodeuwedd* and *Siwan*. As a result they ran the high risk of seeming anachronistic in the mid-twentieth century; grand imposing intellectual structures of the kind to which the resolutely highbrow Lewis was always partial. But it was in the present of Europe, rather than in its past, that he found the rich themes of several of his other final works, and in these – some of which ended up being broadcast or televised – he eschewed stylised verse drama in favour of a more realistic dramaturgy.

In 1954 British newspapers prominently featured the disturbing case of Nicolai Khokhlov. A Russian secret agent, he had been instructed to kill a dissident by offering him a cigarette from a cigarette case that, when opened, would eject a deadly dose of potassium cyanide. Troubled by conscience, Khokhlov confided news of the assignment to his wife. A committed Catholic, she immediately made it obvious that she could not countenance being married to a murderer. At the same time, she fully acknowledged the terrible consequences for her and her baby, as much as for her husband, should he refuse to obey instructions. Racked by conflicting emotions, Khokhlov chose in the end to defect to the United States, thus saving his intended victim's life but sacrificing all that was dear to him in his own. This was exactly the kind of real-life human, moral and spiritual dilemma that was calculated to appeal deeply to Lewis, and he duly explored its complex ramifications in the notable play *Gymerwch chi Sigaret?* Background to the production was Lewis's concerned awareness of the contemporary persecution of the Catholic Church by the communist authorities in Poland.

The typically controversial subject Lewis chose to tackle in *Brad* was the courageous, unsuccessful plot hatched in July 1944, in the wake of the recent Normandy landings, by German officers led by Claus von Stauffenberg. Their intention was to assassinate Hitler and thereafter to liberate occupied France (and if possible Germany) from Nazi oppression. For some, Lewis's treatment of Stauffenberg and his associates as tragic martyrs seemed to assume the inherent nobility of the traditional Prussian Junker class, an attitude balefully consistent with his long-standing admiration for the Welsh gentry and the military. One of his favourite lines came from a late fifteenth-century *cywydd* by Dafydd Nanmor, 'A dyfo o bendefig / A dyf o'i wraidd hyd ei frig' ('He who grows from gentry stock / grows complete from root to top').[69] Consequently, the play provoked predictable criticism from leading Nonconformist figures as well as from the left and the right wings of Welsh politics, both of which appealed to their rival versions of twentieth-century European history. But as Ioan Williams has pointed out in his definitive edition of the play, for Lewis Germany, the country of Goethe, had, prior to the twentieth century, represented all that was best in European culture and indeed all that was best in the inheritance of the pan-European Roman empire. He also felt that the post-war communist empire in eastern Europe, with all its political costs and human calamities, could have been avoided had the assassination plot not miscarried so appallingly.[70]

The state of contemporary Europe, along with its implications for Wales, was also the subject of *Esther*, a play Lewis himself intended to be both a tribute to the Hebraic tradition of Western Christianity and a 'condition of Europe' play, registering an outraged acknowledgement of Christian persecution of European Jews right down to the ultimate atrocity of the Holocaust. It also alludes, in an anachronistic manner that may owe something to the *Verfremdungseffekt* of

UTOPIA

Brecht, to contemporary circumstances such as the threat of imminent nuclear war and the condition of the Welsh as a subject people. Such a people the Jews had been in the Babylonian captivity, such they continue to be in *Esther* within the Persian empire, and such too the Welsh appeared to Lewis to be – a people whose long-term subjugation had rendered them so servile as to prompt them to assent tacitly even in the drowning of Capel Celyn and Cwm Tryweryn. In the play, Esther displays extreme courage (wanting in the Welsh, as Lewis himself felt he had conclusively discovered in 1936 through bitter personal experience) in saving her own people. A heroic challenge to the seemingly unchallengeable power of supreme political authority, at whatever personal cost, by an individual wholly devoted to the service of a higher spiritual imperative, is a recurrent theme of Lewis's late period.

It is duly possible, I find, to be awed by Lewis's theatre, without ever being fully moved or convinced by it. For all his repeated protestations to the contrary, his plays can seem full of a chill, uncompromising moral allegory. He can appear reluctant to immerse himself in the messiness and slipperiness of the human condition, so memorably characterised by Yeats as 'the fury and the mire of human veins'. This may partly have been his defence mechanism against the hideously messy spectacle he'd seen during the war, at the front, of corpses of colleagues being trodden down into the deadly mud by soldiers desperate to find a life-saving foothold. Such harrowing scenes may also have influenced his commitment to the Christian faith and prompted his devotion to the reassuringly solid theological architectonics of the Catholic Church. Lewis's plays are in truth somewhat reminiscent of the 'problem plays' of Shaw – a notable dramatist of the early twentieth century never mentioned either by Lewis or his interpreters. And even his obsession with the theatre of seventeenth-century France, both aristocratic and popular, may have done his creative genius no favours. Given his aspiration, in several of his late plays, to a more realistic theatre, he might have done worse than to turn away from Europe and towards the contemporary United States, whose vulgar culture he so despised. There he could have discovered impressive examples of such theatrical modes and conventions being put to authentically tragic use, in masterpieces such as Arthur Miller's *Death of a Salesman* and *The Crucible*.

France it was, though, that continued to fascinate Lewis to the very end, so that even when he turned his hand to adaptation and translation in his late phase, it was to the culture of France he returned. Thus he circled back to his beginning, because one of his earliest productions had been *Doctor er ei Waethaf* (1924), a translation of Molière's *Le Médecin malgré lui* for Cyfres y Werin. A long-distance range-finder for his later, mature work, it was intended for performance by the innumerable Welsh amateur drama companies anxious to participate in the national competitions sponsored between the two wars by the eccentric Lord Howard de Walden. The hope was that it might wean them off the countless translations of popular English plays which had become their standard fare.

One of the important enabling factors in the remarkable late efflorescence of Lewis's creative imagination was the hospitable interest shown in his work by BBC radio and television in Wales. Several of his original late plays were commissioned for radio broadcast. He collaborated with Emyr Humphreys – himself a major novelist at that time in the full flush of his prime – on a series of radio translations of twentieth-century classics of the theatre of Europe, including a translation of Beckett's *En attendant Godot* in November 1962. Ambitious in scope, the series was deliberately intended by Humphreys, like Cyfres y Werin forty years earlier, to open the windows of Wales towards Europe. It featured plays by the highly distinguished Italian dramatist Ugo Betti, Dino Buzzati (best known as the author of *The Tartar Steppe*), the wildly carnivalesque Spanish playwright Fernando Arrabal – companion in spirit to the Surrealists and heir to the theatre of Artaud – the Swiss Friedrich Dürrenmatt who favoured an epic stage, the ironist Max Frisch and René de Obaldia, who specialised in sophisticated comedy. A decade later, several of these texts were published by the University of Wales Press as part of a series of European works by a number of authors that appeared in two series, Y Ddrama yn Europ and Dramâu'r Byd. Among the authors featured were Chekhov, Jean-Paul Sartre, Jean Anouilh, Federico García Lorca, Luigi Pirandello and Eugène Ionesco.[71] At much the same time, the Welsh-language branch of Yr Academi Gymreig/The Welsh Academy commissioned for publication works by Camus, Gide, Lampedusa, Sartre, Dürrenmatt, Solzhenitsyn and others.

An enigmatic play by an agnostic such as Beckett was calculated to appeal to Lewis, who had early embraced the theology of uncertainty and risk elucidated by Pascal and Kierkegaard, and who in any case was a profound admirer of daring French unbelievers such as André Gide, who defied Welsh as much as French Christians to account convincingly for their lukewarm complacent faith. As for the early appearance of *Godot* (and other 'plays of the absurd' such as those by Ionesco) in the Welsh theatrical repertoire, it might have owed something to the period Emyr Humphreys had spent in the late 1950s working closely with the Hungarian-born producer Martin Esslin in the BBC in London. Esslin it was who actually coined the term 'Theatre of the Absurd' in his important 1962 study.[72] And by translating *Godot*, Lewis gained experience of this kind of theatre that stood him in good stead when fashioning two plays of his own in the same mode: *Yn y Trên* (1965) and *Cell y Grog* (1975).

To the very end, the admiration of Saunders Lewis for any individual who demonstrated an unflinching fidelity to the very highest values, at whatever personal or political cost, remained undimmed. In 1969 he adopted *Colonel Chabert*, a minor novella by Balzac, for radio. In it an old French military hero stubbornly retains his military and moral principles, and with them his honour, despite shameful mistreatment at the hands of a shabby civilian society rife with egotism and greed. But as the disappointed Lewis proceeded through his seventies and into his eighties, he was most often moved to comedy and satire by the spectacle of a contemporary, comfortably unheroic Wales in which a political tribe of opportunists, trimmers and compromisers happily thrived. And in this connection, too, he found a suitable vehicle for his purpose in French theatre. In 1959 he wrote a comic libretto, *Serch Yw'r Doctor*, based on Molière's *L'Amour médecin*, for an opera by Arwel Hughes, but in this case he chose to pitch it more as light comedy than as the scathing satire on the self-congratulation of the medical profession that it had partly been in the original French. The text did, though, license him to show a little of the devil in his nature, as Ioan Williams has appreciatively noted.

The very last play he wrote, in the autumn of 1975 and at eighty-two years of age, was again commissioned for radio and again dealt with a significant event relating to the Second World War. Entitled *1938*, it centred on the conspiracy by Generalmajor Hans Osler, former chief of the General Staff Ludwig Beck, and other high-ranking Wehrmacht officers, to arrest or assassinate Hitler in the event of the invasion of Czechoslovakia.[73] The plot came to nothing because, by ceding the Sudetenland to Germany under the terms of the 1938 Munich agreement, Neville Chamberlain had annulled the invasion threat and thus postponed armed conflict for a year. What fascinated

Lewis, as usual, was the choice faced by the conspirators, between obedience to the supreme state power embodied in the atheistic Hitler, with his claims to represent the German nation, and obedience to moral conscience and a higher, spiritual authority. In the ultimate decision taken, in the wake of Chamberlain's infamous Munich agreement, to abandon the putsch, and thus to compromise with Hitler and an evil state, he saw the first sign of the imminent end of a Christian European civilisation that, he believed, subsequently came with the Second World War.

At his death, Lewis also left behind sketches for several plays, all set in Europe and all centring on the choice mentioned above. In Catherine of Siena's efforts to heal the schism between the papacy at Avignon and the Roman papacy; in the uprising in Palermo, known as the Sicilian Vespers, in the name of local nationalism, to expel the foreign occupying power installed by the pope; and in the unsparing attempt by the Dane Niels Bohr, a passionate pan-European and internationalist, in the early stages of the Second World War, to place the momentous development of the atomic bomb on a collaborative, internationalist footing, Lewis discerned the same moral and spiritual dilemma recurring.

Saunders Lewis's Europeanism was undoubtedly a very rum affair indeed. He was besotted with France to the virtual exclusion of all the other nations of Europe, great and small. He was thoroughly beguiled by France's own idealised image of itself, as the true, sophisticated fount of European culture. He was wilfully blind to so many of the adverse aspects of French history: in the post-war period alone he managed to ignore de Gaulle's blustering nationalism, the late colonial episode involving the *pieds-noirs*, the *colons* and the 'Algérie Française' movement, the continuing evidence of French anti-Semitism, the denial by post-war France of the strong collaborationist streak that had blemished the wartime national character. Although he lived through the crucial Franco-German rapprochement initiative that led to the inaugural phase of the European Community he chose to make no comment. The somewhat uneasy Franco-British *entente cordiale* made spectacularly visible in the joint venture of Concorde is nowhere mentioned by him. And so on and so forth. In truth, for all his militant anti-modernism, Lewis can be regarded as a typical twentieth-century modernist in his sure instinct for such selective aspects of the past, and of a 'foreign' culture, as were most likely to nurture his own creative gifts, both as writer and as politician. His

218

'European Wales' can therefore perhaps best be regarded as his greatest invention, what Wallace Stevens would have termed his 'supreme
fiction'. Nevertheless it remains a towering, magisterial achievement
of much wider sociocultural and sociopolitical resonance; because
it is by far the most significant attempt that has yet been made to
relate Wales meaningfully and productively to the continent and to
encourage it to lend its own voice to what Lewis himself suggestively
termed 'the conversation of Europe.'[74]

Thanks in no small part to Saunders Lewis, a rising generation of
Welsh writers and intellectuals found it natural, by the mid-1930s,
to consider Wales in a European context. When a new periodical,
Heddiw, appeared in 1935, it soon featured mention of the work
already done by Lewis and by Emrys ap Iwan to broaden the cultural horizons of the Nonconformist nation.[75] The 'alternative' Welsh
Europeanism of D. J. Davies, with its influence on the cooperative
initiatives in Scandinavia, is also implicitly acknowledged by Aneirin
Talfan Davies when reviewing Marquis W. Childs's *Sweden: The
Middle Way*.[76] Edited by an emergent cadre of talents, *Heddiw* was far
more liberal and eclectic both in its cultural and its political outlooks
than *Y Llenor*. Thus in 1937 it included a hymn to democracy by
W. H. Reese, dedicated to the memory of John Cornford, the young
communist poet and member of the International Brigade recently
killed near Córdoba.[77] In a later number appeared a review of a new
volume of poetry by two Welsh Young Turks. It began by embracing
the *vers libre* revolution that had been such an important feature of
the modernist revolution across Europe. Rejecting Saunders Lewis's
attempt to treat this form, in *Buchedd Garmon*, as a modification of
traditional Welsh prosody, the author sensibly argues that *vers libre*
was a revolutionary new form, partly pioneered in the USA to meet
the needs of a revolutionary period.[78] A particularly daring essay to
appear in *Heddiw* was Nefydd Owen's study of André Gide, a novelist
already noted to have been one of Saunders Lewis's favourites. Raging
against the puritanism and Philistinism of Welsh letters, which he
deemed were largely to blame for the absence of any major modern
Welsh novel, Owen commended Gide to his readers' attention for his
readiness to engage fearlessly with taboo subjects such as pederasty.
Owen approvingly concluded by echoing Lewis and pronouncing
Gide, unlike the glitteringly superficial showman Oscar Wilde, to have

been a real devil of a sinner, and thus paradoxically worthy of being considered a perverse kind of saint.[79]

In the autumn of 1940, *Heddiw* carried 'Cwymp Candia',[80] a story by Gabriele D'Annunzio translated by B. J. Morse.[81] It is a simple story about how the malicious persecution of the villagers, who refuse to believe her innocent of stealing a silver spoon, drives a poor washerwoman to the edge of madness. What is most notable about it is that it represents the very rare appearance on the Welsh cultural scene of Ben Morse, who sadly remains a largely undiscovered figure in the history of Welsh Europeanism. A native of Gorseinon and a graduate of the University College of Wales, Aberystwyth, Morse (1899–1977), was professor of Italian at University College of Cardiff from 1935 to 1966, and his papers can be consulted in Cardiff University Archives. These include translations of the poetry of Rainer Maria Rilke and a cache of Morse's extensive correspondence with the Rilke family. There are also materials relating to a number of twentieth-century German writers, but particularly extensive are the materials relating to the preparation of his two standard editions of the letters of the mystical and visionary German poet Alfred Mombert (1872–1942), whose poetry had affinities with both Rilke and Stefan George. Morse had spent several years on the continent, in Trieste, Osnabrück and other cities, and he maintained a substantial correspondence with a number of contemporary German and Italian writers.

In 1938 and 1939 Morse published two small selections in the progressive Welsh periodical *Tir Newydd* from letters Rilke had addressed between 1903 and 1905 to a young poet and novelist, Franz Xaver Kapper, the tone of which helps explain why his poetry was to fascinate both the Welsh- and the English-language poets of Wales between the wars. As we shall see, Vernon Watkins was very interested in Rilke, and during the war Alun Lewis addressed a moving poem 'To Rilke' from distant India. In it he ruefully imagined what the poet's reply might have been had he been aware of the Welshman's attempt to speak to him, and he ended up with the vision of the 'simplicity' he, too, had at last discovered, like Vishnu and like Rilke, sadly adding, 'but in Oh a distant land'.[82] When Brenda Chamberlain showed Lewis some poems she was drafting for what eventually became her collection *The Green Heart* he shrewdly advised her to note the kind of vocabulary Rilke had used to address experiences similar to those with which she was wrestling.[83] Later, she even had the opportunity to meet a close female friend of Rilke's, who showed her personal photographs of the poet and some of his letters. She also familiarised herself with Rilke's published letters, an extract from which served her as epigraph for her novel *The Water Castle*, and she took the names of some of the people featured in the letters for characters in that novel. The text also included three quotations from the poet's work, while Chamberlain's manuscripts show her attempting several translations of Rilke's poems.[84] Morse was in turn to dedicate an unpublished translation of Rilke's *The Tale of the Love and Death of Cornet Christoph Rilke* in part to the memory of Alun Lewis.

The major Welsh-language poet, Gwenallt, was another to be attracted to Rilke, and a fine translation of a poem by him (taken from *Das Stundenbuch* and directly preceded in Gwenallt's volume by another translation from Goethe) was included in the major 1939 collection *Ysgubau'r Awen*.[85] Interestingly enough a poem dedicated by Gwenallt to B. J. Morse appeared just a few pages later (*CG*, 102). They had been exact contemporaries at Aberystwyth, when they were both young aspiring poets, and the friendship born of that early bonding was to last for the rest of their lives. Gwenallt's interest in German culture was to be reinforced after the war through his close friendship with the notable German Expressionist artist, F. R. Könekamp, to whom he addressed a splendid poem and who in due course reciprocated by fashioning a striking bust of him (*CG*, 185). A refugee, Könekamp had left Germany in 1933 and settled permanently in Pembrokeshire in 1945.

The interest of Welsh writers in Rilke may well have been due to that strong vein of post-Christian mystical spirituality to which he gave direct expression in those sections of the letters that Morse had chosen for translation. Equally attractive to several of the post-Nonconformist generation in Wales was Rilke's brusque rejection of the traditional Catholicism of his family, centred as he believed it to be on a limp belief in a wan, ineffectual and anti-life Christ. A modernist child of German Romanticism, Rilke developed a radically heterodox post-religious vision that was indebted to German Pietism, neo-Platonism and mysticism that had been important influences on such great precursors of his as Hölderlin. In the letters translated by Morse, for example, Rilke advises his young correspondent to 'seek the depth of things' and thus delve deeper than could be reached by irony. He speaks of works of art as being 'products of the eternal loneliness', and encourages Kapper to move beyond his current agnostic state by conceiving of God, not in the terms of conventional religious belief, but as 'One about to come, One who is near to us from eternity to eternity'.[86]

It is also in these letters that Rilke outlined his early commitment to 'Einsamkeit', the lonely isolation which was necessary for the true artistic temperament. In the first selection of the letters translated by Morse, Rilke presses his correspondent to examine himself carefully to see whether he is truly 'called' to be a poet, because for Rilke such a 'calling' is a form of divine election. That, he adds, is a fate from which the true poet cannot escape in all its burden and greatness, and it requires him to become a world utterly entire in and to himself.[87]

Rilke became the subject of a heated wartime spat between Morse and Kate Bosse-Griffiths, whose life and work is examined in the next chapter. Partly carried out through the pages of *The Listener*, it pertained to the vexed question of Rilke's nationality. Morse passionately held to the view that, having been born in Prague and having spent almost his entire life in Czechoslovakia, Rilke should be accounted Czech. Bosse-Griffiths argued that, on the basis of Rilke's lifelong devotion to the German language, he should be considered German. Their difference of judgement was based, in part, on the distinction between Rilke as a man (Morse) and Rilke as a poet (Bosse-Griffiths). So incensed was Morse (who was rumoured to have acted as a British secret agent during the war) that he intemperately threatened to report Bosse-Griffiths to the police for her pro-German sympathies – a move that seems utterly grotesque given the terrible fate her Jewish family was undergoing in Germany at that very time.[88] Neither Morse nor Bosse-Griffiths seemed willing, however, to face up to Rilke's isolationist view of the artist and his necessary, total dedication to pursuit of his own vision at the expense of family, community and country.[89] Yet this, too, may well have accounted for his attractiveness to a Welsh poet like Alun Lewis.

Immediately after the war, J. Henry Jones published the first edition of his pioneering translation of Rilke poems into Welsh in 1945.[90] Almost forty years later he incorporated these into a more complete collection of verse translations of the poet's work, consolidating his reputation as the authority on Rilke in Welsh.[91] (In his Preface he thanks the family of B. J. Morse for allowing him sight of his unpublished versions of some of the poems.) Jones's versions cover some thirty pages, following an Introduction and followed by brief notes, and their centrepiece is the ten poems of the famous *Duino Elegies*. While accomplished, they rarely catch fire or fully capture the edgy

daring of the hieratic and occult originals. The impressive span of
Jones's linguistic gifts is further evident in the posthumous collection
of his writings edited by Gareth Alban Davies with the cooperation of
his widow. The literatures there represented are Classical Greek and
Latin, English, German (Uhland, Rückert, Storm, Morgenstern and
von Munchhausen in addition to Rilke), Italian (Dante, Ungaretti),
Modern Greek (Cavafy, Lysiotes, Ranggavis, Seferis), and Magyar
(Arany, 'The Welsh Bards').[92]

The second of Jones's volumes was another published in the series
(mentioned above) supported by Yr Academi Gymreig. Yet another
in the same series was the anthology of poetry from many European
languages edited by D. Myrddin Lloyd.[93] Highly eclectic in content,
it drew upon translations by some twenty Welsh-language authors
of the twentieth century, and, in addition to ancient Hebrew, Greek,
Latin (also Ancient Egyptian, Persian, Irish and Scots Gaelic) it featured poems in Modern Greek, Italian, French, Provençal, German,
Spanish, Danish, Russian, Polish and Modern Hebrew. In an earlier anthology of translations, E. T. Griffiths had included his own
version of poems from Provençal, French, Spanish, German and
Italian.[94]

The most striking and incisive politico-cultural article on Europe to
appear in *Heddiw* was an analysis of the plight of the Basques by
Geraint Dyfnallt Owen. The son of the prominent Welsh Independent
minister, Dyfnallt (John Dyfnallt Owen, 1873–1956), he had inherited
his father's cultural catholicity – Dyfnallt's account of his travels in
Brittany, *O Ben Tir Llydaw* (1934) is widely acknowledged to be a
minor Welsh classic.[95] His son had preceded him by publishing a
selection of Breton stories, *Helynt y Pibydd* in 1932.

Geraint Dyfnallt Owen's article in *Heddiw* opened with an exceedingly well-informed analysis of the 'small nations' politics that had
been a feature of European affairs since before the First World War.
His conspectus was wide-ranging. Noting the disgraceful neglect by
the League of Nations of the rights of national minorities, Owen
recalled the period of international admiration for the famous
Norwegian explorer Nansen, who became a passionate supporter
of the League of Nations, and of the great Czech leader Tomás
Masaryk, and of widespread sympathy for the Armenians, Poles,
Finns, Bohemians and others. He also pointed to the vociferous

propaganda about defending the little peoples of Europe that had been so important during World War One. Owen argued that such national minorities as had subsequently gained their independence continued to practise toleration of their own internal minorities, to the discomfort of Europe's major powers. Switzerland had officially become a multilingual state, Holland had recognised the rights of Friesland, the Czechs acknowledged those of German-speakers in the Sudetenland. The French, however, continued to ignore the Bretons, and the Basques had been brutally suppressed by Franco, finding support only among the Bretons. A particular hero to Owen was José Marie de Aristimuno, the scholar who had done so much to revive the native literary culture of Euskadi.[96]

Owen was at that juncture just embarking on what was to develop into a distinguished career, one aspect of which was the catholicity of his European outlook. As early as 1937, he had struck out across Europe, through Ostend, Austria and Hungary, in all of which he discerned troubling signs of impending conflict, and had reached as far as distant Romania. There, in the remote land he had hitherto been accustomed to associate only with romantic stories of colourful gypsies and the gory tale of Dracula, he found only devastating poverty. He recalled the traditional tensions between the majority Romanians and the Hungarian minority in Transylvania. Owen then circled back to Czechoslovakia, arriving there only three days after Masaryk's death, and sensitively noticed there too the uneasy relations existing between the dominant Czech society and the subordinate one of the Slovaks. Moreover, he noted, Czechoslovakia was really a hotchpotch of peoples – Hungarians, Poles, Russians and Jews – and he wondered whether relations between them and the dominant Czech culture were quite as rosy as had been depicted.[97]

During the war, Owen, a gifted linguist, served as a member of the Intelligence Corps and was trained as an interpreter intended for service in the Balkans. His diary of his wartime experiences, *Aeth Deugain Mlynedd Heibio: Dyddiadur Rhyfel*, which covers the period between the summer of 1944 and the end of 1945, eventually appeared in 1985.[98] The troopship on which he embarked (with the vague hope of an eventual posting to Romania) touched port at Algiers, Malta and Naples, where he found himself unexpectedly assigned the duty of protecting Tito (*DR*, 38–45). He was awaiting the arrival of Churchill, and Owen witnessed the preparations for their conference.

During the war, Romania's initial neutrality had been abandoned, under duress, and replaced by a commitment to the Axis cause, and the country provided Germany with the bulk of its oil supplies. But then in August 1944, Romania switched sides to that of the Allies, suffering significant casualties thereafter in the concluding stages of the conflict, at the end of which it found itself, following the period of Russian occupation witnessed by Owen, condemned to be a Soviet satellite. In the summer of 1944, Owen found himself frustratingly stuck in Naples, exploring the ruins of Pompeii far from the action in the Balkans. The diary is full of his scorn for the British army's bungling incompetences, petty tyrannies, general ignorance (particularly of foreign parts and foreign languages) and genius for misdirecting talents and capacities. One of Owen's minor triumphs was his stubborn ascent of Vesuvius. Eventually he was moved to Bari, on the Adriatic coast, where he quickly became aware that his destination was at last to be Romania. Britain had reached an agreement with Stalin that it could send a small corps of 130 men there, in exchange for admitting a similar assignment of Soviet commissioners to Italy. Unfortunately, no one in the British contingent had any Russian, although Romania was now in the rough care of Soviet troops.

Finally arriving in Bucharest in October 1944, Owen immediately sensed the ominous signs everywhere of looming Russian presence. Corruption, he found, was long established and rife. The political scene was highly volatile, and already secret Russian support for Romanian communists was beginning to tell. (During the period when Romania had been a German ally, there had been fierce fighting between the Romanians and the Russians.) The city was also swarming with closet fascists and German and Hungarian spies. Owen himself spent much of his time with the intelligentsia in Bucharest, a cultivated class proud of this non-Slav, 'Latin' country's long history of Western orientation. Several of them had strong personal connections with Britain, and of course the old connection with France had also left its traces. Many were desperate to persuade Britain to side with Romania against the threatening Russian occupying force. Owen's concern was that such fantasies only further encouraged the Romanian population not to set their own dysfunctional political house in order, thus providing the Russians, in due course, with a perfect excuse to intervene. The censoring of the press by the Russians only made things worse. The many small business people with whom Owen mixed were particularly concerned about a communist future. A particular current flashpoint was the northern fringe of Transylvania, a region that was an integral part of Romania but was now placed by the Russians under the control of its Hungarian minority.

The diary naturally reflects Owen's work as an intelligence officer, charged with the responsibility of mixing with the natives of Bucharest and of coolly analysing their political sympathies and views. He was also there to report on the conduct of the Russians who were now in complete control of the country. Consequently the entries record key contemporary events from right across several varied regions – Owen had an opportunity to visit very briefly a desperately impoverished Moldova – and to note the responses of its substantial Hungarian, Jewish, Czech and Serbian minorities. Owen also carefully recorded sound statistics that graphed the way in which Russia was beginning to extract animals, tractors and other commodities from Romania, and he tracked the Russians' forced removal of various ethnic communities. Throughout the diary runs a threat of deep mistrust of the Jews and the part they played in Romanian life, although Owen clearly deplores anti-Semitism, and sombrely mentions the tens of thousands of Jews in the country who had fallen victim to the Nazi regime. He was likewise disturbed by the wholesale deportation to Russia from Transylvania of the Saxons and Schwabians. The Romanians, he dryly noted, seemed very ready to turn a blind eye to such developments. But Owen's duties also naturally allowed him the luxury of viewing films, visiting the theatre and experiencing the rich musical culture of the city. He many times had the pleasure and the privilege of listening to the eminent composer George Enescu perform both his own compositions and works of the great German classical tradition.

Owen witnessed the virtual Russian takeover of the Romanian government in March 1945, involving the dismissal of the police, the disarming of the Romanian army and the paving of the way for a puppet, left-wing government. Even those contingents of the Romanian army still fighting the Germans on the Eastern front were disbanded. As a concession, the Russians announced that Transylvania would, after all, be recognised as a region of Romania. At the same time, news came of the Yalta conference, and of Stalin's ominous insistence that Romania be treated as a wartime co-belligerent. Shortly afterwards, Bucharest was stunned by the announcement of the death of Roosevelt. And Owen viewed with understandable alarm the reinstatement of former fascists in their posts by the communist authorities.

On 8 May he heard from afar of the wild celebrations of VE day in London. A day later he actually witnessed on the streets of the occupied Romanian capital the Red Army's voluble celebrations of the same event. Throughout the diary, Owen is frank about the domineering, scary conduct of wild, undisciplined Russian troops of peasant stock, brutalised alike by their own officers and by their atrocious war experiences. Once he had occasion to leave Bucharest and travel across country along atrocious roads all the way to the Russian border, and he was struck by the terrible devastation left in its wake by war in every region of the countryside. The impressive mountainous terrain of Transylvania, however, remained for ever etched in his memory.

The *Dyddiadur* is more than a riveting account of life, in late war-time, in one of eastern Europe' major, and least known, cities. It offers us a careful, detailed record of the early stages of the Russian programme to turn the eastern half of Europe into a Soviet empire – although Owen remained cautiously optimistic, particularly following the election of Labour to government in Britain, that Russia might refrain from total domination of the country, and rather seek a close alliance with the local Social Democratic Party. He did, however, notice that an important aspect of Russian strategy was selective investment in Romanian industry as prelude to turning the country into a colonial Russian economy. Thanks to various worrying security breaches that he deplored, Owen even gained several unexpected glimpses of top-secret documents, and he was appalled by what he heard of the conduct of the Red Army during its progress through Hungary, Bulgaria and Austria. The 'evil empire' was, however, within four years of its end in 1989 before the diary was to see the light of day, and so its true import has never been properly appreciated. Interestingly enough, in the wake of what he regarded as the grossly unfair and dangerously punitive final peace settlement agreed between the Allied powers, Owen had sketched out the politics of the Cold War period, foreseeing the increasing post-war isolation of a fatally weakened Britain from a continent completely dominated by the rival powers of the USA and the USSR.

Owen's interest in Romania did not end with his departure from Bucharest. In 1949 he published a selection of the folk tales that had been collected in the later nineteenth century by Petre Ispirescu, and then two years later he published *Rwmania: Pennod Mewn Gwleidyddiaeth Grym*, a succinct history of the country beginning

three thousand years back and concluding with a brief analysis of
contemporary Romania as no more than a puppet state within the
Soviet empire that had emerged from the Second World War, a process
to which Owen himself had, of course, found himself sad witness.[99]
This study was completed when he was working with the European
Service of the BBC in London.[100]

Interestingly, though, Owen was not the first writer from Wales
who had acquired first-hand knowledge of the Balkans. In 1938 the
troubled, mercurial 'Anglo-Welsh' writer Nigel Heseltine, a native of
the borderland near Newtown between Wales and England, had published *Scarred Background: A Journey Through Albania*.[101] Reviewing
this volume in *Wales* in 1939, Celia Buckmaster perceptively wrote:
'[this book] would seem to be in the circumstances not so much a
scarred background for Albania, but a scarred background in front
of which Mr Heseltine walks and suffers.'[102] That scarred background
was his own childhood upbringing, an upbringing which was, indeed,
to be not so much described as invisibly inscribed in much of his adult
writing. Consequently, Heseltine could be seen as living his whole
life in masquerade. It was a chronically restless life during which he
saw service not only in Madagascar but in several of the countries of
postcolonial Africa, and he seemed to change wives more often than
he changed clothes.

Of that tiny band of Welsh whose view of Europe extended well
beyond the borders of the powerful nation states crammed into
the western edge of the continent – the band to which Owen and
Heseltine both belonged – the most distinguished by far was Gareth
Jones, who deserves to be honoured as the patron saint of Welsh
journalism.[103] Born in Barry in 1905, he studied French, German and
Russian with distinction first at Aberystwyth and then at Cambridge,
before becoming private secretary to Lloyd George in 1930, interrupt-
ing his service in that post for a period during which he studied the
economics of business in the USA. In 1929 he paid an official visit
to Italy to investigate the measure taken to assist the unemployed,
involving the draining of the Pontine marshes.

From 1930 to 1933 the young Welshman paid three visits to the
USSR, writing articles for various newspapers about Stalin's five-
year plan. The experience provided him with his first inkling that
there were 'starving peasants' in Ukraine, and in October 1930 he
duly flagged this up in the press. In 1933 he was both reporting from
Germany, undertaking an unofficial visit to the Soviet Union and

filing one of the very first reports (appearing in print more or less simultaneously with similar reports by Malcolm Muggeridge) on the extraordinary famine in the Ukraine ('Holodomor', Ukrainian for 'killing by starvation'). This appeared in such US papers as the *New York Evening Post* ('Famine Grips Russia, Millions Dying, Idle On Rise Says Briton . . . Lloyd George's Aid Reports Devastation') and the *Chicago Daily News* ('Russian Famine Now As Great As Starvation Of 1921, Says Secretary of Lloyd George'). 'If it is grave now', Jones wrote, 'and if millions are dying in the villages, as they are, for I did not visit a single village where many had not died, what will be it like in a month's time?'[104] In his *Western Mail* articles he shrewdly tailored his reports to his Welsh readership, attributing the appearance of a communist state, for example, to Russia's never having 'had the Reformation, which affected so deeply the life of Wales', and noting that the Industrial Revolution, in which Wales had played a leading role, had come very late to Russia.[105] The country, he asserted, was far more 'Asiatic' in character than European.

After his first devastating reports, Gareth Jones was a marked man in the Soviet Union, and found himself unable to travel there again. During 1934 his reporting was mostly confined to local affairs in Wales, but the following year, he embarked on a round-the-world tour that, beginning in Japan, alerted him to that country's sinister designs in Manchuria and northern China. The same year, a series of hard-hitting articles by him about the atrocity in Ukraine appeared in a number of Hearst-syndicated papers across the US. These are harrowing in their sensuous evocation of the sights he had seen. He recalled watching an old woman dying of hunger as she moved away from him: 'I stood watching her bent, ugly, tragic figure outlined against the snow.' He spoke of peasants so desperate that they resorted to eating their horses as well as their fodder. And he referred to villages where 'ALL HAVE DIED' and communities where 'HALF HAVE PERISHED'.[106]

It was in 1935 that Gareth Jones, aged only thirty, was killed in Mongolia under mysterious circumstances. While that may possibly have been in consequence of his having discovered too much about the Japanese plans, it seems most probable that his effective assassination by the 'bandits' who had kidnapped him may have been master-minded by a Soviet Union still smarting at his exposure of the murderous consequences of Stalin's catastrophic policies in Ukraine. Since Jones had written many pieces for the *Western Mail*, the paper mourned the passing of its most distinguished journalist, and duly published a collection of his essays in his memory.[107] In the epigraph to that collection, J. L. Garvin is quoted as eloquently observing that Gareth Jones had 'perished on one of the horizons he was always questing'.

On the very first page of the essay on the Eisteddfod with which the *Western Mail* collection opens, Jones records his determination to pierce the romantic fog that has for so long obscured the true facts about the origins of the Welsh and their festival. 'I think', he notes, 'of how maddened I have felt in countries such as Germany when men like Ludendorff have invented fantastic beliefs concerning Thor and Wotan and the ideal nature of the original Teutons and when charlatans have spread pernicious forgeries about peoples like the Jews' (*ISN*, 10). He strongly felt, he adds, 'that such methods are as reprehensible in Wales as in Germany'. A crucial figure in the history of the development of what was in essence a modern festival was Iolo Morganwg, whom Jones neatly describes as a 'curious literary forger', and a 'cross between Chateaubriand, Baron von Münchausen and the Scot Macpherson' (*ISN*, 10). It was the iron integrity of this determination to separate truth from the falsehoods of myth and propaganda alike that was to make Jones at his best such a notably perceptive analyst of political affairs at several key sites across the globe in the early 1930s, and that so sadly led to what was, in a way, his noble and heroic death.

He brought this clear, dispassionate, non-partisan outlook to bear alike on fascist Italy, Nazi Germany, Japan and Stalin's Soviet Union. In one of his *Western Mail* reports he recorded the visit he had paid to Lenin's widow in Moscow. While he clearly shared the sympathy felt by many south Walians of his day for the Bolshevik revolution, he was not to be duped, as were so many socialists as well as communists of the time, into idealising the Stalinist regime. As he slyly noted, Lenin's widow had been 'associated with the opposition to Stalin, and her real relations with the present dictator are not so cordial as they are stated to be in the official press' (*ISN*, 15). After her husband's death she had devoted herself to the improvement of the education system in Soviet Russia, laying great emphasis on the particular need to develop 'polytechnical education' through attaching schools to factories. 'She mentioned the word "production"', Jones ironically recorded, 'in the same tone as a Welsh minister might mention God or religion' (*ISN*, 17). Betraying his own Welsh background, he wondered whether too much stress was being laid in Russia 'upon the material and technical', and 'whether there were not other things, such as liberty and literature and religious freedom, which were infinitely more important' (*ISN*, 17). And he concluded his piece by doubting 'whether a system of education which had no place for freedom of thought would succeed in raising a generation of truly educated men [*sic*] who would think for themselves' (*ISN*, 18).

That even Jones was not, however, immune to false impressions is borne out by his report of his experience of accompanying Hitler in 1933 on a flight from Berlin to Munich. Like so many others, he initially found himself baffled by how such a small, slight and unprepossessing figure could have become 'deified by fourteen million people' (*ISN*, 19). One of Hitler's companions in the travelling party was Dr Goebbels, an influential Rhinelander who was already exerting a sinister influence over the new chancellor. Jones disconcertingly viewed him as a 'little man who laughs all the time. He has a narrow Iberian head and brown eyes which twinkle with wit and intelligence. He looks like the dark, small, narrow-headed, sharp Welsh type which is so often found in the Glamorgan valleys' (*ISN*, 20). His general impression of Hitler's entourage was likewise depressingly favourable. The people in it, he felt, were pleasant, polite and friendly, and not at all 'Prussian'. He ended his piece by explaining that the ominous background to this flight had been the vicious street fighting between Hitler's followers and Germany's communists. It was the consequent desire for revenge, he implied, that had accounted for the fierce, aggressive passion with which Hitler had proceeded to deliver his speech to the Munich crowd at journey's end. 'There are two Hitlers,' was his final verdict, 'the natural boyish Hitler, and the Hitler who is inspired by a tremendous national force, a great Hitler. It is the second Hitler who has stirred Germany to an awakening' (*ISN*, 22).

Had Gareth Jones's reputation rested on this report, then it would have been as short-lived as it would have been unfortunate – one wonders how much his view of Hitler owed to his close association with Lloyd George. It was the remarkable reports he went on to send about Ukraine that were to ensure for him an honoured place in the annals of international journalism. Unlikely though it may seem, he had a strong personal investment in determining the exact condition of the Ukrainian people. His mother had spent a period as English-language tutor to the children of John Hughes, the famous industrialist from

Merthyr who had responded in 1870 to an explicit and pressing invitation from the Tsar to establish a pioneering steel-making plant in what consequently became known as Yuzovka, and is now known as the Ukrainian city of Donetsk.

What Jones found in Ukraine, as he momentously and unflinchingly reported, was widescale famine, starvation on a scale so appalling that to this day no precedent for it has been found in the whole of human history. What is more, it was planned famine, the direct consequence of Stalin's murderous policy to starve Ukrainian peasants, to death if necessary, in order to supply the supposedly more 'progressive' army of industrial workers in the cities of the eastern Soviet Union with sufficient food. Stalin eventually justified his murderous plan by claiming that the peasants had deliberately starved themselves in protest at his enlightened communist policy of collectivising all private farms in the interests of increasing rural production. This was of course the exact opposite in every detail of the truth. It was the policy of collectivisation (implemented in increasingly ruinous stages) that had actually precipitated a disaster that was then compounded and aggravated by the misfortune of failed harvests.

Jones's achievement was all the more remarkable because not only was he one of the very first Western correspondents to file any account of what was a vast human calamity, but because he thereafter had to endure vilification for it from some of the most prominent British and American journalists of the day, most notably the Pulitzer Prize winner Walter Duranty (nowadays sometimes dubbed 'Stalin's Apologist'). These professed to have a superior, and highly positive, understanding of the true social and economic conditions right across the Soviet Union. Eventually, of course, Gareth Jones was not only entirely vindicated but recognised to have been courageously perspicacious in his scrupulously detailed accounts. The latest authoritative survey of the Ukrainian famine is that in Timothy Snyder's classic volume *Bloodlands*. He there soberly estimates that at least three million Ukrainian citizens died of starvation in that period, supporting the general picture with specific details so searingly vivid as to be barely endurable. And he studs his discussion with the highest possible praise for Gareth Jones, whom he openly reveres as the perfect model of a journalist who records experiences with undeviating fairness and honesty. Certainly, there is no more impressive example than his to be found of a truly operative Euro-Welshness.

Notes

1   Well over half of his debut collection, *Caniadau* (Oxford: Fox-Jones and Co., 1907), consisted of translations. They were taken from the German (Heine, Greibel, Ernst Schulze, Arndt, De La Motte, Fouqué, Lenau, Uhland), French (Alfred de Musset, de Jouy), Italian (Vittorelli, Ugo Foscolo), and Breton (F. M. Luzel). For an informative brief study of Morris-Jones's life and work see Allan James, *John Morris-Jones*, Writers of Wales Series (Cardiff: University of Wales Press, 1987).

2   T. Gwynn Jones, *Astudiaethau* (Wrecsam: Hughes a'i Fab, 1936). For the authoritative biography of Gwynn Jones see David Jenkins, *Thomas Gwynn Jones* (Denbigh: Gwasg Gee, 1974).

3   These were subsequently published in *Traethodau* (Caernarfon: Swyddfa'r Herald, 1910).

4   Daniel Rees (trans.), *Gweledigaethau Dante: sef 'La Divina commedia' wedi ei throsi i'r Gymraeg* (Newport: John E. Southall, 1908).

5   See the section of translations and adaptations with which he concludes *Manion* (Wrecsam: Hughes a'i Fab, 1932).

6   See Ioan M. Williams, *Y Mudiad Drama yng Nghymru* (Cardiff: University of Wales Press, 2006).

7   Saunders Lewis, 'Trosi *Faust* i'r Gymraeg', *Y Faner* (30 Awst 1923), reprinted in Gwynn ap Gwilym (ed.), *Meistri a'u Crefft: Ysgrifau Llenyddol gan Saunders Lewis* (Cardiff: University of Wales Press, 1981), 260–2. (Hereafter *MaC*).

8   For a brilliant definitive account of this formative period see Angharad Price, *Ffarwél i Freiburg: Crwydriadau Cynnar T. H. Parry-Williams* (Llandysul: Gwasg Gomer, 2013). Hereafter *Ff*. She notes that Parry-Williams studied Latin, Old Irish, Old German, Old Bulgarian and Gothic at Freiburg as well as *Das Nibelungenlied*, the *Iliad* and the *Odyssey*. All this while pursuing postgraduate research into Celtic philology! See also R. Gerallt Jones, *T. H. Parry-Williams*, Dawn Dweud Series (Cardiff: University of Wales Press, 1999).

9   T. H. Parry-Williams, 'Eryri', in *Awdlau Cadeiriol Detholedig Y Ganrif Hon* (Llundain: Cymdeithas yr Eisteddfod Genedlaethol, 1930), p. 107.

10 For the context of culture shift I believe to be important in this connection, see 'T. Gwynn Jones: The once and future Wales', in M. Wynn Thomas, *The Nations of Wales, 1890–1914* (Cardiff: University of Wales Press, 2016), pp. 185–213.

11 *MaC*, p. 23.

12 *MaC*, p. 25.

13 Tamâs Kablebô and G. M. Ashton (trans.), *Gemau Hwngaria* (Denbigh: Gee, n. d.).

14 Stafford Thomas and T. Pugh Williams (trans.), Maurice Maeterlinck, *Mair Magdalen* (Caerdydd: Llyfrau'r Castell, 1947).

15 Nathaniel Thomas (trans.), Pierre Loti, *Ynys yr Ia* (Swansea: Thomas and Parry, 1927).

16 Gwenda Gruffydd (trans.), Anatole le Braz, *Storïau'r Peilat a Storïau Eraill* (Aberystwyth: Gwasg Aberystwyth, 1930).

17 R. Silyn Roberts (trans.), *Bugail Geifr Lorraine* (Wrexham; Hughes and Son, 1925).
18 R. J. Paul-Williams (trans.), *Storïau'r Meistri* (London: Foyle, 1945).
19 T. Ifor Rees (trans.), René Bazin, *Rousille* (Aberystwyth: Gwasg Aberystwyth, 1935).
20 Rhiannon Davies and T. Ifor Rees (trans.), Henri Troyat, *Y Brawd* (Cymdeithas Lyfrau Ceredigion, 1960).
21 John Edwards (trans.), *Ffloris, 'y nghariad i* (Llandysul: Gwasg Gomer, 1973); Cyril P. Cule (trans.), *Ffloris, Rhamant ac Antur* (Llandysul: Gomer, 1978),
22 John Edwards (trans.), Louis Hémon, *Ar Gwr y Goedwig* (Aberystwyth: Cymdeithas Lyfrau Ceredigion, 1955).
23 Elenid Williams (trans.), Françoise Sagan, *Bonjour tristesse* (Aberystwyth: Cymdeithas Lyfrau Ceredigion, 1970).
24 E. T. Griffiths (trans.), Alain-Fournier, *Y Diriogaeth Goll* (Llandybïe: Christopher Davies, 1969).
25 Gwenda Thompson and T. Ifor Rees (trans.), C. F. Ramuz, *Pan Gwympodd y Mynydd* (Swansea: Gwasg John Penry, 1968).
26 E. T. Griffiths (trans.), Mary Tibaldi Chiesa, *Y Sgarff Felen* (Llandybïe: Gwasg y Dryw, 1966).
27 E. T. Griffiths (trans.), Eduardo de Amicis, *Calon/Cuore* (Denbigh: Gee, 1959); Giovanni Mosca, *Atgofion Dyddiau Ysgol/Ricordi di Scuola* (Swansea: Christopher Davies, 1965).
28 W. Gareth Jones (trans.), Tshingiz Aitmatof, *Ffarwel Gwlsari* (Llandybïe: Llyfrau'r Dryw, 1971).
29 John Grey Davies (trans.), Carmen Martin Gaite, *Rhwng y Llenni* (Swansea: Christopher Davies, 1975); E. T. Griffiths and T. Ifor Rees (trans.), Juan Ramón Jimenez, *Platero a Minnau* (Llandysul: Gomer, 1961), abridged edition.
30 Brenda Wyn Jones (trans.), Stefan Dichev, *Rali* (Llandybïe: Christopher Davies, 1972).
31 Eleutheria Smith (trans.), C. Serracostas, *Tusw o Flodau* (Caernarfon: Llyfrau'r Methodistiaid Calfinaidd, 1969)
32 Dilys Price (trans.), Valère Depauw, *Brad yn y Bryniau/Auftrag in Guernika* (Swansea: Christopher Davies, 1978); John Edwards (trans.), Valère Depauw, *Breiz Atao* (Liverpool: Gwasg y Brython, 1969).
33 Dilys Price and Iswyn Ffowc Elis (trans.), Evi Boegenaes, *Noson y Ddawns/Julleballet* (Llandysul: Gomer, 1965).
34 Meic Stephens, *Linguistic Minorities of Europe* (Llandysul: Gomer. 1976).
35 Elin Garlick (trans.), Marga Minco, *Dail Surion* (originally *Het bittere kruid*) (Llandybïe: Christopher Davies, 1972).
36 Elin Garlick (trans.), Hella S. Haasse, *Fy Ffrind Oedd Wrwg/Oeroeg* (Llandysul: Gomer, 1968); *Y Ffynhonell Gudd /De Verbrogen Bron* (Llandysul: Gomer, 1970); Marnix Gijsen, *Galarnad Annes* (Swansea: Christopher Davies, 1979).
37 Elin Garlick (trans.), Renata Laqueur, *Dyddiadur Belsen* (Swansea: Christopher Davies, 1973).
38 John Elwyn Jones (trans.), Hans Werner Richter, *Ôl Traed yn y Tywod/Spuren im Sand* (Aberystwyth: Cyngor Llyfrau, 1968); Hans Werner Richter, *Pinc*

a Gwyn – Pinc a Coch (Y Bala: Llyfrau'r Faner, 1975); Horst H. Tiedke,
Dyma'r Dyn i Mi/Ein Mann für mich (Bala: Llyfrau'r Faner, 1971); Paul Georg
Kaufmann, *Priodi ar Brawf/Hochzeit Aue Raten* (Swansea: John Penry, 1971);
Otfried Preussler, *Nos Galan/Krabat* (Cardiff: Dref Wen, 1974); Eva Marianne
Gowerius, *Cristina* (Bala: Llyfrau'r Faner, 1973).

[39] John Elwyn Jones (trans.), Gerhart Hauptmann and Heinrich Böll, *Carnifal*
(Bala: Llyfrau'r Faner, 1974); Horst Biernath, *Rhybudd Torfeydd/Achtung –
Kurven* (Bala: Llyfrau'r Faner, 1975); Horst Biernath, *Llond Ceg o Lwc/Ein
Mund voll Glück* (Aberystwyth: Cambrian News, 1978); Jerzy Andrzejewski,
Lludw a Diemont/Popiół (Llandysul: Gomer, 1975); *Storïau Byr o'r Bwyleg*
(Bala: Llyfrau'r Faner, n.d.).

[40] John Edwards (trans.), Theodor Sturm, *Y Goruchwyliwr/Der Schimmelreiter*
(Liverpool: Gwasg y Brython, 1961); Gustav Frenssen, *Y Mab Ieuengaf/
Jörn Uhl* (Swansea: John Penry, 1968), abridged version; G. L. Jones (trans.),
Othmar Franz Lang, *Holl Ddefaid fy Mrawd* (Swansea: John Penry, 1973);
Nina Watkins (trans.), Hans Nicklisch, *Fy Nhad* (Denbigh: Gee, 1970); Rhian
Pritchard (trans.), Barbara Noack, *Dy Dro Di* (Llandysul: Gomer 1978).

[41] E. T. Griffiths (trans.), Carlo Lorenzini [Carlo Collodi], *Yr Hogyn Pren:
Helyntion Pinocio/Avventure di Pinocchio* (Denbigh: Gee, 1938).

[42] Margaret Audrey Griffiths and Rhiain Wyn Jones (trans.), Henri Bosco, *Y
Plentyn a'r Afon* (Denbigh: Gwasg Gee, 1968).

[43] Elin Garlick (trans.), Paul Biegel, *Y Capten Bach* (Cardiff: Gwasg y Dref
Wen, 1974).

[44] Hazel Walford Davies, *Saunders Lewis a Theatr Garthewin* (Llandysul: Gomer,
1995), p. 165.

[45] 'F'Ewythr John', *Y Llenor*, 1 (1922), 18–25. The review by Williams appears
on pp. 71–6.

[46] Insofar as he was implying that close Welsh intellectual contact with Europe
came to an end with the Reformation, Williams was much mistaken. As
R. Tudur Jones was conclusively to demonstrate some fifty years later, the
Reformation actually greatly stimulated the interest of Welsh Protestant
ministers and theologians in the work of their noted confrères on the continent. German Protestant theology in particular came to fascinate the Welsh
Nonconformist pulpit in the nineteenth century (the entry on 'Genesis' in
Thomas Gee's groundbreaking *Gwyddoniadur* (*Encyclopaedia*) of 1855–79
cited the scholarship of no fewer than fourteen German theologians). And
one Welsh scholar of the period (Ioan Pedr/John Peters, 1833–77) walked
most of the way home to Bala all the way from Bavaria, where he had been
consulting the work of some of the most 'advanced' theological thinkers of
the day. R. Tudur Jones, 'O Genefa i'r Bala: Marchnad Rhydd y Diwinyddion',
in Densil Morgan (ed।)., R. Tudur Jones, *Grym y Gair*.

[47] *Y Llenor*, 2 (1923), 197–200.

[48] Ifor Williams (trans.), *Tŷ Dol* (printed and published by Evan Thomas, 1926).

[49] Tom Parry and R. H. Hughes (trans), Henrik Ibsen, *Hedda Gabbler* (Cymdeithas
Ddrama Gymraeg, University College of North Wales, Bangor, 1930).

[50] For the anti-Nonconformist animus of several key Welsh dramatists of this
period, along with their indebtedness to Ibsen, see 'All Change: the new Welsh
drama before the Great War', in M. Wynn Thomas, *Internal Difference:*

Twentieth-Century Writing in Wales (Cardiff: University of Wales Press, 1992), pp. 1–24.

51 *Y Llenor*, 2 (1923), 53–4.

52 The definitive biography of Saunders Lewis is by T. Robin Chapman, *Un Bywyd Ymhlith Llawer: Cofiant Saunders Lewis* (Cardiff: University of Wales Press; Llandysul: Gomer, 2006). See also D. Tecwyn Lloyd, *John Saunders Lewis: Y Gyfrol Gyntaf* (Denbigh: Gee, 1988); Mair Saunders Jones, Ned Thomas and Harri Pritchard Jones (eds), *Saunders Lewis: Letters to Margaret Gilcriest* (Cardiff: University of Wales Press, 1993); Dafydd Ifans (ed.), *Annwyl Kate, Annwyl Saunders – gohebiaeth 1922–1983* (Aberystwyth: National Library of Wales, 1992); *Saunders Lewis: Aspects of his Life and Work* (Aberystwyth: Saunders Lewis Memorial Trust, 1991).

53 Morgan Watkin (1878–1970) began life as a stonemason but went on to study at University College Cardiff, Paris and Zurich, ending up as professor of French and Romance Philology at University College, Cardiff. Among his published works were such controversial titles as 'The French Linguistic Influence on Mediaeval Wales,' and *La Civilisation française dans les Mabinogion.*

54 Percy Mansell Jones (1889–1968) was educated first at University College of Wales, Aberystwyth and then in Paris and Oxford. He spent a period as professor of French at University College of North Wales, Bangor, and subsequently as professor of Modern French Literature at the University of Manchester. During his time at Bangor he is credited with supplying W. G. Sebald with such information about Welsh Nonconformist culture as is found in his great novel *Austerlitz*. Jones was a prolific publisher, and in his autobiography *How They Educated Jones* there are references to meetings with Ezra Pound, André Gide, Ernest Jones and others.

55 R. Geraint Gruffydd (ed.), *Meistri'r Canrifoedd: Ysgrifau ar Hanes Llenyddiaeth Gymraeg gan Saunders Lewis* (Cardiff: University of Wales Press, 1973), pp. 306–24. Hereafter *MC*.

56 See Harri Pritchard Jones (ed.), *Saunders Lewis: A Presentation of His Work* (Springfield, IL: Templegate Publishers, 1993), p. 206.

57 When this poem first saw print in 1973, a fascinating correspondence ensued between the author and the eminent philosopher Dewi Z. Phillips concerning the exact import of this profound poetry. It was during the course of this that Lewis referred Phillips to the writings of the great classic Christian mystics of the late medieval period.

58 For 'Gweddi'r Terfyn' see R. Geraint Gruffydd (ed.), Saunders Lewis, *Cerddi* (Cardiff: University of Wales Press, 1976), p. 53. Lewis's important gloss on the poem appeared in *Y Tyst* (13 June 1974). For an English translation of the poem see 'Prayer at the End', in Joseph Clancy (trans.), Saunders Lewis, *Selected Poems* (Cardiff: University of Wales Press, 1993), p. 46.

59 For a thorough account of Lewis's earlier exposure to France and its literature, first at school and then at university, see 'Saunders Lewis ac Ewrop', in Rhianedd Jewell, *Her a Hawl Cyfieithu Dramâu: Saunders Lewis, Samuel Beckett a Molière* (Cardiff: University of Wales Press, 2017).

60 *Doctor er ei waethaf*, Saunders Lewis's translation of Molière's *Le Médecin malgré lui*, was published by Hughes a'i Fab, Wrexham, 1924. *Serch yw'r*

Doctor, his 1958 pastiche of Molière's *L'Amour médecin*, is held in the National Library of Wales collection NLW ex 2453.

61 *Wrth Aros Godot* (1970), a translation of *En attendant Godot*.

62 *Y Cyrnol Chabert* (1989), a translation of Balzac's novella *Le colonel Chabert* (1832), which was intended as a tribute to the code of honour of the French military.

63 *Amlyn ac Amig* (1940) is based on a medieval translation of the French legend of *Amis et Amiles*.

64 Bruce Griffiths, 'His Theatre', in Alun R. Jones and Gwyn Thomas (eds), *Presenting Saunders Lewis* (Cardiff: University of Wales Press, 1973), pp. 91–2.

65 Frances Wilson Huard (trans.), *Colette Baudoche* (New York: George H. Doran Co., 1918).

66 Densil Morgan (ed.), Saunders Lewis, *Williams Pantycelyn* (Cardiff: University of Wales Press, 2016),

67 'Rhagair', in D. Densil Morgan (ed.), Saunders Lewis, *Williams Pantycelyn* (Cardiff: University Press, 2016), p. ix. Hereafter *WP*.

68 'Nodyn ynghylch Diwinyddiaeth', in Marged Dafydd (ed.), *Ati Ŵyr Irainc, Ysgrifau gan Saunders Lewis* (Cardiff: University of Wales Press, 1986), p. 31.

69 See his seminal 1924 essay on the poet which featured his earliest account of a 'Welsh aesthetic' (*MC*, pp. 80–92).

70 Ioan M. Williams (ed.), *Dramâu Saunders Lewis, Y Casgliad Cyflawn*, Cyfrol II (Cardiff: University of Wales Press, 2000), pp. 3–107. My discussions of Lewis's late plays is heavily indebted to this magnificent edition (along with the same author's *Dramâu Saunders Lewis, Y Casgliad Cyflawn*, Cyfrol I (Cardiff: University of Wales Press, 1996).

71 For the information in this paragraph I am much indebted to Rhianedd Jewell, *Her a Hawl Cyfieithu Dramâu: Saunders Lewis, Samuel Beckett, Molière* (Cardiff: University of Wales Press, 2018). Her study also includes an excellent overview chapter on Saunders Lewis's Europeanness.

72 Martin Esslin, *The Theatre of the Absurd* (Harmondsworth: Penguin, 1962).

73 This incident is the central subject of Robert Harris's popular thriller, *Munich* (London: Hutchinson, 2017).

74 Saunders Lewis, 'The Literary Man's Wales', *The Welsh Outlook* (October 1929), 102–3.

75 See, for example, the articles by Peter Hughes Griffiths, *Heddiw*, 1/2 (September 1936), 11, and Lewis Valentine, 'Emrys ap Iwan', *Heddiw*, 1/1 (April 1936), 10–12, 38).

76 *Heddiw*, 2/2 (March 1937), 79–80.

77 'Gweriniaeth: i goffáu John Cornford', *Heddiw*, 3/1 (August 1937), 12–13.

78 Gwilym R. Jones, 'Y Canu Newydd', *Heddiw*, 3/3 (September 1937), 83–4. Welsh taste still stubbornly went for the conventional, however. A later number of *Heddiw* (3/11) opened with a translation of a slight lyric ('Sur une Morte') by de Musset.

79 Nefydd Owen, 'André Gide', *Heddiw*, 7/2 (February–May 1942), 37–47.

80 B. J. Morse, 'Cwymp Candia,' *Heddiw*, 6/5 (November–December 1940), 12–33. Interestingly, the story was dedicated to the Anglo-Welsh author Glyn Jones and his wife Doreen.

81 The same number also carried a poem, 'Am Bump yn y Bore,' also by Morse: *Heddiw*, 6/5 (November–December 1940), 124.

82 Alun Lewis, 'To Rilke', in the 'Part Three: India' section of *Ha! Ha! Among the Trumpets: Poems in Transit*, collected in Cary Archard (ed.), *The Collected Poems of Alun Lewis* (Bridgend: Seren Books, 1994), 124–5.

83 Jill Piercy, *Brenda Chamberlain, Artist and Writer* (Cardigan: Parthian, 2003), p. 91.

84 Kate Holman, *Brenda Chamberlain*, Writers of Wales (Cardiff: University of Wales Press, 1997), p. 75.

85 'Duw (*Rainer Maria Rilke*)', 'Ysgubau'r Awen', in Christine James (ed.), *Cerddi Gwenallt: Y Casgliad Cyflawn* (Llandysul: Gomer, 2001), p. 86. Hereafter *CG*. Gwenallt also included translations from the Goliardy and Villon in this collection.

86 B. J. Morse, 'Detholion o Lythyrau Rainer Maria Rilke', *Tir Newydd*, 15 (February 1939), 4–7.

87 B. J. Morse, 'Detholion o Lythyrau Rainer Maria Rilke,' *Tir Newydd*, 13 (August 1938), 10–11.

88 J. Gwyn Griffiths, 'Rilke: *Einsamkeit* a Chenedl,' in *Ysgrifau Beirniadol*, XXV (Denbigh: Gee, 1999), pp. 112–25. This volume also contains an article by Bosse-Griffiths, 'Gwaith gan Rilke a fu'n sail i opera fodern yn Dresden', pp. 127–9.

89 T. Pugh Williams brings out this crucial aspect of Rilke's ruthless view of the truly modern artist's responsibilities in his essay on Rilke in Gareth Alban Davies and W. Gareth Jones (eds), *Y Llenor yn Ewrop* (Cardiff: University of Wales Press, 1976), pp. 115–25.

90 J. Henry Jones, *Cyfieithiadau o Rainer Maria Rilke* (Llandysul: Gomer, 1945).

91 J. Henry Jones, *Rainer Maria Rilke* (Cardiff: University of Wales Press, 1984).

92 Gareth Alban Davies (ed.), *Cardi o Fôn: Detholion o Gerddi a Throsiadau John Henry Jones* (Aberystwyth: Cymdeithas Lyfrau Ceredigion), 1991.

93 D. Myrddin Lloyd (ed.), *O Erddi Eraill* (Cardiff: University of Wales Press, 1981).

94 E. T. Griffiths, *Cerddi Estron: Cyfieithwyd o Amryfal Ieithoedd*, Llyfrau'r Dryw (Llandybïe: Christopher Davies, 1966).

95 Dyfnallt [John Dyfnallt Owen], *O Ben Tir Llydaw* (Merthyr Tydfil: Swyddfa'r Tyst, 1934). The volume is dedicated to those who were friends to the Breton cause. During the long period when Dyfnallt acted as editor of his denomination's weekly paper, *Y Tyst*, his editorials regularly included such subjects as his pre-war visits to Danzig and Lucerne, his post-war journey down the Rhine, and a tribute to Goethe as the ultimate representative of the Hellenic mind, which Dyfnallt cannot resist comparing unfavourably to the 'Hebraic' mind of a committed Christian believer. See *Ar y Tŵr* (Swansea: Welsh Independents' Press, 1953), a selection from the editorials by a number of prominent Welsh Independent ministers.

96 'A Phwy yw'r Basgiaid?', *Heddiw*, 3/9 (April 1938), 240–5.

97 'Dwy Seren Wib ar Draws Ewrop', *Tir Newydd*, 13 (August 1938), 14–18.

98 Geraint Dyfnallt Owen, *Aeth Deugain Mlynedd Heibio: Dyddiadur Rhyfel* (Caernaerfon: Gwasg Gwynedd, 1985). Hereafter *DR*.

99 Geraint Dyfnallt Owen, *Y Blaid Hud a Chwedlau Eraill* (Aberystwyth: Gwasg Aberystwyth, 1949); *Rwmania: Pennod Mewn Gwleidyddiaeth Grym* (Aberystwyth: Y Clwb Llyfrau Cymraeg, 1951). The subtitle of the latter volume may be translated as 'A Chapter in the Politics of Power'.

100 The book was reviewed by J. Gwyn Griffiths, and his piece reprinted in J. Gwyn Griffiths, *I Ganol y Frwydr*, Llyfrau'r Dryw (Llandybïe: Christopher Davies, 1971), pp. 113–19.

101 Nigel Heseltine, *Scarred Background: A Journey Through Albania* (London: Lovat Dickson Publishers, 1938). For Heseltine, see 'A Grand Harlequinade: The Border Writing of Nigel Heseltine', in M. Wynn Thomas, *All That is Wales* (Cardiff: University of Wales Press, 2017), pp. 77–97. The fullest account of his remarkable life is that by Rhian Davies, in *Welsh Writing in English*, 11 (2006–7), 69–101.

102 *Wales*, 6/7 (March 1939), 208.

103 In some of what follows I rely heavily on the outstanding website constructed to honour Gareth Jones's remarkable career: to be found at <*garethjones.org*>.

104 Gareth Jones, 'Famine Rules Russia: The 5-Year Plan Has Killed The Bread Supply', *The Evening Standard*, 31 March 1933.

105 Gareth Jones, 'My Thoughts On The Journey To Moscow: Putting The Clock Back By Centuries', *The Western Mail*, 7 April 1933.

106 'There Is No Bread: Gareth Jones Hears Cry Of Hunger All Over Ukraine, Once Russia's Sea Of Grain', *Sunday American/Los Angeles Examiner*, 13 January 1935.

107 Gareth Jones, *In Search of News* (Cardiff: Western Mail and Echo, 1938). Hereafter *ISN*.

7

THE FEMALE EUROPA, THE RHONDDA
EUROPEANS AND WELSH SYMBOLISM

The November–December 1940 issue of the progressive
Welsh-language periodical *Heddiw* included an essay on Nietzsche
and Nazism. It began by conceding that the Third Reich did indeed
have some reason to claim Nietzsche, who had preached the gospel
of the Superman, the Blond Beast and a great future for Europe, as
the visionary philosopher of their movement. But then it proceeded
to quote his approving views on the strongly hybrid, multicultural,
character of the supposedly exclusively Aryan nation of Germany, to
note his admiring description of the Jews as the strongest and most
pure of races, to emphasise his contempt for anti-Semitism and to
show how ardent he was for the intermixing of the Jews even with
the Prussian aristocracy. It then added, however, that the Nazis had
indeed found Nietzsche's emphasis on the right of a Superman and a
class of strong leaders to rule over the passive masses, and his prophecy of a future age, when the minor nations and races of Europe
would all have been either obliterated or assimilated by a superpower,
very much to their malign purpose.[1]

The author of that article had the soundest of reasons to reach
such conclusions. Her name was Kate Bosse-Griffiths, and she had
left Germany shortly before the war because she was of partly Jewish
family. She had also been trained as a Classical scholar, and so was
able to point to the social structure of the Classical world, with its
clear division between a slave underclass and a free ruling class, as
the model for Nietzsche, who had himself been a renowned scholar
of the classics. And in concluding her article with a scathing criticism
of Nietzsche's appalling misogyny ('When you go to your wife, carry

a whip with you'), she was paving the way for the important work she herself was shortly to perform, of providing women's experience with a voice for almost the first time in Welsh-language literature.

Kate Bosse-Griffiths was one of the most remarkable of Welsh Europeans. She was a native of Wittenberg, daughter of a distinguished German physician and a cultivated Jewish mother. Demonstrating a gift early for the classics, she studied at Munich University, with periods in Bonn, Italy and Greece, and also in Berlin, where she later took up a curatorial post at the State Museum. Switching to Egyptology for her postgraduate studies – she was eventually to gain an international reputation, like her future Welsh husband, J. Gwyn Griffiths, as a specialist in ancient Egypt – she also became fluent in Italian (following her period of study there) and (thanks to an early Russian boyfriend) in Russian. Additionally, she knew Spanish, French, modern Greek and a little Swedish. To advance her work in Egyptology she mastered ancient Greek, Latin, Egyptian, Coptic, Classical Arabic and Hebrew. Nazi persecution devastated a large section of her family: one of her brothers spent a period in Buchenwald; her father was forced to leave his hospital post; her aunt committed suicide to save her Aryan husband from having to resign as an army general; both her parents and her sister were imprisoned; and her mother eventually died in Ravensbrück. In anticipation of what was to come, the youthful Käthe Bosse (as she then was) had left for Britain, spending periods at St Andrews, then London (where she mixed with the Bloomsbury set) before finally being made a curator at the Ashmolean Museum in Oxford. There she met and in 1939 married a young Welsh postgraduate and budding Egyptologist, J. Gwyn Griffiths, and the pair moved to live in Griffiths's home township of Pentre, Rhondda, where she immediately began to learn Welsh. Very shortly thereafter she became mother to three children – although one, a baby girl, sadly died.[2]

No sooner had she learned Welsh, it seems, than she also began to produce highly accomplished articles, short stories and novels in her newly acquired language. One of her central preoccupations was the danger presented by marriage to young women of creative talents and intellectual gifts. She found it reassuring that Marie Curie's collaboration on equal terms with her husband in the discovery of radium had been publicly acknowledged. It was, for her, a rare instance of a married women proving able to overcome 'spiritual subjugation'.

But, *pace* Cyril Connolly's famous epigram, she well knew that the 'pram in the hall' was a far greater danger to a talented woman than it was to a talented man.[3]

In 'Crwban', one of her earliest stories, she set out to illustrate this. The heroine, Titania (the significance of the name is obvious), is a strikingly vivacious young Russian who has contracted an unfortunate marriage to Phil, a staid, workaholic Oxford don.[4] She quickly finds the stuffy male atmosphere of the clubbable Senior Common Room stifling. There she is nothing but an amusing exotic. She therefore provides herself with a safety valve in the form of the soirées she regularly organises for refugees from Europe. There she meets Swtja, a quiet young Indian Buddhist, and they form an intense Platonic relationship. On the eve of his final departure, he shyly discloses the image of her he has all along had in his mind. It is of a tortoise whose head has been self-protectively withdrawn into the safety of its shell. Experiencing a shock of self-recognition, Titania impulsively begs that she be allowed to accompany him wherever he is bound. His refusal of her desperate request condemns her to a life that sees her harden into an iron conventionality covered by a mask of impeccable social conformity.[5]

The restless energy occasioned by the confused sexual awakening of a young woman is the subject of the novella *Anesmwyth Hoen*.[6] Escaping her claustrophobically loving home in Wales to study in London, Megan slowly begins to come to terms with her own nature and learns to navigate her complex relations with two men, one an athlete of sound, sensible character, the other, Paul Wilde, considerably older and an experienced womaniser. Previously married, he has lost his wife in a climbing accident in Switzerland – an example of the way in which in this novella Europe becomes a signifier of the precariousness of the ambivalent freedom available to modern women, an aspect of Europe which intensifies in significance in the last third of the novella.

Suppressing, with great difficulty, the sensual feelings excited in her by the suavely predatory Wilde, Megan, who has also joined a group of free-minded young intellectuals, eventually opts for a teaching post in Munich. There she responds eagerly to the enticements of a foreign culture, marvelling at the ways of Bavarian Catholicism, revelling in her new-found freedom to explore the city's cultural riches, enthusiastically learning to ride, and attempting to ski in the Bavarian Alps in the lovingly attentive company of a young Scottish medic.

Finally she and he find themselves swept up in the Dionysiac frenzy of a Munich carnival, fully entering into its intoxicatingly permissive spirit when they don fancy dress, she as a Japanese geisha, he as an Indian magus. The novella culminates with Megan facing the terrible dilemma of whether or not to marry the Scot, who has just been appointed to a medical post in Edinburgh. And in full, deeply troubled, awareness of the implications of her fateful choice she, only recently awakened to the potentialities of her personality and the possibilities of life, consents. It is a momentous and, as the novel implies, a highly dubious, decision, and one to which the new wife and mother Bosse-Griffiths seems to grant only a very qualified, deeply uncertain endorsement.

As its title suggests, 'Fy Chwaer Efa', a long story from the collection of the same name, is about the sisterhood of women, bound in solidarity in their opposition to the imprisoning stereotype of guilty Eve foisted upon them by men.[7] It is a strange, extremely ambitious work, a visionary parable centring on the story of Maia, the beloved daughter whose untimely loss Efa is deeply mourning. It is also a profoundly syncretic work, fusing biblical allegory (Efa's sisters are respectively named Mary, Martha and Magdalen, and in places the phrasing also references the Virgin Mary) with ancient pagan sources featuring the Mother Goddess, at once fiercely destructive and nurturing. Such a deity was worshipped in ancient Egypt, as the poem which acts as Preface to the collection indicates, under the name of Hathor, and, in her benign aspects, was there adored for licensing female joy and sexuality. (Later in life, Bosse-Griffiths was to embrace a radical Christian theology that advocated conceiving of the Deity as reflective of both male and female.) The name Maya/Maia has similar resonances – in Buddhism she is the Buddha's mother, in Hinduism she is a goddess associated with love, and also with extraordinary power and wisdom. Maia first enters Bosse-Griffiths's story as a precocious child and she baffles the women in her family with her disconcerting questions about existence, much in the manner of the boy Jesus who baffled the wisest in the Temple. Thereafter she evolves into a female Redeemer figure, one who has been granted a dream-vision in which she sees a multitude of women being sacrificed on the bloody altar of maleness, a fate to which they assent because custom and tradition have rendered them totally passive and malleable. 'Fy chwaer Efa', published in 1944, thus becomes in part a female pacifist's comment on the male predilection for violence and war.

While there is no mention of Europe in this long story, it does nevertheless bear the unmistakable signs of Bosse-Griffiths's continental origins, being, as Katie Gramich has perceptively noted, a story 'of competing ideas, a dialectical story, betraying the author's intellectual, Germanic and academic background'.[8] As Gramich has further observed, the later novel, *Mae'r Galon wrth y Llyw*, mistakenly published under the name 'Boss Griffith' [*sic*], which daringly treats adultery from a woman's point of view, is similarly a 'novel of ideas' on the German model.[9] Bosse-Griffiths's treatment of women's experience in Wales was consistently informed by her extensive familiarity with the imaging of it in European culture. Thus her main interest on a visit to Brittany is in the intriguing folk festival of the 'Grandmother Saint,' that is St Anne, supposed mother of the Virgin Mary (*TM*, 43–9). She particularly approves of the festival celebrating both mother and daughter – a seminal relationship she had already explored, of course, in 'Fy Chwaer Efa'.

There are many instances in her numerous short occasional essays of the connections she makes between Wales and Europe. Having noted the influence the philosophy of Henri Bergson (himself Jewish as well as French) had had both on European neo-Catholicism and the European left, she concluded her obituary of him with an *englyn* in his memory by J. M. Edwards (*TM*, 105–9). Implicit in her essays on the German peace movements and on the life and work of the important German Expressionist dramatist and pacifist Ernst Toller (who was of Jewish parentage) is her awareness of the powerful Welsh tradition of pacifism to which she and her husband belonged (*TM*, 115–42, 83–9). Examining some of the 300,000 remarkable petroglyphs to be seen in Valcamonica in Alpine Lombardy, she recalls seeing similar ancient marks on stone at Bala (*TM*, 63–7). Behind the gold Celtic torque or gorget worn on the breast of the archdruid of Wales she detects an image of the sun such as she finds, too, in various artefacts and images from Valcamonica to ancient Egypt. Visiting Austria, she points out that it is not much larger in population or in size than Wales, and recalls that it was once part of the territory of a Celtic tribe: her etymologist's eye shows her that the name 'Vienna' derives from a Celtic word closely analogous to the Welsh word for 'gwyn' (white). The continental roots of the Welsh are again evident to her when she visits Hungary, where of course she learns that the country's national epic is based on the legend of the massacre of the Welsh bards by Edward I (*TM*, 157–8, 159–60, 161–4). And she opens the interesting essay in which she discloses her impressive familiarity with the works of Nikos Kazantzakis with a quotation from a poem by her great friend Pennar Davies (*TM*, 193–203).

Europe, as the great ancient source of empowering wisdom about the condition of women, features prominently in the remarkable opening story in Bosse-Griffiths's late collection *Cariadau* that explores several different forms of human love. 'Y Stori Gyfriniol' concerns the 'mystical' experience gained near Pompeii by Alun Rabaiotti, an eighteen-year-old Welshman of Italian descent.[10] Given a chance to visit his father's homeland, he journeys to Rome where a visit to the Sistine Chapel stuns him with an exposure to the reverent worship of the Virgin Mary. Although immensely impressed by the majesty of the occasion, he is repelled by such adoration of what to him is an evidently nonsensical sublime virginity. In it he sees a denial of the procreative energies of life. As if by reaction, he next acquires, by accident, a small ivory carving of a dolphin, believing that it cradles a naked Venus. On closer inspection, however, he discovers to his horror that it is in fact a pornographic carving of a sexual act featuring two men, one of whom is having intercourse with a woman, while the other submits to fellatio. Bewildered and disgusted, he feels stranded between two equally repellent extremes, one glorifying sexlessness, the other revelling in what he regards as a humanly degrading, bestial sexuality. Redemption finally comes for Alun in the form of an image he sees depicted on the walls of a ruined pre-Christian villa. It depicts a young woman being prepared for her marriage by a crowd of older, experienced women. Terrified at what is to come – which is represented by an erect phallus – she buries her head in a companion's arms. For the young man, this is the revelatory moment both of his and her awakening. Because what is imaged is the awed and fearful reverence which is due to the great creative, procreative power of life and which is manifest in human (and most specifically female) sexuality.

Another story in the collection is a debate about the condition of women in the form of a narrative about Helen of Troy at the moment when her lover Paris has ignominiously fled the field of battle, leaving Menelaus victorious and Troy doomed (*C*, 72–90). The kernel of the story is the debate between two rival versions of womanhood. The one, voiced by the ageing Hecuba, mother of Paris, sees women as destined to serve others selflessly – hence her plea to Helen to accompany her to the temple to pray for the women of Troy. The other, voiced by Helen herself, sees women as solely devoted to the cultivation of beauty and as powerless to act save by inspiring men to action. Obviously implicit in the story is the message that women allow themselves to be confined to two equally unsatisfactory roles. They are thus prevented by their social conditioning from developing a fully mature, responsible understanding of their female powers.

That the voice of women's experience in Welsh-language Wales should have become clearly and unmistakably heard for one of the first times only thanks to the mediation of Europe should come as no surprise. Europe had for some time seemed the continent of libera-tion for female Welsh creative talents. But for her disastrous marriage to the controlling Ernest Jones, Morfydd Llwyn Owen might have realised her dream of studying music in Russia. Although she made it to Paris, Gwen John ended up emotionally enslaved to the equally controlling Auguste Rodin, and her experience was imaginatively explored decades later by the leading Welsh women's writer Manon Rhys in her notable novel *Cysgodion*.[11] It was during wartime nurs-ing service in France that the Davies sisters of Gregynog, renowned collectors of the Impressionists, first became aware of their work and that of the Post-Impressionists. Then there is the case of the Welsh-Argentinian Lynette Roberts, who settled in the rural west Wales village of Llanybri at just the same time that Bosse-Griffiths was making her equally unlikely home in Pentre. No wonder that poor Roberts, starved of sun and culture alike, was desperately confiding to her journal by the summer of 1940, 'I felt like running off to France and selling my British status.'[12]

Several other female writers of the inter-war period are worth closer examination in this European connection. Dorothy Edwards had devoured continental literature when young, and was deeply influ-enced by Turgenev in particular.[13] She also became proficient in Greek, German and Russian. A brief period in Vienna proved frus-trating because she was strictly chaperoned by her mother, and her stories accordingly often associate Europe with the illusory promise of freedom and self-fulfilment. In her short story 'Days', the young rural innocent Bessie, whose approach through the grass sets the composer Alexander Sorel humming a few bars of *L'Après-midi d'un faune* to himself, yearns to 'go into service' in France and to travel.[14] On the other hand, when, having entered her thirties, Mary in 'La Penseuse' finally makes it to Holland, it is only to find herself imprisoned within the same intellectually stimulating but emotionally frustrating relationship that she had experienced when a youngster in her home village. In this case, therefore, Europe has flattered a woman only to deceive (*R*, 197–215).

Edwards herself had been impelled to visit Europe largely by her youthful ambitions to become an opera singer. Accordingly, the classical music of the European tradition becomes one of the most important, and most complex, signifiers of female experience in her curiously abstracted stories – when she writes of a man seemingly 'listening all the time to something intensely illuminating but scarcely audible' she exactly captures the atmosphere of her curiously inconsequential and scrupulously noncommittal fictions (*R*, 1). Thus, once again we find the continent being associated with the ambivalent process of female sensuous awakening and with cunning male exploitation of it. In 'Rhapsody', the creepy Mr Everett surreptitiously undermines his ailing wife and (platonically) seduces the governess, Antonia, by inveigling her into singing Mozart, Beethoven, Schumann and (climactically) Bellini's 'Casta Diva' for his swooning pleasure on a regular basis. Chopin and Wolf are the composers who do the damage in 'A Country House', in which a wife becomes unconsciously alienated from her husband by innocently delighting in the company of an engineer whose singing complements her own dexterity at the piano (*R*, 27–44).

Time after time, the susceptibility of women to the sensuous allure of great European music serves only to deliver them into the hands of manipulative men. But in 'The Conquered' it is the state of the Welsh nation that is obliquely referenced through the playing of Chopin's 'Polish Songs' and Brahms's 'Nachtigall', the music evoking a melancholy that 'was the melancholy of impotence, not of power.' (*R*, 45–60). It is, though, a Welsh woman who sings the former for an English man, and the quoted phrase could also be applied to the part played by melancholy music in the 'conquest' of women in general by men in Edwards's stories. In 'Cultivated People', however, the emphasis is elsewhere. Here the German spinster Miss Wolff's exceptional prowess on the violin serves only to weave a complex web of emotions imperceptibly entangling not only herself but a married couple and a bachelor who becomes her hapless suitor. In this case, European music played by a woman arouses in a man unsuspected feelings to which it is the sensible, practical woman, for once, who is stoutly immune (*R*, 79–95).

Eluned Phillips, a native of Cenarth, was much the same age as Edwards and in the early 1930s she left her rural home village and headed for Paris, where she enthusiastically involved herself in the racy bohemian life of the Left Bank artists and writers.[15] She formed a close acquaintance there with Edith Piaf (in whose quarters she met Jean Cocteau and others), and for the rest of her life Phillips was to view Piaf as her own alter ego, a soul as impulsive and tempestuous as herself. She several times addressed poems to her, characterising her as a 'flame devouring time in the flesh in a dreadful storm' in 'Trioleg yr Oet' (*OA*, 55) and dedicating one section of her Eisteddfod entry of 1967, 'Corlannau', to her memory.

The most troubled, and troubling, of Phillips's continental escapades was her romantic involvement with a passionate young Breton nationalist, who ended up imprisoned and tortured during the Second World War on suspicion of being a German collaborator. Many Breton nationalists had indeed been persuaded by their political convictions to cooperate with the Germans occupiers, and Rob Stradling has examined the support some of them received from sympathetic Welsh nationalists such as Kate Roberts and her husband.[16] Phillips enthusiastically contributed to this underground network of support provided by Welsh patriots, even going so far as to hide some of the nationalists who were en route to refuge in Ireland in the tiny village of Cenarth.

The lifelong relationship of the artist-writer Brenda Chamberlain with Europe began when, as a teenager, she spent a period visiting Copenhagen.[17] Most important to her thereafter were Germany (thanks to her intense, long-lasting relationship with Karl von Laer, the blonde, blue-eyed Westphalian whom she first met as a young man) and Greece (her extended period of living on the island of Hydra was terminated only by the notorious right-wing military coup engineered by the Greek Colonels, who ruled from 1967 to 1974). In her experience, the relationship between Wales and Europe seems to have been a dialectical one. While Bangor remained her base, an assured (but stiflingly claustrophobic) source of material and emotional support, it was the continent that came to represent imaginative freedom, fulfilment and hazardous emotional daring. Indeed, influenced by the paintings of Gauguin, Cézanne and Matisse, she could view even the hardy Welsh islanders of Bardsey, where she lived with a French companion for a dozen years, as of originally Iberian stock. Hence her highly stylised treatment of them in her art and in her important prose work *Tide-Race*. She was naturally attracted to creatures such as the mythical man-horse the Centaur, and that beguiling amphibian the seal, which is ubiquitous in *Tide-Race*.[18] Chamberlain's early interest in Personalism, and in particular the variant of it that derived from the philosophy of the Russian/Ukrainian Nikolai Berdyaev (and Jacques Maritain), remains to be explored. It placed great emphasis on personal freedom and respect for individual creativity, and in the immediate aftermath of the Second World War a poem of hers ('White Water') appeared in the periodical *Transformation Three*, a collection of Personalist writings edited by Stefan Schimanski and Henry Treece that Chamberlain signed and retained in her personal possession until her death.[19]

Her poetry collection *The Green Heart* is bilateral in character, like its author. Some poems are solidly grounded in shrewd observations of the community around Llanllechid, the Snowdonian village that was Chamberlain's home before and during the war. But others are in a different vein. In these, owing much to the poetry of Rilke, she associates personal liberation with her Muse, Karl von Laer, the young Prussian with whom she had so loved climbing the crags of Snowdonia. He it is who may be invoked in a poem such as 'You, who in April laughed' as 'a green god in the sun', who 'sang in the bowel-rock below me / Words unknown'. Chamberlain knew no German, and so felt that what she heard was 'familiar-strange'.[20] Several of the mythopoeic poems that implicitly celebrate the exotic von Laer's radiant, transfiguring presence in her mountain fastness are as recklessly sensual as any passage in the *Song of Solomon*: 'For joy my head is crowned / With stags' horn mosses. / Feet have no weight / Upon the shining hill' (*GH*, 19), she writes, and sexual arousal is everywhere inscribed in her electric response to her environment: 'I have touched the spring in the rock; / Quenched thirst from many waters' (*GH*, 22). While the landscape of Snowdonia is her staple landscape of passion, some of the poems (a few influenced by her later prolonged residence on Bardsey Island) are ocean-drenched, with her imaginary lover now a fisherman who 'was salt, and very rib of his boat / Eager to plunge an oar into black night'. (*GH*, 25).

The sequence entitled 'The Green Heart' is specifically dedicated to von Laer, and draws extensively on their prolonged correspondence. The first part pictures him lonely and desolate on the cold, cloudy, distant coast of the Baltic, and in it she implicitly images herself now as *his* Muse, an imaginary presence both reconciling von Laer to the

deadness of his sodden surroundings and promising new life. This
arrives in the Second Part, when she journeys to his 'water castle'
at Oberbehme bearing 'gifts', 'the honey of my body, the constancy
of my mind' (*GH*, 54). What follows is ecstatic poetry edged with
despair and desperation. Theirs is to be a kind of mystical marriage,
but one fraught with risk and ending in a separation in which she
pleads to be allowed to be for ever cherished in memory as his 'Green
Heart'. There is therefore a sense in which Wales and Europe become
in this volume not just two contrasting locations but the two poles
of her nature, doomed to be forever irreconcilable. The third section
is accordingly a suite of poems acknowledging the finality of separation, in which the Second World War serves as both occasion and
metaphor for a sundering of their respective worlds. The gulf can now
be spanned only by the fragile bridge of their love, and the poems that
are its precious medium.

At the beginning of her autobiographical novel *The Water-Castle*,
closely modelled on her actual visit to Karl's home, a 'baroque Schloss'
in the Harz mountains, Klaus (i.e. Karl) hyperbolically observes that
she has 'written more poetry about Germany than have her native
poets', thereby implicitly signalling, she believes, that she is as spiritually at home there as he is.[21] The novel is psychological in character,
tracing the processes whereby 'Elizabeth' (Chamberlain) schemes to
alienate Klaus's affections from his wife, and in the process distances
herself irrevocably from her own husband, Antoine. At one point
she identifies with Flaubert's poet-mistress Louise Colet (*W*, 106),
recalling the novelist's question to her: 'What is the colour of your
dream?' Elizabeth's overheated relationship with Klaus likewise inhab-
its a feverishly dreamlike inner realm from which his broad-hipped
'brood mare' of a wife is of course excluded. Although the inevitable
parting duly comes, the novel ends with Elizabeth's belated realisation
that she 'had, as a girl of twenty, given [her] soul for ever into [Klaus/
Karl's] keeping' (*W*, 150).

If the German Karl is Chamberlain's intensely imagined European
soulmate, for her alter ego we might turn to another region entirely
of the continent. When she read in a newspaper of the recovery of
a statue of Demeter from the depths of the sea off Asia Minor, her
imagination immediately resonated to this image of 'conserved force'
raised 'from the seabed / where the dark centuries held her', so that
she could once again, 'with salt-burned gaze / [give], under an old
sun, solace'.[22] The poem was eventually published in *Poems with*

Drawings, a volume furnished with an epigraph from the letters of
Rilke. Chamberlain entered the realm of Demeter, and of the other
celebrated divinities of ancient Greek mythology, in person when
she took up residence on the small Greek island of Hydra. There, in
due course, she found another male muse in the person of the charismatic dancer Roberto Saragas. So mesmerising did she find his fluid,
improvisatory movements in the Martha Graham tradition that she
attempted to develop a special visual notation for them, compressing
a rapid series of gestures into a single, multifoliate image exultantly
expressive of the ingeniously inventive repertoire of totally free movement. In his dance she saw 'rhythm' depicted, contrasting it with the
mere 'motion' that obsessed the inhabitants of the machine age.

'Here for me', Chamberlain wrote in her engrossing journal of
her life on Hydra, *A Rope of Vines* (the epigraph this time is taken
from Thomas Mann), 'the Welsh sea has joined its fountain-head, the
maternal middle-ocean that hisses round promontories of pale-boned
islands.'[23] She imagines that in this locality she too, like Demeter, has
at last 'surfaced, and it is the light of the world above around in the
mittelmeer that fills and nourishes me' (*RV*, 15). The Mediterranean
(the mid-land sea) is here transformed into the 'middle-ocean,' the
'mittelmeer', intermediate between the world below and the world
above. Like the Great Mother, it is the source of all life, of all earthly
existence. And it is out of this element that Chamberlain is accordingly brought to new, ambivalent birth, most particularly as a woman.

Even on this island she finds herself confronting 'the great cleavage
in [her] nature' (*RV*, 28), recognising in herself an instinct to retreat
from the press of the world (she spends a period of respite in an
Orthodox nunnery 'for a stocktaking of the spirit') and a contrary
impulse to emerge 'clad in nothing but her skin', to 'stretch content-
edly, unfolding from a man's arms, her legs released from his, to face
the challenging world'. All around her she sees the same struggle
being enacted between these two alternatives – the monastery and
the *agora* – that frame a woman's life; and it is the life lived by the
women, not by the men, that primarily monopolises Chamberlain's
attention on Hydra, an island whose harshly revealing light is shadowed by dark. It is through a comment by Dostoevsky that she finds
her way out of her impasse: 'For a woman, all resurrection, all salvation, from whatever perdition, lies in love; in fact, it is her only way to
it' (*RV*, 92). But in the freedom to love there inevitably lies the probability of suffering, and the last third of *A Rope of Vines* dramatises

Chamberlain's suffering for and with Leonidas, a close friend unfairly accused of manslaughter.

Chamberlain herself suffered most grievously when the junta's military coup – whose human atrocities she glimpsed when she visited a penal settlement and sought to dramatise it in her unpublished play *The Protagonists* – effectively banished her for ever from Hydra. Forced to retreat to Bangor, she felt ever more frustrated, her vital freedom had been drastically curtailed, her life cruelly diminished, her imagination crippled. Breakdown ensued in due course, and that culminated sadly in Brenda Chamberlain's suicide in July 1971. For her, as for the other Welsh women authors mentioned above, Europe was Europa, the continent of female experience in all its bliss and bale.

At the end of 1940, *Heddiw* carried a sonnet by Kate Bosse-Griffiths entitled 'Moel Cadwgan'. It opened with an impression of the western slopes of the Rhondda Fawr, up which terraced houses, grey-haired as geriatrics, laboriously climbed. It then proceeded to contrast these miners' cottages with the hill above, on which shone the sun of whose light and warmth the toiling miners were deprived. Finally it noted how the gravestone slabs in a neighbouring cemetery resembled the bones whitening on the mountain slopes of sheep who had strayed too far from the flock.[24]

'Moel Cadwgan' is the name of the mountain separating the upper reaches of the Rhondda Fawr (and the village of Pentre) from the Rhondda Fach (and the village of Maerdy). On the slopes of the mountain nestled 'Cadwgan,' the house that was home to the newly weds Kate Bosse-Griffiths and J. Gwyn Griffiths from 1939 to 1943. It in turn gave its name to the 'Cadwgan group', a coterie of young, lively, free-thinking writers and intellectuals who congregated there. As J. Gwyn Griffiths was to record much later, the model for such a grouping was taken partly from such celebrated continental examples as the French *salons* and the informal circle formed briefly in Weimar by Goethe, Herder, Schiller and Richter.[25] Its members were all enthusiastic cosmopolitans, as well as campaigning nationalists and pacifists, and the frank intellectual debates they held carried overtones of sensuality and of sexuality. All in all they must have seemed a thoroughly rum group to their neighbours in a proletarian valley whose own utopian radicalism had always run in the direction of socialism, Marxism and anarchism. Moreover, they had disconcertingly eclectic cultural interests. Three were learned classicists, two specialists in Egyptology and the ancient cultures of the Mediterranean and the Middle East, and two were German refugees steeped in European culture. The narrow upper reaches of the Rhondda valley could scarcely have been expected comfortably to contain their strikingly catholic outlooks.

These young intellectuals found it entirely natural to regard the whole of European culture as their province, to view Europe in the light of its long, ancient history, and to include Wales within their ambitious ken. A fictional portrait of the group was painted over twenty years later in *Meibion Darogan* (1968), a novel by one of Cadwgan's most brilliant talents, Pennar Davies. The only son in an ordinary working-class family in Mountain Ash (Aberpennar), in the Cynon valley, Davies early displayed remarkable intellectual talents that eventually led him to Oxford and Yale. On his return to Wales he turned himself into an accomplished Welsh-speaker before unexpectedly committing himself to a lifetime's service with the Annibynwyr, the Welsh denomination of Independents. His exceptional learning – comfortably embracing ancient civilisations, Classical culture, a wide range of European literatures and the whole spectrum of Christian theology – won him the awed respect of his peers. Appointed professor of Church History at Bala-Bangor at a young age, he went on to become a beloved and revered principal of Swansea Memorial College. At the same time he was active in politics with Plaid Cymru, and the author not only of many impressive theological and devotional works but also of several unorthodox volumes of poetry and creative prose in many of which the European bent of his mind became very evident.[26]

His novel of ideas, *Meibion Darogan*, captures, with mingled sympathy and amusement, the intellectual antics of this odd-ball group of young intellectuals defiantly meeting under hostile conditions in the most unlikely of locations.[27] It conveys its almost incestuous coterie character; its exhilarating yet arrogant intellectualism; the heady, hot-house atmosphere in which sexual and creative desires mingled and ambiguously thrived; and the general atmosphere of permissiveness that helped young talents break free of stiflingly respectable social and cultural conventions. And central to the work, as it was central to the discussions, was the problematical nature of art, an issue explored in the novel through a fourfold portrait of the artist – as actor (Eurof Powell), as musician (Edryd Simon), as novelist (Heddwyn Lewis) and as female dramatist (Serena Francis).[28]

Like all of Pennar Davies's unconventional fiction, *Meibion Darogan* is a work of indeterminate genre and of enigmatic character. In his prefatory note, for instance, Davies suggests that his ostensibly realist fiction may be better understood as a retrospective dramatisation of a wartime dialogue the young fledgling author had been conducting with himself; an exploration of the different personae he had at that early, inchoate phase in his artistic development been tempted to adopt. The novel is certainly conscious of its confusingly mixed, and largely European, ancestry – of its descent from the confessional mode of Augustine and Rousseau to which Dostoevsky gave a dizzying fictional twist; from novels of ideas such as Thomas Mann's *The Magic Mountain* and the same author's extraordinary portrait of an artist in *Doctor Faustus*; from great cartographies of the soul beginning with Dante's *Divine Comedy* and ending with Goethe's *Faust*; and from the turbid records of the psycho-sexual life, including the novels of de Sade, the poetry of the Decadents, and the pseudo-scientific ideas of Freud and other members of his Viennese circle. The novel's self-conscious relation to these and many other paradigms may be fairly taken as evidence that it is the work of a European intellectual in search of an answering Welsh intelligentsia.

As for its textual practices, the novel's ironic refusal to allow the reader ready means of self-orientation – baffling him/her with its cool web of discourse, its tonal indeterminacy and its calmly alienating procedures – is Davies's way of breaking with the chapel concept of fiction as didactic in intent, a means of comfortably reinforcing moral assumptions. In keeping with the practice of modern psychotherapists and of a radical Marxist dramaturge such as Brecht, his aim is to bring the reader to the simultaneity of a revelatory new understanding of text, born of unmediated personal encounter with it, and also of self, through the act of defamiliarisation. The act of reading consequently becomes reintegrated with wider life experiences in a way that Davies's reading in such Christian Existentialists as Kierkegaard had caused him to value highly.

In *Meibion Darogan* the characters are left to tangle, as best they can, with each other and with their own desires whilst the author looks on with amusement and with some sympathetic bemusement. We are coolly insinuated into the slippery innards of the text and of its characters, learning that human psychology is not only labyrinthine but metamorphic, so that its complexities are ubiquitously self-altering and so endlessly elusive. The challenge which, as a

Christian, Davies attempts to accept is that of confronting this reality
without either defensively retreating to simplistic ethical distinctions
or capitulating to laissez-faire moral relativism. The former Davies,
the defiantly heterodox Nonconformist preacher, sees as the failure
of a Welsh establishment Nonconformity devoted to didacticism; the
latter he regards as the failure of the modern secular world.[29]

Several of the characters in *Meibion Darogan* exhibit clear
symptoms of Europeanism. Thus the aspiring young composer
Edryd Simon secretly hopes to compose a messianic work that will
save Wales from extinction. He also believes passionately in Henri
Bergson's concept of the *élan vital*, feeling its pulse in Beethoven's
music, and he imagines such a force to be pent up, awaiting creative release, in all human beings. As for Neddwyn Lewis, a young
trainee minister and hopeful rookie of a writer, he is a connoisseur
of psychic extremity, holding to a kind of pseudo-Baudelairean or
sub-Dostoevskian belief that man becomes spiritually alive only in
those strange twilight regions where extreme evil can unexpectedly
reverse itself into saintly good, as Saunders Lewis felt it might do in
the case of André Gide. For Neddwyn Lewis, important writers are
the great transgressives who dare to explore these tenebrous regions
of the human psyche in their works, oftentimes at the expense of their
personal relations.

In this novel, then, the sophisticated culture of Europe is implicitly treated by Davies as the great laboratory of the human spirit. It
stands both as an antithesis of, and an antidote to, that crass model of
humanity that underlies the far more powerful global culture of what
Davies, in another of his fictions, satirically dubbed 'Anglo-Sacsonia'.
This, of course, was the commercially and technologically powerful
culture of post-war Anglo-Americanism, which Davies regarded as
the great enemy of the human spirit and the even greater enemy of
a small, fragile, powerless culture such as the Welsh-language culture with which he so passionately identified and which he valiantly
defended. His dystopian novel *Anadl O'r Uchelder* is accordingly
the dark twin of *Meibion Darogan*. It replaces the latter's strain
of European utopianism with a fantastic vision, in the manner of
Nineteen Eighty-Four, of a future when a totalitarian Anglo-Saxon
empire has become all-powerful. Wales, governed by an American
gauleiter, has fallen helpless victim to this rapaciously capitalist
empire, seduced and totally overwhelmed by its immense power and
crude vitality. Welsh religious culture has been completely cheapened

and commercialised by the importation of powerful techniques of persuasion modelled on those of tub-thumping and greedily money-garnering American evangelists. No wonder that in his Preface Davies described his work as a specimen of the apocalypse of the twentieth century.[30]

In his capaciously European outlook, Davies displays an impressive cultural eclecticism and ecumenism that is conspicuously evidenced in his unorthodox poetry. For him, Europe stood in part for that boldness of imaginative life he found so sorely wanting in parochial, philistine and puritan Wales. A poem from his last collection, *Llef* (1987), begins by vividly recalling how in boyhood he used to imagine ponies running wild on the hills above his mining village. It next brings to mind Epona, the Celtic goddess of the horse, before regretting how her creatures ended up tamed into the docile drudges and racehorses of the modern day. Finally, it ends by joyfully celebrating the restoration to the horse of all its original glorious wildness, unbridled and riotous, in the celebrated works of the Expressionist painter Franz Marc.[31]

Having begun in a mining family where his father was fatally attracted to drink and his siblings were all ordinary valley girls, Pennar's personal journey led to release through his own imaginative awakening and spectacular educational successes. Dreamily lost in his own world from a very young age, he had always seemed peculiar and exotic in his drab working-class surroundings. Therefore it was no surprise that in the early years of adulthood he was attracted to Nietzsche's notorious concept of the Superman, and of the artist as set apart and uniquely licensed to transgress. His early antipathy to Dylan Thomas seems to have been clearly related to his associating Thomas with exactly the lifestyle he himself had with such difficulty chosen to renounce.

Davies's fiction duly enacted his struggle with this temptation, which was again for him, as for other members of the Cadwgan group, associated with the sophisticated cultural scene in Europe. Homoeroticism functioned as one signifier of the unconventional artist nature. Thus in *Meibion Darogan* the young dramatist Serena, mysteriously invalid, is powerfully attracted to her maid. And in the strange short story 'Y Dyn a'r Llygoden Fawr' an account of a Russian scientist's infatuation with a male lover is counterpointed by a report on an experiment that involves training rats to submit passively to his commands. It is a fable both of political authoritarianism and of the totalitarianism implicit in the Superman cult.[32] As for Davies's story 'Prifardd Cysefin', it is a sympathetic comedy loosely modelled on his own dreams of superiority as a young working-class author. Tal Cohen (part-Jewish) is a gauche young man, embarrassingly short in stature (although his name ironically means 'tall') and altogether physically unprepossessing but full of an overweening belief in his unappreciated poetic talent. He is potentially the equal in genius, at least in his own sadly disordered mind, of Dante and Goethe and Tolstoy. Tal is in short (so to speak) an artistic *Übermensch*, a Promethean soul secretly feeding his dreams of personal aggran-disement on the poetry of Rubén Dario and filling his ears with the intoxicating sound of Mahler and Beethoven.[33]

Pennar Davies's marriage to Rosemarie Wolff, a German national, undoubtedly enriched his knowledge of her country's culture and deepened his admiration of it. In 1983 he published a comprehensive collection of translations from German poetry. Beginning with the period of the Niebelungen, they tracked all the important phases of the country's poetic culture (with inclusion of occasional materials from Austria and Switzerland) down to the First World War. Among the poets of the late nineteenth and early twentieth centuries featured were Friedrich Nietzsche, Christian Morgenstern, August Stramm and Hugo von Hofmannsthal. The collection ended with a particu-larly fine Welsh version of a poem by Georg Trakl, and for each poet in the volume Davies furnished a pen portrait and description of his period. An Introduction provided a brief overview of the history of German poetry, and in an interesting Preface the editor noted that in translating he had in every case adhered strictly to the precise verse form of the original. He added that his anthology was modelled on a previous one that had been prepared for publication by T. Pugh Williams in the early 1950s. While that had failed to see the light of day, among those who had contributed to it were Silvan Evans, Elfed, John Morris-Jones, T. Gwynn Jones, T. H. Parry-Williams, Ifor L. Evans and J. Gwyn Griffiths. This list gives us some idea of the extent of interest there had been in Wales between the wars in Germany's poetic culture.[34]

Also married to a German national – Kate Bosse-Griffiths – J. Gwyn Griffiths was no doubt similarly culturally advantaged. He evidently acquired an impressive mastery of the country's literary culture, as is clear from his long 1969 essay, 'O'r Balcon i'r Arena'.[35] In the course of vigorously arguing against the conception of 'pure poetry', untarnished by social commitments – a concept he blames partly on such French authors as Gautier, Flaubert and Mallarmé – he ranges widely, and approvingly, across the German literary landscape. His survey includes an analysis of the equally pernicious poetry of political propaganda promoted by the Nazis. Not that his references to European culture are limited to France and Germany. His essay includes mention of some of the great nineteenth-century Russians and of such Italian poets as Giosuè Carducci (*IGF*, 38–9).

By the early 1970s there was increasing talk of the UK, under the premiership of Edward Heath, joining the European Economic Community at long last. That Pennar Davies's response to this possibility was lukewarm and inclined to the sceptical is evidenced in a long poem he wrote in 1971 in response to a Welsh Arts Council commission.[36] Entitled 'Mae Cymru'n Mynd i Europ', it opened with sardonic reflections on the condescending supposition by UK politicians that they would be (as the title of the poem had it) leading Wales to Europe. Hardly so, was Davies's tart response. After all, Wales would be the oldest of the nations that had so far joined the Community. Indeed, the origins of Wales as a national community, could be said to have predated the very concept of a modern Europe. Davies then proceeds to survey his country's history from pre-Christian times onwards, noting along the way how, along with the saints of Ireland, the saints of Wales had not only been instrumental in Christianising Europe but also in reintroducing Classical learning to the continent. Europe had come to Wales in the form of the Normans, but in the same period European culture had, through the poetry of Ovid in particular, enriched the poetry of Dafydd ap Gwilym. Owain Glyndŵr's European aspirations for a Welsh polity, a Welsh Church and a Welsh university were well chronicled.

Thus Davies traces the interlinkages between Wales and Europe down to the present. However, to him, the European Community as constituted seems to be more akin to a betrayal of Wales's age-old European dreams than a fulfilment of them. Along with the leaders of Plaid Cymru, of which he was a very active member, Davies believes the Community's version of Europe to be based on the worship of two pagan gods: Mammon and Moloch. And so he ends his poem with the hope not that Wales will be led to Europe, but rather that Europe will be led to recognise a Wales that still remains stubbornly faithful to Europe's better self. Wales, he sonorously concludes, is 'calon y wir Europ' ('the heart of the true Europe').

The youngest member of Cylch Cadwgan was Gareth Alban Davies. Still a sixth-former studying French and Spanish for A-level at Porth County School at the time, he then spent three years working underground as a conscripted Bevin boy miner before resuming his education at Queen's College, Oxford. Subsequently he was appointed to a post in the University of Leeds, where he finished his career as a distinguished professor of Spanish, specialising in the poetry of the golden age of Spanish culture. His non-academic output included three volumes of poetry, each including a high percentage of poems relating to locations on the continent, many of them, naturally, in Spain, but that also span Europe from Moscow and the Moselle to Lugo (Galicia) and Venice. And in 1965 he published, jointly with his wife Caryl, a Welsh translation of André Gide's *La Symphonie pastorale* under the title *Y Deillion*.[37] He is an important and unconventional poet, whose achievement remains largely unappreciated.

In his poetry, as in his professional life, Davies opened himself up completely to a country very different from his own in culture, as in climate. But rarely did he lose sight of Wales in the process. Instead he often instinctively used it as his point of reference. As autumn rain starts falling in Madrid, dripping from gutter to ground as if in glittering exultation ('a'r diferion yn orfoledd at y llawr'), he sees the greenness of Wales in its every drop.[38] When witnessing the solemn marking of Easter in El Escorial, he draws an unexpected parallel between the elaborate rituals of the sombre Catholic service conducted in the majestic monastery (every picture and image hooded, the priests like stunned ants busily coaxing Christ from the dead, and then the blaze of floodlights bringing colours leaping back to life) and the simple Nonconformist worship of his family, companionably gathered to read the Book of Job around the heat of a kitchen stove. Both occasions, he realises, are acknowledgements that God makes himself available in the little love that binds humans together in a royal ministry, protecting them from the devilish confusion of the pines ('a'n deil . . . rhag dryswch dieflig y pin') that shake so violently in the cutting wind of April.[39]

On another visit to El Escorial, he regrets that the arrival of spring there is delayed by the cold wind, slyly adding that it will eventually turn up as tardily as a Welsh Nonconformist minister arriving late for a preaching engagement (*T*, 21). Overhearing priests, enveloped in black from top to toe, busily gossiping in Lugo, he translates their banal chatter into the colloquial Welsh idioms of chapel ministers chewing the cud in his native Rhondda (*T*, 37). It is the monumental Escorial, too, that supplies a setting for another Welsh reminiscence. It describes a middle-aged woman (probably his wife, Caryl) watching a group of children crossing the simple courtyard in front of the huge monastery and being borne back in memory to the occasion when she watched two little Welsh children playing in the same foreign space, as shadow crept slowly across it and a breeze arrived to harvest the afternoon.[40]

As he joins in dancing the *Sardana* in Barcelona, Gareth Alban Davies implicitly associates the Welsh with the Catalans in their stubborn repeated defiance of the several arrogant cultures that have attempted to silence their language (*T*, 62). The flow of the Duero river in Tordesillas, its course fringed with poplars that seem nailed in place to torture the great arid waste, prompts the realisation that the word 'Duero' is related to 'dŵr', the Welsh word for water (*T*, 83). Even in distant Santiago de Chile, he and his family fall to discussing the minutiae of the Welsh language, oblivious of their immediate environment, and do so with all the intensity of people intoxicated by the perfume of their own obsessions (*T*, 73).

The son of a prominent Welsh Congregationalist minister, Davies naturally gravitated to notable religious sites and responded to celebrations of great religious festivals. On many such visits he was reverently impressed by the majesty of the spectacle. But he also repeatedly drew attention to the repugnant alignment of religion with brute power evident in grand, overpowering cathedrals that trumpeted in their paintings and their carven images the glorious victories of the *Reconquista*, the violent expulsion of the Moors from Spain that ended in 1492. He similarly deplored the disquieting tendency in Spanish Catholicism to linger lovingly over the traces of agony limned for the adoration of the multitude in the writhing body of the crucified Christ. In a poem recording an Easter he spent in 1991 in Artá, Majorca, he falls to cursing the cross, with its fetishised image of the suffering Christ (*GC*, 12), and he does so in a volume, *Galar y Culfor*, that pointedly contains many poems in memory of humble Welsh Nonconformist ministers and ordinary chapel members whose faith was of an entirely different temper. There is therefore a significant sense in which we find in Davies's poetry, for all its undoubtedly catholic Europeanism, a sophisticated late twentieth-century variant of the Nonconformist view of Europe advertised by O. M. Edwards in his classic volume *O'r Bala i Geneva*, examined in an earlier chapter.

When he attends again to the churches of Catholic Spain, the strong egalitarian instincts trained in Gareth Alban Davies by his Welsh chapel background and early proletarian surroundings in the Rhondda valley often become evident, as he homes in on humble, humanising details. He responds sympathetically to the worship of the Virgin Mary because it is clearly an expression of the desperate yearning of humans for love and compassion. 'Mary is crucified', he powerfully writes in 'Y *Rosario* yn Laguardia, La Rioja', 'on the torture of our humanity' ('Croeshoelir Mair / ar artaith ein dynoldeb'). She is fashioned out of 'the rags of our anxieties' into a 'rag-doll of graciousness' (*CG*, 53). In the same poem, he warms to the whisper of the wings of ordinary pigeons, a simple daily sound he hears competing with the anxious twittering in the church of the birds of faith. Mary is also viewed approvingly by him as providing a gentle and welcome feminine contrast to the *machismo* of the Spanish male, strikingly imaged in the form of a bull he sees leading a docile herd with his rampantly potent testicles proudly swinging to impress a herd of heifers in a neighbouring field (*CG*, 24). As for the nun whose mummified body is on display in a convent at Agreda, it is not so much for her rigidly cloistered piety that he admires her as for the empowering skill with which she deployed her virginity to influential political, as well as religious, effect (*CG*, 54).

The colourful boldness and sensuous opulence of some of Gareth Alban Davies's images strongly suggests that he had been influenced by the startling Latin extravagances of some of Spain's most celebrated *modernista* poets, such as Lorca, whose description of New York as a modern metropolis in which at dawn a 'gust of black pigeons washed their feet in rotten waters' came to his mind when he visited the city (*CG*, 67). And his comprehensive mastery of the Spanish poetic tradition became fully manifest when in 1990 he published an anthology of translations from the twelfth to the twentieth centuries. The Introduction provides an impressive sweep of the whole of Spain's poetic landscape during the course of which Davies makes several suggestive references to comparable aspects and phases of Welsh history and culture. He notes the presence of the Celts on the Iberian peninsula, particularly in Galicia, the region that still bears their name; in Spain's exposure to the multiple influences of several outside cultures (including most obviously the Jewish and the Islamic) he detects a hugely magnified image of the Welsh experience, and in both instances he notes how multiculturalism and multilingualism left beneficial traces on the 'indigenous' culture; Spain, he notes, experienced an important literary renaissance at the beginning of the twentieth century, as too did Wales, and he suggests that both these renaissances were in part enabled by such factors as a newly educated population, a revival of scholarship, a revivifying injection of foreign influence and a political awakening; finally, he emphasises that Spain, like Wales, had always existed at a remove from the influential centres of cultural production.

Gareth Alban Davies's excellent body of translations appeared, as did the German anthology by Pennar Davies already mentioned, in a series of translations produced under the auspices of the Welsh-language section of Yr Academi Gymreig. From its inception in 1959, this highly select and culturally influential Welsh Academy of distinguished writers (consciously modelled on the Académie Française) had adopted the aim of introducing major European writers to Welsh attention. In this context, translation, as Gareth Alban Davies noted in his Preface, took on an exalted missionary role. It was in the same spirit that, along with the Russian specialist W. Gareth Jones, he edited in 1976 a collection of essays on prominent European writers. Following an overview of twentieth-century literature, the volume included discussions of André Gide, Franz Kafka, Malraux, Jean-Paul Sartre, Albert Camus, the New Novel, Boris Pasternak, Paul Valéry, Rainer Marie Rilke, Paul Claudel, Federico García Lorca, Bertolt Brecht, and Ionesco, Beckett and the Theatre of the Absurd.[41]

In 1953 the members of the Cadwgan circle jointly published a short anthology of their poems. Two of those with a clear European orientation were by J. Gwyn Griffiths. In the first, he welcomed as 'the Messiah of a new Europe' the pianist imprisoned in Lübeck in a camp for Latvian, Lithuanian and Estonian refugees who, according to report, had defied the Nazis with his playing.[42] In the second he riffed on a line by Gabriele D'Annunzio to produce a poem crammed with typically adventurous images. The coming of wild dawn takes on the aspect, in the mind's sieve, of a great rat, a grey murderer, the nadir of the feast (*CG*, 67). Much later in life, Griffiths displayed the extraordinary eclecticism of his scholarship and scope of his imagination when, during the course of reviewing a volume of Welsh translations from the Polish by T. Hudson Williams, he enthusiastically digresses to recommend the culture of Czechoslovakia to his readers (*IGF*, 170–5). In particular, he chooses to pay attention to the dramatist and novelist Karel Čapek, to whom he attributes the coinage of the term 'robot'. It was, argues Griffiths, the very term needed to describe the kind of automaton to which the totalitarian machine age threatened to reduce the human being. He ends by hailing Čapek as a champion of the people, a pacifist, nationalist and humanist who, in his *Letters from Holland* (1933) had displayed an instinctive sympathy for small nations. 'If the shop is small', he had written, 'then it leaves no room for rubbish.'

With the departure of J. Gwyn Griffiths and Kate Bosse-Griffiths for Bala the Cadwgan circle dispersed, but the members still retained close creative contact with each other. In their new locality the pair soon found another kindred spirit in Euros Bowen. Son of a Nonconformist minister and a native of the Rhondda Fawr like Gwyn Griffiths, Bowen had, following extensive theological training, entered the priesthood with the Church in Wales, and the prolific and frequently controversial poetry he was eventually to produce clearly bore the marks of the sacramentalism to which he became devoted. Shortly after the arrival of the Griffithses in the neighbourhood, Bowen launched a new periodical, *Y Fflam*, with the aim of providing young writers with a platform denied them by the established literary periodicals still dominated by the old guard. Soon after it had begun to establish itself, J. Gwyn Griffiths and his old close friend Pennar Davies began to take an ever-increasing role in *Y Fflam*'s editorial decisions.

In August 1949 a major article on contemporary literature in France and Wales appeared, written by another member of Cadwgan, Gareth Alban Davies, by then an undergraduate at Queen's College, Oxford.[43] Using famous passages by Eliot from 'Tradition and the Individual Talent' and 'The Function of Criticism at the Present Time' as his warrant, Davies argued strongly for recognising that Welsh literature formed a part of the literary culture of Europe and that it should accordingly also be fully informed of it and by it. Fair-mindedly noting that European culture had usually been mediated to the Welsh by English culture, Davies warned against over-reliance on this, because, in the very act of transmitting the culture of Europe, England was bound to filter it through its own highly distinctive cultural sensibility. Direct, unmediated access to Europe was therefore imperative for the health of the Welsh literary tradition.

In Davies's opinion, French authors should be of particular interest and value to Welsh writers because there was a natural affinity between the literatures of France and Wales. And of all literary movements, that of French Symbolism was most pertinent to current Welsh needs. Among the defining features of Symbolism were its treatment of symbols as an indispensable medium for accessing the transcendent, and the priority it placed on the musicality of poetry. Words were to be chosen, as Mallarmé had insisted and demonstrated, exclusively for their colour and suggestive sound. About this credo Davies had his doubts; hence his preference of Paul Valéry over the nineteenth-century French Symbolist masters, because he had anchored words once more in meaning and thus healed the breach between poetry and everyday life. But Valéry had, Davies approvingly noted, fully accepted and capitalised on the seminal perception of the Symbolists that poetry derived from, spoke to, and spoke from the mysterious human unconscious. Valéry had succeeded in fusing this vital new insight with the beliefs and practices of the great French classical tradition. In this lay his value for Wales. Because the central Welsh literary tradition had also been soundly based on classical models and had also highly prized sound without fetishising it.

Alongside Valéry Davies placed Proust as a salutary model of achievement for the Welsh. For all the unhealthy neuroticism of his self-obsession, Proust had fully grasped the implications of Freud's new, subtle, nuanced understanding of the human psyche in all its dark and labyrinthine depths, and had evolved the means of incorporating this in the form of a revolutionary fiction. So far, only Saunders Lewis, John Gwilym Jones and, to a lesser extent, Kate Bosse-Griffiths had attempted anything similar in Wales, and their work had therefore necessarily involved an exploration of the sexual insights of Freud. This had been deplored by the critics. As a corrective to their puritanism, Davies recommended the example of another French novelist, Jules Romains, in his novel *Psyche*. Totally frank about human sexuality, it nevertheless treated it in a non-titillating, even unerotic, way, thus continuing the robust French tradition famously instanced by Rabelais and Voltaire. This, Davies argued, would prove a powerful antidote to the puritan philistinism that bedevilled Welsh culture.

Finally, Davies turned to the plays of the Catholic Paul Claudel. For him, these offered a valuable corrective to the limiting theatre of realism, in that they emphasised the connection of the human to the divine and thus satisfied what Davies viewed as a primal, primary human need. While recognising Saunders Lewis's debt to Claudel, Davies regretted that Lewis had not learned from the Frenchman the value of a non-realistic drama, the importance of which for Wales lay not least in that it did not tie the dramatist to the language of everyday life. Vital aspects of everyday life in Wales were being lived primarily through the medium of English, a fact that was an obvious hindrance to the development of a convincingly realistic Welsh-language theatre. Davies concluded his important article by expressing the hope that he had drawn attention to aspects and achievements of recent French literature that should help advance the vital aim of replacing Wales on the map of Europe, and of enabling Wales both to benefit from and to contribute to European culture.

Davies's article attracted a vigorous riposte. A year later, Bobi Jones, at the time a Young Turk but destined to become a considerable, highly adventurous Welsh-language poet, contributed an essay in which he attacked Symbolism (defined by him with a characteristically cavalier vagueness) for being archaic and decadent. In his view, it tended towards escapism and resulted in a limiting and specialising of lexicon, and thus a weakening of poetic discourse. In the modern form towards which, he regretted, some modern Welsh poets were inclining, it was the product of French culture. It had originated in France partly as a kind of extreme reaction against the classic 'realism' of the traditional high culture of French letters, and partly as a reaction against the empiricism of the great nineteenth-century novelists, most particularly the scientism of the naturalists.[44] Jones's essay was a companion piece to another in which he debated the virtues of Symbolism with another young emergent poet of the time, T. Glynne Davies, who held that Welsh Symbolism (of which he approved) was the product of a reaction against the culture's recent tendency to reduce poetry to propaganda.[45] Jones's final counterblast was that in so far as it embraced Symbolism enthusiastically, Welsh poetry was running the risk of going the way of French poetry and ending up in the anarchy of Surrealism.

These may seem like the stale and sterile intellectual debates of a long-ago yesteryear. But they are more interesting and significant than that. They are the telling symptoms of a new cultural movement. They show how intensely interested a young post-war generation of Welsh writers was in French Symbolism. Bobi Jones went on to be as good as his word, eschewing Symbolism for a much more hybrid poetic, acrobatic in its daring leaps of association and characterised by high-risk fusions of different registers and vocabularies, in the process generating his own unconventional vocabulary of Symbolism. As has already been seen, Gareth Alban Davies moved on from French to Spanish literature, his professional studies in the latter circling back in his poetic practice to a variant of Symbolism via such major figures of the *modernismo* movement as Lorca. But the poet to bear the marks of French Symbolism most evidently was Euros Bowen, the founding editor of *Y Fflam*, who had first turned to poetry, perhaps not entirely coincidentally, just two years before Gareth Alban Davies's essay appeared in his periodical.

In Bowen's case, his interest in Symbolism may well have been mediated by his enthusiasm for the neo-Symbolist poetry of Dylan Thomas, the self-styled 'Rimbaud of Cwmdonkin Drive' (a subject to be discussed in a future chapter). Shortly after Thomas's passing, he dedicated an *englyn* to his memory, invoking him as a Dionysiac figure who had reaped the harvest of poetry so enthusiastically that his lips had turned red and, drunk on the grape, he had dropped dead, leaving wine widowed (*D*, 19). In his chosen manner of expression, so Bowen believed, Thomas had revealed himself to be a European, rather than an English, poet.[46] Behind the memorial *englyn* there lies, one suspects, an allusion to Baudelaire's warning to the poet that permanent intoxication was the only reliable protection against becoming a prisoner of time[47] (*D*, 277). Bowen quoted this Baudelairean apophthegm in a note to a poem he composed in response to it, bearing the title 'Sobri' ('Sobering up'). Flight from time is there affirmed to be already implicit in the history of stars and birds, and to be palpable in moments of silence and stillness, as when stars steady the hours of night, a bird meditates on the tip of an ash tree at midday, and sobriety claims the imagination's chamber (*D*, 155).

Bowen resembled Baudelaire in his love of the prose poem. Sight of the renowned stained-glass windows of Chartres moved him to an extravaganza of synaesthesia, again in the manner of the great French poet: 'I listened to them striking up their chords on wall and pillar, in the bays and on the floor. / I saw the musical instruments in the windows, an intense violin blue, red impassioned trumpets, a yellow fluting alternating with harps in their setting bright and gay.'[48] His whole approach to the poetic imagination was clearly informed by the credo Baudelaire had announced in his celebrated sonnet

'Correspondances' – acknowledged by Bowen in one of his commen-
taries and duly translated by him – in which the intermingling of the
senses enables unique symbolic apprehension of the secret underlying
unity of all creation. Time after time Bowen transfigured the world
in this fashion in his torrent of poems. For him, sunflowers are to be
viewed in the manner of Van Gogh, as being 'like a yellow emotion
on the blue wave of trees; like a sea-shell intent on oystered pearls:
// Like drops of lemon rain on the high windows of the wood: like a
deep whirlpool circling to the acclaim of bannered rocks' (*EB*, 39).
'When the wind is green', he elsewhere writes, 'seaweed in the sea, /
the ivy's flesh, / and the glass of the lake's windows // When the wind
is yellow, / sand and shells, / and the moon on the floor of the lake'
(*D*, 214). Rimbaud's famous remark about *dérèglement de tous les
sens* comes to mind.

As was the case with Baudelaire, Bowen's aim was, he explained
in 'Y Gelfyddyd' (the Art), to use the products of the mortal mind
of art to reveal the secret creative sources of all of creation, It was a
glimpse of the ultimate mystery – what Mallarmé had termed 'sens
mystérieux de l'existence' – he added, that lent colour to the images
in poems (*D*, 224). In a series of crucial essays, in which he defended
his difficult poetry from the charge of wilful obscurity, he spelt out
his poetic credo, at the heart of which lay his religious reverence for
image and symbol. And religious it truly was, because Euros Bowen
saw his work as poet as a natural extension of his work in the priesthood. At the very centre of the act of worship, as of the act of writing
and reading a poem, lay ritual and sacrament, both indispensable
means, for him as an Anglican priest, of communicating with ultimate
spiritual reality. As a poet he was, Bowen insisted, not a Symbolist
(which he equated with an occult atheism) but a devout Christian
Sacramentalist.

In the matter of the symbol, he adopted the view that, evolving out
of the theories of the great German Romantics and other sources, it
had found its refined, sophisticated form in the credo and practice of
the French Symbolists. In the realm of the creative imagination, he
asserted, the image was one with the essence of things. Therefore to
be intimate with the image was to become inward with reality itself.
Hence the necessity for the true poet to think symbolically – Bowen
was, consciously or not, echoing the views of Dylan Thomas and of
the Hart Crane who spoke about trusting to the 'logic of symbols', a
phrase closely echoed by Bowen in his own formulation, 'rhesymeg

y dychymyg'. A poem, he explained with more than a hint of impatience to a sceptical and philistine Welsh Nonconformist readership brought up on a strict diet of didacticism, was best thought of as a 'river of symbols', carrying the mind of the reader on its flood towards a different world from that of mundane apprehension and communication.[49]

These were all views fully consistent with French Symbolist doctrine, and Bowen was fully aware of that. Indeed, in 1980, at the request of Yr Academi Gymreig, he edited a volume of his own masterly translations from the poetry of Baudelaire, Mallarmé, Rimbaud, Verlaine, Corbière, Laforgue, Valéry and Claudel. In the Introduction he furnished a succinct, trenchant account of the movement and its philosophy, along with a brief pen portrait of its main poetic practitioners. He is careful to distinguish between the different inflections given to the core ideas of Symbolism by these key figures. The translations that follow are in effect embedded in an impressive essay in which Bowen traverses the whole mental landscape of the Symbolist movement.

Bowen's relationship to the French Symbolists was a deeply complex and conflicted affair, and one that led him repeatedly and heatedly to deny that he was one of their company. At bottom, his denial may well have come from his instinctive understanding, as a Welsh poet of some originality, that, as André Gide had put it in a remark Bowen quoted in his Introduction to his volume of translations, 'L'influence ne crée pas, elle éveille' ('Influence never creates, it only excites', *BSF*, 3). But additional to this was Bowen's Christian unease at some of the more extreme tendencies apparent in the work of all the great Symbolists, with the belated exception of Claudel. He felt a mixture of admiration and repugnance for Baudelaire, for example, a poet whose own peculiar vision of original sin led to his emphasising the close affinity between divinity and Satanism, in the creation as in human nature. In his two-part poem on the poet he both compares and contrasts him with Dafydd ap Gwilym. Like the great Welsh poet, the Frenchman, too, had rebelled against the restrictive moral outlook of the Church (a rebellion exemplified in Dafydd's work by his debates with 'Y Brawd Llwyd', a Greyfriar). But unlike the Welshman, Baudelaire had, by way of reaction, allowed himself to be seduced by the fatal allure of sinful, ultimately syphilitic, flesh (*D*, 2256).

Bowen, as a confirmed Christian incarnationist, was also disapproving of the tendency of the greatest Symbolists to treat the given, visible world, glorious in all its ambivalent character and manifest imperfections, as a mere springboard towards some more pure transcendent reality. There are some occasions when, as in his two poems to the swan, he seems to be engaging obliquely with key Symbolist texts (*D*, 5, 189). He had translated the famous poems by Baudelaire and Mallarmé on the same subject (*BSF*, 24, 42), pointing out that, while very different, both treated the swan as a symbol of the poet's alienation from the ordinary world and proof of his complete devotion to the transcendent realm of beauty. This reading of the swan is specifically repudiated by Bowen, who sees the bird (with, in the second poem, more than a nod to Yeats's 'Wild Swans at Coole') as dazzlingly bright, inevitably transient, evidence of the presence of divine creativity abroad in all common things and creatures. While Bowen's swan, too, is ultimately a visitor from a superior spiritual realm, it does not offer transport to the transcendent. Instead this swan on Bala Lake brings with it for mortals the gift of discerning the signature of the divine perfection legible under the dull surface of surrounding mundane reality. Hence the poem's opening lines. These rapturously acknowledge the swan's power to bestow the gift of new (in)sight on a human observer who thereby acquires the visionary ability to glimpse significance and mystery everywhere. Except that at this crucial point Bowen uses the active continuous present tense of the verb 'to signify' ('argoeli') where normally the noun-form ('argoel') would have been employed. He thus underlines the permanent dynamics of this new, transfiguring, act of looking enabled by the visitation of the swan.

Another devotee of the symbol was Euros Bowen's contemporary Vernon Watkins, close friend and poetic confidant of Dylan Thomas. Watkins was nothing if not a visionary poet, humbly apprenticed to the great literary culture of Europe, but also keeping proud, aloof company with those Immortals whom he regarded as the elect of the ages, those 'poets, in whom truth lives' – from Dante through Blake to Hölderlin and Heine and the other great German Romantics, and from the French Symbolists to George, Rilke – and, of course, the incomparable Yeats. For him, poetry had to be exalted, rapt, time-defying, fixated on eternity; rhythmically it had to be ritualistic, incantatory and consciousness-altering; sonically it had to become the echo-chamber of the soul – a word Watkins was not shy about

using; and, of course, the native language of soul poetry was symbolism, since he was convinced that the ultimate, eternal truths cannot
be rationally known; they can only be imaginatively symbolised.
And whereas Dylan Thomas, that serpent in Watkins's bosom, was
a Freudian Symbolist, Watkins was incorrigibly Jungian, believing
in the persistence, the recurrence, in every person's unconscious, of
archaic images embodying eternal, universal truths.

Watkins's natural habitat was the southern coast of the Gower
peninsula. The cliffs there are limestone, and Watkins was a passionate lover of limestone landscapes. They were the veritable landscapes
of the soul, honeycombed as they were by secret caves and cavities,
and carrying deep within themselves underground pools and streams
that occasionally glinted unpredictably and mysteriously to the surface. The map of such a landscape's deep interior was nothing like
its familiar geographical surface appearance. Limestone landscape
thus emblematised temporal mortal existence, which also carried in
its secret depths perennial truths that occasionally manifested themselves to the initiate and could be expressed only through the esoteric
vocabulary of image and symbol uniquely available to art. This vocabulary was the great carrier of a perennial philosophy, universal to all
civilisations, surviving by metamorphosing anew from millennium to
millennium. These myths, symbols, and images belonged to the deep
grammar of the human soul. Watkins therefore felt that the ancients
of all ages and cultures were his closest contemporaries.

Watkins was another poet who accorded the swan pride of place
in a visionary poem. But in his case the swan, in all its glory, seemed
in the end to signify only the debased and derivative state of mortal
existence. The swan's presence therefore aroused in him only a yearning dream for that 'original white, by which the ravishing bird looks
wan', as Watkins puts it in his magnificent poem 'Music of Colours:
White Blossom'[50] (*CP*, 101). This is an example of Watkins's meta-
physic of sound, itself of course a key Symbolist rhetorical device
– the attenuation of 'swan' to 'wan' verbally emblematises the difference between mortal and divine standards of purity and thus
highlights man's impoverished sense of what constitutes perfection.
Man mistakes what is at best 'wan' for the authentic 'swan'. Here
again we have a Welsh poem haunted by French Symbolist poetry.

Scattered throughout Watkins's hefty *Collected Poems* are his trib-
utes to the great European masters he so reverently admired. That
they were the guardian angels of his imagination becomes apparent

in the long wartime poem he wrote for his godchild, born in Paris in a 'wailing time' (*CP*, 94). At the heart of the poem, as if to ward off despair, he invoked 'the great [European] interpreters of lyric judgment' (*CP*, 96): Dante, Hans Christian Andersen, Hölderlin (his words 'secret and proud, / Like a lion, like a fawn', *CP*, 97), and Kierkegaard ('world-moving . . . with an intellectual blade, / Piercing the inmost shade / Of Sophoclean death'). A visit to Venice sees him summoning up the Tuscan ghosts of 'Dante and Guido . . . / They rise from sandgrains where they seemed forgotten' (*CP*, 178). Swedenborg, the occult Christian Platonist, is celebrated in a poem mocking grave robbers intent on gold and totally unaware of that true treasure, 'the interior psalm / Intended for God alone' (*CP*, 247). As for the collection tellingly entitled *Affinities* (1962), it included a memorial poem for Heine ('Your footstep crossed the sun, / And where you stepped the world was changed', *CP*, 300) and two for Watkins's beloved Hölderlin, one of the most important and intimate of his personal muses, perhaps because he had known the anguish of breakdown and mental derangement as had Watkins himself.[51]

The German was for him, as the first poem dedicated to his memory affirmed, a 'poet of godlike stillness, anchorite, / Son of the world God made before man sinned', and for him love 'was . . . as to the birds their flight' (299). Glancing, perhaps, at the source of Watkins's own poetic vision in mental suffering, in his long second poem he identified in Hölderlin a Sophoclean awareness that 'a wound was in the nature of man', that 'joy had a tragic base' and that 'the wound of love was his, the unhealing wound' (*CP*, 305). For Watkins, Hölderlin's tortured 'fragments' had even outshone the majestic achievements of his great contemporaries at Weimar, Goethe and Schiller. He had ended up, imprisoned but left with a language 'torn in fragments', testifying to 'the glory / Accessible only to faith, miraculous bridges, / Visions too great for men without the cadence / And broken utterance of our elected guide'. (*CP*, 310). Watkins was also attracted to another afflicted soul, the 'rhythmic demigod', Nijinsky (*CP*, 290). The ode to his memory claimed that in his sublime dancing, 'the grace of Mallarmé's Faun / Smiled, you brought to Gautier's perfection life, / Valéry dreamed, and waking / Saw in your dance his divine Narcissus' (*CP*, 290).

Throughout his career, Watkins worked on translations from major European poets and after his death several were published by Enitharmon in a slim volume edited by Ruth Pryor and introduced by Michael Hamburger. It included extracts from the *Iliad,* the *Purgatorio* and the *Paradiso,* and a range of poems in French, Italian and German – a language with which Watkins had been familiar from an early age as his mother had been a student of the language who had spent a study period living in the country. The translations from the German included a striking rendering of one of Rilke's best-known poems, on the 'Archaic Torso of Apollo', which ends with the imperative exhortation attributed to the statue for any observer to 'change your life', a phrase that might also be said to epitomise Watkins's own urgent and visionary poetic.[52] In an essay by Watkins on translation reproduced in the volume, he argues for a poet's mode of translation being superior to a scholar's, because 'a poet . . . seeks the migration of mysteries of language from one country to another' (*SVT*, 16). Translation, he stated, was one of 'the most nourishing arts' (*SVT*, 17). He added 'of all the major European languages German is the one best adapted to translation into English' (*SVT*, 19).

Notes

1   Kate Bosse-Griffiths, 'Nietzsche a Natsïaeth', *Heddiw,* 6/5 (November–December 1940), 139–41.
2   See the remarkable, prize-winning family memoir by her son, Heini Gruffudd, *Yr Erlid* (Tal-y-Bont: Y Lolfa, 2012), translated as *A Haven from Hitler: A Young Woman's Escape from Nazi Germany to Wales* (Tal-y-Bont: Y Lolfa, 2014).
3   'Madame Curie', in J. Gwyn Griffiths (ed.), *Teithiau'r Meddwl: Kate Bosse-Griffiths* (Talybont: Y Lolfa, 2004), 90–7. Hereafter *TM.*
4   For an overview of Bosse-Griffiths's output see Bethan Eleri Hicks, 'Astudiaeth o Yrfa Lenyddol Kate Bosse-Griffiths' (MA thesis, Swansea University, 2001).
5   'Crwban', *Heddiw,* 6/9 (May 1941), 263–7.
6   Kate Bosse-Griffiths, *Anesmwyth Hoen* (Llandybïe: Llyfrau'r Dryw, 1941).
7   Kate Bosse-Griffiths, *Fy Chwaer Efa* (Llandybïe: Llyfrau Pawb, 1944).
8   Katie Gramich, *Twentieth-Century Women's Writing in Wales* (Cardiff: University of Wales Press, 2007), p. 66.
9   Kate Bosse Griffith (*sic*), *Mae'r galon wrth y Llyw* (Llandysul: Gomer, 1957).
10 Kate Bosse-Griffiths, *Cariadau* (Talybont: Y Lolfa, 1995), pp. 1–20. Hereafter *C.*
11 Manon Rhys, *Cysgodion* (Llandysul: Gomer, 1993).
12 Patrick McGuinness (ed.), *Lynette Roberts: Diaries, Letters and Recollections* (Manchester: Carcanet, 2008), p. 117.
13 The standard study is Claire Flay, *Dorothy Edwards*, Writers of Wales Series (Cardiff: University of Wales Press, 2011).

14 'Days', in Dorothy Edwards, *Rhapsody*, Library of Wales Series (Cardigan: Parthian Books, 2007), pp. 155–94. Hereafter *R*.

15 See Menna Elfyn, *Optimist Absoliwt: Cofiant Eluned Phillips* (Llandysul: Gomer, 2016). Hereafter *OA*.

16 Rob Stradling, 'Breton Collaborators and the Welsh Llenorion,' *Planet* (Winter 2014).

17 There are two standard studies of Chamberlain's life and work: Kate Holman, *Brenda Chamberlain*, Library of Wales Series (Cardiff: University of Wales Press, 1997) and Jill Piercy, *Brenda Chamberlain, Artist and Writer* (Cardigan: Parthian, 2013).

18 Brenda Chamberlain, *Tide Race* (London: Hodder and Stoughton, 1962; reprinted Bridgend: Seren Books, 1987).

19 Brenda Chamberlain, 'White Water', in Stefan Schimanski and Henry Treece (eds), *Transformation Three* (London: Lindsay Drummond, n.d.), p. 103. The volume also included a poem by John Ormond Thomas and an article on Dylan Thomas's poetry. The volume came into my possession through my late aunt, Joan Rees, a friend and patron of Chamberlain's.

20 Brenda Chamberlain, *The Green Heart* (London: Oxford University Press, 1958), p. 13. Hereafter *GH*.

21 Brenda Chamberlain, *The Water-Castle* (London: Hodder and Stoughton, 1964), p. 11. Hereafter *W*.

22 Brenda Chamberlain, *Poems with Drawings* (London: Enitharmon, 1969), p. 30.

23 Brenda Chamberlain, *A Rope of Vines* (London: Hodder and Stoughton, 1965), p. 14. Hereafter *RV*.

24 'Moel Cadwgan', *Heddiw*, 6/5 (November–December 1940), 139.

25 J. Gwyn Griffiths, '*Meibion Cadwgan*, Pennar Davies a Chylch Cadwgan', in *I Ganol y Frwydr*, Llyfrau'r Dryw (Llandybïe: Christopher Davies, 1970), pp. 213–25.

26 For a penetrating discussion of Pennar Davies the author, see John Rowlands, 'Y Llenor Eigmatig', in Dewi Eirug Davies (ed.), *Pennar Davies: Cyfrol Deyrnged* (Swanea: Tŷ John Penry, 1981), pp. 15–29. The best overview of Davies's life and career is D. Densil Morgan, *Pennar Davies*, Dawn Dweud Series (Cardiff: University of Wales Press, 2003).

27 Parts of the discussion that follows draw on my study of Pennar Davies and the Cadwgan circle in M. Wynn Thomas, 'Portraits of the Artist as a Young Welshman', in *Corresponding Cultures: The Two Literatures of Wales* (Cardiff: University of Wales Press, 1999), pp. 94–9.

28 For an account of the novel in relation to Pennar Davies and Cylch Cadwgan, see '*Meibion Darogan*, Pennar Davies a Cylch Cadwgan', in J. Gwyn Griffiths, *I Ganol y Frwydr: Efrydiau Llenyddol* (Llandybïe: Gwasg Y Dryw, 1970), pp. 230–2;

29 For an alternative fictional portrait of Cylch Cadwgan, see Rhydwen Williams, *Adar y Gwanwyn* (Swansea: Christopher Davies, 1972).

30 For a discussion of the novel see M. Wynn Thomas (ed.), *Gweld Sêr: Cymru a Chanrif America* (Cardiff: University of Wales Press, 2001), pp. 18–19.

31 'Y Meirch', in Pennar Davies, *Llef* (Llandybïe: Cyhoeddiadau Barddas, 1987), pp. 21–4.

32 'Y Dyn a'r Llygoden Fawr', first published in *Heddiw*, 6/9 (May 1941), 268–73, collected in *Caregl Nwyf* (Llandybïe: Christopher Davies and Llyfrau'r Dryw, n.d.), pp. 35–43.
33 'Prifardd Cysefin', in Pennar Davies, *Llais y Durtur* (Llandysul: Gomer, 1985), pp. 70–84.
34 Pennar Davies (trans.), *Yr Awen Almaeneg: Blodeugerdd o Farddoniaeth Almaeneg o'r dechreuadau hyd at drothwy'r Rhyfel Byd Cyntaf* (Cardiff: University of Wales Press on behalf of the Academi Gymreig, 1983).
35 'O'r Balcon i'r Arena', in J. Gwyn Griffiths, *I Ganol y Frwydr* (Llandybïe: Llyfrau'r Dryw, 1970), pp. 11–51. Hereafter *IGF*.
36 'Mae Cymru'n Mynd i Ewrop', in *Clywch y Beirdd* (Cardiff: Welsh Arts Council, limited edition, 1971). The council had invited ten poets to produce new poems to be read aloud at that year's National Eisteddfod at Bangor.
37 Caryl Davies and Gareth Alban Davies (trans.), André Gide, *Y Deillion/ Symphonie Pastorale* (Cardiff: University of Wales Press for Yr Academi Gymreig, 1965).
38 'Yr Hydref ym Madrid, 1951', in Gareth Alban Davies, *Balad Lewsyn a'r Môr* (Denbigh: Gwasg Gee, 1964), p. 15. Hereafter *BLM*.
39 'Y Pasg yn El Escorial', in Gareth Alban Davies, *Trigain* (Llandysul: Gomer, 1986), p. 19. Hereafter *T*.
40 'El Escorial – wrth y Fynachlog', in Gareth Alban Davies, *Galar y Culfor* (Llandybïe: Gwasg Dinefwr, 1992), p. 56. Hereafter *GC*.
41 Gareth Alban Davies and W. Gareth Jones (eds), *Y Llenor yn Ewrop* (Cardiff: University of Wales Press, 1976).
42 *Cerddi Cadwgan* (no publication details, 1953), p. 63. Hereafter *CG*.
43 Gareth Alban Davies, 'Llenyddiaeth Gyfoes Ffrainc', *Y Fflam*, 8 (August 1949), 25–32.
44 Bobi Jones, 'Simboliaeth', *Y Fflam*, 9 (August 1950), 3–6.
45 Bobi Jones and T. Glynne Davies, 'Trafod Simboliaeth', *Y Fflam*, 9 (August 1950), 36–8.
46 'Barddoniaeth Dywyll', *Taliesin*, 10 (July 1965), 29.
47 'Dylan Thomas', in Euros Bowen, *Detholion* (Llandysul: Gomer, 1984), p. 19. Hereafter *D*.
48 'Yn Chartres/In Chartres', Euros Bowen's translation of his own poem, in Cynthia Davies and Saunders Davies (eds), *Euros Bowen: Priest-Poet/ Bardd-Offeiriad* (Penarth: Church in Wales publications), pp. 46–7. Hereafter *EB*.
49 His most important statements along these lines occur in 'Barddoniaeth Dywyll', and 'Trafod Cerddi', *Taliesin*, 9 (March, 1965), 31–2.
50 Ruth Pryor (ed.), Vernon Watkins, *Collected Poems* (Ipswich: Golgonooza Press, 1986), p. 101. Hereafter *CP*.
51 For Watkins and Hölderlin, see Ian Hilton, 'Vernon Watkins and Hölderlin', *Poetry Wales*, 12/4 (Spring 1977), 101–17; Ian Hilton, 'Vernon Watkins as translator', in Leslie Norris (ed.), *Vernon Watkins, 1906–1967* (London: Faber and Faber, 1970), pp. 74–89; H. M. Waidson, 'Vernon Watkins and German Literature', *Anglo-Welsh Review*, 21/47 (1972), 124–37.
52 Ruth Pryor (ed.), *Vernon Watkins: Selected Verse Translations* (London: Enitharmon, 1977), p. 73. Hereafter *SVT*.

8

SURREALISM, THE WAR AND AFTER

In November 1937 an essay entitled 'Nodiadau ar Surrealistiaeth' ('Notes on Surrealism') appeared in the pages of *Tir Newydd*, the progressive new Welsh-language journal intended to appeal in particular to the intellectuals of the Cardiff area, and thus consciously metropolitan in its outlook.[1] Its author was Glyn Jones, a talented young poet and fiction writer – as well as a frustrated painter – from the old, distinguished industrial town of Merthyr. He was a close early friend of Dylan Thomas and akin to him in his dedication to the kind of bold, late modernist experimentations in writing that was anathema to the Welsh-language cultural establishment of the time. Such experimentation naturally found very few anglophone sympathisers among the heavily industrialised proletarian society of the south Wales coalfield.

A native of Merthyr, Jones had but a basic grasp of the colloquial Welsh still spoken by a few in his industrial district, until he settled in Cardiff as a young teacher and decided to attend night classes in Welsh literature taught by none other than Saunders Lewis. He then used his newly reinforced grasp of the language to explore its literature, particularly its rich medieval bardic tradition, and subsequently fashioned his own distinctive brand of Welsh modernism partly through fusing this Welsh-language cultural inheritance with what he had learned from mainstream modernism. It early became clear to him that a Welsh Europeanism could be viable and creatively productive only insofar as it was grounded from the beginning in a secure familiarity with both the anglophone and the Welsh-language literary traditions of his own country. In this, of course, he was the opposite of Dylan Thomas.

As he noted, Jones had been stimulated to write his essay for *Tir Newydd* in the wake of the controversial International Surrealist Exhibition held in the summer of 1936 in the New Burlington Galleries in London. He was left clearly unimpressed by the fashionable outcry surrounding it, early intuiting the shameless exhibitionism and ingenious promotional strategies that marked the spread of the movement from France. His exposure to Surrealism may well have predated the exhibition, as in 1932 he had spent a summer vacation with a friend in Paris, wandering Montparnasse as well as visiting the great art galleries of the city (*CS*, xxxvii).

In his carefully considered essay, Jones distinguished between those aspects of the Surrealist movement that were contemporary and thus new, and those aspects that could be said to instance one mode of seeing and writing that had always been part of the repertoire of the artist. It was obviously to the latter that Jones was attracted, and much the same could be claimed of his friend Dylan Thomas. Both recognised in Surrealism cleverly packaged instances of the kind of extravagant and fantastical productions with which they, as young writers, had already been experimenting and to which they had been independently introduced by much older writers. Predecessors acknowledged by the Surrealists themselves, Jones pointed out, included Swift, de Sade, Baudelaire, Hugo, Uccello, El Greco and Cézanne, and he quoted Pound's remark that 'The twelfth century [*sic*] had surrealism in plenty . . . The first "Arp" is in Bergamo; painted by Cosima [*sic*] Tura' (*TN*, 12). To these Jones added other examples of his own, such as Blake, Carroll and Lear, William Morris, Rossetti, some old folk rhymes and ballads, nursery rhymes and some poems for children. Rimbaud could not have produced word combinations more bizarre and unexpected than were haphazardly thrown up by a game of 'Consequences', and as for the Marx Brothers, their films, like other popular products of the cinema, were full of Surrealist gags and comic business.

Jones thus effortlessly demonstrated how fully familiar he was with the history of artistic culture, and how comfortable and natural it was for him to move from high culture to popular culture, from Breton and Éluard to nursery rhymes, from Europe to Britain and so on to the USA. His Europeanism was therefore not a precious cult, or a cherished cultural and political ideal, as it still was for some of the leading Welsh-language writers and intellectuals of his day. Indeed, he might even be said to take for granted his own creative relationship to it as a Welsh writer. His Europeanism was certainly one – if only one – source of fruitful examples, exactly as it was for Dylan Thomas.

In his short, highly condensed essay, Jones demonstrates his understanding of the cultural etiology of continental Surrealism. He explains how it originated in the (for him) anti-art antics of the sterile nihilistic movement of Dada; how the influence of Freud enabled Aragon, Éluard, Breton and others to develop a practice that involved a kind of spontaneous mapping through art of the chaotic under-world of the unconscious; how an artist such as Miró discovered the potential of collage to capture, through free, random expression, the serendipity of subliminal mental processes; how Surrealists had come to trumpet (unconvincingly) their sympathies for a utopian communism or anarchism, and for a radical democracy; and how conservative modernists of the old school, such as Eliot, Pound and Wyndham Lewis, had increasingly voiced their impatience with the manifold irresponsibilities of a Surrealist movement they regarded as meretricious and trivial.

In his conclusion, Jones made it clear he viewed Surrealism as no more than a stimulating and diverting artistic fad, doomed in the end to extinction because of its narrow philosophy. But he also conceded it could act as very useful 'gwrtaith', that is a fertiliser for the imagination, and it is in that very regard, one suspects, that both he and Dylan Thomas found it useful for their purposes. Surrealism, to change the metaphor, served both writers as a magic magnifying glass through which to view their own world.

After all, some aspects of Surrealism appeared completely familiar and natural to Glyn Jones and other Valleys writers. Their own native environment was itself outrageously bizarre, replete with incongru-ous juxtapositions and insanely mixed elements. Above the grime of the dark Valleys rose the green sunlit uplands of the bald hills with their exaltation of skylarks; the tangled bric-a-brac of the pithead machinery could have been sculptures devised by Man Ray, Marcel Duchamp or Hans Arp; carnival time brought in its wake marchers dressed as Moroccan soldiers complete with fez and blaring bazookas; trailing behind came a disciplined horde of blacked-up children whose comb mouth-organs produced a prodigiously raucous din; working-men's institutes provided the most unlikely of platforms for grand Italian opera; when the miners walked home at the end of their shifts through the streets with coal-blackened faces, they resembled strange foreign products not only of the mines but also of the dark Freudian underworld of the human psyche; as for the ethnically mixed population, it generated a wild babble of tongues and accents; the hooters that punctuated the working day had about them an ominous mournful banshee ring; and the dream-world of Hollywood cinema peddled romantic fantasies grotesquely at variance with the hard working lives of their eager viewers. All this and more constituted the ordinary rich Surrealism of the everyday in the society that Glyn Jones was proud to call his own and which he chose to celebrate in poetry and prose.

These were the 'crooked valley[s]' in which he defiantly gloried in a poem that appeared alongside Dylan Thomas's thoroughly Surrealist 'Prologue to an Adventure'. The two pieces were prominently featured in the launch issue of Keidrych Rhys's aggressively avant-garde periodical *Wales*. Simply entitled 'Scene', Jones's poem appeared the same year as his essay for *Tir Newydd*. In it he declared that 'I hear my heart speak to the bleaky sky', and fiercely identified with his natal environment: 'Coal and the valleys were my lucky egg . . . / my lonely burning flesh / Smokes up this sky-hook like a plunging fish.'[2] Such lines naturally assume a Dalí-esque quality.[3] After he'd moved away from Merthyr to teach in a slum district of Cardiff, Jones likened the experience of listening to a record of a choir from one of his beloved Valleys to 'cuddling the Nile of sounds between the steel / Lids of a needle's eye'. He found himself reluctantly responding to the massed voices 'hymning / That honeyed hooey, those bloodshot fairy-tales'.[4]

Jones's creative imagination developed in the borderland where two contrasting cultures met. Such zones are natural breeding grounds for the Surreal. Under such conditions, the mores and conventions of one of the two cultures cannot help but seem peculiar, even bizarre, when viewed in the perspective of the other. Even in Merthyr, Jones grew up with the bewildering weekly experience of sitting in chapel, listening to the pulpit rhetoric and related histrionics of a minister preaching in Welsh, a language he could barely understand. For him, as for Dylan Thomas who was subjected to the same experience, it must have been somewhat odd, even hallucinogenic, like watching a silent film with a sound-track suddenly added in a foreign tongue. Rhys Davies was another 'Valleys' writer, like Glyn Jones, who likewise found attending a largely unintelligible service in a Welsh chapel extremely rum.

Nor was this 'borderland' experience confined to the Valleys. It was replicated in Dylan Thomas's Swansea, a town where, of a Saturday night, the colourful rowdies of the surrounding, Welsh-speaking, areas of heavy industry descended on the more 'sophisticated' English-speaking townies among whom were sheltered products of respectable middle-class districts like Thomas's native Uplands. No wonder a story like 'Where Tawe Flows' in *Portrait of the Artist as a Young Dog* is replete with surreal effects. There was also the ancient area of the Welsh March. There the 'borderland' phenomenon left its mark on the mind of a writer like Nigel Heseltine. His thoroughly zany collection of short stories, *Tales of the Squirearchy* (1946), records the surreal antics of the eccentric remnants of the decaying local gentry who in his day still haunted those localities of rural Montgomeryshire where Wales fades into England.[5] His 1930s poetry was full enough of Surrealist imagery for a selection of it to be included (alongside that of Keidrych Rhys, another Welshman and close associate of Dylan Thomas) in an anthology published in Virginia, in the US, under the title *Seven Poets of the New Apocalypse*.

Even more of a culture shock for Glyn Jones's developing imagination was the annual migration when he and his parents took off from their home in Merthyr to spend part of the summer holidays in the old family region of Llansteffan and Llanybri, in rural Carmarthenshire. Jones remained haunted by that human version of transhumance for the whole of his life, variously translating the experience into golden idyll and surreal comedy, sometimes with distinctly dark overtones. His short stories, many of which are set in rural west Wales, are loaded with surreal effects, particularly when describing the physical peculiarities of people. The features of Wil Thomas, in the story of that name, are worthy of being captured in a film by Buñuel, for example. The miner has lost one eye, leaving 'the flesh all round red as though the eye-hole had been cut in his skin with a scissors'.[6] As for his wife, 'her lips were tight . . . and hard as a couple of pebbles' (*CS*, 57). A sinister stranger in 'The Four-Loaded Man' has a nose that is 'narrow and bony, a thick pink claw, sharp-hooked like a rose-thorn, and his heavy bottom lip hung down the bright purple-black of tracing paper' (*CS*, 120). A rural vicar in 'Price-Parry' has eye-brows that are 'black reaping-hooks' (*CS*, 161), and as for the terrifying Jordan in the masterly story of that name, who brings a heavy stick down on a dog's head 'until . . . the brains came out', he has finger-nails 'as green as grass' (*CS*, 206).

In her illuminating discussion of the subject, Laura Wainwright sees Glyn Jones as 'consciously adapting elements of European Surrealist art to a Welsh context',[7] and persuasively juxtaposes

passages and aspects from the stories with images by artists such as
Oscar Dominguez, Salvador Dalí, Giorgio De Chirico and Franz von
Stück to reinforce her point. As she points out, Jones's stories are
full of eruptions from the unconscious, many of them heavily laden
with sexual overtones, and she provides instances where he combined
observational detachment with bizarre details in the classic Surrealist
manner:

> He looked down and gazed with absorption at the spine that had moved
> upward with such rapid growth and saw it enter his breast-skin like a
> spear-head; he watched it without resistance slowly thrusting its green
> blade upwards as it grew into him, tearing off its vivid juicy flesh as it
> entered.[8]

In another story, 'the Wanderer,' Jones writes how 'through the blue
birdhole of sleep a sea-dove flew bringing its dreams like a beakful
of infinity'.[9] As Wainwright shows, Jones also occasionally placed his
characteristic hallucinatory effects at the service of an insurrectionary
social (and socialist) politics, an act again consistent with the sociopolitical aims of several of the most influential European proponents
and practitioners of Surrealism.

Stimulating though Glyn Jones evidently found European
Surrealism, however, and much though he may have gained as a writer
from studying it, he had entertained deep misgivings about it from
the beginning, as his essay for *Tir Newydd* made clear. Most particularly, he objected to its complete abandonment of both analytical
reason and creative imagination to the wild, dictatorial impulses of
the unconscious, a fixed objection that had artistic, moral and political roots. Nor were his interests in the progressive cultural aspects
of continental modernism limited to Surrealism. As Wainwright and
others have pointed out, early in his career as a poet he was attracted
to Symbolism, although here again he would have no truck with it in
its original French form because it specifically refused ever to engage
with social realities. He was, though, influenced by its trust in image
and symbol as quintessential vehicles of poetic expression. He, too,
chose to think in symbols and to develop his poems accordingly,
as when in 'Rant' he writes of how 'Time bites brightness from / A
moon's heart', while 'Slamming our sashes, throttling down the wrist,
/ Night comes for cock owls and shoos out the bats / Across a planet
streaming ghosts' (*CP*, 8). Nor were his European inclinations devoid

of any understanding of the potential of Europe for a writer with a specific commitment to Wales. Study with Saunders Lewis had made him fully aware of the cultural and nationalist aspects of his tutor's pro-European bias, and also made him cautiously sympathetic to it, although as a lifelong socialist he could not possibly accept the political (or for that matter the religious) elements in Lewis's conservative brand of Welsh Europeanism. As Jones wrote in a 1937 letter to Keidrych Rhys, 'Saunders is in some ways the Pound of Wales – trying single-handed it seems to me to break the narrow parochial tradition of Welsh literature and criticism and prejudice, point all the time to France and the Middle Ages and to England even' (*CS*, xxix). There was also the immediate, personal matter of his own poetic needs. Instinctively attracted to aestheticism (to the end of his life he favoured coloured ties) he harboured a strong social conscience that made it impossible to commit itself wholeheartedly to it, and through his carefully selective response to both Symbolism and Surrealism, and by means of a skilful adaptation of both to his own distinctively Welsh purpose, he was able to effect a synthesis perfectly suited both to his conscience and to his artistic practice.

Dylan Thomas, Glyn Jones's early friend, was troubled by no such scruples and so was free to exploit Symbolism and Surrealism as fancy dictated. As was the case with Jones, Thomas's imagination seems to have been naturally attuned to Surrealism from its earliest development, partly because of those sociocultural factors in his environment that have already been mentioned and partly from a temperamental taste for verbal contortions and theatrical effects of all kinds. Nostalgically recalling in a convivial letter to Daniel Jones the wild menagerie of characters and outlandish incidents they had invented when young teenagers in suburban Swansea, he wrote:

> I can't believe that Percy, who droppeth gently, can have dropped out of the world, that the 'Badger Beneath my Vest,' and 'Homage to Admiral Beatty' are a song and a boat of the past, that Miguel-y-Bradshaw, Waldo Carpet, Xmas Pulpit, Paul America, Winter Vaux, Tonenbach, and Bram, and all that miscellaneous colony of geniuses, our little men, can have died on us; that the one-legged grandmother – remember the panama-hat-shaped birds, from the Suez Canal, who pecked at her atlas-bone – doesn't still take photographs of Birmingham.[10]

As an adult, his theatre of the absurd ran easily to black humour – ' Mr [Neville] Chamberlain is crazy about modern verse, and I shall send a photograph of myself, in bowler and gasmask, rhyming womb with tomb' (*CL*, 325). It is an image worthy of Magritte. He unforgettably described the world as 'a chapter of accidents written in a dream by a professor of mathematics who has forgotten all formulas but the wrong one that 2 & 2 make 5' (*CL*, 528). His distinctive version of Surrealism was little more than an honest transcription of the serendipitous character of ordinary reality, a faithful tracing of the crazy paving of the human mind and of the anarchic world of the psyche.

When therefore Thomas encountered Surrealism in its fully fledged form in continental art, as he did when visiting the 1936 exhibition in London, he did so as a veteran, and his response was accordingly knowing and camp – as was his response to all forms of modernist experimentation. As the story goes, he wandered amongst the viewing guests with a tea bag dangling on a piece of string, and enquired of all and sundry whether they'd prefer it weak or strong. True or not, it is an incident that perfectly captures Thomas's arch way with Surrealism, and also explains why he could never simply succumb to its allure – his caginess being reinforced by his iron commitment to the practice of poetry as a complex conscious craft and not as a spontaneous product of the poet's unconscious.

This prevenience may partly account for Thomas's vehement denials that he was a Surrealist, although he certainly seemed such to many of his contemporaries. In the first of three letters in which he explicitly addressed the subject, he assured Richard Church that he had 'very little idea of what surrealism was, until quite recently I had never heard of it' (*CL*, 205). He could not read French, he went on to explain, and so French poetry was a closed book to him. Letters to Henry Treece, whose pioneering Study *A Dog Among the Fairies* was shortly to explore the issue of Thomas and Surrealism, and to whom he dismissed Surrealism as a 'highbrow parlour game' (*CL*, 282, 298,302), and Edith Sitwell, to whom he insisted he had no interest in 'clever things' like Surrealism (*CL*, 210) passionately labour the same point. And while admitting he had read at the International Surrealist Exhibition in London in 1936, he protested (disingenuously?) that he couldn't understand why he'd been invited (*CL*, 230, 231). There may be at least some truth in all these adamant assertions – he was genuinely averse to all labels and movements, and allergic to elaborate theorising – although it's by no means the first time for Thomas to provide grounds for suspecting he was protesting all too much. He was ready enough to admit to a familiarity with the poetry

of George Barker and David Gascoyne, the latter the most committed
and crusading of British Surrealist poets.

The briefest examination of almost any one of his early poems
makes it immediately clear why he was so consistently suspected by
friend and foe alike of Surrealist sympathies, as does the briefest
glance at any one of the grotesque stories set in rural west Wales that
he wrote in the 1930s. The 'Altarwise by Owlight' sequence of sonnets
in particular is packed with notorious examples of his outré imagery:
'Which sixth of wind blew out the burning gentry? / (Questions are
hunchbacks to the poker marrow). / What of a bamboo man among
your acres? / Corset the boneyards for a crooked boy?' and so on.[11]
Thomas's defence always involved emphasising that, contrary to
first impressions, such lines were actually soundly underpinned by
traditional syntax, and that the total effect was the result of conscious, elaborate artifice consistent with the customary ground rules
of grammar.

The early Thomas was also strongly suspected, not without good
reason, of being indebted to French Symbolist poets, notwithstand-
ing his stated lack of French. His friendships with Daniel Jones and
Vernon Watkins, both of whom were very well informed about continental modernism, added to the translations and discussions of
continental writers readily available in the various poetry journals
of the period in which he either published or showed an interest,
provided him with information more than enough for his own mag-
pie creative purposes. Self-mocking though it might have been, his
throwaway description of himself as 'the Rimbaud of Cwmdonkin
Drive' (*CL*, 487) does seem to betray more than a passing familiarity
with those aspects of the French poet's life, as well as of his work,
that Thomas would have recognised as relevant to his own deepest
fears and aspirations: his early burn-out, followed by a premature
death; his view of true poetry as originating in a deliberately induced
'derangement' of the senses, a state greatly facilitated by alcohol; and
his devotion to the arcane truths accessible only through the committed deployment of symbols. Here again, though, as in the case
of the Surrealists, he strongly objected to Rimbaud's addiction to an
impenetrable private lexicon of images, so that 'reading him and his
satellites, we feel as though [we] were intruding into a private party
in which nearly every sentence has a family meaning that escapes us'
(*CL*, 98). He was writing to Glyn Jones, who would have shared his
misgivings, rooted as they were, like his own, in a characteristically

(left-wing) Welsh commitment to a poetry, however necessarily obscure, of demonstrable social worth and usefulness.

Thomas was certainly aware very early of the work of the Symbolists. In a letter written at the age of nineteen to his friend Trevor Hughes he described him, in a burst of lyrical excess, as 'one of the dark-eyed company of Poe and Thompson, Nerval & Baudelaire, Rilke and Verlaine' (*CL*, 17). Earlier that same year (1933), Thomas had contributed a short essay on Symbolism to the *South Wales Evening Post*, a discussion culled directly from the *Encyclopaedia Britannica*. In an excellent survey both of Thomas's indebtedness to Symbolism and his practise of a Symbolist poetic, Nathalie Wourm concluded by persuasively arguing that the year or so during which Thomas displayed a particularly intense interest in the great French Symbolist poets coincided with a remarkable surge in his own early poetic environment.[12]

The precise relationship between Dylan Thomas and European modernism remains a vexed and contested subject. His has recently been labelled a modernism of the margins,[13] and an attempt has been made by James Keery and Vincent Sherry to characterise his sensibility as modernist, 'taking the crisis-time of the Second World War and the Apocalyptic poetry that consummates it as points of reference in political and literary history'.[14] What is clear is that Thomas (unlike, say, Saunders Lewis or the members of the Cadwgan group) was not beguiled by the glamour of European culture, partly because he was not a devotee of high culture at all. A vivid passage from *Return Journey* captures the creatively inflammable mix of high culture and popular, demotic culture that Thomas favoured, and that supplied him with the vocabulary even of his most Sibylline poems. He is recalling the halcyon days of his youth when he sat in Swansea's Kardomah café with his cronies, 'drinking coffee-dashes and arguing the toss . . . [about] music and poetry and politics, Einstein and Epstein, Stravinsky and Greta Garbo, death and religion, Picasso and girls'.[15] No wonder that he was, if anything, far more at ease, as his later life amply confirmed, with the democratic culture of the United States than he was with the aristocratic, and bourgeois, culture of a stuffy old Europe.

Thomas could never, therefore, have subscribed to that enthusiastic view of Europe expressed by David Gascoyne, for whom 'the tradition of modern English poetry is . . . quite different from the tradition of Hölderlin, Rimbaud, Rilke, Lorca, Jouve, – I belong to Europe before I belong to England.'[16] And by the very same token he would have been unable to proclaim himself a Welsh European, as implicitly did Glyn Jones for example. For him, the literary cultures of Europe were never more than a handy resource of models that were of occasional use to his own individual creative purposes. They certainly did not represent cultural liberation, enlargement or enrichment.

Service on the continent during the Second World War left a profound impression on some Welsh writers. One such was Alun Llywelyn-Williams, whose post-war poetry included many attempts to digest the experience he had undergone. Born into a middle-class family in Cardiff, Llywelyn-Williams became fully literate in Welsh only through studying the language, first at school and then at university. But even as he began to fall in love with the language and its long literary tradition, his impatience grew with those grand survivors of the great Welsh-language literary renaissance of the early twentieth century who still resolutely refused to take any account in their works of the experience of the Welsh proletariat, or of the lives lived by the urban Welsh (like his own family), or of the gathering sociopolitical crisis evident both in the depressed south Wales Valleys and in the rise of fascism on the continent. 'Very little [of their work] had any bearing, or so it seemed to me, on the life of the Wales that I knew in cosmopolitan Cardiff and industrialised Glamorgan and Monmouthshire', he later wrote.[17] So, when he began to write poetry himself, he reinforced its urban outlook and its radical politics (he was attracted to Marxism for a brief period) by launching a new youthful periodical, *Tir Newydd*, to remedy the glaring cultural deficit of the Welsh-language literary establishment.

As a young man in the 1930s faced with the growing probability of involvement in an annihilating war, Llywelyn-Williams was naturally fixated on the contemporary European scene. One of his early poems, written shortly after the aerial bombing of Guernica, has him seeking the vantage point of a local mountain top. He is intent on rising above the narrow outlook of his self-absorbed society so as to keep an eye on events elsewhere upon which, he knows, the future of that society depends.

> A war over the sea, the splendid museum
> is being violently plundered, and the stars are angered by the drone
>   of planes,

listen to the wail of our struggle, and the people of Spain
mourning the sweeping away of their withered ones.[18]

This passage includes references to the two aspects of Europe that
deeply mattered to the young Llywelyn-Williams. It is a 'splendid
museum', containing the priceless treasure of Western civilisation;
and it is a continent of ordinary working people, whose lives are now
being devastated by war. Llywelyn-Williams's passionate interest in
the Spanish Civil War was, like that of Cyril Cule, based on a recognition of the intimate bond between the proletariat of the south Wales
Valleys and the proletariat of Spain's several industrial regions. But he
also realised that aerial warfare, such as was being 'pioneered' by the
Luftwaffe over Guernica, was the great social leveller, in several senses
of the latter word. The incident had demonstrated that the whole
of Wales, from the Valleys of the south to what Llywelyn-Williams
elsewhere invoked as the 'slopes of Snowdonia', would be as helplessly
vulnerable to such an attack as Guernica had been. Pan-European
solidarity was therefore the only means of avoiding pan-European
catastrophe. He felt despair 'for Wales helplessly entangled in the
cataclysm . . . and for the whole of human civilization' (*AW2*, 174–5).
    Wartime experience with the Royal Welch Fusiliers both reinforced
and refined Llywelyn-Williams's dual response to Europe. Particularly
influential was the period he spent in occupied Germany, as is evident
from 'On a Visit'.[19] Written in the first person, the poem recalls the
occasion when, while serving in Germany, he had come upon a great
house standing on the sunlit slope of a valley 'steep and secret with
quiet pine-trees'. Reluctantly admitted by the scrupulously courteous
owner, a Baron, he was shown the house's war wounds – room upon
room whose windows had been removed by bomb-blast so that 'the
east wind stung / and vomited snowflakes onto carpet and / mirror
and chest'. Insufficiently chastened even by this very evident image of
devastation, he had insisted, in an inexplicable spirit of perversity, on
being led through to the family's inner sanctum of the living-room.
Taken there by his visibly discomfited host, he warmed to the homely
signs he saw of decent, civilised living; the elderly wife seated near
the generous fire, the firelight intermittently illuminating a picture
of Christ on the wall, a handsome piano piled high with copies of
classical music. Seeing Liszt and Chopin lying side by side he'd been
moved to enthuse, praising music's power to cross national boundaries and to bring peoples together. But he'd stopped abruptly upon

seeing the tears gathering in the woman's eyes, 'like a lake filling up
with stars'. He'd realised, too late, that the piano reminded this couple
of their lost son. Embarrassed then by his guest's embarrassment, the
host had asked forgiveness for such 'discourteous bearing', and had
explained, 'we do not wish to share our pain with anyone.' All three
had then stood silent, 'till the man turned to the piano as though
challenging its power':

> For a moment, he sat there, humbly praying
> before seeking the tune; then the graceful music flowed
> from his hand, prelude and dance and song so
> bitterly sad, so carelessly cheerful and gentle and full of
> mercy until the sound blended into a communion
> where angels walked, healing our hurt and setting free
> our captive hours.[20]

The poem dramatises the difficulties of making 'living contact' during wartime, even with those in the occupied territories who are one's
natural allies. Implicit in the poem – and a crucial factor in the whole
drama – is the narrator's status as an officer in the liberating army.
He unconsciously trades on his authority when he insists on gaining
admittance to his host's living-room, the last refuge of private, domes-
tic feelings. And in the process he is, of course, taking unfair advantage
of the code of aristocratic courtesy by which the Baron is bound.

As the pattern of the poem makes clear, the result is an intrusion
into the intimate life of the family that is as violent and as destructive
as the bomb blast. The supposed 'ally' suddenly, in the ignorance of
his arrogance, becomes the enemy. It may well be that in this incident
we are being shown the kind of wartime experience that caused Alun
Llywelyn-Williams's outlook to change in the way he himself later
described. In his poem 'Remembering the Thirties', he recalled his
pre-war certainty that he, an enlightened socialist, was on the side
of the angels who were fighting the twin evil empires of fascism and
capitalism: 'For this we were born // to confidence in the destruction
of false idols.' He had likewise been convinced that he would be fighting to preserve 'the splendid museum'; all that was best in Western
civilization; the values that were so richly instanced in the wealth of
European culture. But he emerged from the war with the very different
conviction that he was essentially no different from the enemy – that
human nature was always piebald:

The saving grace was the discovery in war, in the midst of its evil destruc-
tiveness, of the astonishing power of the human power to survive and to
triumph. What the war really gave me, I suppose, was a salutary direct
experience of human suffering and folly of which I had hitherto been
a mere passive observer, and a realisation that they are inherent in the
human condition everywhere at all times. They are prerequisite and
inescapable conditions for the exercise of love and compassion, for our
awareness of joy and our attainment of wisdom, because good and evil
are inextricably intermingled. Ideologies, and political systems, even forms
of religion, are propitia[to]ry ephemeral supports in the face of forces
that transcend time and space, but poetry though it can't attempt any
solutions to the eternal paradox of human life can at least celebrate its
mystery and its magic and articulate our occasional glimpses of universal
truth. (*AW2*, 174)

At the end of 'On a Visit', music – in the form of works by two of
the great masters of the European musical tradition – is shown as
performing the pseudo-religious office ascribed in the prose comment
to poetry, and in the process music becomes a form of redemptive
communion between the visitor and his 'hosts'. Living contact has
occurred, against all the odds. It is as if the original situation had been
turned inside out: strangers from different cultures, brought together
initially by the most inauspicious of circumstances, and relating to
each other at first only in unfortunate, blundering ways, are eventually joined together in a moment of genuine mutuality. Moreover this
ambivalent aspect of the whole story is inscribed from the beginning
in the style of the poem. It is written as if the events recalled were
almost a dream, and it is written in a distanced way in a style of discourse that is formal, dignified, courteous. On one level this style of
presentation can be said to encode the spirit of elaborate, defensive-
cum-aggressive *politesse* that governs most of the visit. But on another
level the style enacts the inner meaning of the story; bringing out its
ritualistic, ceremonial aspects; showing it to be a vision, an initiation
into a state of deeper psychological and spiritual understanding. The
style therefore speaks to us of Dante, of the courtly society of the
Mabinogion, of strange meetings that are simultaneously ancient and
modern.

A concern for the plight of ordinary people – the other aspect
already evident in the pre-war Welsh Europeanism of Alun
Llywelyn-Williams, not least in his response to the plight of the
Basque civilians at Guernica – also surfaces in some of the poems

that came out of his war experiences. In one such poem, he records his reactions to an episode he had experienced in one of Berlin's greatest railway stations. There, amidst the rubble that was all that was left of the capital of the Third Reich, he had spotted one of wartime's most ubiquitous civilian casualties – a young woman left homeless, destitute and defenceless. His involuntary response is to see in her ('Inge') the very image of the desolate Heledd, supposed author of the great ninth-century Welsh-language lament, in the form of a series of *englynion*, for the total destruction of the palace and realm of her brother, Cynddylan, who had been lord of Pengwern and overlord of the region of Powys in north-east Wales. The most famous of the *englynion* traditionally attributed (probably mistakenly) to her is 'Stafell Cynddylan ys tywyll heno':

> Dark is Cynddylan's hall tonight
>   With no fire, no bed.
> I weep awhile, then am silent.[21]

It is to this that Llywelyn-Williams alludes in the opening lines of his own poem:

> Heledd and Inge, when the torches are red –
> Inge, or Heledd, which one? deceiving us are the years –
> see us meeting, at some interweaving of the swift threads,
> the far travellers by chance beneath the clock.[22]

By the end of the poem, he has homed sympathetically in on the sordid price that women have always had to pay, in times of war, for mere survival:

> Sharp is the breeze, Heledd, do not shiver, do not weep,
> take courage, hidden on the handy bed of the rubble,
> as a gift for savouring the cigarette, for sucking the chocolate,
> you can reach out your love to the lonely conqueror.

By this point, it is not the old Welsh poem that is helping Llywelyn-Williams focus empathically on a modern war situation, it is the contemporary plight of Inge that is allowing him to imagine, and to speak of, the sexual exploitation that would also have been Heledd's fate, but that was of course denied expression in 'her' poem. And so, by the end of his poem, he has difficulty in expelling Heledd's

importunate ghost so that once more he can squarely view Inge, but
even as he achieves this refocusing he seems to hear, in distant, war-
ravaged Berlin, the mocking, triumphant screech of 'Eryr Pengwern',
the eagle that, in another of Heledd's famous *englynion*, had gorged
itself in the aftermath of the carnage on the feast of dead flesh:

> A gross, pompous city this has always been,
> and fit to be ruined,
> and have you heard, Heledd – no, wounded Inge –
> the greedy eagle's fierce laughter,
> have you seen, in his half-closed eyes,
> the predestined image of all our frail cities?

By the end of the war, Llywelyn-Williams had come to view the struggle between barbarity and civilization not as a struggle between the
Allies and the Axis countries, but rather as a struggle ongoing within
the lives of every individual. He strongly felt his own complicity, even
as liberating conqueror, in what had become of the Germany that
had, after all, been one of the great cradles of European civilisation.
In viewing the condition of Inge, he not only sympathises with her as
an eternal victim; he knows himself to have been partly responsible
for her piteous condition. Hence, too, his fusion of her image with
that of the Welsh Heledd, for whose lamentable fate in all likelihood
the Welsh themselves, rather than some 'enemy' people, had, after
all, been responsible.

    'Lehrter Bahnhof' was the first of three linked poems all related to
Llywelyn-Williams's experiences in August 1945 in a Berlin that had
but very recently been liberated. Here it is of Olwen he is reminded,
the legendary woman of the *Mabinogi* in whose every footstep a clo-
ver reputedly sprang up. In her dancing, therefore, she represents
the hope that life will once more recover, even in the wake of the
most devastating of destructive catastrophes. Art – in this case the
art of dance – will always exhibit the triumphant, miraculous power
of transforming the darkest despair into the verdant freshness of
hope. And by art Llywelyn-Williams has in mind not only what is
usually meant by 'the arts', but also all the healing 'arts of life' as
practised every day by ordinary men and women – of whom Inge is
of course one.

    As for 'On a Visit', it, too, is a meditation on the deeply human
vulnerabilities, strengths and resilience, of European culture. After

all, Llywelyn-Williams had entered the war believing that 'a second world war meant quite literally the end of European civilization as we knew it' (*AW2*, 173). The concluding lines of 'Ar Ymweliad', when the Baron reluctantly plays the piano, humbly and tentatively suggest that European civilisation may have survived the war after all, although in a vastly chastened form. The poem is an implicit voicing of the beliefs Alun Llywelyn-Williams had recorded before the war in an editorial for *Tir Newydd*, during the course of defending the relevance of poetry to the acute crises of the time. 'The whole culture of Europe is in imminent danger', he had written, and such should be an issue 'of immense importance to every poet – and yet there is scarcely an echo of all these problems in the contemporary poetry of Wales.'

    After the war, he returned to the same concerns but this time identified in the more local terms appropriate to radically different post-war circumstances. Now his concern was in some part for the future of the Welsh language, whose literary tradition he regarded as a marginal, but far from insignificant, example of the richness of the ancient cultural heritage of Europe. He was also worried for the future of a dynamic new bicultural Wales that had begun 'at least to some extent . . . to enter fully into the common heritage of the nations' and even 'to offer its own contribution in kind'. This Wales, he felt, was 'coming of age culturally at a time when European culture has lost its stability and sense of direction and is itself undergoing a prolonged crisis of disillusion and fragmentation. The capitalist civilisation and its culture are still under threat of dissolution' (*AW2*, 176–7).

    The writer whose work was most extensively influenced by wartime experience of Europe was probably Emyr Humphreys. Born in 1919, he had been converted to nationalism by the Penyberth incident, when he was only a sixth former. Simultaneously, he had become fascinated not only by the actions but also by the ideas of Saunders Lewis, and had arranged for every wartime issue of *Y Faner* that carried 'Cwrs y Byd', Lewis's controversial column on contemporary political affairs, to reach him even where he served, first in Egypt and then in Italy. Decades later he was to recall the surreal experience of reading Lewis's words in this foreign environment: 'While you are privileged with a little solitude in your sweaty sleeping quarters in the Administrative block', he wrote of his time in Florence, 'you read

successive numbers of "Cwrs y Byd" . . . far into the hot night.'[23] Even
before the war, he had already become a convinced Welsh Europhile
in the Lewis tradition, having adopted the view that the Welsh had
been a part of Europe from their inception as a national collective.
He had also accepted Lewis's opinion that in order to preserve its
cultural distinctiveness Wales needed to bypass English literature and
reconnect itself creatively with the literatures of the continent.

A couple of years after he'd returned from Italy, Humphreys
published an imaginary conversation between Saunders Lewis and
Llywelyn ein Llyw Olaf (the last native prince of Wales, killed 1282)
in the Welsh avant-garde periodical *Wales*. It ended with Lewis summarising the state of Europe at the war's end, in the process obviously
voicing Humphreys's own reading of the situation. 'From the West
a new Mammon has arisen', Lewis explains, 'obscene with wealth,
from the east another barbarian horde is spreading from Asia and
Europe, ruined Europe, like a vacuum, draws them together for mad
collision.' England has a 'weak, well-meaning government sprung
from the common people', and is in thrall to the 'money-masters'
of the great western Mammon. As for Wales, 'whose frontiers have
shrunk to a partition in Welsh minds, [it] is a villa on Vesuvius, gently
shaking'.[24] Several years earlier, Humphreys had already captured
the deranged, violently disarranged state of Europe's great cultures
in a poem published in Wales whose title – 'Piecepomb for Vjayday'
– and grotesque lexical neologisms had deliberately evoked James
Joyce's *Pomes Penyeach* (1927).[25] There he notes the arrival of a
new 'Arithmatic atomic. / Endglow – American gnomic / Lumps my
wellearned bell burned sleep', and invites his reader to 'Pity me, who
sting on the sleet corner / Of the burst and disembowelled city', while
viewing the 'Wawning of a new unfettered world'.

By 1949, Humphreys had recent first-hand experience of the
'vacuum' of a post-war Europe eviscerated by war. A conscientious
objector, and therefore a non-combatant, he trained for service with
the Save the Children Fund, acquiring experience in Egypt, then land-
ing in Sicily before following in the wake of the bloody advance of
the Allied forces up through the Italian peninsula. Years later, he
was to recall his experience as a twenty-five-year-old in the Welsh
poem 'Cymodi â Ffawd', remembering arrival by jeep in Dongo, the
place where Mussolini and his mistress had been shot before their
corpses were transferred to Milan, where they were strung up by their
feet, heads hanging down in the stifling heat, their corpses like steers

awaiting flaying; hastily dug shallow graves everywhere, abandoned tanks and bayonets rusting in the sun, the sound of insects filling the air like anxiety; and arriving at the Alpine frontier, suddenly aware that nothing he had to say could endure like the rocks, and no cry he could utter that would not start an avalanche (*HCP*, 156–7).

In the aftermath of war, he helped run a large camp in the heart of old Florence for displaced persons numbering over 7,000 inmates, in the process becoming fluent in Italian and a devotee for life of the culture of Italy. As will become apparent later, this period of service left a positive, deep and complex impression on him as a creative writer, but in the notes he kept at the time, a selection from which appeared in *Wales*, he tended to concentrate on the dark aspects of human nature that were liable to surface under such conditions. 'One begins to believe', he wrote,

> that honesty doesn't exist outside the imagination and that selfishness is the hand and brain of life. It needs an Elizabethan to do justice to Europe today, another Webster. For we are too much like cold fish caught in a net swivelling an eye over the expiring species.[26]

Humphreys duly set his second novel, *The Voice of a Stranger*, in a camp for displaced persons in post-war Italy, and given his admiration for Jacobean drama, it is not surprising that his text runs readily to melodrama and is laced with violent intrigue. His service in Florence had made him aware of the ruthless efficiency displayed by the communists amidst the anarchic chaos of civilian life. In the novel, circumstances conspire to highlight the tragic consequences for an individual life of events that bring the cold discipline of an ideological commitment to revolutionise society by destroying all 'sentimental' intimate human relationships into direct, disastrous conflict with a 'bourgeois' romantic love interest.

Just as Renaissance Italy had been routinely characterised in Jacobean drama as home to the sly duplicitousness in every aspect of human affairs notoriously advocated and codified by Machiavelli, so Humphreys, too, painted a not dissimilar picture of Italy in the immediate aftermath of war. In *The Voice of a Stranger* he pitched Williams, a naive young product of Welsh Nonconformity, into the midst of this tortuous and murky milieu in which former support-ers of fascism were busily, and cynically, reinventing themselves as ardent supporters of the new liberal democratic order being ushered in under the powerful auspices of occupying British, and above all American, forces. All and sundry were also scrambling to take full advantage, often via a thriving black market, of the largesse suddenly made available by the many foreign agencies assisting Italy to recover and to rebuild its shattered social and economic structures. And then there was the allure – that a homesick Williams finds irresistible in the novel – of attractive young flesh rendered helpless, vulnerable and thus readily available, amidst the total collapse of all social and moral order.

This key narrative stratagem of exposing a Welsh innocent to the ancient practised wiliness of Italy, and to the dark, amoral arts of survival was to be repeated several times over the next sixty years by Humphreys, not only in his novels and short stories but also in his poetry. In several instances, the most skilled and memorable practitioners of the unscrupulous art of survival are old women who have learned it the hard way, by living as best they could through the turbulent events of twentieth-century Italian history. One such in the late novel *The Gift of a Daughter* is an ancient, heavily bejewelled marchesa, a viciously scheming old crone who is a survivor from the Mussolini era and therefore as well used to being socially and politically complaisant as her son is to being sexually obliging. Another such character is the old woman in the poem 'Cara Signora', who spends her days recalling how in a bygone age the 'principe' himself used to pay his respects to her, and moaning about the lack of respect now being shown her by her daughter-in-law, who is characterised by her as a scheming bitch, but is actually a harmless infants' teacher whose worst vice is an addiction to chocolate. The old woman 'sits in front of her door like a black idol, / A prisoner in paradise', complaining that she is 'sitting like a sick cat / In the sun moulting and struggling for breath / As useless as a cough' (*HCP*, 162–4).

As a ravaged Europe slowly began to recover during the 1950s, so a sophisticated international set of business people, artistic drifters and fashionable intellectuals emerged who were well used to travelling casually around the continent. By the end of the century tourist travel had become an ordinary mass experience, and Humphreys's later fiction often centred on Welsh participation in it. But it was in *The Italian Wife*, a novel that made no mention of Wales and was partly set in Italy, as the title suggested, that he first turned his attention to a peripatetic lifestyle that in the 1950s was still the prerogative of the rich.

Richard Miller is a wealthy publisher married to Paola, an Italian wife a dozen years his junior, and he has a son from his first marriage, Chris, who is only some ten years younger than his stepmother. An unscrupulous opportunist, with a keen eye for the main chance, whether it comes his way in the attractive person of a young woman or of a political crisis, Miller no longer owes any sincere allegiance to his native culture, background or class, for all his advantageous membership of the Labour Party, and he has carefully distanced himself from his Jewish background. Paola is a far more sensitive and inherently decent character, whose misfortune it is to have married a boorish, selfish husband and to have fallen in love with his son. Her retreat to Italy and to the supportive company of her sister Cecilia, to whom she reluctantly confides her infatuation, marks the beginning of the novel's exploration, in its later stages, of the ruthless, scheming side of clannish Italian family relationships. That is implicitly contrasted with the strained relations within Miller's atomised nuclear family. The novel also touches on other features of the European scene in this period, such as the former Nazis boldly apparent and thriving in Germany and Austria, and before concluding, it glances dismissively at the growing belief in some quarters that the Age of Europe is drawing to a close and being superseded by the advent of the East. Such an outlook had been very much in vogue between the wars, thanks to Oswald Spengler's *The Decline of the West*, and it returned to fashion after the war, this time in the form represented by dubious Indian gurus, the forerunners of those who were to mesmerise the Beatles and their rock kin in the later 1960s and 1970s.

When working on *The Italian Wife* Humphreys was also busy commissioning and producing plays for *Y Theatr yn Ewrop*. This was the radio series, already examined in some detail in a previous chapter, of translations into Welsh of several of the most adventurous classics of twentieth-century European theatre. His association with Martin Esslin at this time brought what the latter had termed 'The Theatre of the Absurd' very much into focus, and among the works that resulted were Saunders Lewis's translation of *Waiting for Godot* and translations of plays by Dürrenmatt and Brecht. This was also the period of his introduction to Brecht's celebrated concept of the *Verfremdungseffekt*, a revolutionary theory at the time that was reflected in his growing fictional practice of neutral presentation of both characters and actions.

After *The Italian Wife*, Europe was not to figure significantly again in Humphreys's fiction for almost forty years. But throughout that period he paid frequent, lengthy visits to Italy in particular, consistently accounting himself a Welsh European and a novelist whose fictional techniques were consciously aligned with the best European, rather than English, practice. His wartime experience of working in the heart of the old city of Florence had afforded him splendid opportunities for cultural self-education, as had his visits to other regions of post-war Italy. His recollections of this period included an hour spent during a visit to Rome lying on his back surveying Michelangelo's great ceiling in an otherwise totally deserted Sistine Chapel. As for the uprooted condition of the displaced persons with whom he worked, it permanently underlined for him the complex necessities of an intimate attachment to place, faced daily as he was with Italian peasants desperate to return to their land in Abruzzo. But it also brought him into intimate contact with Jewish refugees from central Europe, equally desperate to emigrate to a totally new life in Palestine. Rootedness on the one hand, a deep desire for the freedom to escape to a new country and into a new selfhood on the other: his fiction was eventually to explore both impulses with equal understanding and sympathy.

Humphreys gained further first-hand experience of Europe through a period spent in Klagenfurt and Salzburg in the early 1950s and through regular visits paid later in life to his brother, who ended his days as an Anglican canon ministering to the spiritual needs of expat Brits sunning themselves in the Algarve and nearby Estoril. Humphreys skewered such Brits in his late poem 'Marvao', in which the speaker professes himself 'as comfortable / As a cockroach', complacently adding that 'Nothing / Matters all that much. Except the booze / and the sun. And my dividends / Of course', before announcing in self-satisfied conclusion that 'I've gone native more or less / Without the lingo' (*HCP*, 202). But Humphreys's Welsh Europeanism has always been firmly centred in his beloved Italy. For him, it is 'the home of European culture as a whole – the source of Latin, the source of medieval civilisation' (*CR*, 134). During the time he spent there, he got to know Elio Vittorini, and came to admire Leonardo Sciascia, the great Sicilian writer, while Montale and Ungaretti became important to him, as did Primo Levi and Italo Calvino.

'Pirandello and Verga', Humphreys has noted, 'are modern writers of the novella tradition that stretches back to Boccaccio.' In his late period, he repeatedly favours the *novella* form. And Dante, above all others, has been one of the major presences throughout his life. He confesses to a love of *paese* – the equivalent of *brogarwch* ('attachment to locality') that makes Italy, like Wales, 'a continent not a country . . . that includes an infinite number of regional variations and local dialects' (*CR*, 134). Above all, he can identify with Italy because, like Wales – and like modern Germany, he interestingly adds – it is a 'defeated nation', its nationalism chastened accordingly. Humphreys strongly approves of that, contrasting such an attitude to the swagger of the *soi-disant* 'undefeated' French.

'To be more European, we need first to be more Welsh' (*CR*, 149). Thus Humphreys concluded his frequently scathing essay on that sometime BBC cultural eminence, the Welshman Huw Wheldon. Humphreys devoted most of his creative energies during the middle period of his long career as a writer to attempting to make his people 'more Welsh' by employing a range of fictional means to make them aware of themselves as a distinct people with a long, complex history. But then, when he was well into his seventies, he specifically began to place Wales once more in relation to Europe. This shift in emphasis first became apparent in *Unconditional Surrender* (1996), a novel devoted to the retrospective examination of the state of Wales at the end of the Second World War in which he reflected on the range of possibilities that seemed available to the country at that historic moment.

Whereas several of his late works feature instances of the Welsh going into Europe, *Unconditional Surrender* is primarily concerned with examples of Europe coming to Wales. The action is set in the immediate post-war period and mediated through the consciousnesses of two central characters, one of whom is Cecilia von Leiten, a German countess conveniently 'elderly' at fifty-seven. Complete with purloined family jewels, she has found 'refuge' (as she euphemistically puts it) in Wales, but then restive fellow residents of the north Wales Residential Home for Decayed Gentlewomen in which she has been settled begin maliciously to campaign for her repatriation. It becomes evident, as the novel proceeds, that the countess is torn in her attitude to the war and its prelude. On the one hand, the subterfuges she has been so skilfully practising and the lies and half-truths in which she has liberally indulged mean that she lives in constant terror of any revelation of the complex truth about her German background – which includes a

family history of fellow-travelling with the Nazi Party. On the other
hand, she cannot bring herself to relinquish her 'right' to the estates
of her late husband and to such wealth as they represented. The family jewels, the pride and joy of her 'old age', are treasure she can use
to influence people, even to buy their 'affection', but they are also a
tangible link with her personal past and guarantor, in her eyes, of her
continuing right to inherited privileges she cannot bring herself to
relinquish. Yet her claim to them is extremely dubious. She had been
persuaded by her then second husband, a rackety Anglo-Irishman
who worked in the film industry, to 'abscond with the family silver',
to the outrage of relatives who are now intent on reclaiming it.[27]

Given to occasionally voicing a nostalgia, like that of her late
'Oma' ('grandmother'), for the Austro-Hungarian empire, the countess is actually unwilling to disavow her German identity, arguing
disingenuously and yet truthfully that Bach, Schubert and Goethe
had nothing to do with Nazism. Hers is therefore a cultural nationalism that chimes in some ways with that of Meg and Griff, two young
ardent and idealistic campaigners for Plaid Cymru in the general
election of 1945. They harbour a utopian dream that post-war Wales
will choose to access and mobilise important aspects of its past in
order to participate in the international building of a new post-war
world order.

Through the case of Cecilia, Humphreys is therefore able, not
for the first time, to subject his own strong cultural commitments to
sceptical cross-examination, as he is also able to reflect on the ambivalent consequences and indeed sinister pitfalls of such a deep devotion
to the past as he is elsewhere anxious to inculcate in his culturally
amnesiac people. A sardonic note in this connection is struck at the
very end of the novel, where we learn that the countess has ensured
her long-term stay in Wales by moving into the rectory in order to
assist the antiquarian rector in completing his history of the local
parish. It is a partnership that seems to represent a retreat into a
highly selective and carefully managed version of the past by a Welsh
man and a German woman, both of whom are seeking refuge from
a recent history whose monstrous character stands rawly revealed in
newsreels featuring the death camps, and from the urgent challenges
and ambiguous opportunities of a beckoning post-war future.

In contrast with the countess, Karl, a young German prisoner of
war, is rabidly anti-nationalist and eager to renounce all his cultural
allegiances. For him, the future is everything, and its opportunities

to be grasped at any price – including the price of lasting human relationships. Having made Meg pregnant, Karl then takes advantage of her disillusionment, at the decisive rejection of Plaid Cymru by the Welsh electorate, to persuade her to join him in the adventure of creating a new Europe out of the wreck of the old, which is vividly recorded in newspaper photographs:

> Bremen is a waste land licked by a black river. The ruins of Nürnberg stretch over two pages like a bloated corpse being eaten by blind worms. There is no noise of explosion, but the centre of Cologne has become a black and white catastrophe. Broken bridges sag and sink into water that has lost the ability to flow. Railway tracks bend and buckle into the ground like a shower of arrows aimed at the devils of hell. (*US*, 93)

Meg chooses to enter this landscape of devastation, believing it is ultimately redeemable, rather than remain in a Wales sinking hopelessly back into its customary lethargy, passivity and torpor, but her partnership with Karl proves to be short-lived. Her middle-aged mother is similarly moved to embark on an unconventional continental adventure, and the novel ends with news of them both working as volunteers in a centre for refugees.

Not the least intriguing aspect of *Unconditional Surrender* is that it concludes with these two characters making a choice diametrically opposite to that which Emyr Humphreys himself made at the conclusion of his period of service in Florence. Strongly tempted to remain in Italy, where as a young author he could safely adopt a detached 'balcony' view of life, he determined instead to return to Wales, primarily because he had already found his future wife there, but also because he sensed that removal from his native soil would in the end disadvantage him as a writer. Commenting on this choice fifty years later, he was to observe that whereas it was fine for a writer of upper-class background, such as the great Italian novelist Alberto Moravia, to survey the teeming plebeian life of the Italian streets from on high, it was a privilege denied him (*CR*, 55).

Two years after *Unconditional Surrender* he published *The Gift of a Daughter*, a novel a substantial part of which is set in Italy. Humphreys's lifelong friend was Basil MacTaggart, a cosmopolitan multicultural figure to whom he had first grown close when the two were training in wartime London for work with the Save the Children Fund, and a talented linguist in whose company he subsequently ran the Displaced Persons' Camp in Florence. Settling in Italy thereafter, MacTaggart had acquired extensive amateur knowledge of what remained of Etruscan culture. As Humphreys came gradually to benefit from his friend's expertise, so he began to perceive parallels between the eventual fate of the Etruscans and that of the Celts. In both cases, such traces as remained of what had once been major civilisations had disappeared almost completely by the twentieth century. All that was left in the one case was the extraordinary tombs, complete with funerary artefacts, that so fascinated both professional and amateur archaeologists, and in the other a marginal 'remnant' culture such as stubbornly lingered on in Wales, thanks to the survival of the Welsh language. And Wales could also furnish an even older example of a vanished civilisation, that of the anonymous Neolithic people who constructed the impressive passage tomb of Bryn Celli Ddu on Anglesey. Both this funerary site and those of the Etruscans figure large in *The Gift of a Daughter*, serving to link Wales closely with Italy.

The novel is one of the most intensely European of all of Humphreys's novels, not least because around half the action is located on the continent. Italy is the refuge to which Aled, an academic classicist, and his wife Marian repair in the aftermath of the unbearable loss of their talented, rebellious young daughter. They are drawn there by the imposing figure of Aled's old friend Muzio. He is a decayed aristocrat of impeccable manners, considerable learning, and a wealth of weary and wary worldly experience such as only life in a country as ancient and as chronically and cynically steeped in intrigue as Italy would, it is implied, be capable of producing. One of Muzio's interests is Etruscan remains, and through the fascination Aled too develops with their ancient burial sites and funerary practices Humphreys is able to explore the potentially fatal attraction of the past for the present. The bookish Welsh academic, whose present is already threateningly ghosted, and in some ways dangerously governed by his memories of his dead daughter, becomes self-destructively obsessed with the Italy of both Etruscan and Classical times, in both of which he mistakenly supposes he detects useful parallels with his own present situation.

In the beautiful young local girl, Grazia, both Aled and Marian think they detect a similarity to beloved features of their own lost past. In her passionate youthful hopefulness Marian believes she discerns more than a passing resemblance to her own younger campaigning self. Grazia reminds Aled on the other hand of his beloved daughter, prompting in him an urge to protect her even as her nubile beauty reawakens in his blindly infatuated middle-aged self sexual instincts that are otherwise beginning to weaken.

Husband and wife construct a heroic narrative that involves plucking Grazia from the clutches of her claustrophobic extended family and domineering father. Their plan is to provide her with the education that her intelligence deserves and that would grant her freedom to develop as she wishes. But the implementation of their somewhat histrionic plan – it involves subterfuge and disguise engineered by Prue, Muzio's no-nonsense English wife, who is actually an opera singer – triggers another of the subjects that recur in Humphreys's fiction: the right to freedom of self-development that has become a cardinal principle of a highly individualistic modern Anglo-American culture, versus the embeddedness in family and in local community that characterised traditional European societies. The latter values are obviously imperative if local, regional cultures, such as those that have always thrived in Italy, and that even precariously survive in rural Wales, are to withstand the powerful forces of global homogenisation. A related theme is that of complete, unfettered, global freedom of movement on the one hand and on the other the respect for fixed inherited boundaries, limited but also inevitably limiting, without which distinctive societies and cultures cannot continue to exist.

As for the bearing the history of ancient Rome has on these contemporary proceedings, that emerges from Aled's growing interest in the Rome and Byzantium of the sixth century when the Byzantine emperor Justinian and his controversial empress Theodora, originally a courtesan of low birth, were seeking to reclaim control of Rome from Theodosia, daughter of Theodoric, a Goth-turned-Roman. Aled sees a parallel in this situation to the way he thinks the USA is seeking to impose its power on the old countries of Europe. But he also begins slowly to identify himself after a fashion with Procopius. Sometime obedient scribe to Justinian, the official had turned against his master in his later years and written a bilious and notorious *Secret History* of his time, full of lubricious details about the scandalous antics of both Justinian and the libidinous Theodora. Procopius is thus presented by Humphreys as a rogue variant on the dissident figure he has always so admired.

For a period, Aled fancies himself to be, like Procopius, an undercover agent secretly working to undermine and expose the moral corruption he slowly detects in Italy. This decadence is apparent in the torrid affair that Prue, Muzio's wife, is openly conducting with the priapic Luzio, who is Muzio's secret half-brother and irresistibly macho estate manager. And it is differently evident in the violence Grazia's father is willing to exert to maintain his domination over his cowed family and clan. Even Muzio himself is gradually realised by Aled to be sexually impotent and accordingly complaisant in his wife's affair.

But by the end of the novel it has become evident that Aled is not remotely up to remedying weaknesses that are not peculiar to Italy but in many respects inherent in the human condition. As his wife – who has turned out to be considerably more pragmatically resourceful and effective than he in handling the situation – remarks to him with a mixture of sympathy and condescension, he is much too gentle a soul to survive in the world of intricately devious family politics in which he has become entangled in Italy. Aled therefore returns to Wales and to his first love, *De Consolatione Philosophiae* (*The Consolation of Philosophy*), written in prison in the early sixth century by the politician-turned-philosopher Boethius, after he had been sentenced to death by the king he had once loyally and obsequiously served.

Through Aled's application of the struggle between Justinian and Theodosia to the modern crisis of Europe, then, Humphreys explores that struggle for supremacy between European and American culture that he has long regarded as a crucial feature of the late twentieth century, both in Wales and across the countries of Europe at large. He reflected on this crucial issue at length during the course of an interview printed in *Conversations and Reflections*:

> If you want to maintain an identity, the first step you must take is linguistic, and unless you have the supreme power invested in the language you have no hope whatsoever of maintaining your identity . . . It is a practical truth that all the European nations have got to come to terms with in the twenty-first century when American English is set – perhaps along with Chinese – to dominate the world. Neither of these is European in its centre of gravity, and therefore the European situation is a very special one, which is going to become ever more apparent. Because insofar as language is fundamental to identity, every European nation, large or small, will have to grapple with this question. The only alternative is a kind of globalization which will eventually extinguish their separate identity, and I cannot see any other outcome in western civilization myself . . . the only choice is whether this is going to be a European Wales or American Wales.

If it's going to be an American Wales then it's going to be in even greater
danger than it is in being a minor part of Britain. (*CR*, 133)

Elsewhere in the same volume he recalled how during his youth and
early manhood the threat had come from the powerful, endlessly
aggrandising, empires of Britain, Nazi Germany and the Soviet
Union, all of which had disappeared off the political map by the
end of the twentieth century. But their passing had seen the rise in
their place of the cultural and political empire of the USA to global
dominance, and this now posed the major threat to all the countries of Europe, Wales included. A complicating factor in the Welsh
case was that it was tied very closely to a post-imperial England that
was likewise 'experiencing its own distinctive set of difficulties that
are also post-imperial [but] these are not of much help to the different post-colonial problems of Wales. That', he added, 'is why I keep
emphasising Wales's need of Europe' (*CR*, 189).

These were matters on which Humphreys had long been brooding,
both directly and indirectly, in his creative work. He realised early in
his career that such a cultural stance as his, which he believed to be
typical of all those who worked in the beleaguered cultures of post-
war Europe, necessarily made a dissident of the writer. And to be a
dissident inescapably meant challenging power in its established form,
which was always a risk. This is the theme of 'A Roman Dream',
one of the poems in his important sequence 'Ancestor Worship'. In
this chilling poem, a scholar serving a Roman emperor maddened by
supreme power – as Caligula most notoriously was – is seductively
'persuaded' to do the decent thing and commit suicide – by a method
the quivering scholar is suavely left by the drunken emperor to choose
for himself (*HCP*, 78–9). The poem was written when the Cold War
was at its height, and American hegemony very evident in Europe as
it was across the whole of the 'free world'. At that time the parallels
between imperial Rome and an imperial USA (originally intended,
of course, by its eighteenth-century founders to be the 'new Rome')
were widely remarked upon by dissident American poets and com-
mentators from Allen Ginsberg to Gore Vidal.

The awesome assimilative power of twentieth-century American
culture, in both its benign and malign aspects, is one of the themes
of *The Anchor Tree*. The only one of Humphreys's novels to be set
in the States, it functions thereby partly as an oblique meditation on
the ambivalent relations between America and Europe, including a

European Wales. In the plot of the novel he takes the rough diamond of the United States and, like an expert cutter, shapes it so as to bring out the coldly glittering multifacetedness of that fascinating society's relationship to its founding dreams. Morgan Rees Dale, a young Welsh historian, sets out to research, excavate and, if possible, restore the physical remains of the ideal Christian community established in Pennsylvania by his ancestor Robert Morgan Reece in 1795. Humphreys is here drawing on the impressive history of Morgan John Rhys, a Baptist minister who was a fervent supporter of the French Revolution and who in 1794, sickened by the repressions of Pitt's notorious government, emigrated to the United States. As a step towards realising his dream of a free Welsh settlement he purchased a tract of land in western Pennsylvania which he called Cambria, and anticipated its eventually replacing the original, old Cambria he had left behind. There he established his own church and established a mission to the Native Americans.

In the novel, Reece's Cambria Nova turns out, however, to have long been supplanted by the thriving small town of Idrisburg, established by his fellow countryman and rival, Oliver Lloyd. 'Idrisburg flourished on the hilltop, nourished by aggressive commerce, industry, healthy greed, competition, compromise and original sin. The ruins of the second City of Brotherly Love were lost in the silent forest.'[28] Lloyd had been a hard-headed Calvinist, whereas Reece had been a Christian perfectibilist. There seems to be little doubt which of them has been sourly vindicated by the course of American history. Moreover, America's savage, property-based ethic of ruthless competitive individualism is shown at its most seedy and sinister in the character of the violent, shotgun-toting redneck Heber S. Hayes, the scavenging owner of the wrecked-car dump under which Cambria Nova is buried:

> Well let me tell you somethin'. Every fuckin' inch of this land is mine and I ain't intendin' no fancy societies treadin' all over it. I didn't get shot in that war just to have a load of Jews and Germans crawlin' all over my land. So you get the hell out of here right this goddam'd minute. The whole lot of you. (*AT*, 71)

The ultimate fate of an American Wales, and indeed of an Americanised Europe, is, then, starkly revealed in this account of the rapacious values by which the USA is governed.

But something of the incorrigible idealism of America – magnetic, naive, vulnerable, yet also ultimately deadly – is embodied in the beautiful young Judith, with whom Morgan Dale becomes ridiculously and dangerously infatuated. As one who was, when a baby, plucked to safety by American troops from the ruins of wartime Germany, Judith is a figure that emblematises the ambiguous relationship between America and Europe in the novel. The American forces that undoubtedly saved Europe, as they had saved her, were also the forces responsible for the evil inferno of Dresden, and in the very act of liberating Europe they were also, with good-natured egotism, appropriating it for their own purposes. The post-war Marshall Plan for the rebuilding of Europe was similarly double-edged; genuinely well intentioned and generous yet also calculatingly self-interested. The American economy could best thrive if a revitalised Europe, sufficiently reinforced by States support to resist the lure of communism, provided a ready market for its products. And with them unavoidably came the most powerful of all of the US's export products: its irresistibly seductive popular culture.

As he moved into his eighties, Humphreys began to realise he no longer possessed either the physical or the creative energies needed to construct and sustain an ambitious novel. He turned instead to the novella, which he regarded as a quintessentially European form most exquisitely employed by Chekhov, and to short story collections. He used these forms in part to examine the relationship of a new generation of the Welsh middle class to a Europe now made easily accessible, rendered highly familiar by cheap popular travel and bound together by a variety of international businesses, government agencies and commercial ventures. He himself continued to 'believe in the benefits of the European Union for Wales and Welshness and the Welsh language' (*CR*, 183), even while sadly recognising that the Union had settled into a form nothing like that for which he had originally hoped, in which due recognition would have been accorded not merely to the powerful established nation states but also to minority nationalities and subordinated peoples. Some of his stories also demonstrate concern as to the highly superficial and culturally levelling terms in which people, including the Welsh, were now prone to experience a Europe that had largely become a mere tourist attraction, holiday playground and attractive location for ageing and wealthy expats, unreconstructedly 'British' and intent on soaking up the sun. His own outlook was of course very different. 'We are all Europeans and we need to know more about each other's languages and cultures' (*CR*, 183).

He was also interested in the way in which the Europe of the past, as well as the present, could function for some of the Welsh as a 'forest' through which they could wander, 'discovering things about themselves' (*CR*, 184). Such, he pointed out, was the case with Menna, in the story of that name from *Ghosts and Strangers*, who toys with the idea of writing a novel about a Cathar girl from the Middle Ages because her story seems to chime with her own experiences.[29] But then there was the danger that Europe would serve only to encourage a generation of Welsh who were already largely culturally deracinated and ignorant of their own history to travel pointlessly around. Such is sadly the case with Gwion in 'Ghosts and Strangers'. He is a lifelong professional gardener, who loses his bearings completely when, on her death, his wealthy wife leaves him with means sufficient for him to wander around Europe, with the supposed aim of broadening his narrow horizons (*GS*, 27–80).

The early part of the action in the late novella *The Shop* occurs in the Alentejo region of Portugal, and includes a visit to the cromlechs at Almendres. Eddie Lloyd is the son of a Swiss mother and a Welsh father, Orlando Lloyd (full name Hubert Cynddylan Vaughan-Lloyd), sometime matinée idol, grand Shakespearean actor of the old school of rodomontade, and blithe, aged philanderer. The resentful Eddie, 'a burgeoning international bureaucrat' (*S*, 50), camps in a gloomy flat in Rome while his ineffably self-regarding and condescending father, although reliant on his son's financial support, is comfortably holed up in a luxurious apartment in fashionable Juan-les-Pins, coastal resort and spa in Antibes.

As the action unfolds, Eddie, who at the outset is virtually wholly ignorant of the land of his father's birth, finds himself reluctantly involved, via his lover, Bethan Mair Nichols, in a scheme to save and restore a relic of traditional rural, Welsh-speaking culture. A widely travelled stills photographer, Bethan Mair has become jaded through repeated exposure, thanks to her extensive international travel, to the threat posed by global culture to distinctive local communities. But then she becomes entranced by the romantic story of her own family past, and while she remains in that state she succeeds in attaching Eddie, too, to her project of cultural restitution through modern adaptation. In the process, he cuts his ties with his line manager, a German who represents the new cynical pan-European elite of international civil servants and media hustlers, as much at their ease in Copenhagen as in Rome, in France as in Spain. However, just as Eddie is resolving to cut his ties with such a world, Bethan Mair is drawn back into it, thanks to the flattering approaches of Jens, a pretentious Danish director anxious to exploit her family's romantic story for commercial gain. But finally, owing to an unexpected disaster that puts paid to her hopes, she applies her feckless, restless energies instead to a commission to 'make a series of documentary films on the present state of racial and class relations in seven major English cities. (*S*, 223). Poor Eddie is therefore left behind to make what he will of the original Welsh project.

This complex story thus poses a series of questions about how that which has traditionally made Wales distinctive may still be respected and rendered viable in a European world dominated by global capital, culturally trivialised by an international media industry and honeycombed by ceaseless travel. Viewed in this dark perspective there seems to be little left of a Europe corrupted by postmodernity that could be of service to Wales. As for Bethan Mair's story, it seems to follow a familiar culturally destructive trajectory, and to be nothing but a repeat, but now in a Europe-wide context, of the usual flight of Welsh talent to the seat of power, wealth and influence that had first begun way back in Tudor times. She and her generation are drawn in the direction of whatever green pastures media cameras can discover in the culturally undifferentiated landscape of Europe. And despite her loudly voiced misgivings about the theatrical falsifications of the media industry, Bethan Mair, it seems, has been reproducing all along in her imagination nothing but a stagy, folksy version of traditional Welsh village life. *The Shop* is in many ways a bleak, disillusioned and disturbing treatment of what has become of Humphreys's lifelong commitment to a Wales in Europe.

Unlike Bethan Mair Nichols, Humphreys never simplifies or sentimentalises when dealing with the past, partly perhaps because of his experience of the traumatic state of post-war Europe with its vast armies of displaced persons. That experience left him with an understanding of the urgent need felt by so many at that grim time to escape the past by forgetting it so as to start over anew. Such memories operate in his writing to counterbalance and qualify his understanding of the totally different situation in Wales, where a distinctive break with the past could signal the end of any distinctive cultural identity, even while an obsession with it could disable the Welsh from meeting the challenge of present and future.

It is the former state of willed amnesia, though, that receives his sympathetic attention in 'An Ethnic Tremor', a story in *Old People are a Problem* that features the journey reluctantly undertaken for the sake of her Welsh-American granddaughter, Megan, by Siri Lloyd to that northern region of Slovenia that had been occupied by German families such as her own before the war.[30] There she comes painfully face to face with memories of her lover, a young Chetnik who was eventually caught and killed by Tito's forces. It is an encounter the full force and import of which Megan, a typical young American whose interest in the past is purely academic rather than bred in the bone, naturally finds it impossible fully to comprehend. And Humphreys's sympathy for displaced persons, developed early, morphs easily into his late sympathy for refugees and asylum seekers like the Azerbaijani children whose company little Ruthie much prefers to that of her chillingly ambitious and indifferent parents in 'Looking after Ruthie', again from *Old People are a Problem*.

Just as Henry James developed a fruitful fascination with the fate of culpably innocent young Americans at large in a wily and cynical old Europe, so Humphreys has, late in life, developed an interest in the Welsh likewise newly let loose on the continent. Most of them, too, travel dangerously encumbered by the remnants of a puritan chapel culture that in its declining decades had cultivated its own innocent dreams and illusions about the duties and potentialities of human nature. They are accordingly ill prepared to encounter an Italy whose Catholicism is thin cover for an underlying pagan sensuousness and opportunism.

Such is the basic scenario in 'Vannenburg's Ghost', a story from the collection *The Woman at the Window* which was published when Humphreys was in his ninetieth year.[31] It features the mannered exchanges between Griffiths, a Welshman on the verge of retirement from the international civil service in Geneva, and his old friend Marloff, a sophisticated White Russian well used to affectionately teasing him for his unreconstructed puritan tendency to confuse morals with mores, and to rush to judgement where it would be wisest simply to maintain a knowingly objective protective distance. Together they contemplate the implications of a story Marloff relates concerning an attractive rich young German widow settled in Italy, who ends up an alcoholic controlled by her lecherous and amoral gardener, Mario, and his equally scheming wife, Giusi. By the end of the story, it is clear that in contemplating eventual retirement in their vicinity, Griffiths is in fact considering placing himself in an alien environment he as a Welshman would be ill equipped to survive undamaged, for all his carefully acquired worldly sophistication.

The Europe that had seemed to leading Welsh-language writers and intellectuals of the inter-war period something of a promised land, comes, then, in several of these late stories to serve as a continent of dangerous disappointments and a sinister site for self-destruction for a supposedly 'liberated' and glibly internationalist generation of Welsh men and women. In 'The Comet' (*WW*, 65–90) Hefin, a successful, self-indulgent young man sustained in his seemingly idyllic Balearic retreat by the practical and resourceful Swiss Giselle, spends much of his time waging a permanent war against his suavely successful father Bryn Tanat, an ageing, self-satisfied Welsh Labour MP. It is a story in which Humphreys distributes his satiric disdain fairly equally between the unattractive Welsh pair, in the process also mocking Hefin's ostentatious fashionable concern for the welfare of the planet.

The darker logic of the story is revealed in its ending, where Hefin, who has already contrived an 'accidental' blow to the head that conveniently rendered it impossible for him to collect his father from the airport, manages to damage himself again – this time possibly permanently – by falling, in a drunken stupor, over the edge of the parapet of the roof garden where he has just been reciting his bombastic 'poetic' elegy for all doomed planetary life. His is manifestly an impotently introjected rage of frustration; a self-destructive urge that implicitly leaves the story reflecting pessimistically on the Welsh condition.

The aged Humphreys seems often to sense parallels between the confused, disjointed Europe of the late twentieth century and the Europe of the immediate post-war period he had come to know intimately during his time in Florence. Some of his stories accordingly return us to that earlier period. The female survivor in 'Luigi', a sad, desolate sliver of a story, is Sylvana, a young Italian girl who quickly deploys her charms to seduce a British major in the dangerous aftermath of the final defeat of Mussolini and his grandiose legions (*WW*, 91–102). As for poor Luigi, Sylvana's would-be suitor and something of an inoffensive local mummy's boy, he is left the helpless, hapless

victim of a fascist 'cause' in which he had never believed but which
he had been forced to serve briefly and catastrophically because of
family pressure. The story begins and ends with him seeking lonely
shelter in a graveyard, a grim comment on the casual human debris
of war. In his lonely, bewildered way, Luigi, the isolated fugitive, is
a person as displaced as those Emyr Humphreys had looked after
fifty years earlier in his Florentine camp. And in finding himself cut
adrift from his moorings even in his own familiar local surroundings,
he is suggestive of the populations of contemporary Europe, including Wales, who have in effect found themselves becoming culturally
deracinated even while remaining completely *in situ* in their own
communities.

The ardent Europeanism of Saunders Lewis, which had captivated
Emyr Humphreys when young, had been based on the assumption,
not unreasonable at the time, that a Welsh culture seriously weakened
over a long period by subordination to, and occlusion by, English culture could recover something of its inherent strength and confidence
by reconnecting itself to the rich, powerful, safely established cultures
of Europe. How different, then, is the European outlook of Emyr
Humphreys in his later years. But he still regarded it as imperative
that Wales remain within the European family that was underpinned
by the European Union. Indeed, he anticipated and much feared
the Brexit outcome almost twenty years before it actually happened,
because he foresaw that, in the final painful stages of its adjustments
to its drastically diminished post-imperial situation, an Anglo-Britain
would make one more attempt to establish itself as a significant independent player on the global scene. Its first attempt at playing at such
a new role resulted in the debacle of Suez. Humphreys intuited that
its second attempt would result in something like what has transpired
with Brexit. Speaking in 2002 he reflected on the common plight of
Wales's two linguistic cultures:

> Both of our linguistic cultures are suffering from the same vitamin defi-
> ciencies, so to speak, and so their growth is stunted. Our bilingual society
> is no healthier in this respect than is our monolingual society – which is
> a very serious problem, because we are all of us so readily recruited to
> the service of the British media and communications industry which is
> currently struggling to perpetuate what is left of the English imperial
> mentality: despising the European Union and grudgingly admiring the
> United States for commandeering their role and language. (*CR*, 190)

It was against this threatening background that Humphreys insisted Wales needed to understand that its position in this post-imperial order was diametrically opposite to that of England. Whereas England's reflex reaction was to turn its back on Europe, Wales desperately needed to stay close to the countries of Europe, not because those countries and their cultures were strong, as they had seemed in Lewis's time, but because they were weak, just like Wales, weakened by the implacable penetration of a global Anglo-American culture. He therefore now conceived of the relationship Wales urgently needed to forge with Europe as constituting part of an alliance of mutual solidarity and resistance, a common front formed by languages and cultures right across Europe, all of which were greatly at risk of erasure. Anglophone Wales, he argued, needed to participate in such an alliance quite as much as did Welsh-language Wales, because the distinctiveness of both would soon be obliterated once Wales opted (as, of course, it sadly did) to throw in its lot with a post-imperial England. It is this seriously weakened state of a contemporary Europe inclusive of Wales that has therefore preoccupied him in his late stories and novellas.

Notes

[1] Glyn Jones, 'Nodiadau ar Surrealistiaeth', *Tir Newydd*, 10 (November 1937), 11. Hereafter *TN*.

[2] 'Scene', *Wales*, 1 (Summer, 1937), 7.

[3] Several of the other contributions to this number also bore the marks of Surrealism, most notably a poem by Nigel Heseltine (see below).

[4] Meic Stephens (ed.), *The Collected Poems of Glyn Jones* (Cardiff: University of Wales Press, 1996), p. 13. Hereafter *CP*.

[5] For Heseltine and *Tales of the Squirearchy* see '"A Grand Harlequinade": The Border Writing of Nigel Heseltine', in M. Wynn Thomas, *All That is Wales* (Cardiff: University of Wales Press, 2017), pp. 77–98.

[6] Tony Brown (ed.), *Collected Stories of Glyn Jones* (Cardiff: University of Wales Press, 1999), p. 57. Hereafter *CS*.

[7] Laura Wainwright, 'The European Dimension in Glyn Jones', *Almanac: Yearbook of Welsh Writing in English*, 12 (2007–8), 55–88; 58.

[8] The passage occurs in 'The Kiss' and is quoted in Wainwright, 'The European Dimension', 56.

[9] From 'The Wanderer,' and quoted in Wainwright, 'The European Dimension', 59.

[10] Paul Ferris (ed.), *Dylan Thomas: The Collected Letters* (London: Dent, 1985), p. 196. Hereafter *CL*.

[11] Dylan Thomas, *Collected Poems 1934–1952* (London: Dent, 1964), p. 73.

12   Nathalie Wourm, 'Dylan Thomas and the French Symbolists', *Welsh Writing in English: A Yearbook of Critical Essays*, 5 (1999), 27–41.

13   Chris Wigginton, *Modernism from the Margins: The 1930s Poetry of Louis MacNeice and Dylan Thomas* (Cardiff: University of Wales Press, 2007). This study includes a chapter on 'Dylan Thomas: Modernism and Surrealism in the 1930s', pp. 28–50.

14   Edward Allen (ed.), *Reading Dylan Thomas* (Edinburgh: Edinburgh University Press, 2019), p. 236.

15   'Return Journey', in Dylan Thomas, *Quite Early One Morning: Poems, Stories, Essays* (London: Dent, 1974), p. 81.

16   Quoted by Keery in Allen, *Reading Dylan Thomas*, p. 182.

17   Alun Llywelyn-Williams, autobiographical essay in Meic Stephens (ed.), *The Artist in Wales*, 2 (Llandysul: Gomer, 1973), p. 171. Hereafter *AW2*.

18   Alun Llywelyn-Williams, *Cerddi, 1934–1942* (London: Foyle, 1944), p. 19. The translation is mine.

19   Part of the discussion that follows draws on materials from my chapter on Alun Llywelyn-Williams and Alun Lewis in *Internal Difference: Literature in Twentieth-Century Wales* (Cardiff: University of Wales Press, 1992), pp. 62ff.

20   'Ar Ymweliad', in *Pont y Caniedydd* (Denbigh: Gee, 1956), pp. 26–8. The translation comes from R. Gerallt Jones (trans.), *Poetry of Wales, 1930–1970* (Llandysul: Gomer, 1982), pp. 167–9.

21   Tony Conran (trans.), 'Cynddylan's Hall', in *The Penguin Book of Welsh Verse* (Harmondsworth: Penguin, 1967), p. 197.

22   Joseph Clancy, 'In Berlin – August 1945: I. Lehrter Bahnhof', in Clancy (trans.), *Twentieth-Century Welsh Poems* (Llandysul: Gomer, 1982), pp. 169–70.

23   *Conversations and Reflections* (Cardiff: University of Wales Press, 2004), p. 86. Hereafter *CR*.

24   'Imaginary Encounter', *Wales*, 31 (October 1949), 34.

25   'Piecepomb for Vjayday', *Wales*, VI/2 (June 1946), 6. This is one of several poems by Humphreys published in *Wales* and not reprinted in his *Collected Poems* (Hereafter *HCP*).

26   'A Season in Florence', *Wales*, 24 (Winter 1946), 120–4,

27   Emyr Humphreys, *Unconditional Surrender* (Bridgend: Seren, 1996), p. 80. Hereafter *US*.

28   *The Anchor Tree* (London: Dent, 1980), p. 183. Hereafter *AT*.

29   'Menna', in *Ghosts and Strangers* (Bridgend: Seren, 2001). Hereafter *GS*.

30   *Old People are a Problem* (Bridgend: Seren, 2003). Hereafter *OPP*.

31   *The Woman at the Window* (Bridgend: Seren, 2009). Hereafter *WW*.

9

ONWARDS TOWARDS UNION

One of the earliest memories of Roland Mathias, an important anglophone poet of the Wales of the post-war period, was of standing at the age of five on a couch placed under a high window in an upstairs apartment in Cologne, where his father was serving as an army chaplain, and watching the tugs fussing about on the Rhine below. Many decades later he would recall the incident in the form of an accomplished short story, central to which is the lingering innocent romance of this mysteriously significant mental image, which had become for the adult Mathias his own personal equivalent of one of Wordsworth's redemptive 'spots of time':

> Tugs with trains of barges trailing across the stream like tails they couldn't wag properly, and sometimes great rafts, filling the river from shore to shore, with little huts like dog-kennels on them and men paddling out of them across the patterned logs.[1]

In the story, this recollection is attributed to a traumatised young German survivor of the Second World War whose attempt to settle in a complacently victorious England is frustrated by the visceral distaste he feels for its vulgar Anglo-American culture, and whose memories of his native Germany are almost literally bedevilled by nightmare memories both of the Nazis and of the apocalyptic aftermath of the bombing of Cologne by the Allies – there were 262 raids in all conducted on the city. As for the young man's half-guilty memory of the Rhine tugs, it is for him the saving remnant of a faith that the dignified decencies of the ordinary can somehow survive even at the very heart of the utterly monstrous. It is his assurance that, *pace*

W. B. Yeats, the ceremony of innocence can never really be drowned. This was the difficult belief to which Mathias, a committed Christian who had been a conscientious objector during the Second World War, also remained true throughout his impressive life. What is interesting to note in the present context is that when he was looking for an objective correlative for this core conviction it was to Europe that he instinctively chose to turn.

This was no isolated choice. It was one repeated many times by Mathias in his singular, and often forbiddingly difficult poems. Time after time Europe provided him with occasions and locations for profound self-scrutiny and self-reorientation. It also provided him with valuable means of reflecting obliquely on his own Welshness. Such an identification mattered immensely to him but, thanks to the complexity of his case (he had spent long periods living outside the country, including in army barracks and while studying at public school and at Oxford), he repeatedly strove to understand it and felt he constantly had to earn it. Accordingly several of his continental poems are attempts to get his personal bearings, and since Mathias, with a first in History at Oxford, was an erudite, quirky historian, it was natural for him to look to the past for illumination.

A period as a visiting scholar at Brest University allowed him to research ancient 'Celtic' links between Wales and Brittany. His strong connections with Pembrokeshire led to a particular interest in the Celtic St Guenole, reputed to have sailed from his native Brittany to Pembrokeshire, where he is remembered as Winwaloe. Mathias accordingly dubbed him a 'Channel Saint' in a brief poem celebrating one who had, like himself, been an outsider who had come to Wales and been fully accepted.[2] In Brittany, too, Mathias found a parallel to the Welsh rural experience of evisceration of rural culture as the young left in their droves for greener pastures:

> Only
> Grandmothers, stiff with the coiffe
> And rheumatics, stand absurd
> In the gooseberry patch, rapt
> In a habit of Sundays. (*CPRM*, 201)

He ominously entitled the poem 'A Celtic Death', grimly noting the appropriateness of the region's name: 'Finistère' (*Finis terrae*: land's end, or end of the earth).

A majestic, diapasonic elegy for the Celts is prompted by Mathias's visit to La Tène, where, to his mingled disgust and fear, he finds all the magnificent cultural artefacts laid out in vulgar display in sepulchral cabinets for the gratification of the gawping, avaricious 'vandals' of the present day. So where in all this dead matter, he wonders, can he find the living spirit of the Celts?

> The ceramic masters
> Of Europe, the uncompromised chasers whose spirals
> Match real with unreal, whose imagined receding faces
> Trade with the fox, whose earth-god horns at the stag, Esus
> Become Cernunnos, where are they? (*CPRM*, 209–10)

His concluding fear is that the authentic Celt is for ever 'lost, his antique designs of faith / And mystery tidied-up in this dried-out marsh'. Mathias, a Christian believer deeply committed to honouring in his life and in his writings the demanding moral principles of the Welsh Nonconformist tradition that had sustained his chaplain father, clearly discerns in the museum artefacts of La Tène the equivalent of the empty sepulchral chapels that litter the Welsh landscape.

Mathias undertook a typically severe and rigorous audit of his Welsh chapel values at three continental sites. Like many another Welsh Nonconformist before him, he was fascinated by the sensuousness and languor of southern Europe. For him, it was both attractive and morally sapping. 'The Path to Fontana Amorosa' records a northern puritan male's ambivalent response to the 'feminised' landscape of ancient Mediterranean cult and culture. Setting out on the path to the Baths of Aphrodite in Cyprus, Mathias uneasily allows himself to be seduced by the lushness of the landscape in this, 'the white goddess's country' (*CPRM*, 257). Wantoning in abundance, the whole coastline, as 'reckless' as it is 'magical', seems to beckon him towards 'the spring / Where the gush is all women's abandon' (*CPRM*, 257). But, warned by the corpses of snake and lizard, he reaffirms the fidelity of his allegiance to the realm of self-disciplined order by choosing not to proceed to the sacred site. As two contrasting poems show, Mathias is much more comfortable in the bracingly testing mountainous terrain of northern Europe. The harsh music of Alpine grasshoppers is for Mathias the only true song of a lapsarian earth, trustworthy and durable:

> Patently
> It is the grasshoppers I
> Must listen to, as they intersperse
> A hard leg-music with mad
> Travels from tussock to bleaker
> Tuft, to broken stick or random
> Protuberant stone. (*CPRM*, 273–4)

This 'hard leg-music' is fitting accompaniment to mankind's errant and erratic ways.

Companion to this is an account of a day trip to an Alpine valley on the Swiss border in 'A Field at Vallorcines', which ends by admiring the humble, unostentatious 'grace' (the religious overtones of the term would have been important to Mathias) of the little train station from which he will return down the steep slope:

> It has borne
> The faces of doubt, the comings and goings
> Of millions. We shall stand there solid in
> The goodly counsel with which a world back we set out. (*CPRM*, 268)

Contained in that resonant phrase 'goodly counsel' is another deliberate tribute to Mathias's biblical background.

One of Mathias's closest friends and associates was Raymond Garlick. The two first met when Mathias was headmaster of Pembroke Dock Grammar School and Garlick a new young appointment to the staff there.[3] It soon became apparent that they shared a secret passion for what in those days was called 'Anglo-Welsh Literature'. Beginning by starting a new magazine devoted to the subject and punningly called *Dock Leaves* – it evolved into the major organ *The Anglo-Welsh Review* – they went on to produce, both singly and jointly, a body of critical and historical studies of this literature for the next half-century, in the process laying firm foundations for the academic study which became known as 'Welsh Writing in English'.

Like Mathias, Garlick was also a very accomplished poet. He was a gentle, shy man, formal and courteous in manner and elegantly courtly in his unfailingly dapper appearance. These qualities of character duly found expression in a poetry whose fastidious formalism he attributed, in several personal poems, to his self-image as a 'cripple',

misshapen from an early age. He had spent long, lonely periods as
a sensitive child undergoing painful hospital treatment at a distance
from his parents, and this had bred in him a strong inner resolve, self-
control, and emotional detachment:

> Mister to most, a formal man
> (lives raised in splints grow stiff, no doubt,
> training themselves to a handrailed plan
>
> of plotted movements, fixed, foreseen),
> for me a poem is first a frame.
> Form is the cane on which I lean.[4]

A Londoner by birth, Garlick identified strongly with Wales, having
spent idyllic childhood holidays visiting his paternal grandparents at
Deganwy, and he settled in the country following his period of undergraduate study at the University College of North Wales, Bangor.
While never comfortable speaking Welsh, he became a passionately
committed supporter of the language and a courageous advocate for
the law-breaking campaign on its behalf – non-violent in character,
which was extremely important to the pacifist Garlick – waged by
Cymdeithas yr Iaith Gymraeg from the late 1960s onwards. There was
a strong personal component to his involvement: he had a wife, son
and sister-in-law who were active in the ranks of the society.

Garlick had been awakened early to what he was to call 'a sense
of Europe'. While studying at Bangor he had become friendly with
a much older and very experienced Dutch student there, and this
afforded him an initial acquaintance with the continent that was
quickly deepened through his courtship of a young Anglesey girl,
Elin Hughes. She had become fluent in French thanks to the friendship she had formed, as a young girl, with a community of nuns from
France who were resident in a nearby convent at Holyhead. Once they
were married, the pair became enthusiastic pro-Europeans, travelling
extensively on the continent during their spare time.

Eventually, following a period when Garlick taught at county
schools first in Pembroke Dock and then in Ffestiniog, the pair settled for seven years in Holland, where Garlick had obtained a post
at the International School in Eerde Castle. The place seemed to be a
physical palimpsest of European history. Situated on the edge of the
forest of Ommen, it was a 'double-moated château in the Louis XIV

manner, raised in 1745 upon the foundations of castles going back
to the ninth century. It is the countryside of Thomas à Kempis, the
classical expression of its serene lyricism.'⁵ He found that the 'avenued
Holland', with its neat pattern of enclosed polders, and the disciplined
orderliness of the Dutch way of life, were perfectly suited to his own
reserved temperament. That so much of the land had been reclaimed
from the sea through human industry and ingenuity also appealed
to one who had known what it was to have to struggle to recover
psychological equilibrium following the physical and mental trau-
mas of his childhood. He wrote a poem celebrating the astonishing
achievement of Cornelius Lely, who in 1891 had conceived the idea
of draining the Zuidersee, the great shallow inland sea at the heart
of the Netherlands. As a result, 1,700 square kilometers of what had
been the sea bed were turned into fertile arable land. Lely, Garlick
believed, was far more worthy of poetic celebration than those violent
'louts', the braggart warriors who had been accorded eternal fame in
the *Iliad*: 'I sing Lely / who burnt no tower / but brought the sea-floor
/ into flower. (*SE*, 38).

Most of the poems set in Holland implicitly or explicitly referenced Wales by frequently pointed and poignant contrast. Deeply
appreciative of the peaceful calm of the contemporary Netherlands,
Garlick was always mindful of its violent past. Alarmed by the activities of the Free Wales Army at the time of the investiture of the
Prince of Wales, Garlick fervently prayed that his adopted country be
spared the agony of birth into nationhood through a 'terrible beauty':

> I have lived where blood
> had flooded down men's hands.
> Though I look for a Wales
> free as the Netherlands,
> a freedom hacked out of here
> is a freedom without worth,
> a terror without beauty.
> Here it must come to birth
> not as a pterodactyl
> flailing archaic wings,
> but the dove that broods on chaos –
> wise as a thousand springs. (*SE*, 92–3)

In another poem of the same period, he meditates on the Fourth
of May, the date set apart in Holland for commemoration of those

there who had suffered during those terrible years of Nazi occupation when the Dutch nation had known 'the shock of blood, and the
smell of fear'. It opens with his siting himself 'in this country / the
size of Wales' (albeit with five times the population), and it ends with
an intensely protective prayer for his beloved country; 'Don't let the
nails // of crucifixion / be hammered there – / employed by hands /
half unaware' (*SE*, 91).

The very flatness of the Low Countries, vividly contrasting as it
did with the mountainous Eryri which Garlick so loved, underlined
the exhilarating fact that he was living at the extreme end of a long
highway that led right across the vast expanse of a whole continent.
For him, this beckoning vista represented welcome escape both from
the insularity (psychological as much as physical) of little 'Albion' and
from the internecine struggles within Wales itself. 'To be European',
he declared, 'is first to be not / an island.' It is to know that 'the mind's
neat plot, // the dust you set your roses in, / squares out in hectares /
to Berne and Berlin' (*SE*, 63).

Implicit in such a declaration, of course, was the acknowledgement that 'Europeanness' was not a matter of physical location but
rather a state of mind. As such, it was every bit as possible for a native
of Wales to be a European as it was for a resident of Holland. Except
for one great obstacle, which came in the gigantic looming form of
an intervening England: not the actual physical land of England, but
rather the pro-Englishness, ingrained in the Welsh by centuries of colonisation, that continued to prevent effectual Welsh contact, through
exercise of intellect and imagination, with the cultural resources of the
continent. Garlick repeatedly addressed this condition in his poetry,
boldly trying, for example in the poem 'Capitals', to insert Cardiff,
with an affected nonchalance, into a list of some of Europe's greatest capital cities – Moscow, Madrid, Dublin, Rome, Paris, Bonn,
Amsterdam. The poem ends with a revealing invocation of the names
of some of the most celebrated Welsh Europeans:

> Europe,
> young Ap Iwan's yard,
> Gruffydd Robert's vision's scope,
> Morgan Llwyd's hoist petard:
> source to which our ballads grope –
> context, compass-card
> and hope. (*SE*, 64–5)

Another strategy he employed was to reference Camelot and the Arthurian romances as examples of Wales's valuable past contribution to European culture. 'No troops for us', the poem rather brashly and unconvincingly asserts, 'no occupied zone. / Wales in Europe / is in the bone' (*SE*, 67). Wishful thinking indeed, as Garlick was sadly very well aware.

Having joined his wife in the Church of Rome on their marriage, Garlick remained a member of it for over thirty years. During that time his view of Wales's relation to Europe was significantly influenced by his Catholicism. He admired Saunders Lewis, addressing a congratulatory poem to him following the famous lecture he'd delivered at Newtown in which he controversially portrayed the Methodist Ann Griffiths as heir to the great European mystics of the late medieval period; and he shared Lewis's view that Wales was the natural heir of the pan-European Roman empire. In his long early radio poem 'Blaenau Observed' he recalled how Wales had been 'formed and nursed to nationhood by Rome' (*SE*, 27). Accordingly he viewed Caernarfon, site of the key legionary fortress of Segontium, as marking the beginning of the famous Roman road of Sarn Helen, and he came to feel, on a visit to Rome, that many of the Eternal City's roads 'led to Wales'.

Garlick developed a particular interest in, and felt a particular affinity for, those Welsh Recusant priests who had relocated to the continent. The most famous, of course, was Gruffydd Robert. Having settled in Milan, where he became Cardinal Borromeo's right-hand man, Robert, a great Renaissance humanist, proceeded to prepare and publish the first-ever grammar of the Welsh language, prefacing it with a famous essay in which he professed his undying love for his native tongue and his ardent wish to ensure it would become a sophisticated contemporary language equipped to deal with the most advanced learning.

So in 'Blaenau Observed' Garlick imagined Gruffydd Robert, 'canon of Milan', setting his Grammar aside 'on the window seat', and seeming to hear 'Welsh voices in the lane' (*SE*, 170). Robert featured in several other of his Welsh European poems, particularly in 'Mirrors'. Passing the famous Biblioteca Ambrosiana in the heart of Milan, a legacy of Borromeo's project of the Counter-Reformation, he imagines that he sees 'all Anglesey spread out / and like a map'. Stopped in his tracks by the unexpected vision, he turns back, enters the great Renaissance library, and calls up an original copy of Robert's great Grammar. There, sitting at a table just two streets away from the famous cathedral in which Robert served as canon, he found himself magically transported, by 'the dead / black letter, foxed and flecked', over the thousand miles to Holyhead (*SE*, 87).

Robert was not the only one of the generation of Welsh Recusant priests who had relocated to Europe to attract Garlick's sympathetic attention. Cassano all'Ionio is a small town deep in Calabria, located on the coast in the instep of Italy. It was there of all places that Owen Lewis fetched up as 'lord bishop'. An 'old Welsh abbé' of the Renaissance, he has long been forgotten in his native Wales:

> Precisely. That is why I try to fan
> the embers of his name, long dead, alive.
> He was, you see, a European man. (*SE*, 88)

Much nearer his home in Holland, Garlick found occasion for reflection on modern Wales's complete indifference to Europe when he visited Louvain for a graduation ceremony at the ancient university there. Viewing the procession of academic dignitaries, his eye is caught by the short, thickset stature of the Rector Magnificus, wrapped in all the dignity of his 'red / and Roman purple'. A proud, serene Fleming, he beams on the crowd whose 'roars are thrown / like sticks of hand-grenades' around his fearless head. Much impressed by the scene, Garlick is moved to view this dignified and self-possessed Flemish university chancellor against the turbulent background of the language struggle ongoing back home in Wales, and to see in him, equally at home as he comfortably is in French and in Flemish, a monitory example for the stubborn, arrogant and aggressively hostile monoglot anglophone majority in his adopted country:

> Observe him, Wales.
> The image is clear:
> bilingualism's
> grenadier
>
> is what is pacing
> through Louvain town –
> coming to turn you upside down. (*SE*, 95)

'For some of us you see', Garlick wrote, 'Wales is another word for peace / . . . We like our castles ruined.'[6] It is a touchingly flattering conviction, born in part of Garlick's experience, as a pacifist, of keeping company over a long period of years with some of the country's most celebrated of principled pacifists, most notably including the great Waldo Williams. It was this (doubtlessly misguided) vision of Wales that had helped form, as he explained in an autobiographical essay, his highly idealistic sense of the country's natural connection with Europe:

> Listening to Marcia Draak, Professor of Welsh at Amsterdam and Utrecht, lecturing in Dutch upon Celtic Literature at the University of Utrecht, I realised that because it was a culture of peace, of intellect and the arts, Welsh civilization had preserved this sense of Europe, which seemed much more tenuous in cultures preoccupied with the introverting and divisive values of power. (*AW*, 93)

The conviction was strengthened further as he witnessed the resolution shown by the young activist members of Cymdeithas yr Iaith Gymraeg in adhering to their non-violent principles even in the face of considerable provocation from a police force that was far less inclined at times to observe such niceties. Garlick found himself shocked to the core at the 'violence of the law', in the very rough treatment meted out by the police to a large crowd of protesters, including his son Iestyn, who had gathered on 8 May 1971 outside the Guildhall in Swansea, 'the bitter city'. They were there to support their inoffensive comrades who were standing trial for defacing, and removing, monoglot English road signs. Admitted to the courtroom, Garlick was appalled anew by the conduct of the judge administering the law of England and felt he was watching, he noted with a nod at Ginsberg, 'the alienation/ of the finest minds of a generation' (*GSP*, 130).

His sympathy was completely with the protesters, not only because of the involvement of several members of his immediate family, but because the many years of living in the Netherlands and of failing to become fluent in Dutch had brought home to him that 'the long nerve of identity / Runs through a language' (*GSP*, 153). This, he further realised with typical fair-mindedness, was true not only of the identity of Welsh-speakers but also of the 'Anglo-Welsh', 'whose true Welsh mind / Speaks only English' (*GSP*, 153). Despondent that in 1979 the Welsh had chosen 'to become / Colonials by referendum' (*GSP*, 157), he nevertheless retained a faith that the Anglo-Welsh, as well as the speakers of Welsh, would eventually rally to the common cause of preserving a Welsh identity that, Garlick conceded, had come to seem a far more problematic concept than being Dutch had for the inhabitants of the Netherlands.

When Wales at last accompanied the rest of the UK into Europe in 1973, Garlick was commissioned by the BBC to write a radio ode to celebrate the occasion. He began with the pointed comment, addressed to fellow Europeans but with the English very particularly in mind. 'You will not expect celebrations here', he told them, because for the Welsh the event represented nothing but 'a people / ascending to their origins at last'. 'From the incarnation of the Lord / the year two hundred and twelve', he continued, 'we entered / Europe; by the edict / of Caracalla / becoming Roman citizens. Before / ever England was, we were. And still we are.' For Wales, he nonchalantly added, 'It's an old affair – / Wales went in with Gaul, you see, / with Arthur a late entry. / A couple of millenniums / we've been in.'[7] Raymond Garlick remained faithful to that particular vision of Wales in Europe until the end of his life.

More different poets could scarcely be imagined than the courteous, reserved, schoolmasterly Mathias and his friend the courtly, formal Raymond Garlick on the one hand and Harri Webb, the rumbustious and maverick Falstaffian extrovert on the other. Webb was best known for outrageously amusing popular verses, comic and sharply satiric, written for performance in pub sessions enticingly entitled 'Poems and Pints'. A cunning manipulator of his own public persona, he set out to puncture what he believed to be the somnolence of the colonised and cowed working population of his native south Wales and to remedy their woeful ignorance of their own history. Contrary to the knockabout plebeian image he cultivated in his popular verses, the maverick Webb was in fact sophisticated, intelligent, multilingual and highly cultured after a deliberately unorthodox fashion. He translated poems from several European languages throughout his career, drawing his examples not from the familiar mainstream cultural sources but from the 'marginal' poetry produced in some of Europe's minority languages. An avowed, campaigning nationalist and champion of the Welsh language, he aimed thereby to put Wales in what seemed to him its appropriate pan-European setting.

In the autobiographical sketch he contributed to *Planet* in 1976, Webb warmly recalled his superb French teacher at his Swansea

secondary school who not only infused in him a passion for that
language and its literature but also provided him with 'acquaintance
with Europe's central and seminal culture . . . a liberation, not least
from the hick provincialism that characterises so many of the claims
made for Eng. Lit.'[8] Simultaneously learning Spanish, he came across
Lorca,

> a poet of my own day, a poet of his own people, killed, as far as I could
> make out, simply because he was such a poet. His death seemed part
> of the poetry itself. It meant more to me than anything I had encoun-
> tered so far in the three literatures with which I was beginning to become
> acquainted. (WP, 28)

Years later, when visiting Cairo on leave from the Malta convoy, Webb
picked up Aragon's *Le Crêve-Coeur*.

> I knew of him as a surrealist, a communist, a literary manifestant. Here
> he suddenly was as a poet of action and feeling, of involvement and
> immediate communication, a man who loved his country deeply and was
> scalded by her shame. It was another revelation of what real poetry was
> all about. (WP, 28)

Webb's vision of Europe was not of a union of the existent large
nation states writ thereby even larger, but of a plural community of
cultures and peoples both large and small. He therefore gravitated
towards poets 'of the margins'. Among such were Frédéric Mistral
(1830–1914), a leader of Le Félibrige, a movement devoted to the
Provençal language (WP, 117); Antioco Casula (1878–1957), nick-
named Montanura (WP, 118); the Breton poet, Paol Keineg; and the
poet from the Galician region of north-west Spain, Manuel Mañam,
whose patriotic poem to his native region opens by defiantly asserting
that 'Galicia is her people, nothing more, / Where there is no people,
there cannot / Be Galicia'.[9] He also adapted a poem in memory of
the Polish-German communist Rosa Luxemburg (*CPHW*, 143) by
André Benedetto (1934–2009). He was a theatre director and Marxist
poet who was writer-director at the Nouvelle Compaignie/Théâtre des
Carmes at Avignon, a community theatre dedicated to addressing the
issues of the Occitania region of France. Webb's particular favourite, though, was Lorca, the great Spanish Marxist poet of the 1930s
who drew inspiration primarily from his native region of Andalusia.
Particularly attractive for Webb, as for many other poets of his period

and later, were those ballads and romances in which Lorca drew on the rich popular legacy of Andalusian gypsy songs.

Committed to radical left-wing politics and working within a Plaid Cymru that had moved far to the left by the 1960s from its original conservative political position under Saunders Lewis and his associates, Webb admired writers of like mind, such as the great Chilean poet, Pablo Neruda. Webb's *Collected Poems* includes a translation into Welsh (*CPHW*, 271–84) of one of Neruda's most famous poems that stretches over thirteen pages. A celebration of Machu Picchu, perched high among the majestic peaks of the Andes, it discovers in this ancient site, as in the whole magnificent land of Chile, exhilarating evidence of a potential for liberating the oppressed masses of South America. In the classic study by Frantz Fanon, *Les Damnés de la Terre/The Wretched of the Earth*, Webb found a definitive analysis of the different stages of the anti-colonial struggle that he believed could profitably be applied to the Welsh situation. As an Algerian, Fanon was a passionate supporter of the violent struggle being waged by African Algerians during the 1950s against the arrogantly repressive French colonists, the *colons*, who believed they were the agents of the *Mission civilatrice*. 'The colons of rich lands / For whom life was sweet / Privileged and serene,' Webb wrote in his tribute 'For Franz [*sic*] Fanon',

> Saw no end to the long peace
> Nor the coming of their dark.
> I often think of the scene
> As I walk in St Mary's Street
> As I walk in Cathays Park. (*CPHW*, 137)

In the early 1960s, when he was in his prime and very active in Plaid Cymru circles, Webb gathered around him a commune of sorts in Garth Newydd, a large empty house in Merthyr. Its members were untamed nationalist activists like himself, and during this time Radio Free Wales, an illegal radio station, frequently took to the air from the attic of the property. Among those living there was Meic Stephens, a young teacher and poet keen to publish poetry by some of Wales's young anglophone authors. A few years later, Stephens switched from working outside the system to working inside it, when he was appointed the first director of literature of the Welsh Arts Council, a post he proceeded to fill with immense distinction for the next thirty years. A graduate in French like Webb himself, whose literary executor he eventually became, Stephens also shared his passion for Europe's smaller peoples and languages. When, therefore, he published his pioneering study of the *Linguistic Minorities of Western Europe* in 1976, Webb responded with a typically rousing chorus of verses to be sung to the tune of Widccombc Fair:

> Meic Stephens, Meic Stephens, lend me your great book
> (In the name of George Steiner and Noam Chom-sky),
> For I'm stuck for a word and I must have a look
> At Friulan, Galician, Jurassian, Alsatian,
> North Frisian, Aostan,
> And the Flemish of Westhoek and all,
> And the Flemish of Westhoek and all! (*CPHW*, 285)

And so this lively squib proceeds for another three verses, during which it also lists Breznhoneg, Albannaich, Kernewek, Sydslesvig, Eskuarra Slovenska, Carinthian, Croatian, Valdostsan, Utsitan, Sardinian and Lusatian.

As well as being an impressive introduction to the field, Stephens's large volume (it runs to over 700 pages) now stands as important testimony to the new interest in Europe that had been steadily gaining ground amongst writers and intellectuals, particularly those of a nationalist bent, in the wake of the cultural and political reorientation that had occurred in the Wales of the 1960s. In his Preface, Stephens explained that his aim was to 'describe the cultural and political situation of over fifty linguistic minorities in sixteen states of Western Europe'. By 'linguistic minorities', he proceeded to explain, he meant a community in which a language was spoken that was not 'the language of the State's citizens'.[10] He then distinguished between such of those sub-state languages as were indigenous to the regions in which they were spoken and others that were 'outliers', so to speak, of majority, state, languages spoken elsewhere. His study, he added, was exclusively confined to the former, and it included a substantial chapter on Wales and the Welsh language.

Stephens ended his Preface with an open acknowledgement that he himself was 'a Welshman of Socialist convictions who supported the national movement in my own country' (*LME*, xvii). He might have added that while he was a product of anglophone industrial south Wales, he had, while studying at the University of Wales,

Aberystwyth, mastered the Welsh language thoroughly and been involved in peaceful, law-breaking campaigns on its behalf. His was therefore very much the passionate identification of a convert with a language he had elected to acquire. His Preface was followed by a substantial Introduction which traced the history of a linguistically defined nationalism from its origins in the Germany and France of the eighteenth century right down to the book's present. It concluded with a clarion call 'to move towards a united but federal Europe which, across State frontiers, will permit and encourage the free development of all its regions and peoples' (*LME*, xxv).

Stephens's identification of himself as both a nationalist and a socialist is a reminder that from the 1960s onwards Plaid Cymru was becoming steadily more radical in its political policies, ending up well to the left of the conservative Labour Party that had dominated Welsh politics since the 1920s. With this shift, by the 1970s, went a burgeoning interest in cooperation with social movements for reform of like radical tendency across western Europe. The idea began to form of a very broad and diverse 'common front' of such pan-European initiatives under the ideological auspices of what became known as the 'New Left'. As capacious and nebulous as it proved ideologically fruitful, this fashionable label of the day referred to a spectrum of neo-Marxist, or even post-Marxist, causes and was characterised, as the *Encyclopaedia Britannica* entry on the subject explains, by 'an extension of the traditional left's focus on class struggle to acknowledge multiple forms and bases of oppression, including race and gender'. To instances of this sort, some of the young members of Plaid Cymru of the 1970s, including those who had been roused to illegal actions by Saunders Lewis's historic 1962 radio broadcast 'Tynged yr Iaith', added their own experience of a settled state of cultural oppression involving potentially terminal discrimination against the Welsh language.

The largely unofficial movement of Plaid towards the left was officially confirmed by the party when a special report by leading figures concluded in 1979 that Plaid should hereafter declare its commitment to a moderate form of 'devolved socialism', strongly localist in emphasis.[11] Such a platform represented in some ways an updated version of the communitarian politics of D. J. Davies in the 1930s, averse though he had been, like Gwynfor Evans after him, to the socialist label. It was, however, an even more radical model that was in the end adopted by the party, partly as a result of promptings by Dafydd Elis Thomas and others. Firmly embedded in traditional class politics, this version boldly stated the aim of turning an independent Wales into an avowedly socialist democracy. The majority of Plaid members proved responsive to this dramatic new initiative at the time, partly because of the perceived failure of the party to deliver self-government in the devolution vote of 1979, a failure some attributed to its anachronistic ideology.

The new policy advocated cooperation with enlightened elements even within the old enemy ranks of the Welsh Labour Party, The aim was to prepare the ground for a truly socialist Wales by moving politics on beyond existing narrow party ideologies and animosities. It also anticipated the formation of a broad front with a wide range of 'progressive' initiatives, from grass-root movements to a variety of radical causes. In these important respects, the new official platform of Plaid brought it into line with the operations of the New Left. The tracing of the consequences of this approach would, however, involve moving beyond the scope of the present volume in order to study the Wales of the Thatcherite decade of the eighties that saw, for instance, the creation of the National Left, the publishing of such periodicals as *Arcade* and *Radical Wales* along with the fervid intellectual debates of the influential coteries that supported them, the emergence of a women's movement within Plaid Cymru, the party's active support, alongside the unions and the Labour Party, for the miners' strike, and involvement in a number of local direct actions against factory closures and the like.

By the late 1970s such stirrings within Plaid Cymru had attracted the attention, and eventually elicited the committed support, of Raymond Williams, the Cambridge don and cultural theorist of international renown who hailed from Pandy, near Abergavenny. One of Williams's central contentions was that, contrary to official Marxist theory, culture should not be treated as a mere epiphenomenon and regarded as simply a by-product and useful symptom of the underlying economic relations that were the real agents of social development and political structures. Taking his cue from Gramsci and other European intellectuals who were highly influential in British New Left circles, Williams first borrowed from anthropologists and sociologists a definition of culture according to which it signified every aspect of the way of life of a given community, from the banal

to the arcane. He then proceeded to argue that culture, properly conceived, was not a mere passive reflector of socio-economic realities
but an agent active in determining their character and their development. This was obviously a view calculated to appeal to writers and
intellectuals with an interest in the creative arts. It also spoke to that
segment of the young Welsh intelligentsia deeply concerned to protect
and develop the Welsh language that had been the primary carrier of
a Welsh cultural identity down the centuries. Furthermore, it provided
them with grounds for relating their own struggles to those of similarly imperilled national linguistic cultures across Europe.

Disillusioned by the late 1970s with a traditional British Labour
Party whose timid practise of what passed for a socialist programme
had been exposed during the years of the Harold Wilson government, concerned at evidence of the growing power of a new populist
consumer capitalism that was to usher in the Thatcher years, and
somewhat mistrustful of the will of the British working class to effect
change according to the classic Marxist model, Williams cast around
elsewhere for signs of hope. He found it in the form of the 'growing
points' of an alternative, genuinely socialist future politics evident
for him in a number of different initiatives and locations traditionally considered ephemeral and peripheral by Marxists. This search
it was that brought him 'home' not just to Wales, but to a Wales he
now began to view in a European context, as he duly explained in an
influential series of interviews conducted by the *New Left Review*:

> Suddenly England, bourgeois England, wasn't my point of reference any
> more. I was a Welsh European . . . I want the Welsh people – still a radical
> and cultured people – to defeat, override or bypass bourgeois England;
> the alternatives follow from the intricacies. That connects, for me, with
> the sense in my work that I am now necessarily European; that the people
> to the left and on the left of the French and Italian Communist parties,
> the German and Scandinavian comrades, the communist dissidents from
> the East, like Bahro, are my kind of people; the people I come from and
> belong to, and my more conscious Welshness is, as I feel it, my way of
> learning these connections.[12]

Following Williams's use of the term, 'Welsh European' (previously
used by Saunders Lewis) became a mantra for many on the left in
Wales. But long before he made it fashionable, such a concept, understood in much the same terms as Williams himself intended, had
not only been adopted but actively implemented in creative practice

by several Welsh intellectuals, foremost amongst whom was Ned
Thomas, who both admired Williams and was admired by him.

'All Europe went into the making of Kurtz', wrote Conrad bleakly.
The same might more positively if hyperbolically be said of Ned
Thomas. During the period covered by this volume, his major contribution to the creation of a European consciousness amongst the
Welsh was the launch of the periodical *Planet* (subsequently entitled
'The Welsh Internationalist') in 1970 and his work as editor throughout the first period of its publication, ending in 1979. But fully to
appreciate the context for this seminal initiative, and the vision behind
it, one needs to be aware of the important account Thomas was later
to offer of his peripatetic life in his award-winning 'memoir of a
period', *Bydoedd*.[13]

The opening section ends where it began, with the author pondering a photograph of his ten-year-old self on a bike in a corner
of post-war Germany and playing with his blonde friend Marianne.
Behind them both, the adult Thomas realises, stretched a world
that they did not know but that had brought them together from
very different, distant spheres: the vast ruined landscape of post-
war Europe. And between first viewing of this photograph and its
later reviewing, Ned Thomas offers us a portrait of his boyhood
self as an Innocent Abroad; leaving his grandparents' Anglesey for
a north-west Germany under British occupation; accompanying his
father in official, chauffeur-driven cars while the locals fed logs into
the boilers of their steam-driven vehicles; collecting the stamps of
countries whose identities had changed several times in a few years;
visiting a reservoir the boy could not know had been the target of
the Dam Busters raid. These personal recollections are an exercise in
endless adjustments of perspective entailing reorientation and redefi-
nition. From the outset, we are shown that for Ned Thomas humans
live in a world which is itself a plurality of worlds, each distinct yet
interconnected – his father recognises something of his south Wales
in the Ruhr. (Waldo Williams's 'Mewn Dau Gae' has always been
Ned Thomas's touchstone poem, with its great mystical vision of
the secret netting/knitting of all humanity together.) To register this
intricate interconnectedness in the marrow of one's being from an
early age is to grow into an active, practising Europhile and ardent
multiculturalist.

By such subtleties and nuances of reflection does this remarkable memoir proceed. Plain recollections are haloed by complexities
of implication, deferrals of understanding: some individuals met
seem double agents on closer acquaintance. Kierkegaard noted that
'We live life forwards but understand it backwards'; 'we need two
lives, one to have the experiences, the other to understand them',
writes Ned Thomas, and understanding is, as he shows, a matter of
making connections. His memoir is a constant attempt to collapse
recollection and mature reflection into one, with his second chapter
devoted to a revisiting (in person and through documents) of the
boyhood Germany of the first chapter. Into focus (and tropes from
film and theatre recur) comes the 'cold and starving' life for Germans
in the British zone; the social confusion; the policy of denazification,
thwarted by the messiness of reality; innocent families ejected from
requisitioned homes. With all this the young boy had been innocently
complicit, unaware even of the contrasting histories of two of his
tutors.

Ned Thomas has lived through interesting times in interesting
places, recalled in the text with lyrical delicacy, discriminating intelligence and political shrewdness. Stints at the University of Salamanca
and Moscow University afforded insights into the Byzantine worlds
of Franco's Spain and Soviet society. Alive to the paradoxes of both
individuals and systems, he passes no simple judgements but leaves
us with a vivid sense of the precious singularity and irreducible complexity of periods and places and people. Deeply familiar with the
situation both of the Basques and the Catalans, and alert to the lessons they teach, he is too scrupulous to suppose that they offer Wales
any simple blueprint for advancement. The difference between the
cultural profile of FC Barcelona and Cardiff City is greater even than
the vast gulf between the clubs' talents.

No better recommendation than *Bydoedd* could be imagined
of that preservation of cultural and linguistic variety to which
Ned Thomas has so impressively devoted his entire life. As a self-
styled 'unorthodox' intellectual of the post-war left, a product of
the Hoggart era, he warms nostalgically to the valuable human and
political role played in oppressive regimes by what consumer society
now derisively labels a minority 'elitist high culture'. Left implicit
is the difficult question of what purchase, if any, such values can
continue to have on our populist, levelling age with its craven adoration of mass taste. And such a question strikes even at the heart

of Ned Thomas's Europhilia: Europe Inc., that wealthy capitalists'
club of established nation states, is a travesty of the European ideal
of a plurality of peoples to which his memoir bears such eloquent
testimony. And cheap tourism is more likely to lead to universal com-
modification than to linguistic tolerance. A pivotal experience in this
memoir is his return to Wales from London at the end of the 1960s.
In Llwynpiod, deep in the Cardiganshire countryside, he found a
generous-spirited, culturally rich, chapel-educated, politically active
and thoroughly Welsh-speaking community that embodied, and thus
resonantly reaffirmed, the values by which he has lived his life. But
what price such a community now?

It was that return to Wales, with the wealth of European experience that had antedated it, that prompted Ned Thomas to launch
Planet in 1970. The subtitle of 'The Welsh Internationalist', added
later, clearly signalled an intention to foster intellectual relations
between Wales and the world at large, but the bulk of the international
articles carried by the cultural periodical featured European locations
and issues. Instead of being singled out for editorial promotion, such
essays were deliberately, one might even say casually, interspersed with
others addressing many different aspects of the contemporary Welsh
cultural scene. The overall result, deliberately contrived, was the 'nor-
malisation' of the practice of viewing Wales in a European context.

There was a specific political background to the production of
Planet which needs mentioning. It was signalled by the cartoon of
the former Secretary State for Wales, George Thomas, on the cover of
the first number, prelude to an opening article by the editor entitled
'The George Thomas Era'. It characterised the recent state of affairs
in Wales during Thomas's term in office, from 1968 to 1970, as one
of turmoil, demonstrations, direct action and protest –

> Pembrey and Cwm Dulas, the farmers and the Rural Development Board,
> and many campaigns of the Welsh Language Society. It was also the time
> of the bombs, the first maimings by explosive charges, and on the morn-
> ing of the Investiture of the Prince of Wales, the first deaths, however
> unintended, in the name of the Welsh language movement.[14]

Such a climate of protest, it continued, was also to be found abroad,
in such instances as 'Negro [*sic*] violence in the United States, or
Protestants fighting Catholics in Northern Ireland'. Conflicts inherent
in the very structure of Welsh society, it added, had surfaced in the

form of violent confrontations, and the established animosity between Labour and the nationalist movements was preventing a constructive address of the crisis.

George Thomas was the very embodiment of this problem, implacably hostile, as his unpleasant record proved him to be, to any form of national sentiment or language movement. He was later to revel in his role as Speaker of the House of Commons and to gloat over his elevation to the peerage as Lord Thomas of Tonypandy: obviously, the Tonypandy riots had not been in vain. As for his period as secretary of state for Wales in the Wilson government, 'The George Thomas Era', as Ned Thomas scathingly termed it, 'gave one the impression of living in a boisterous and dissident satrapy which an adroit manipulator had been asked to handle' (NT, p. 6). As was noted on the back cover of the second number of *Planet*, Thomas duly replied in character, dismissing the periodical as 'Arrogant, conceited nonsense . . . will be read by Nationalists . . . needs to broaden its philosophy.'[15]

At its inception, then, *Planet* pledged itself to an attempt to reconcile socialism with nationalism in Wales, with the overall aim of securing an effective degree of self-government. But it went further. It deliberately noted that 'the fossilization of socialism is not something peculiar to Wales or to Britain', thus preparing the way for a programme of international comparisons, primarily drawn from European experience, in line with the editor's contention that Wales needed to begin to extricate itself from the British political system within which it had for too long been disadvantageously embedded, as had been amply demonstrated in the 'George Thomas era'.

Another important aspect of the *Planet* programme was its ambition to forge a common front between the two language communities of modern Wales, based on mutual respect and a shared ground of cultural understanding. In an interview with John Tripp in issue number 9, Meic Stephens recalled the way *Planet* first came to be launched. Shortly after his appointment as inaugural literature director of the Welsh Arts Council in 1967 he had made it one of his priorities to enable the publication of an English-language periodical that would address the arts and current affairs. Following discussions with Ned Thomas, then newly returned to Wales after a period editing the UK government's official Russian-language periodical *Anglia*, an application was received and approved for launching *Planet*, which Stephens characterised as 'a magazine which discusses the culture of Wales' in English. 'As it happens', Stephens continued,

[it] had a left-wing, nationalist, but non-party bias. If it offends in some
quarters, it may be that the brouhaha is caused by those who are hearing,
for the first time, what the Welsh-language magazines like *Taliesin* and *Y
Genhinen* have been saying for years. It must be embarrassing, I suppose,
to have an intelligent, articulate and radical magazine focussing attention,
in English so that the majority can hear, on topics of the day.[16]

Stephens and Thomas shared a perception that the divisions
between the two linguistic communities of Wales derived partly
from the lack of any opportunity for a mutual exchange of information between them. Ned Thomas was at that time attempting to heal
this breach not only through the agency of *Planet*, but also through
the publication of his little volume, *The Welsh Extremist*, a brilliant
attempt to explain to non-Welsh-speakers, both within Wales and
outside the country, the cultural background of the Welsh-language
campaigns of non-violent law-breaking that were at the time garner-
ing a lot of hostile media attention and polarising public opinion.
Viewed in this context, *Planet*'s commitment to the fostering of a
vision of Wales as operating within a multilingual and multicultural
European context was a natural corollary of its aim of fostering a
correspondingly eirenic and eclectic vision of multilingualism and
multiculturalism at home.

One of the hopeful central arguments of *Planet* from the outset was that the large established nation states of Europe were on
the brink of a process of decentralisation which would allow for the
re-emergence of the national regions of which they were actually
composed. The aim of the periodical was not merely to reflect on
this process but actively to promote it wherever possible. The second issue included an article by Paul Sérant, author of *La France
des Minorités*, on 'The Rise of French Regionalism'. It began by
dismissing de Gaulle's 1969 proposal to divide the country into
regions that did not correspond to the existing regional communities of 'French Flanders, Brittany, the French Basque country, the
various *langue d'oc* regions of southern France known collectively
as "*l'Occitanie*", French Catalonia, Corsica, and finally Alsace and
the German-speaking Moselle district'.[17] Then, having offered a brief
overview of the various movements within several of these national
regions that were agitating for change, he concluded by asserting:

It would be disastrous to try to replace the sovereignty of the European
nation-states by a new, centralised, unitary super-state. Europe in the

future can and must be a Europe of regions in which the central authority will respect the natural differences and individualities of the different
communities.

Given *Planet*'s mission, it was natural that it should wish to associate itself with the evidence submitted by Patricia Elton Mayo to
the Crowther Commission (subsequently renamed the Kilbrandon
Enquiry), whose official title was the 'Royal Commission on the
Constitution (United Kingdom)'. Initiated in April 1969 by Harold
Wilson's Labour government, it finally submitted its report in
October 1973, recommending the adoption of devolved assemblies
for Scotland and Wales rather than the more radical options of a federal or confederal structure. The leading Welsh representatives on the
committee were Sir Alun Talfan Davies and Sir Ben Bowen Thomas.
  Patricia Elton Mayo was a sociologist who would become best
known for her study *The Roots of Identity* (1974). In the evidence
she submitted to the Crowther Commission she compared the heavily
centralised constitutional structure of the United Kingdom adversely
with that which had long been operative in the flourishing federal state
of Switzerland and subsequently adopted by West Germany.[18] While
recognising in separatist movements such as those of Wales, Brittany
and Occitanie 'the resurgence of old nationalities which would like to
be recognized as such in a future European organisation', she argued
that they were also fuelled by the feelings of disempowerment common to all 'marginal' areas of Europe that were remote from the
administrative centres where all the key decisions were made. In
France, Mayo acerbically noted, 'care is taken to mutilate the real
local groups with an indigenous life of its own, viewed as a subver-
sive threat to the French state' (PEM, 30). The situation in Britain
was not so extreme, and was the result of the creep of administrative
precedent rather than of ideological dogma. But it was now time to
dismantle the present structure in favour of a devolved model which
recognised that 'governmental systems rather than being imposed
from the top downwards' should be 'built upwards from communities
with a cultural, historic, and economic life of their own' (PEM, 30).
  Planet was always keen to report on any developments in Europe,
past or present, that would seem to have a bearing on the situation in
Wales. Issue 3, for example, included an excellent, detailed account by
Goronwy Glyn Hughes on the very long and vexed history of Czech–
Slovak relations and the continuing tensions that existed between the

two different national communities currently yoked together, voluntarily but also very uneasily.[19] The same issue also featured a short
story by the Bulgarian short story writer Nikolai Haitov, whose work
continues to be recognised by UNESCO.[20] In the introductory note
supplied by the translator, Mina Bohana, Haitov is praised for his
depiction of life in the rural and mountainous district of the Rodopi
mountains, in the south of Bulgaria, which was at that time part of
the Soviet empire. He is thus doubly commended – as a committed
regionalist within an occupied country that is itself one of the 'fringe'
countries of Europe.

Robin Okey's article on 'Yugoslavia – the Background to Cultural
Policy' was another example of attention being paid to a country that,
like Czechoslovakia, had been cobbled together – in this case largely
by the adroit manoeuvrings of Marshal Tito – out of several constituent nationalities in the form of a south Slav alliance.[21] The collapse
of the Habsburg empire at the end of the First World War had made
possible the fusion of Serbia and Croatia with a group of the smaller
national collectives of Macedonia, Montenegro, Bosnia-Herzegovina
and Slovenia, along with their non-Slav minorities. Denied political
expression by the dominant Serbia during the inter-war years, these
other peoples were granted formal recognition only when Yugoslavia
re-emerged after the Second World War as a communist state that,
despite being a satellite of the Soviet empire, continued to enjoy a
very significant degree of self-government thanks to the wiliness of
the Marshal.

In his article, Okey was particularly approving of the remarkable
strides towards the development of an intra-cultural infrastructure
that had been enabled in these several different sub-state national
regions by the Tito regime. The overall aim, Okey stressed, was to
'release the energies of the people for the building of socialism' (RO,
45), and it was this that had commended what was an enlightened
cultural programme to a resolutely communist government. Yugoslavs
had thus been taught 'to place a positive value on the nation', even
while they remained wary of the dangers of an unbridled nationalism. In this fundamental respect, Yugoslavia contrasted with Britain,
where national collectives had been traditionally disregarded by an
anglocentric state intent on the valorisation of the individual and
the exaltation of the law. Thus within a British political system that
insisted on the primacy of the supposedly unitary state, Wales continued, so Okey concluded, to enjoy far less influence than did not

only Slovenia and Macedonia in Yugoslavia but even minorities such as the Albanians and Hungarians in that country.[22]

As had long been the case with most Welsh texts that had a pronounced European bent, *Planet* had a tendency to fret over the state of the 'sister' region of Brittany. In a measured article, Dewi Morris Jones surveyed the vexed, and in some ways sorry, history of various national movements there during the century, noting the damage that had been done by the pro-fascist and collaborationist activists associated with the right wing of the PNB (Parti National Breton) and its periodical *Breiz Atao* during the Second World War. A postwar revival of national sentiment began belatedly and timidly around 1957, eventually spawning the UDB (Union Démocratique Bretonne), a strongly anti-capitalist, anti-bourgeois left-wing party sometimes criticised for being too French and centralist in its outlook. Jones noted how very difficult indeed it was for Bretons to gain an overview of contemporary affairs in Brittany, so heavily centralised, and selectively biased, were the established media industries there. Jones concluded with the hope that 'the connection of Breton politics with fascist-tainted conservatism is being gradually lost as there spreads an increased understanding of the colonial situation and this is seen as the initial step towards a free and European Brittany'.[23]

One of the wartime collaborators had been Morvan Lebesque, a leading Breton patriot. But by the 1960s he had become a respected journalist and television critic, and was also known to have been a friend of Albert Camus. His autobiography was published in 1970, the year of his death, and three years later an extract from it appeared in *Planet*.[24] He recounted how, following his commitment to the politics of the left as a teenager, he had been ashamed of belonging to the 'retarded' region of Brittany, and had been utterly scornful of the local 'lingo'. Instructed by his parents to despise his fellow Bretons, he had treated them as his 'negroes'.

His conversion had been sudden, beginning with a fascination with what, for him at the time, was an unintelligible Breton phrase. This had led to a crash course in Breton history and culture that filled him with excitement at the ancient romance of the life of the 'proletariat' of Brittany. Discovery of a major Breton text convinced him that 'If only for such a work as this, one does not have the right to stifle the *still living* language of this people' (ML, 9). It was the discovery of 'the matter of Brittany' that released the writer in him, and he set out to experience the Breton countryside for himself, with an intimacy possible only to a cyclist. Reacting against the infantilisation of Brittany that had been the outcome of nineteenth-century folklorism, and regretting that the region had become severed, thanks partly to its peripheral geographical position, from 'the European axis, the rich Rhine–Rhône boulevard' (ML, 13) he gradually learned to wed his liberationist left-wing politics to the cause of Breton self-government. In the process he shed the conventional left-wing shibboleth that to abandon localism and to adopt a human universalism was the only way to effect social progress:

> All that my generation had predicted, the following generation would disprove. It was *first of all* as Algerians, Vietnamese, – and Flemings and Québecois – that men would receive their salvation. Wars of liberation, federalism gaining ground step by step, regionalism in the heart of con- stituted States, everywhere the divorce of the Idea and the Land would cease; and in France itself, the centralisation which we believed to be unshakeable would be disputed and decline. (ML, 19)

Whereas the trajectory of Lebesque's career had been from rejection of local identity to celebratory acceptance of it, that of the distinguished philosopher Miguel de Unamuno had been in pre- cisely the opposite direction. As Esyllt Thomas Lawrence explained in her article on 'The Ambivalent Basque', having been an enthu- siastic Basque nationalist in his teens, Unamuno had become an equally enthusiastic Castilian centralist in his adulthood.[25] Obviously ill at ease with this volte-face, Lawrence strove hard, but somewhat unconvincingly, to argue that, appearances very much to the con- trary, Unamuno had to the end been haunted by residual feelings of attachment to his natal region, finding evidence of this in his 'dis- placed' enthusiasm for the Catalan language, which he actually took the trouble to learn. As for his desertion of Euskadi, she attributed it partly to his failure to acquire fluency in the Basque language, a failure which, she writes with a conscious eye on anglicised Wales, resulted in an 'unfocussed resentment, even veiled hatred, against the language . . . mixed with a complex uneasiness and fear leading to a longing for the language to disappear and, with it, all sense of linguistic obligation' (ETL, 40).

The most famous contributor to *Planet* by far was Jean-Paul Sartre. His article, translated from the original Basque, appeared in the December 1971/January 1972 issue.[26] It related to the 1969

show trial staged by Franco's regime in Burgos that condemned sixteen ETA members to death for their fatal attack on a brutal police
superintendent who had strong wartime connections with the Nazis.
The trial had succeeded, however, only in drawing attention to the
national, ethnic and linguistic oppression of the Basque people by
a violently repressive fascist state. As a doyen of the left in France,
Sartre had supported the Algerians in their liberation struggle and
had written the introduction to Frantz Fanon's classic *Les Damnés
de la Terre*.

A pioneer of what was to become known as post-colonial criticism, Sartre begins his article by claiming that

> what the trials have done is to arouse consciences inside and outside of
> Spain by revealing to many people for the first time the existence of the
> Basque nation, and established this fact as by no means unique. All big
> nations contain interior colonies within frontiers they themselves have
> drawn. (JPS, 3)

For Sartre, the trials had served to remind him of the 'jacobin cen-
tralism' of his own country of France, a country that itself included
'interior colonies' such as Brittany, Alsace, Occitania and, above all,
that part of the Basque country that lay on the French side of the
Pyrenees. Nor was France by any means a unique case.

> In Yugoslavia, France, Spain, Northern Ireland, Belgium, Canada and
> elsewhere, social conflicts have begun to take on an ethnic dimension.
> Provinces declare themselves nations and more or less openly claim the
> status of nations. It has become clear that the present frontiers correspond
> to the interests of the dominant classes and not to popular aspiration,
> that the unity of which the great powers are so proud is a cloak for
> the oppression of peoples and for the overt or covert use of repressive
> violence . . .
> [The rebirth of a Basque people evident in the Burgos trials] could
> not have taken place if the so-called provinces had not had a national
> existence which for centuries the conquerors had tried to suppress and
> obstruct and conceal, but had remained in being, an historic and funda-
> mental tie between the people. (JPS, 4–6)

Having surveyed the recent history of the Basque country, Sartre then
proceeds to inquire whether what is happening there can be classed
as an anti-colonial struggle. While admitting the paradox that the

industrialised Basque region is much wealthier than a largely impoverished and rural Castilian Spain, and that therefore the economic statistics do not demonstrate that the Basques have been disadvantaged and damaged by the exploitation of their resources for the benefit of the Spanish state, Sartre argues that in this particular case colonial relations are manifest instead in the state's 'pillaging' of the Basque economy through disproportionately heavy taxation and the denial to the region of key economic investments. The Madrid government is deliberately undermining the region by facilitating massive emigration and immigration. It has also taken extensive steps to repress the language and culture of Euskadi, and in this connection Sartre draws a comparison with the case of Brittany.

He is harsh in his judgement of the response of the left, both within the Basque country and elsewhere, to this state of affairs, deploring its rigid adherence to the conventional Marxist model of class struggle. In the case of Euskadi, Sartre insists (and here his argument closely parallels that advanced by Ned Thomas as the *raison d'être* of *Planet*) that 'independence and socialism are two sides of the same coin' (JPS, 14). The first step is to ensure that the proletariat becomes 'aware of its colonised condition' (JPS, 15). Moreover, Sartre is adamant that, given the savage nature of Franco's Spain, the Basques can advance to freedom only by engaging in an armed struggle, and the final section of his article is devoted to a description of the different phases to date of such a campaign of targeted violence. It culminates in a call for 'a cultural revolution, which will create a socialist man [*sic*], on the foundations of his land, his language, and his renovated customs' (JPS, 20). A few years later, the publication of a study of 'internal colonisation' by the American sociologist Michael Hechter prompted Phil Williams to revisit Sartre's article and to find in it reassurance that 'the nationalist parties are the most powerful vehicle for social change in Western Europe today, and once nationalist movements reach a certain strength growth is irreversible except by the crude physical destruction of their cultural base'.[27]

The translator of Sartre's piece was Harri Webb, who contributed an essay of his own on Galicia, another of the regions of the Atlantic seaboard of Spain, to *Planet* in August 1974.[28] Opening with a comment on the distinctive landscape of the region that brought Brittany to his mind, Webb proceeded to mention briefly the possibility of early Celtic settlement there, and noted how the Franco regime was

prepared to tolerate such a badge of identity because it carried with
it no separatist political threat. He then summarised the history of
the region. Having coalesced into a people at much the same time as
the Welsh, the Galicians had soon been politically assimilated by a
dominant Castile, after which they had shared in the common history of the whole Iberian peninsula. All that had survived to set them
apart was the Galician language, which, Webb pointed out, 'is more
closely related to Portuguese than to Castilian' (HW, 49).

Over time the language had produced a distinctive literary tradition, centred on the lyric rather than on the epic mode that prevailed
in Castile. Once this tradition had died out, the language had managed to survive only as a patois until a literary revival during the
nineteenth century had seen it fitted for modern expression. Webb
ended by drawing several comparisons between Galicia and Wales,
ranging from the core rural poverty he detected in both regions,
despite the vigorous development of trade and industry in some of
their areas, to the problem of extensive emigration and the political
quietism that continued to characterise both subservient societies.
He remained hopeful, however, that the eventual end of the Franco
regime might well see the Galicians begin, like the Basques, to agitate for the radical reshaping of the political structure of the Iberian
peninsula.

The time spent by Ned Thomas in Spain naturally inclined him to
pay particular attention to the situation in that country – Catalonia
was featured by the magazine in 1977[29] – with the attendant risk of
skewing the impression given of the politico-cultural map of Europe.
The winter, 1974/75 issue of *Planet* carried another essay on the
Basque country, in the form of a detailed, authoritative study of
'ETA and the Basque problem'.[30] It began with a frank admission of
the racist and reactionary elements of a national movement which
(rather like that of the early Plaid Cymru under Saunders Lewis) had
run the risk of totally ignoring the actual, complex social composition
of the region. It then shrewdly assessed the dilemma faced by all the
liberationist movements in the region. They had to choose between
adopting an ideology that was militantly anti-capitalist, class-based
and attractive to their working-class supporters, and an ideology
primarily centred on nationalist aspirations, the approach that was
actually favoured by the majority of activists.

Very important in the latter regard, the article points out, had
been a growing awareness of the link between Basque nationhood

and the Basque language, and anger at Franco's ruthless suppression of the latter. Support for ETA had grown in strength partly owing to the movement's success in fusing a proletarian sense of class grievance with a bourgeois commitment to a defence of language and culture. This allowed it to proclaim itself to be 'a socialist movement of national liberation' – at this point the parallel with *Planet*'s own programme for Wales became very evident – and to make common cause with freedom struggles from Algeria to Cuba. The article ended with a scrupulously detailed mapping of the seemingly innumerable tendencies and factions by which ETA itself was internally riven, which made it 'the noisiest, the most thoughtful politically and the most divided aspect of Basque nationalism' (JLH, 65).

The savage struggle within Franco's fascist Spain between the Madrid government and the various national regions served the useful purpose for *Planet* of advertising, in the most extreme (and therefore one might add, with the Welsh context in mind, one of the most misleading) of terms, the evils of the centralised politics to which the magazine was itself implacably opposed. *Planet* 28 duly opened with a clarion call, blazoned in large print, by Ned Thomas to Wales to 'Remember Euskadi'. It drew attention to Franco's continuing military 'occupation' of what had been recognised by the republicans during the Spanish Civil War as an 'independent state', explaining that ETA violence needed to be viewed against this savage background. 'Meanwhile', Thomas pointedly commented, 'the West debates the admission of Spain to NATO – for the better defence of democracy.'[31] *Planet* revisited the Basque question after the death of Franco in an article that noted how cultural activities had consequently been much improved while political progress was still beset by the internal divisions of the Basque country. The discussion also emphasised how in Euskadi 'the impetus for much of the cultural and language movement appears to come from the direction of the Basque left', a message that would no doubt have heartened *Planet* readers desperate to forge such links in Wales between the nationalist and socialist movements as the periodical repeatedly and ardently favoured.[32]

Such was the supposed Spanish bias of *Planet* that it led to gibes about the periodical's imaginary 'Basque of the Month' feature. But this Hispanic tendency was to some degree offset by a conscious effort to survey the many other European countries where national regions harboured ambitions for greater powers of self-determination.

Attention was paid to Corsica by Meic Stephens, who traced the island's history of occupation by a lengthy sequence of foreign invaders, terminating with France wresting control of the island from the Genoese in the later eighteenth century. Subsequently Corsica was formally incorporated into the centralist state that was the supreme creation of the little Corsican corporal, Napoleon.[33] Neglect duly followed, as tended to happen to all of France's 'marginal' national regions, until a concerted effort was at last made in the 1960s to improve agricultural production and to create the infrastructure needed to support a tourist trade. Attempts, current at the time of the article's writing, to strengthen and safeguard the island's distinct linguistic heritage and to secure a degree of autonomy were proceeding against a worrying background of immigration, most notably in the form of the resettlement there of some of Algeria's *pieds-noirs*, or French colonists. Although Stephens did not directly say so, he clearly intended a comparison with Wales, since the acquisition of homes by the English in the Welsh countryside was beginning to offer a similar outside threat to established communities and their culture.

While some of the regional issues within Europe that were addressed in *Planet* could indeed *prima facie* seem amusingly and self-indulgently arcane, on closer inspection they usually proved to have yielded up trenchant articles that included illuminating comparisons with Wales. A case in point is Ioan Bowen Rees's succinct essay on 'The Jura Question'.[34] It reported on the agitation within a federal Switzerland for a greater degree of autonomy for the small Francophone Jura region that had been contained for a century and a half within the much larger Germanic canton of Berne. Commending the Swiss government for the sensible way in which it had quickly moved to defuse the issue by allowing one section of the Jura to split off to form a new canton, Rees pointed out how unimaginable it was that the British state would respond in similarly enlightened fashion to the claims of Wales and Scotland for a greater degree of self-government. Switzerland, Rees concluded, offered 'a prototype for a federal Europe of regions', and the 'resurrection of the Jura' was a step in that direction (IBR, 13).

The connections made by *Planet* could sometimes be very unexpected. A sketch of 'the Sorbs of Lusatia' featured 'one of the smallest nations of Europe'. Numbering in total only about 70,00 people, this community still managed to survive within its narrow confines some fifty miles south-east of Berlin and to maintain their distinctive language (roughly categorised as West Slavonic) and its culture, while remaining firmly embedded in the powerful German state. This tiny, rather exotic, ethnic Slav minority might have seemed rather too negligible and peripheral a phenomenon to receive much attention even from *Planet*, indefatigable though the magazine's pursuit was of the goal of mapping a Europe of the regions. But this essay, by Gerald Stone, ended by reporting that the great nineteenth-century champion of the Sorbs had been a German from Hanover named Georg Sauerwein; and his passion for threatened minority cultures had been kindled during the period when, following completion of a degree at Göttingen University, he had spent three years in Wales as a guest of Lady Llanover, during which time he had acquired complete fluency in the Welsh language.[35]

Planet was interested not only in minority peoples, languages and literatures but also in prominent European writers and intellectuals whose work seemed relevant to Wales. During his early years as literature director of the Arts Council, the budget available for distribution by Meic Stephens was sufficiently generous for him to introduce into his programme a scheme that would bring prominent international writers to Wales for a short period and allow them to tour around the country. Eugène Ionesco was the first such writer to be invited, Friedrich Dürrenmatt the second, and their visits were duly reported in *Planet* in articles that endeavoured to convey the relevance of their thought and writing to the Welsh cultural situation.[36]

Ionesco turned out to be formal, 'cerebral and rather intimidating', while the Swiss proved to be 'warm, jolly, roly poly', and agreeably prolix, 'taking pleasure in assaulting a question as though it were one of his own mountains, looking for the best route up but trying a number in order to make a point fully'.[37] The Romanian at least had the grace to profess, in an interview, an interest in the 'seriousness' of Welsh literature, while clearly regarding the approach to theatrical performance in the country as still much too 'literary' and insufficiently innovative. In the 'national consciousness' he had discovered in Wales lay, he flatteringly suggested, an important 'hope for the Western world':

> Britain has won the war but lost her empire. Now a new Celtic culture is being created: this is one of the only hopes for the future, that a Western

world in crisis is finding new philosophical beginning. I am clearly speaking of Brittany as well as Wales.[38]

In a personal statement, Dürrenmatt reflected on the complex implications of being a native speaker of the Berne dialect of Swiss German who wrote his plays in standard German while actually choosing to live in the French-speaking part of Switzerland. He wryly noted how the French Swiss prided themselves on their cultural superiority, since they spoke a language that the 'proper' French had long grandly viewed as the natural medium for the highest human intelligence and therefore as the 'universal' language of human experience. German, by contrast, took no pride in its linguistic purity and correctness, celebrating instead the rich variety of local dialects that constituted the language as actually spoken throughout the many different regions of the country. As a writer, he confessed that he instinctively warmed to the pliability of German and its hospitality to a range of lexical registers and modes of expression. Moreover, he loved the feeling that the foreign linguistic environment of his home in French Switzerland meant that the German in which he thought and wrote was a private language, exclusively personal to him. He simply could not imagine living in a country where he, as a writer, actually had to share his language with the population at large.[39]

One prominent European thinker of the day whose ideas seemed perfectly suited to *Planet* was Ivan Illich. Born in Vienna to a father who was a Dalmatian engineer and a mother who was a Sephardic Jew, Illich, who was fluent in ten languages, entered the Catholic priesthood after studying a range of subjects – histology and crystallography, history and theology – at a number of prestigious European universities. A radical libertarian with a strong anarchist streak, and a turbulent priest constantly at loggerheads with the Catholic authorities, he proceeded to develop a highly controversial reputation both in Europe and in the United States. This was based on his impassioned attacks, which antagonized those on both the Left and the Right of the political spectrum, on what he regarded as the 'institutionalisation' of the human mind. The result, he argued, was the promotion of conformist thinking, the deadening of individual creative capacity, and the cultivation of an infantile dependency on impersonal processes. This pernicious process, so damaging to every form of distinctive individual development, was in Illich's opinion consequent on the insidiously manipulative mass organisations that dominated most contemporary fields of organised social activity. Regardless of whether they were state-controlled or private ventures, these organisations were in essence bureaucratic initiatives under the control of self-certifying elites. These powerful, controlling 'treatment institutions' ranged from the field of medicine, through education, to the world of work, and further included key activities relating to human control of the natural environment.

Illich's ideas were attractive not only to the enthusiasts of the counter-cultural movement in the USA but also to those in Europe who were casting around for a radical programme of social reform and reconstruction in the wake of the 1968 *événements*, the violently disruptive student revolt across Paris's most prestigious institutions of higher education. They also appealed, as Paul Luke pointed out in his article on the subject for *Planet*, to Breton devolutionists because Illich did not only favour decentralisation; he also advocated what he called 'autogestion'.[40] Luke glossed this as representing

> a desire to cease to define democracy narrowly and mechanically as the shifting of government from the centre to the periphery, and to equate democracy with the opening up of the economy and *all* configurations of power [by placing] the emphasis back with the individual. (PL, 1)

(The concept would later return to favour under the label of 'subsidiarity'.) Luke concluded his article by suggesting that Illich's ideas contained 'various elements of the community-based socialism which a number of Welsh devolutionists have attempted to depict and achieve', and he argued that 'the sooner the Welsh devolutionists are able to recognise, with Illich, the real obstacles to the realisation of a decentralised society, the better' (PL, 5).

There was, though, one significant European intellectual of the day who lived much closer to home than Illich, to some of whose ideas he would no doubt have been sympathetic. Indeed, Illich himself characterised Leopold Kohr after his death as 'a funny bird – meek, fey, droll, and incisive', and noted that he was 'unassuming' and even 'radically humble'. Kohr's description of himself as a 'philosophical anarchist' would apply equally to Illich. He was an Austrian economist and political scientist who had been based for decades in Puerto Rico before relocating to Aberystwyth to be near his close friend Alwyn D. Rees, a distinguished academic and campaigning editor of the influential Welsh periodical *Barn*. Resident there from 1968 to 1977, he adapted the influential critique of 'bigness' he had first outlined in his 1955 study *The Breakdown of Nations* to suit the condition of Wales and to support campaigns, led by Plaid Cymru, for a greater degree of Welsh control over its own social, economic and political affairs.

Kohr liked to claim he had come to realise early that there was no necessary correlation between bigness and a thriving social organism or cultural production of the highest quality through having been born and raised in the tiny Austrian village of Oberndorf. For him, the discovery that 'Stille Nacht', the nineteenth-century Christmas carol of worldwide fame, had been composed by the local priest to be sung by the choir of the village church had been a revelation: small communities, it was clear, could produce great cultural riches. Oberndorf was located in the Salzburg district, and Kohr never tired of emphasising how small had been that town, too, when it had pro-vided the genius of the youthful Mozart with invaluable sustenance.

His initial mistrust of what he was to call 'the cult of bigness' had been confirmed during the period he'd spent in Spain as a freelance journalist covering the Civil War. There he became a close friend of George Orwell and an acquaintance of André Malraux and Ernest Hemingway. He also developed a respect for the political sophistica-tion not only of Catalonia but of several of the other regions of Spain. As an Austrian of Jewish descent, he had first-hand knowledge of the evils of a powerful centralised state with complete control over every aspect of economic, political, social and cultural life. He had been forced to flee abroad to escape Nazi oppression, so it was little wonder he went on to advocate the dismantling of all such oppres-sive structures.

No sooner had he settled in Aberystwyth than Kohr became a close friend of Gwynfor Evans, whose adviser he became on con-structing a Plaid Cymru programme for basing any future government of Wales on a sound basis of small local initiatives and progressive communitarian efforts. Shortly afterwards, he dedicated the little volume he entitled *Is Wales Viable?* to Evans 'in admiration'.[41] In his introduction to the book, Alwyn D. Rees accurately pinpointed the premise on which Kohr had based his affirmative answer to the question posed in his title. For Kohr, Rees pointed out, 'provincial prosperity in the prosperity of a large political unit diminishes with the distance between the province and the centre of government'.

The only remedy for such 'inbuilt inequality' was 'the division of large states into their more manageable component parts', and this diagnosis predisposed Kohr as Rees said, 'favourably towards "separatism" wherever it manifests itself' (LK, 11). As stated in his lucid little book, his preference was for Welsh 'separatism', but within the framework of an economic 'common market' that would include the other nations of the United Kingdom.

Rees also pointed to the unconventional basic strategy deployed by Kohr to advance his central argument. Rather than relying on statistical analysis, in the classic manner of Economic Studies, he preferred to multiply analogies. Many of these involved comparison of the economic condition of a dependent Wales with that of some of Europe's small but thriving independent nations, most particularly the federalised state of Switzerland. It was precisely this unconventional mode of proceeding that, as Rees had anticipated, attracted criticism from the mainstream economist Eirian Thomas in a review in *Planet*. For Thomas, 'a valid and meaningful appraisal of economic viability, whether it be of a project, firm or an entire economy requires as much factual material as possible.' For want of such material, Kohr's arguments were doomed to be unconvincing.[42]

The ideas championed by Illich and Kohr were very evidently at work in an essay by Yves Person, arguing 'Against the Nation-State', that had originally been published in a French socialist publication.[43] Person turned to the concept of an *ethnie* – at that time a new term borrowed from social anthropology – to emphasise (in New Left fashion) that the production and maintenance of distinctive cultural communities had always been a primary human activity, not a secondary one, as supposed by classic Marxist thinkers. Recovery of this truth was vital to the success of socialism, as it allowed it to position itself in opposition to the 'massification' process upon which modern capitalist society depended and which could result only in a destructive uniformity. 'We must struggle for creativity, for diversity, against massification', Person argued, echoing Illich. 'The *ethnies* or nationalities are not a decoration, for if the *mega-ethnie* is ever imposed, the creatures who emerge will no longer be human' (YP, 3).

The direction of Wales's future relations with Europe was becoming clear by the time that Ned Thomas's term as *Planet*'s founding editor was drawing to its close. Under the leadership of Edward Heath, the UK had been belatedly admitted to the European Union, the decision confirmed by the referendum of 1975, and direct election of representatives of the European Parliament followed in 1979. Anticipating the latter development, *Planet* included in 1977 an essay by Elizabeth Jones, entitled 'The New Europe', that explained the key developing institutions of contemporary Europe. In it she carefully distinguished between the European Community and the Council of Europe, a slightly older and completely independent body, many of whose decisions and initiatives, however, impacted on the EU. The latter, she reported, had recently adopted a Social Charter designed to protect the rights of workers across Europe.[44]

By January 1978, the Council of Europe, meeting at Bordeaux and including representatives of all twenty-six of the democratic countries of Europe, had adopted a seminal declaration about the responsibility of the European Union to ensure equitable support for the many sub-state regions of which Europe in practice consisted.[45] It was replete with observations that applied directly to Wales. It stressed that 'the region is the most appropriate framework for preserving and enhancing the regional and cultural heritage and its traditions, since it is closer to the inhabitants and hence more familiar with their needs than any central administration in a frequently distant capital'; it appreciated that constructive recognition for the regions and support for their vital distinctiveness would not only require proper funding but would involve the provision of legislative and administrative resources sufficient to enable 'active participation in the spheres of education and research, cultural activities' and the like; denying that such regional support would inevitably lead to 'national dismemberment', the declaration emphasised that 'the region is the ideal context for trans-frontier co-operation to mitigate the divisive effects of the national frontiers which scar the face of Europe'. Finally, it urged 'the creation of a European second chamber composed of local and regional representatives.'

Soon after publishing this exhilarating Declaration, Ned Thomas stepped down as editor of *Planet* and for decades afterwards devoted himself to the work of turning the fine words recorded in Bordeaux into real actions at European level from which Wales could benefit. He criss-crossed Europe and was one of the first of the Welsh to appreciate that membership of the Union could afford his country exciting access to a number of funding schemes designed to support the economy and the culture of Europe's many regions. Accordingly, he learned to navigate the frequently tortuous and arcane routes through the Brussels bureaucracy that eventually led to the relevant resources.

As Thomas's career therefore illustrates, from the late 1970s onwards Wales became embedded in an intricate pan-European system in a way and to a degree that earlier generations could not possibly have foreseen. Meanwhile, thanks to increasingly cheap and easy forms of travel, the Welsh public at large began to visit Europe's holiday resorts, tourist spots and honey pots in ever-increasing numbers. This resulted in a superficial, sometimes even blasé familiarity with continental countries and locations that would once have been deemed distant and highly exotic. The popular media, too, soon began to take Europe for granted and to feature casual extensive coverage of a wide range of contemporary events there, in particular highly popular sporting and cultural activities. Meanwhile the English language seemed well set to become the lingua franca of the whole continent, so that the people of Wales soon lost interest even in attempting such elementary mastery of 'foreign' languages (French, German, Spanish) as had once been possible in the old grammar school system. They became, as a result, ever more insularly anglophone, culturally Anglo-American, and accordingly indifferent to, and ignorant of, inherited markers of cultural difference, including those of Wales itself.

The inexorable advance of an immensely powerful mass consumer culture eroded respect for those traditional signifiers of supreme quality that were the products of the high culture of a refined European civilisation. Moreover, high culture itself came to be contemptuously debunked as nothing but the precious preserve of a tiny privileged class of the socially elite. All these revolutionary trends were aided and abetted by the increasing dominance being exerted by the popular entertainment industry of the USA over the collective mind of the UK and, albeit to a lesser extent, of Europe. All this meant that the cultural values in the light of which Welsh writers and intellectuals had for long been viewing European culture were thoroughly undermined, and in effect discarded. As for the Union itself, it steadily hardened into a pragmatic alliance of established state powers united primarily by a recognition of mutual economic interests although also haunted by grim memories of a long common continental past of murderous international strife, and accordingly idealistically committed to jointly ensuring a harmonious future.

In short, the story of Wales's relationship with Europe took on an entirely different complexion roughly from 1980 onwards, for better and no doubt also for worse. In the process it acquired a complexity

that would require a very considerable effort to map. And that is why
this present study has chosen to terminate in 1979.

Notes

1   Sam Adams (ed.), *Collected Stories of Roland Mathias* (Cardiff: University
    of Wales Press. 2001), p. 70.
2   Sam Adams (ed.), *Collected Poems of Roland Mathias* (Cardiff: University of
    Wales Press, 2002), p. 199. Hereafter *CPRM*. See also p. 242.
3   A useful summary of Garlick's life and career may be found in Don
    Dale-Jones, *Raymond Garlick* (Cardiff: University of Wales Press, 1996).
4   Raymond Garlick, *A Sense of Europe: Collected Poems, 1954–1968* (Llandysul:
    Gomer, 1968), p. 104. Hereafter *SE*.
5   Raymond Garlick, autobiographical essay in Meic Stephens (ed.), *Artists in
    Wales* (Llandysul: Gomer, 1973), pp. 94–7; p. 92. Hereafter *AW*.
6   Raymond Garlick, *Collected Poems, 1946–1986* (Llandysul: Gomer, 1987),
    p. 123. Hereafter *GCP*.
7   'Fanfare for Europe', in Raymond Garlick, *Incense* (Llandysul: Gomer, 1976),
    p. 11.
8   Harri Webb, 'Webb's Progress', *Planet*, 30 (January 1976), 23–8; 28. Hereafter
    WP.
9   Meic Stephens (ed.), *Collected Poems of Harri Webb* (Llandysul: Gomer,
    1995), p. 233. Hereafter *CPHW*.
10 Meic Stephens, *The Linguistic Minorities of Europe* (Llandysul: Gomer, 1976),
    p. xiii. Hereafter *LME*.
11 See Richard Wyn Jones, *Rhoi Cymru'n Gyntaf: Syniadaeth Plaid Cymru*,
    Cyfrol 1 (Cardiff: University of Wales Press, 2007), Chapter 4.
12 Daniel G. Williams (ed.), Raymond Williams, *Who Speaks for Wales: Nation,
    Culture, Identity* (Cardiff: University of Wales Press, 2003), p. 136.
13 Ned Thomas, *Bydoedd* (Talybont: Y Lolfa, 2010).
14 *Planet*, 1 (August/September 1970), 4. Herafter NT.
15 *Planet*, 2 (October/November, 2010).
16 John Tripp/Meic Stephens, 'Under Two Hats', *Planet*, 9 (December 1971/
    January 1972), 56.
17 Paul Sérant, 'The Rise of French Regionalism', *Planet*, 2 (October/November
    1970), 16–19.
18 Patricia Elton Mayo, 'Constitutional Background of Separatist Movements',
    Planet, 7 (August/September 1971), 29–31. Hereafter PEM.
19 Goronwy Glyn Hughes, 'Lightning on the Tatras', *Planet*, 3 (December/
    January 1971), 32–9.
20 Mina Bohana (trans.), Nicolai Haitov, 'Paths', *Planet*, 56 (August/September
    1970), 56–63.
21 Robin Okey, 'Yugoslovia – the Background to Cultural Policy', *Planet*, 20
    (Autumn 1973), 41–8. Hereafter RO.
22 A companion piece in some ways to Okey's article was E. Glyn Lewis's discus-
    sion of 'Language Contact in the U.S.S.R. and Wales', *Planet*, 20 (Autumn

1973), 53–64. The following issue of *Planet* (January 1974) was largely dedicated to essays on Russia.

23 Dewi Morris Jones, 'Left Wing Nationalism in Brittany', *Planet*, 7 (August/September 1971), 21–8. The same author later contributed an article on the state of the Breton language: 'The Struggle for Breton', *Planet*, 36 (February/March 1977), 22–4.

24 Morvan Lebesque, 'Becoming a Breton', *Planet*, 17 (April/May 1973), 3–20. Hereafter ML.

25 Esyllt Thomas Lawrence, 'Unamuno the Ambivalent Basque,' *Planet*, 11 (May 1972), 34–43. Hereafter ETL.

26 Jean-Paul Sartre, 'The Burgos Trials', *Planet*, 9 (December 1971/January 1972), 3–20. Hereafter JPS.

27 Phil Williams, 'The Internal Colony', *Planet*, 37/38 (May 1977), 60–5.

28 Harri Webb, 'Galicia', *Planet*, 24/25 (August 1974), 47–53. Hereafter HW.

29 Miquel Strubell, 'Catalunya – Back in the Running', *Planet*, 39 (August 1977), 2–7.

30 John Ll. Hollyman, 'ETA and the Basque Problem', *Planet*, 26/27 (Winter 1974/75), 51–66. Hereafter JLH.

31 Ned Thomas, 'Remember Euskadi', *Planet*, 28 (August 1975), 1.

32 Glenn Heinmiller, 'Euskadi since the Elections', *Planet*, 41 (March 1978), 14–17.

33 Meic Stephens, 'The Corsican Struggle', *Planet*, 29 (October 1975), 1–6.

34 Ioan Bowen Rees, 'The Jura Question', *Planet*, 31 (March 1976), 11–13. Hereafter IBR.

35 Gerald Stone, 'The Sorbs of Lusatia', *Planet*, 34 (November 1976), 30–5.

36 A later issue of *Planet* carried a brief pen portrait of the celebrated Swedish children's author Astrid Lingren, who also spent a period in Wales under this visiting writers' scheme. Janet Watts, 'Astrid Lingren', *Planet*, 44 (August 1978), 47–9.

37 Beata Lipman, 'Après Dürrenmatt', *Planet*, 35 (December 1976), 24–35.

38 'M. Ionesco in conversation with Beata Lipman', *Planet*, 26/27 (Winter 1974/75), 9–13; 10.

39 Friedrich Dürrenmatt, 'Language Registers', *Planet*, 34 (November 1976), 12–13.

40 Paul Luke, 'Illich and the Devolutionists', *Planet*, 33 (August 1976), 1–5. Hereafter PL.

41 Leopold Kohr, *Is Wales Viable?* (Llandybïe: Christopher Davies, 1971). Hereafter LK.

42 Eirian Thomas, 'Employment versus Wage-Rates', *Planet*, 9 (December 1971/January 1972), 92–6.

43 Yves Person, 'Against the Nation-State', *Planet*, 37/38 (May 1977), 1–8. Hereafter YP.

44 Elizabeth Jones, 'The New Europe', *Planet*, 40 (November 1977), 15–20.

45 'The Bordeaux Declaration', *Planet*, 43 (June 1978), 11–16.

INDEX